Essentials of **Psychological Assessment** Series

verything you need to know to administer, score, and inter

I'd like to order the following *Essentials*

- ☐ WAIS®-IV Assessment, Second Edition (w/CD-R
- ☐ WJ III™ Cognitive Abilities Assessment, Second
- ☐ Cross-Battery Assessment, Third Edition (w/CD-F
- ☐ Nonverbal Assessment / 978-0-471-38318-5 • $40.0
- ☐ PAI® Assessment / 978-0-471-08463-1 • $40.00
- ☐ CAS Assessment / 978-0-471-29015-5 • $40.00
- ☐ MMPI®-2 Assessment, Second Edition / 978-0-470-92323-8 • $40.00
- ☐ Myers-Briggs Type Indicator® Assessment, Second Edition / 978-0-470-34390-6 • $40.00
- ☐ Rorschach® Assessment / 978-0-471-33146-9 • $40.00
- ☐ Millon™ Inventories Assessment, Third Edition / 978-0-470-16862-2 • $40.00
- ☐ TAT and Other Storytelling Assessments, Second Edition / 978-0-470-28192-5 • $40.00
- ☐ MMPI-A™ Assessment / 978-0-471-39815-8 • $40.00
- ☐ NEPSY®-II Assessment / 978-0-470-43691-2 • $40.00
- ☐ Neuropsychological Assessment, Second Edition / 978-0-470-43747-6 • $40.00
- ☐ Essentials of WJ® IV Tests of Achievement • 978-1-118-79915-4 • $40.00
- ☐ Evidence-Based Academic Interventions / 978-0-470-20632-4 • $40.00
- ☐ WRAML2 and TOMAL-2 Assessment / 978-0-470-17911-6 • $40.00
- ☐ WMS®-IV Assessment / 978-0-470-62196-7 • $40.00
- ☐ Behavioral Assessment / 978-0-471-35367-6 • $40.00
- ☐ Forensic Psychological Assessment, Second Edition / 978-0-470-55168-4 • $40.00
- ☐ Bayley Scales of Infant Development II Assessment / 978-0-471-32651-9 • $40.00
- ☐ Career Interest Assessment / 978-0-471-35365-2 • $40.00
- ☐ WPPSI™-IV Assessment (w/CD-ROM) / 978-1-11838062-8 • $50.00
- ☐ 16PF® Assessment / 978-0-471-23424-1 • $40.00
- ☐ Assessment Report Writing / 978-0-471-39487-7 • $40.00
- ☐ Stanford-Binet Intelligence Scales (SB5) Assessment / 978-0-471-22404-4 • $40.00
- ☐ WISC®-IV Assessment, Second Edition (w/CD-ROM) / 978-0-470-18915-3 • $50.00
- ☐ KABC-II Assessment / 978-0-471-66733-9 • $40.00
- ☐ WIAT®-III and KTEA-II Assessment (w/CD-ROM) / 978-0-470-55169-1 • $50.00
- ☐ Processing Assessment, Second Edition (w/CD-ROM) / 978-1-118-36820-6 • $50.00
- ☐ School Neuropsychological Assessment, Second Edition (w/CD-ROM) / 978-1-118-17584-2 • $50.00
- ☐ Cognitive Assessment with KAIT & Other Kaufman Measures / 978-0-471-38317-8 • $40.00
- ☐ Assessment with Brief Intelligence Tests / 978-0-471-26412-5 • $40.00
- ☐ Creativity Assessment / 978-0-470-13742-0 • $40.00
- ☐ WNV™ Assessment / 978-0-470-28467-4 • $40.00
- ☐ DAS-II® Assessment (w/CD-ROM) / 978-0-470-22520-2 • $50.00
- ☐ Executive Functions Assessment (w/CD-ROM) / 978-0-470-42202-1 • $50.00
- ☐ Conners Behavior Assessments™ / 978-0-470-34633-4 • $40.00
- ☐ Temperament Assessment / 978-0-470-44447-4 • $40.00
- ☐ Response to Intervention / 978-0-470-56663-3 • $40.00
- ☐ Specific Learning Disability Identification / 978-0-470-58760-7 • $40.00
- ☐ IDEA for Assessment Professionals (w/CD-ROM) / 978-0-470-87392-2 • $50.00
- ☐ Dyslexia Assessment and Intervention / 978-0-470-92760-1 • $40.00
- ☐ Autism Spectrum Disorders Evaluation and Assessment / 978-0-470-62194-3 • $40.00
- ☐ Planning, Selecting, and Tailoring Interventions for Unique Learners (w/CD-ROM) 978-1-118-36821-3 • $50.00
- ☐ ADHD Assessment for Children and Adolescents / 978-1-118-11270-0 • $40.00

Please complete the order form on the back.
To order by phone, call toll free 1-877-762-2974
To order online: www.wiley.com/essentials
To order by mail: refer to order form on next page

 **WILEY**

Essentials

of **Psychological Assessment** Series

ORDER FORM

Please send this order form with your payment (credit card or check) to:
Wiley, Attn: Customer Care, 10475 Crosspoint Blvd., Indianapolis, IN 46256

QUANTITY	TITLE	ISBN	PRICE
_____	_____	_____	_____
_____	_____	_____	_____
_____	_____	_____	_____
_____	_____	_____	_____
_____	_____	_____	_____

Shipping Charges:	Surface	2-Day	1-Day
First item	$5.00	$10.50	$17.50
Each additional item	$3.00	$3.00	$4.00

For orders greater than 15 items,
please contact Customer Care at 1-877-762-2974.

ORDER AMOUNT _____

SHIPPING CHARGES _____

SALES TAX _____

TOTAL ENCLOSED _____

NAME_____

AFFILIATION_____

ADDRESS_____

CITY/STATE/ZIP _____

TELEPHONE _____

EMAIL_____

❑ Please add me to your e-mailing list

PAYMENT METHOD:

❑ Check/Money Order   ❑ Visa   ❑ Mastercard   ❑ AmEx

Card Number _____ Exp. Date _____

Cardholder Name *(Please print)* _____

Signature _____

*Make checks payable to **John Wiley & Sons**. Credit card orders invalid if not signed.*
All orders subject to credit approval. • Prices subject to change.

Essentials of
WPPSI™-IV Assessment

Essentials of Psychological Assessment Series
Series Editors, Alan S. Kaufman and Nadeen L. Kaufman

Essentials

of WPPSI™-IV Assessment

Susan Engi Raiford
Diane L. Coalson

WILEY

Cover image: © Greg Kuchik/Getty Images
Cover design: Wiley

This book is printed on acid-free paper. ⊚

Copyright © 2014 by John Wiley & Sons, Inc. All rights reserved.

Published by John Wiley & Sons, Inc., Hoboken, New Jersey.
Published simultaneously in Canada.

This publication is designed to provide accurate and authoritative information in regard to the subject matter covered. It is sold with the understanding that the publisher is not engaged in rendering professional services. If legal, accounting, medical, psychological, or any other expert assistance is required, the services of a competent professional person should be sought.

Designations used by companies to distinguish their products are often claimed as trademarks. In all instances where John Wiley & Sons, Inc. is aware of a claim, the product names appear in initial capital or all capital letters. Readers, however, should contact the appropriate companies for more complete information regarding trademarks and registration.

For general information on our other products and services please contact our Customer Care Department within the United States at (800) 762-2974, outside the United States at (317) 572-3993 or fax (317) 572-4002.

Wiley publishes in a variety of print and electronic formats and by print-on-demand. Some material included with standard print versions of this book may not be included in e-books or in print-on-demand. If this book refers to media such as a CD or DVD that is not included in the version you purchased, you may download this material at http://booksupport.wiley.com. For more information about Wiley products, visit www.wiley.com.

Library of Congress Cataloging-in-Publication Data:
Raiford, Susan Engi.
  Essentials of WPPSI-IV assessment / Susan Engi Raiford, Diane L. Coalson.
     pages   cm.—(Essentials of psychological assessment)
  Includes bibliographical references and index.
  ISBN 978-1-118-38062-8 (pbk.)
  ISBN 978-1-118-70540-7 (ebk.)
  ISBN 978-1-118-86981-9 (ebk.)
  1. Wechsler Preschool and Primary Scale of Intelligence.   2. Children—Intelligence testing.   3. Child development—Testing.   I. Coalson, Diane L.   II. Title.
  BF432.5.W424R35 2014
  155.42'3393—dc23   2014002696

Printed in the United States of America

SKY10033019_020222

CONTENTS

SERIES PREFACE

I n the *Essentials of Psychological Assessment* series, we have attempted to provide the reader with books that will deliver key practical information in the most efficient and accessible style. The series features instruments in a variety of domains, such as cognition, personality, education, and neuropsychology. For the experienced clinician, books in the series offer a concise yet thorough way to master utilization of the continuously evolving supply of new and revised instruments, as well as a convenient method for keeping up-to-date on the tried-and-true measures. The novice will find here a prioritized assembly of all the information and techniques that must be at one's fingertips to begin the complicated process of individual psychological diagnosis.

Wherever feasible, visual shortcuts to highlight key points are utilized alongside systematic, step-by-step guidelines. Chapters are focused and succinct. Topics are targeted for an easy understanding of the essentials of administration, scoring, interpretation, and clinical application. Theory and research are continually woven into the fabric of each book, but always to enhance clinical inference, never to sidetrack or overwhelm. We have long been advocates of "intelligent" testing—the notion that a profile of test scores is meaningless unless it is brought to life by the clinical observations and astute detective work of knowledgeable examiners. Test profiles must be used to make a difference in the child's or adult's life, or why bother to test? We want this series to help our readers become the best intelligent testers they can be.

In *Essentials of WPPSI-IV Assessment*, Susie Engi Raiford and Diane L. Coalson—the WPPSI-IV research directors—offer an insider's perspective on the scale's conceptualization, development, administration, and scoring. New Behind the Scenes boxes are incorporated to provide unprecedented insight into the new subtests and the test development process.

Anyone who assesses young children is well familiar with the inherent challenges of obtaining accurate and adequate test data for this challenging population. The authors, who have rich clinical as well as research experience, apply an interpretive approach that is flexible to the real constraints and challenges that practitioners encounter when testing younger children. The approach describes performance in both normative and intrapersonal contexts and facilitates interpretive case formulations from multiple theoretical and clinical perspectives. In addition to coverage of the published composite scores, several additional composite scores aimed at facilitating WPPSI-IV interpretation from a variety of theoretical approaches are supplied; these extra composite scores are especially valuable in those situations where the published comparison scores may not be available or appropriate for a specific child.

The companion CD-ROM automates the basic interpretive approach that is described in Chapter 4 of this book using software that automates derivation and analysis of these newly developed scores. Tools are also supplied in the CD-ROM to enhance WPPSI-IV administration and report writing.

We are excited to add *Essentials of WPPSI-IV Assessment* to our book series. Of special value is the fact that Drs. Raiford and Coalson are Wechsler experts across the entire age range; they were also research directors for the development and standardization of the WAIS-IV and are currently serving that same key function for the WISC-V.

Alan S. Kaufman, PhD, and Nadeen L. Kaufman, EdD, Series Editors
Yale Child Study Center, Yale University School of Medicine

ACKNOWLEDGMENTS

We are indebted to a number of individuals upon completion of this book. We wish to acknowledge those who provided book content first and foremost. Drs. Ron Dumont and John Willis authored Chapter 5, which reviews the pros and cons of the WPPSI-IV. We appreciate their objective evaluation, which will be helpful to readers in evaluation of the test. We are grateful to Mark Engi for his expert advice about the psychometric analyses performed in Chapter 6, which reviews the demographic group differences in WPPSI-IV scores. We appreciate Dr. Kristina Breaux and Cliff Wigtil for their clinical acumen in the areas of learning disabilities and intellectual giftedness, respectively, and for coauthoring the illustrative case reports in Chapter 8. We thank Stephanie Tong, Erik Gallemore, and Kathleen Rollins for providing the Test Yourself questions for seven of the eight chapters. We are thankful to Dr. Ou Zhang, who developed the norms for the seven additional composite scores that appear on the CD and in the WPPSI-IV Interpretive Assistant 1.0, and for Dr. J. J. Zhu, who reviewed and confirmed the quality of his work. We are grateful to Dr. Tommie Cayton for reading and commenting on all content, and for his encouragement of our professional development.

We wish to acknowledge the support of some outstanding colleagues at Pearson, without whom this book would not have been possible. We thank William Schryver, senior licensing specialist at Pearson, for his speedy, expert handling of the numerous permissions requests we submitted. We are grateful to Paula Oles, director of Q-global at Pearson, and Tiffany Jen, UX intern at Pearson, for providing us with high-quality art that illustrates use of the WPPSI-IV Scoring Assistant on Q-global. We are also appreciative of Dr. Larry Weiss, vice president of test development at Pearson, for approving our use of the WPPSI-IV final data.

We are also grateful to the outstanding professionals at John Wiley & Sons who were instrumental in this book's completion. We appreciate Marquita Flemming for her review of the initial proposal and support of it to the board at Wiley, and her support of us as we strove to complete the manuscript. We are grateful to our editorial program coordinator, Sherry Wasserman, who deserves recognition for her expertise and guidance in manuscript preparation. We greatly appreciate Tom Caruso for serving as production editor, and we thank the team at Cape Cod Compositors for their excellent copyediting services.

On a personal note, we wish to thank our loving spouses Robert Raiford and David Shafer for carrying the responsibilities of family and home so that we could be free to write. We are especially grateful to Robert for the many evenings and weekends he cared for their son, George, so Susie could work on the book. Most importantly, we are indebted to Drs. Alan and Nadeen Kaufman for agreeing to give us an opportunity to write our very own book about the WPPSI-IV and for providing guidance, review, and encouragement throughout the process. We appreciate them for creating the *Essentials* series and for their collective, ground-breaking work on the *Intelligent Testing With the WISC-R* and *Intelligent Testing With the WISC-III* books, and on numerous *Essentials* volumes (with Elizabeth Lichtenberger and Dawn Flanagan) on the Wechsler intelligence scales. Finally, we wish to thank Dr. David Wechsler. We hope that he would be proud of our work on the WPPSI-IV, and of this book.

Susan Engi Raiford and
Diane L. Coalson

One

OVERVIEW

The Wechsler Preschool and Primary Scale of Intelligence–Fourth Edition (WPPSI-IV; Wechsler, 2012) continues the progressive trend of recent Wechsler intelligence scale revisions that mirror contemporary advances in intelligence theory, neuropsychology, cognitive neuroscience, and psychometric methodology. Major modifications have been made to both the content and structure to reflect these advances. Primary index scores provide reliable and valid estimates of ability in several distinct but related areas of cognitive functioning, including verbal comprehension, visual-spatial ability, fluid reasoning, working memory, and processing speed. A Full Scale IQ score also is available to represent the child's overall level of ability across these cognitive domains. A number of new, ancillary index scores (e.g., Vocabulary Acquisition Index, Nonverbal Index) are available to represent vocabulary acquisition, global intellectual ability, and cognitive proficiency in more specific clinical situations, such as referrals for suspected language delays, preliteracy concerns, school readiness, or evaluations of children who may have limited levels of English language fluency.

WPPSI-IV scores can be interpreted from both a normative and an intrapersonal perspective. They most often are used from a normative perspective; that is, to describe a child's cognitive ability by comparing the child's scores to those obtained by children of approximately the same age (i.e., comparison to a normative reference group). A child's intrapersonal pattern of cognitive strengths and weaknesses can be evaluated by comparing scores to an overall indicator of performance, or to one another. The score comparison approach has been reorganized and expanded for the WPPSI-IV, with increased comparison score options (e.g., the mean primary index score, the Full Scale IQ, the mean scaled score for the primary index subtests). When combined with the availability of numerous theoretically and practically based index scores (termed *ancillary* index scores in the published test), the WPPSI-IV interpretive approach allows a thorough evaluation of a child's pattern of cognitive strengths and weaknesses that can be tailored to the unique clinical situation each child presents.

Similar to authors of previous books within the *Essentials* series (e.g., Flanagan & Kaufman, 2009; Lichtenberger & Kaufman, 2004, 2013), our goal for this book is to provide a go-to reference for both novice and proficient practitioners using the WPPSI-IV. Administration, scoring, and interpretive information is clearly and succinctly covered in successive chapters, incorporating the familiar Rapid Reference, Caution, and Don't Forget boxes that are hallmark features of the *Essentials* series. We also include Behind the Scenes boxes that offer helpful insights into the test development process as we were the WPPSI-IV research directors. Test questions are included at the conclusion of each chapter to highlight critical content.

The CD included with this book contains appendix matter, such as administration aids, interpretive tables, and normative data for a number of additional index scores not available within the published test. These additional index scores were developed to meet interpretive needs stemming from varied practical and theoretical perspectives (e.g., Cattell-Horn-Carroll [CHC] and neuropsychological). The CD also includes the WPPSI-IV Interpretive Assistant 1.0, scoring software that calculates norms for the additional index scores and walks the practitioner through our interpretive approach (see Chapter 4), including numerous score comparisons not available in the published test that can more fully inform interpretation.

HISTORICAL FOUNDATIONS OF EARLY CHILDHOOD ASSESSMENT

Assessment of preschoolers and young children is a unique and specialized endeavor, different from that experienced with older children, adolescents, and adults. Similarly, some of the historical foundations for early childhood assessment are shared with school-age children and adults, whereas others are unique to young children of preschool age. The following sections include a brief history of key scientific and societal influences on early childhood assessment. For more comprehensive coverage of these topics, the reader is referred to Ford, Kozey, and Negreiros (2012); Kelley and Surbeck (2007); and Wortham (2012).

The recognition of childhood as a unique stage in the life cycle was a critical precursor for increasing our understanding of children's growth and development. Although early publications emphasized this difference and the importance of rearing and educating children (e.g., Locke, 1692; Rousseau, 1762), systematic efforts to study the cognitive development of young children did not begin until the latter part of the 19th century, when increased societal attention in European countries was directed toward the health and welfare of young children. This focus spawned an era referred to as the Child Study Movement, in which attempts were made to apply the scientific method to the study of children. G. Stanley Hall and Lawrence Frank played pivotal roles in bringing this movement to the United States, with Hall establishing the first major child study center at Clark University in Massachusetts in 1893. Frank further entrenched the movement in educational institutions by establishing numerous child study centers at universities across the United States, with funding provided by the Laura Spelman Rockefeller Memorial (Wortham, 2012).

The Child Study Movement produced considerable knowledge and understanding of social, emotional, and cognitive childhood development, but the program's reliance on primarily observational data from children in a wide variety of group settings limited its acceptance by psychologists and other members of the scientific community. Despite the movement's lost momentum in the early 20th century, Hall's students, including Lewis Terman, Arnold Gesell, and John Dewey, continued to serve as pioneers in the more scientifically based field of child psychology that was beginning to take root in the United States. Terman was instrumental in adapting the Binet measures for extensive use in the United States, and Gesell defined and described the characteristic behaviors arising at specific periods during early childhood development (Gesell & Amatruda, 1941). Dewey focused on educational reform and improving educational programs aimed at young children (Wortham, 2012).

Concurrent with the Child Study Movement, progress in the study of childhood intelligence was occurring in the standardized testing field. The influx of students with diverse backgrounds that resulted from compulsory schooling in France and the United States produced a need for a method to classify children for proper educational placement. Alfred Binet and Theodore Simon were among those commissioned to devise a means for identifying children who were unlikely to benefit from formal education in the Paris schools. Binet and Simon produced their first 30-item intelligence scale for this purpose in 1905. Items were ordered by increasing difficulty, and were scored using a pass/fail criterion. Although somewhat crude psychometrically relative to today's standards, the original Binet-Simon scale and its subsequent revisions (Binet, 1911; Binet & Simon, 1908) represented major advances over the obsolete, sensory-based intelligence measures, and incorporated mental tasks that measured reasoning, comprehension, and judgment (Boake, 2002). The Binet scales emphasized the need for a standard administration, simple scoring, and evidence that a test serves its intended purpose (e.g., to identify children with low cognitive ability).

Multiple translations of the Binet scales were completed in the United States, including a well-known version by Goddard and colleagues at the Vineland

Training School (Goddard, 1916) and one by Kuhlmann (1912) that attempted to lower the age range to 2 months by including additional items. Shortly before World War I (in 1916), Terman revised the Binet scale at Stanford. His revision expanded the age range upward to adulthood and replaced the mental age score with the intelligence quotient (IQ). The 1937 Terman-Merrill revision of the Stanford-Binet included a number of new preschool-level items as well as additional nonverbal and memory items.

Intelligence tests for young children that were available in the early part of the 20th century generally failed to capture the complexities and uniqueness of early childhood intelligence, and instead focused on the developmental trajectories of mental and physical skills (Lichtenberger & Kaufman, 2004). A number of intelligence tests for infants and preschoolers published in the middle of the 20th century, including the Cattell Infant Intelligence Scale (Cattell, 1940), the Full Range Picture Vocabulary Test (Ammons & Ammons, 1948), and the Leiter International Performance Scale (Leiter, 1948). Despite increasing options, Terman's adaptation and translation of Binet and Simon's intelligence test, the Stanford-Binet Intelligence Scales (1937) remained entrenched as the preferred intelligence measure in the United States for children until the latter part of the 20th century (Lichtenberger & Kaufman, 2004).

Prior to the emergence of the Child Study Movement and the rise of standardized testing, prevalent views of intelligence posited that it was a genetically determined, immutable trait that was manifested behaviorally through sensory functions (Kelley & Surbeck, 2007). Binet was one of the first to question this basic assumption, but the heredity versus environment debate would continue for more than 40 years, when the preponderance of evidence suggested an environmental role in cognitive development. The influential writings of Piaget (1952) were indicative of this fundamental shift in thought, due to his emphasis on the interaction between the child and his or her environment in shaping progression through the mental developmental stages. In line with Piaget's theory and mounting evidence in support of the environment's role in cognitive development, educators had also noted a persistent pattern of lower performance in children from poor backgrounds (Kelley & Surbeck, 2007). Thus, a renewed focus on the health and welfare of young children ensued, culminating in new social programs and educational legislation that included the Head Start program.

Head Start was the primary federal program established to improve the academic performance of children from economically disadvantaged homes, as well as English language learners. A wide variety of Head Start programs were established throughout the United States, ranging from traditional nursery schools to highly structured academic settings; however, all federally funded programs were required to provide proof of their effectiveness. This requirement resulted in a tremendous increase in the number of available instruments, with more than 200 childhood measures published between 1960 and 1980 (Kelley & Surbeck, 2007; Wortham, 2012). Publications of comprehensive intelligence measures for young children during this time period included the McCarthy Scales of Children's Abilities (McCarthy, 1972), and the Wechsler Preschool and Primary Scale of Intelligence (WPPSI; Wechsler, 1967). Relative to their predecessors, the available instruments for preschoolers were improved, but not as psychometrically sound or as developmentally appropriate as those for older children and adults.

The Education for All Handicapped Children Act of 1975 (PL 94-142) made a profound impact on early childhood assessment by requiring that a free public education be provided to all children aged 3–21, regardless of handicap. The law also stipulated that children with handicaps between the ages of 6 and 21 be placed in the least restrictive educational environment based on placement decisions derived from nondiscriminatory evaluations. Similar recommendations were made, but not required, for children between the ages of 3 and 5. Subsequent amendments passed in 1986 (PL 99-457) addressed this shortcoming through creation of the Federal School Program, which extended the rights to children with disabilities between the ages of 3 and 5 (Wortham, 2012). The 1986 amendments also offered financial incentives to states for the provision of early childhood intervention programs for children from birth to 3 years of age (Ford et al., 2012).

More recent legislation such as the Americans with Disabilities Act (1990) further defined the requirements of special education and added the categories of autism and traumatic brain injury. Goals of the legislation included maximal inclusion and integration of children with disabilities into all educational areas, and the requirement that all childhood programs be prepared to serve children with disabilities (Wortham, 2012). In 1997, Congress reauthorized the Education for All Children Act of 1975, requiring states to include special education students in the yearly state testing and to publicly report the results. The No Child Left Behind Act of 2001 (NCLB) and the Individuals with Disabilities Improvement Act of 2004 further specified the requirement by noting that 95% of children with disabilities must participate in the testing. The effects of this legislation and the resulting initiatives have yet to be evaluated to determine if the needs of these children are being met in the intended manner. Regardless of the findings, the importance of developing reliable and valid measures of mental abilities for children with and without disabilities has received continued support over the past 50 years from changes in social policy and educational legislation.

Today, there are numerous measures of intellectual or cognitive ability available for use with preschoolers and young children. Rapid Reference 1.1 lists the most

≣ Rapid Reference 1.1

21st Century Preschool Intelligence Measures

Measure	Common Abbreviation	Publication Information	Age Range	Primary Scores
Wechsler Preschool and Primary Scale of Intelligence– Fourth Edition	WPPSI-IV	Wechsler, 2012: Pearson	2:6–3:11 (Younger Battery) 4:0–7:7 (Older Battery)	Full Scale IQ Verbal Comprehension Index Visual Spatial Index Fluid Reasoning Index Working Memory Index Processing Speed Index Verbal Acquisition Index Nonverbal Index General Ability Index Cognitive Proficiency Index
Differential Ability Scales–Second Edition	DAS-II	Elliott, 2007: Pearson	2:5–3:5 (Early Years Lower Level) 3:6–6:11 (Early Years Upper Level)	General Conceptual Ability Special Nonverbal Composite Verbal Nonverbal Reasoning Spatial Working Memory Processing Speed School Readiness

Measure	Common Abbreviation	Publication Information	Age Range	Primary Scores
Woodcock–Johnson Tests of Cognitive Ability–Third Edition Normative Update	WJ III COG NU	Woodcock, McGrew, & Mather, 2007: Riverside	2:0–5:11 (Early Development Battery)	General Intellectual Ability Gc: crystallized knowledge Gv: visual–spatial ability Gf: fluid reasoning Gsm: short-term memory Gq: quantitative knowledge
Stanford–Binet Intelligence Scales for Early Childhood, Fifth Edition	Early SB5	Roid, 2005: Pro-Ed	2:0–7:3 (Early SB5)	Full Scale IQ Abbreviated Battery IQ Verbal IQ Nonverbal IQ Knowledge Visual–Spatial Processing Fluid Reasoning Working Memory Quantitative Reasoning
Kaufman Assessment Battery for Children–Second Edition	KABC-II	A. S. Kaufman & Kaufman, 2004: Pearson	3:0–3:11 (5 Subtests) 4:0–6:11 (10 Subtests)	Mental Processing Index Fluid–Crystallized Index Knowledge Nonverbal Index Sequential Simultaneous Learning
Reynolds Intellectual Assessment Scales	RIAS	Reynolds & Kamphaus, 2003:	3:0–94 (All Subtests)	Composite Intelligence Index

(continued)

Measure	Common Abbreviation	Publication Information	Age Range	Primary Scores
		Psychological Assessment Resources		Verbal Intelligence Index Nonverbal Intelligence Index Composite Memory Index

commonly used measures that have published since 2000, as well as some basic descriptive information. A thorough review of these measures is beyond the scope of this chapter; however, Ford et al. (2012) include a concise summary of each scale's strengths and weaknesses.

HISTORICAL FOUNDATIONS OF THE WPPSI-IV

Excellent accounts of the historical foundations of intelligence testing have been written (e.g., Goldstein & Beers, 2003; R. J. Sternberg, 2000; Wasserman, 2012), and the reader is referred to these sources to gain a greater understanding of historical developments in this area. As with most texts on the Wechsler intelligence scales, we have elected to include a brief section describing the historical foundations of the Wechsler scales, despite the possibility that the inclusion of such information may serve to perpetuate a misperception that the scales are outdated. It is our contention that Wechsler's foresight to define intelligence in practical terms allowed the necessary flexibility for continuous revisions to the scales in light of advances in theory, research, and the measurement of intelligence (Coalson, Raiford, Saklofske, & Weiss, 2010). His 1939 definition of intelligence is still relevant today and continues to appear in the most recent revisions of his scales (Wechsler, 2003, 2008, 2012). Wechsler defined intelligence as

the aggregate or global capacity of the individual to act purposefully, to think rationally, and to deal effectively with his [or her] environment. It is global because it characterizes the individual's behavior as a whole; it is an aggregate because it is composed of elements or abilities which, though not entirely independent, are qualitatively differentiable.

(Wechsler, 1944, p. 3)

Wechsler thus supported the existence of general or global intelligence, but also acknowledged that general intelligence is composed of qualitatively different abilities (e.g., verbal comprehension, visual–perceptual skills, and reasoning ability). He believed that intelligence was more than just cognitive abilities and that nonintellective, conative factors such as curiosity, drive, and persistence contributed to the expression of intelligence (Wechsler, 1950). His astute clinical skills were evident in his selection of subtests for his batteries, all of which have been shown to measure important factors of intelligence since their introduction (Carroll, 1993, 2012; Horn & Blankson, 2012; W. J. Schneider & McGrew, 2012).

Consistent with Wechsler's definition of intelligence, results of comprehensive factor-analytic investigations of cognitive ability measures suggest overwhelming evidence for a general intelligence factor at the apex of a hierarchical construct that is composed of a set of related but distinguishable cognitive abilities (Carroll, 1993, 2012). Intelligence appears to be composed of 8 to 10 broad domains that are, in turn, composed of more specific abilities (Carroll, 1993; Horn & Noll, 1997). Additional research is needed to determine whether all of these domains are present in young children. Although some research suggests that the number of intelligence factors is reduced in young children relative to older children and adults (Morgan, Rothlisberg, McIntosh, & Hunt, 2009; Ward, Rothlisberg, McIntosh, & Bradley, 2011), other studies suggest that more differentiation among young children's cognitive abilities exists than was once believed (e.g., S. B. Kaufman, Reynolds, Liu, Kaufman, & McGrew, 2012; Kuwajima & Sawaguchi, 2010; Morgan et al., 2009; W. Schneider, Schumann-Hengsteler, & Sodian, 2005).

As indicated in Rapid Reference 1.2, the WPPSI-IV retains a number of subtests with origins in 20th century measures, supplying additional evidence of Wechsler's impressive clinical judgment when selecting the subtests to include in his original scales.

Extensive testing of military recruits during World War I raised questions about the limitations and weaknesses of early intelligence tests. In particular, concerns with the validity of IQ scores across the age range and for specific ethnic and socioeconomic groups were noted, as well as the increasing factor-analytic evidence suggesting that intelligence was composed of several abilities. Such was the atmosphere when David Wechsler entered the field of test development. Wechsler's clinical experiences as a psychological examiner for military recruits and his psychometric training under Charles Spearman and Karl Pearson led him to develop an adult intelligence scale that addressed some of the shortcomings he had personally observed (Boake, 2002).

≡ Rapid Reference 1.2

Origins of WPPSI-IV Subtests

Subtest	Origin	First WPPSI Edition
Information	Army Alpha Group Examination	WPPSI
Similarities	*Stanford-Binet*	WPPSI
Vocabulary	*Stanford-Binet*	WPPSI
Comprehension	*Stanford-Binet*	WPPSI
	Army Alpha Group Examination	
Receptive Vocabulary	*Stanford-Binet*	WPPSI-III
Picture Naming	*Stanford-Binet*	WPPSI-III
Block Design	*Army Performance Scale*	WPPSI
	Kohs Block Design (1923)	
Object Assembly	*Pintner-Paterson performance tests (1917)*	WPPSI-R
	Army Performance Scale	
Matrix Reasoning	*Raven's Progressive Matrices (1938)*	WPPSI-III
Picture Concepts	Novel task developed by Pearson	WPPSI-III
Picture Memory	Novel task developed by Pearson	WPPSI-IV
Zoo Locations	Novel task developed by Pearson	WPPSI-IV
Bug Search	Schneider and Shiffrin (1977)	WPPSI-IV
	Sternberg (1966)	
Cancellation	Albert (1973)	WPPSI-IV
	WISC-IV Cancellation	
Animal Coding	*Substitution Test* (Kirkpatrick, 1909)	WPPSI-IV

His first test, the Wechsler-Bellevue Intelligence Scale (Wechsler, 1939) possessed important advantages relative to its competitors, including both verbal and nonverbal measures in a single test. More importantly, Wechsler introduced the use of deviation IQs, which offered increased score comparability across measures and improved accuracy, interpretability, and clinical utility. Wechsler subsequently published a downward extension of the Wechsler-Bellevue scale as the Wechsler Intelligence Scale for Children (WISC, 1949), which was designed for children ages 5 to 15. There were few changes from the adult form of the scale, although easier items had been added to extend the test's floor. The Wechsler-Bellevue was revised again in 1955 and published as the Wechsler Adult Intelligence Scale (WAIS). In response to the increasing societal and clinical needs for measures of early childhood intelligence, the WPPSI (Wechsler, 1967) was developed for children between the ages of 4 years 0 months and 6 years 6 months. The Wechsler intelligence scales rose to a level of prominence among assessment measures, with continuous revisions spanning over 70 years.

The first revision of the WPPSI (WPPSI-R; Wechsler, 1989) extended the age range to children between the ages of 3 years 0 months and 7 years 3 months, and retained all of the original WPPSI subtests (Information, Comprehension, Arithmetic, Vocabulary, Similarities, Sentences, Geometric Design, Block Design, Mazes, Picture Completion, and Animal House [renamed Animal Pegs]). Easier and more difficult items were developed to extend the floors and ceilings of several retained subtests, and Object Assembly was added. Although children were administered every subtest in both WPPSI and WPPSI-R, age-determined start points were introduced to reduce administration time. Subsequent factor-analytic studies supported a two-factor model of intelligence for both scales, including both Verbal and Performance factors (Carlson & Reynolds, 1981; Gyurke, Stone, & Beyer, 1990; B. Schneider & Gervais, 1991; Silverstein, 1969; Stone, Gridley, & Gyurke, 1991).

The subsequent revision of the WPPSI-R resulted in the *Wechsler Preschool and Primary Scale of Intelligence–Third Edition* (WPPSI-III; Wechsler, 2002), a scale with more dramatic differences from its predecessor than those in the previous revision. The most obvious change in the WPPSI-III was the division of the covered age range into two age bands with different subtest batteries; ages 2:6 to 3:11 and ages 4:0 to 7:3. Five WPPSI-R subtests were dropped for the WPPSI-III, including Arithmetic, Animal Pegs, Geometric Design, Mazes, and Sentences. These subtests were replaced with five new subtests that were more developmentally appropriate and designed to measure constructs that were shown to be important aspects of intelligence. Similar to previous revisions of the WISC and WAIS, the Coding and Symbol Search subtests were added to the WPPSI-III as measures of processing speed. Word Reasoning, Matrix Reasoning, and Picture Concepts were added as new measures of fluid reasoning.

Revisions to the Wechsler intelligence scales are based on psychometric and theoretical advances, as well as clinical research and practical need: They are not based on fundamental changes to Wechsler's definition of intelligence or any single theory of intelligence or cognitive development. Regrettably, we never had the opportunity to meet or work with David Wechsler. However, based on his accomplishments and writings, we believe he would have embraced advancements in the development of his instruments, based on guidance from contemporary theories of intelligence, child development, neuroscience, and other related fields.

We are confident he would have insisted on the abundant evidence of psychometric quality and clinical utility. The changes in the WPPSI-IV continue to reflect this revision trend and are detailed in subsequent sections of this chapter.

DEVELOPMENT OF THE WPPSI-IV

Key Revisions

A variety of issues precipitated the WPPSI-IV revision. The *WPPSI-IV Technical and Interpretive Manual* (*Technical and Interpretive Manual*; Wechsler, 2012) discusses these issues in detail on pages 19–31. Rapid Reference 1.3 lists the key revision features broadly and specifically.

≡ Rapid Reference 1.3

Broad and Detailed Key Revisions

Broad Key Revision	Detailed Key Revisions
Updated theoretical foundations	• Incorporate and consider research on contemporary structural intelligence models • Incorporate and consider neurodevelopmental and neurocognitive research • Incorporate and consider working memory models and research
Increased developmental appropriateness	• Improve the developmental appropriateness of manipulatives • Improve the developmental appropriateness of instructions • Improve the developmental appropriateness of the Processing Speed subtests
Increased user friendliness	• Enhance item security • Improve user friendliness of materials and packaging • Minimize testing time • Improve user friendliness of administration and scoring • Reduce length of discontinue rules
Improved psychometric properties	• Improve psychometric properties of items and scoring rules • Update the norming method • Increase evidence of reliability and validity

Broad Key Revision	Detailed Key Revisions
	• Improve subtest floors and ceilings
	• Reduce item bias
	• Expand critical value significance level options
Enhance clinical utility	• Improve the clinical utility of the test structure
	• Organize the score differences comparison methodology to maximize clinical utility
	• Extend the age range upward
	• Reduce the expressive language requirements necessary to obtain a composite score
	• Provide ancillary index scores with specific clinical applications
	• Increase the number of special group studies
	• Provide statistical linkage to a measure of achievement, and build in a pattern of strengths and weaknesses analysis

Subtests

Practitioners who used the WPPSI-III will find many of the same core Wechsler subtests are present but substantively revised (with many new items and in some cases new procedures). They also will notice a number of new subtests, a modified test structure, more composite scores, and a new approach to score analysis on the Record Form.

New Subtests

There are five new subtests:

1. Picture Memory, a visual Working Memory subtest that utilizes proactive interference rather than sequencing to introduce cognitive processing demands necessary for measuring working memory.
2. Zoo Locations, a visual-spatial Working Memory subtest that also relies on proactive interference to introduce cognitive processing demands.
3. Bug Search, a timed visual matching Processing Speed subtest inspired by WPPSI-III Symbol Search.
4. Cancellation, a speeded visual search Processing Speed subtest inspired by WISC-IV (Wechsler, 2003) Cancellation.
5. Animal Coding, a timed visual paired associates Processing Speed subtest inspired by WPPSI-III Coding and WPPSI-R Animal Pegs.

Information about the development of these new subtests that provides insight into the test development process appears in the Behind the Scenes boxes in Chapter 2 of this book.

Dropped Subtests

Four subtests were removed from the WPPSI-III complement prior to WPPSI-IV development. These subtests were removed for varying reasons:

- Word Reasoning was dropped because it conceptually overlapped with the Vocabulary subtest, it lacked evidence of measuring fluid reasoning (which was the original intent), and it was strongly associated with the Information subtest to the point of psychometric redundancy. Furthermore, it was not well liked by children and not rated highly by practitioners for its clinical utility. It was retained for the prior edition because of its superior floors relative to Similarities and Comprehension, which were substantially improved for this revision. Thus, it was no longer necessary.
- Picture Completion was deleted because it was desirable to reduce the emphasis of the test on speeded performance and fine visual detail discrimination, and to make room for the Working Memory subtests.
- Symbol Search and Coding were removed to make room for the new Processing Speed subtests, which measure similar constructs in that domain but are more developmentally appropriate and reduce greatly the reliance on fine motor skills. Notably, both of these subtests had a naturally occurring floor that couldn't be overcome without redesigning the tasks; hence, the new subtests were developed.

Retained Subtests

For ages 2:6 to 3:11, five WPPSI-III subtests were retained. For ages 4:0 to 7:7, 10 subtests were retained. Rapid Reference 1.4 lists the retained subtests by age band and examples of changes made to those subtests. The revisions are more specifically detailed in Chapters 2 and 3 of this book.

Subtest Descriptions and Expert References on Constructs Measured and Abilities Engaged

Rapid Reference 1.5 provides a description of all subtests, reproduced by permission from the test publisher. New subtests are indicated with an asterisk. The age range for each subtest is also listed, as not all subtests are available for children aged 2:6 to 3:11. Rapid Reference 1.6 provides information on the constructs and abilities ascribed to each subtest.

≡ Rapid Reference 1.4

....

Retained Subtests by Age Band and Changes

Subtest	Ages	Changes
Information	2:6–7:7	New and revised items and scoring criteria
		Updated with more child-appropriate and contemporary questions
		Reduced total items and shorter discontinue rule
Similarities	4:0–7:7	New and revised items and scoring criteria
		Introduced picture items to improve the subtest floor
		Reduced total items and shorter discontinue rule
Vocabulary	4:0–7:7	New and revised items and scoring criteria
		Reduced total items and shorter discontinue rule
Comprehension	4:0–7:7	New and revised items and scoring criteria
		Introduced picture items to improve the subtest floor
		Updated with more child-appropriate and contemporary questions
		Shorter discontinue rule
Receptive Vocabulary	2:6–7:7	New and revised items
		Reduced total items and shorter discontinue rule
Picture Naming	2:6–7:7	New and revised items
		Reduced total items and shorter discontinue rule
Block Design	2:6–7:7	New and revised items
		Increased teaching and transition between one-color and two-color blocks
		New items to extend the ceiling
		Reduced total items and shorter discontinue rule
Object Assembly	2:6–7:7	New and revised items
		New item to extend the subtest ceiling
		Reduced total items and shorter discontinue rule
Matrix Reasoning	4:0–7:7	New and revised items
		Reduced total items and shorter discontinue rule
Picture Concepts	4:0–7:7	New and revised items
		Reduced total items and shorter discontinue rule

≡ Rapid Reference 1.5

Subtest Abbreviations, Descriptions, and Age Ranges

Subtest	Abbreviation	Description	Age Range
Information	IN	For picture items, the child selects the response option that best answers a question about a general-knowledge topic. For verbal items, the child answers questions about a broad range of general-knowledge topics.	2:6–7:7
Similarities	SI	For picture items, the child selects the response option that is from the same category as two other depicted objects. For verbal items, the child is read two words that represent common objects or concepts and describes how they are similar.	4:0–7:7
Vocabulary	VC	For picture items, the child names the depicted object. For verbal items, the child defines words that are read aloud.	4:0–7:7
Comprehension	CO	For picture items, the child selects the response option that represents the best response to a general principle or social situation. For verbal items, the child answers questions based on his or her understanding of general principles and social situations.	4:0–7:7
Receptive Vocabulary	RV	The child selects the response option that best represents the word the examiner reads aloud.	2:6–7:7
Picture Naming	PN	The child names depicted objects.	2:6–7:7
Block Design	BD	Working within a specified time limit, the child views a model and/or a picture and uses one- or two-color blocks to re-create the design.	2:6–7:7

Subtest	Abbreviation	Description	Age Range
Object Assembly	OA	Working within a specified time limit, the child assembles the pieces of a puzzle to create a representation of an identified object.	2:6–7:7
Matrix Reasoning	MR	The child views an incomplete matrix and selects the response option that completes the matrix.	4:0–7:7
Picture Concepts	PC	The child views two or three rows of pictures and selects one picture from each row to form a group with a common characteristic.	4:0–7:7
Picture Memory*	PM	The child views a stimulus page of one or more pictures for a specified time and then selects the pictures from options on a response page.	2:6–7:7
Zoo Locations*	ZL	The child views one or more animal cards placed on a zoo layout for a specified time and then places each card in the previously viewed locations.	2:6–7:7
Bug Search*	BS	Working within a specified time limit, the child marks the bug in the search group that matches the target bug.	4:0–7:7
Cancellation*	CA	Working within a specified time limit, the child scans two arrangements of objects (one random, one structured) and marks target objects.	4:0–7:7
Animal Coding*	AC	Working within a specified time limit and using a key, the child marks shapes that correspond to pictured animals.	4:0–7:7

*New subtest

Source: Table 1.1 of the WPPSI-IV Administration and Scoring Manual.
Wechsler Preschool and Primary Scale of Intelligence–Fourth Edition (WPPSI-IV). Copyright © 2012 NCS Pearson, Inc. Reproduced with permission. All rights reserved.
"Wechsler Preschool and Primary Scale of Intelligence" and "WPPSI" are trademarks, in the United States and/or other countries, of Pearson Education, Inc., or its affiliates.

≡ Rapid Reference 1.6

WPPSI-IV Subtest Constructs and Abilities

Subtest	Rationale
Information	Designed to measure: Acquisition, retention, and retrieval of general facts
	Related to: Crystallized ability, Gc-K0 (general information), and retention and retrieval of learned information, Glr
	May also involve: Auditory perception, verbal expression
Similarities	Designed to measure: Verbal concept formation and abstract reasoning
	Related to: Crystallized ability, associative and categorical thinking, Gf-I (induction), concept recognition and generation
	May also involve: Auditory perception and verbal expression
Vocabulary	Designed to measure: Word knowledge, verbal concept formation
	Related to: Crystallized ability, Gc-VL (lexical knowledge), fund of knowledge, learning, verbal expression, long-term memory
	May also involve: Auditory perception, auditory comprehension, abstract thinking, expressive vocabulary
Comprehension	Designed to measure: Verbal reasoning, verbal conceptualization, verbal comprehension, verbal expression, practical knowledge, judgment
	Related to: Crystallized ability (Gc), understanding of societal standards and conventional behavior, social judgment, Glr, common sense
	May also involve: Auditory perception
Receptive Vocabulary	Designed to measure: Word knowledge, verbal concept formation, receptive vocabulary
	Related to: Crystallized ability, Gc-VL (lexical knowledge), fund of knowledge, learning, verbal expression, long-term memory
	May also involve: Visual perception, auditory comprehension
Picture Naming	Designed to measure: Word knowledge, verbal concept formation, expressive vocabulary
	Related to: Crystallized ability, Gc-VL (lexical knowledge), fund of knowledge, learning, verbal expression, long-term memory
	May also involve: Visual and auditory perception

Subtest	Rationale
Block Design	Designed to measure: Visual–spatial processing, analysis and synthesis of abstract visual stimuli
	Related to: Gv-SR (spatial relations), Gv-Vz (visualization), Gv-CS (closure speed), mental rotation, nonverbal reasoning, visual perception, simultaneous processing, problem solving, cognitive flexibility, planning
	May also involve: Visual–motor coordination
Object Assembly	Designed to measure: Visual–spatial processing, analysis and synthesis of meaningful visual stimuli
	Related to: Gv-SR, Gv-Vz, Gv-CS, mental rotation, nonverbal reasoning, visual perception, simultaneous processing, problem solving, cognitive flexibility, planning
	May also involve: Visual–motor coordination
Matrix Reasoning	Designed to measure: Fluid reasoning/intelligence, classification ability, inductive reasoning
	Related to: Gf-I (induction), Gf-RG (general sequential reasoning), simultaneous and successive processing, planning, metacognition, problem solving, cognitive flexibility, reasoning, planning
	May also involve: Visual perception
Picture Concepts	Designed to measure: Fluid reasoning/intelligence, classification ability, inductive reasoning
	Related to: Gf-I, Gf-RG, simultaneous and successive processing, planning, metacognition, concept recognition and generation, problem solving, cognitive flexibility, reasoning, planning
	May also involve: Gc (crystallized ability), acquired knowledge
Picture Memory	Designed to measure: Visual working memory, ability to withstand proactive interference
	Related to: Gsm-MW (working memory capacity), Gsm-MS (memory span), Gv-MV (visual memory), attention, simultaneous and successive processing, planning and metacognition, visual immediate memory for pictures, response inhibition
	May also involve: Visual perception
Zoo Locations	Designed to measure: Visual–spatial working memory, ability to withstand proactive interference
	Related to: Gsm-MW (working memory capacity), Gsm-MS (memory span), Gv-MV (visual memory), attention, simultaneous and successive processing, planning and metacognition, visual immediate memory for pictures and spatial locations, response inhibition
	May also involve: Visual perception, visual–motor construction

(continued)

Subtest	Rationale
Bug Search	Designed to measure: Processing speed, simple visual discrimination
	Related to: Gs-P (perceptual speed), Gs-R9 (rate of test taking), simultaneous processing, planning and metacognition, speed and efficiency, selective and sustained attention, visual scanning and tracking, visual immediate memory for pictures, response inhibition
	May also involve: Visual–motor skills
Cancellation	Designed to measure: Processing speed
	Related to: Gs-P (perceptual speed), Gs-R9 (rate of test taking), simultaneous processing, planning and metacognition, speed and efficiency, selective and sustained attention, visual scanning and tracking, visual immediate memory for pictures, response inhibition, classification ability
	May also involve: Visual–motor skills, acquired knowledge
Animal Coding	Designed to measure: Processing speed
	Related to: Gs-P (perceptual speed), Gs-R9 (rate of test taking), simultaneous processing, planning and metacognition, speed and efficiency, selective and sustained attention, visual scanning and tracking, visual immediate memory for pictures and objects, response inhibition, visual associative memory
	May also involve: Visual–motor skills

Note. References: Carroll, 1993; Flanagan, Alfonso, and Ortiz, 2012; Flanagan, Alfonso, Ortiz, and Dynda, 2010; Groth-Marnat, 2003; Lichtenberger and Kaufman, 2004, 2013; Miller, 2010, 2013; Sattler, 2008; W. J. Schneider and McGrew, 2012.

Subtest Terminology

The WPPSI-IV categorizes subtests into three categories—core, supplemental, and optional—that indicate a subtest's status in relation to a given composite score. The categorical assignment sometimes differs across the two age bands (i.e., 2:6–3:11 and 4:0–7:7) as well as across different composite scores. Furthermore, unlike the WISC-IV and the WAIS-IV (Wechsler, 2008), subtests that are core for a given index score are not necessarily core for the Full Scale IQ, because the Full Scale IQ is not derived from every subtest that is a core index subtest.

Core subtests are used to derive the composite score normative information and values. Supplemental subtests are provided to allow assessment of additional intellectual ability constructs, and can be used in some situations as substitutes for core subtests when a necessary subtest score is missing. Optional subtests are included to complement the existing intellectual ability information, but cannot substitute for a missing or invalid core subtest.

Composite Scores

Composite Score Terminology

The 10 composite scores from the published test are described in detail in Chapter 4 of this book. Practitioners who used the WPPSI-III will notice important changes to the composite score terminology. Some scores were renamed, and new scores were created.

The most obvious change is that the names Verbal IQ and Performance IQ are no longer in use. This elimination began with the WISC-IV and WAIS-IV, and the terms are now completely phased out. The Verbal IQ was renamed as the Verbal Comprehension Index. For children aged 2:6 to 3:11, the Performance IQ is renamed the Visual Spatial Index; for those ages it is derived from the same subtests that contributed to that score. However, for children 4:0 to 7:7, the Performance IQ as it stood no longer exists. In its place for these ages there are now two scores, the Visual Spatial Index and the Fluid Reasoning Index. The WPPSI-III Performance IQ formerly was derived from subtests that now contribute to these two separate index scores. The WPPSI-III Processing Speed Quotient was renamed the Processing Speed Index, as was done previously on the WISC-IV and the WAIS-IV, to improve consistency across the different scales. Finally, the WPPSI-III General Language Composite is now termed the Vocabulary Acquisition Index to better represent the skills measured by its contributing subtests.

The published test divides the nine index scores into primary and ancillary categories. The primary index scores are thus termed because they are based on factor-analytic evidence and represent the main constructs measured within the test. The ancillary index scores are designed for use in specific practical and clinical situations.

The published composite scores are listed, with their abbreviations (used in some tables in this book and throughout the published manuals), in Rapid Reference 1.7. Because not all subtests are appropriate or available for ages 2:6 to 3:11, there are fewer composite scores available for younger children (seven). The age range for each composite score is therefore listed, along with the index score categorical membership (primary or ancillary).

Test Structure

The age range covered by the WPPSI-IV includes periods of great cognitive growth and development. For this reason, the battery is different for the two age bands (ages 2:6 to 3:11 and ages 4:0 to 7:7), and the composite scores for each age band are composed of different subtests.

⩰ Rapid Reference 1.7

Published Composite Score Abbreviations and Age Range

Composite Score	Abbreviation	Age Range	Index Score Category
Verbal Comprehension Index	VCI	2:6–7:7	Primary
Visual Spatial Index	VSI	2:6–7:7	Primary
Fluid Reasoning Index	FRI	4:0–7:7	Primary
Working Memory Index	WMI	2:6–7:7	Primary
Processing Speed Index	PSI	4:0–7:7	Primary
Full Scale IQ	FSIQ	2:6–7:7	n/a
Vocabulary Acquisition Index	VAI	2:6–7:7	Ancillary
Nonverbal Index	NVI	2:6–7:7	Ancillary
General Ability Index	GAI	2:6–7:7	Ancillary
Cognitive Proficiency Index	CPI	4:0–7:7	Ancillary

The 2:6 to 3:11 Age Band

For children aged 2:6 to 3:11, there are three primary index scores available (i.e., the Verbal Comprehension Index, Visual Spatial Index, and Working Memory Index), as well as a Full Scale IQ and three ancillary index scores (i.e., the Vocabulary Acquisition Index, Nonverbal Index, and General Ability Index). Each composite score is derived from the core subtests on the corresponding scale. If a subtest is listed on a scale in Figure 1.1, it does not indicate that it can automatically substitute for all core subtests on the scale. Refer to Chapter 3 of this book and to the *Administration and Scoring Manual* for in-depth discussion of the substitution, proration, and invalidation rules, which differ substantially from the WPPSI-III, WISC-IV, and WAIS-IV. Figure 1.1 depicts the test framework for 2:6 to 3:11. Subtests listed in bold font for a given scale are core to the corresponding composite score. Subtests that appear in italic font are supplemental for that scale. If no subtests are listed in italics, there are no supplemental subtests for that scale. Rapid Reference 1.1 provides the core subtest composition of the published composite scores, by age band.

Ages 2:6–3:11

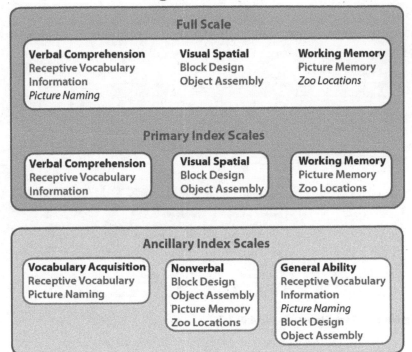

Full Scale

Verbal Comprehension
Receptive Vocabulary
Information
Picture Naming

Visual Spatial
Block Design
Object Assembly

Working Memory
Picture Memory
Zoo Locations

Primary Index Scales

Verbal Comprehension
Receptive Vocabulary
Information

Visual Spatial
Block Design
Object Assembly

Working Memory
Picture Memory
Zoo Locations

Ancillary Index Scales

Vocabulary Acquisition
Receptive Vocabulary
Picture Naming

Nonverbal
Block Design
Object Assembly
Picture Memory
Zoo Locations

General Ability
Receptive Vocabulary
Information
Picture Naming
Block Design
Object Assembly

Figure 1.1 Test Structure for 2:6–3:11

The 4:0 to 7:7 Age Band

For children aged 4:0 to 7:7, there are five primary index scores available (i.e., the Verbal Comprehension Index, Visual Spatial Index, Fluid Reasoning Index, Working Memory Index, and Processing Speed Index), as well as a Full Scale IQ and four ancillary index scores (i.e., the Vocabulary Acquisition Index, Nonverbal Index, General Ability Index, and Cognitive Proficiency Index). Each composite score is derived from the core subtests on the corresponding scale. As with the younger age band, if a subtest is listed on a scale in Figure 1.2, it

Ages 4:0–7:7

Full Scale

Verbal Comprehension	Visual Spatial	Fluid Reasoning	Working Memory	Processing Speed
Information	Block Design	Matrix Reasoning	Picture Memory	Bug Search
Similarities	*Object Assembly*	Picture Concepts	Zoo Locations	Cancellation
Vocabulary				*Animal Coding*
Comprehension				

Primary Index Scales

Verbal Comprehension	Visual Spatial	Fluid Reasoning	Working Memory	Processing Speed
Information	Block Design	Matrix Reasoning	Picture Memory	Bug Search
Similarities	Object Assembly	Picture Concepts	Zoo Locations	Cancellation

Ancillary Index Scales

Vocabulary Acquisition	Nonverbal	General Ability	Cognitive Proficiency
Receptive Vocabulary	Block Design	Information	Picture Memory
Picture Naming	*Object Assembly*	Similarities	Zoo Locations
	Matrix Reasoning	Vocabulary	Bug Search
	Picture Concepts	*Comprehension*	Cancellation
	Picture Memory	Block Design	*Animal Coding*
	Zoo Locations	*Object Assembly*	
	Bug Search	Matrix Reasoning	
	Cancellation	Picture Concepts	
	Animal Coding		

Figure 1.2 Test Structure for 4:0–7:7

does not indicate that it can automatically substitute for all core subtests on the scale. Refer to Chapter 3 of this book and to the *Administration and Scoring Manual* for in-depth discussion of the substitution, proration, and invalidation rules, which differ substantially from the WPPSI-III, WISC-IV, and WAIS-IV. Figure 1.2 depicts the test framework for 4:0 to 7:7. Subtests listed in bold font for a given scale are core to the corresponding composite score. Subtests that appear in italic font are supplemental for that scale. If no subtests are listed in italics, there are no supplemental subtests for that scale.

Subtest Composition of Published Composite Scores

Rapid Reference 1.8 lists the core subtests for the published composite scores for each age band.

≡ Rapid Reference 1.8

Core Subtest Composition of Published Composite Scores, by Age Band

Subtest	VCI	VSI	FRI	WMI	PSI	FSIQ	VAI	NVI	GAI	CPI
IN	Y, O					Y, O			Y, O	
SI	O					O			O	
RV	Y					Y	Y, O		Y	
PN							Y, O			
BD		Y, O				Y, O		Y, O	Y, O	
OA		Y, O				Y		Y	Y	
MR			O			O		O	O	
PC			O					O		
PM				Y, O		Y, O		Y, O		O
ZL				Y, O				Y		O
BS					O	O		O		O
CA					O					O

Note. Y = core FSIQ subtest for ages 2:6–3:11, O = core FSIQ subtest for ages 4:0–7:7. Abbreviations are IN = Information, SI = Similarities, RV = Receptive Vocabulary, PN = Picture Naming, BD = Block Design, OA = Object Assembly, MR = Matrix Reasoning, PC = Picture Concepts, PM = Picture Memory, ZL = Zoo Locations, BS = Bug Search, CA = Cancellation, VCI = Verbal Comprehension Index, VSI = Visual Spatial Index, FRI = Fluid Reasoning Index, WMI = Working Memory Index, PSI = Processing Speed Index, FSIQ = Full Scale IQ, VAI = Vocabulary Acquisition Index, NVI = Nonverbal Index, GAI = General Ability Index, CPI = Cognitive Proficiency Index.

Additional Index Scores in This Book and on the Accompanying CD

There are a number of additional index scores provided in this book and on the accompanying CD. The additional index scores were developed based upon specific theoretical approaches and practical considerations. The norms for these additional index scores are available on the CD that accompanies this book, which contains appendix matter and the WPPSI-IV Interpretive Assistant 1.0. Rapid Reference 1.9 provides a summary of the subtest composition of the additional index scores. Supporting technical evidence for these additional index scores is provided in Chapter 4 of this book.

≡ Rapid Reference 1.9

Subtest Composition of Additional Index Scores

Subtest	Gc-K0	Gc-VL	Gf-Verbal	WKI	CRGI	CVI	CEI
IN	✓					✓	
SI			✓		✓	✓	
VC		✓		✓		✓	✓
CO	✓		✓			✓	✓
RV		✓					
PN		✓		✓			
PC					✓		

Note. IN = Information, SI = Similarities, VC = Vocabulary, CO = Comprehension, RV = Receptive Vocabulary, PN = Picture Naming, PC = Picture Concepts. Gc-K0 = Gc narrow ability of general information, Gc-VL = Gc narrow ability of lexical knowledge, Gf-Verbal = inductive reasoning with verbal stimuli, WKI = Word Knowledge Index, CRGI = Concept Recognition and Generation Index, CVI = Comprehensive Verbal Index, CEI = Complex Expressive Index.

VALIDITY

Factor Analytic Studies

As noted, the WPPSI-IV test structure represents a substantial revision relative to the WPPSI-III. With 4 subtests having been deleted and 5 added, the WPPSI-IV is composed of 7 subtests for 2:6 to 3:11 and 15 subtests for 4:0 to 7:7. As with the WISC-IV and the WAIS-IV before, the structure focuses on the primary-index scores as the primary level of interpretation because they are supported by factor analysis, as well as by clinical and practical utility.

The *Technical and Interpretive Manual* reports the results of several confirmatory factor analytic studies that each support the hierarchical three-factor structure for the younger age band, and the hierarchical five-factor structure for the older age band.

The studies were conducted by age band on two sets of subtests: first on all subtests, then on all primary index subtests. The younger age band results supported a hierarchical three-factor structure with the Full Scale at the apex and separate factors for Verbal Comprehension, Visual Spatial, and Working Memory, with each subtest loading on its expected factor and no cross loadings or correlated error permitted.

The older age band results indicated a hierarchical five-factor structure with the Full Scale at the apex and separate factors for Verbal Comprehension, Visual

Spatial, Fluid Reasoning, Working Memory, and Processing Speed. Each subtest loaded on its expected factor. The model fit was excellent, but examination of modification indices and residuals suggested that two nested subfactors were present within the Verbal Comprehension factor. One subfactor, labeled *Broad/Expressive*, contained Information, Similarities, Vocabulary, and Comprehension. The second subfactor, labeled *Focused/Simple*, contained Receptive Vocabulary and Picture Naming. The groupings were theoretically meaningful because the first contained subtests that required more expressive responses and were not limited to lexical knowledge, and the second contained subtests that required little to no expressive responses and were focused on word meanings only. The Focused/Simple factor provides some factor-analytic support for the Vocabulary Acquisition Index at these ages, and the Broad/Expressive subfactor supports permitting only Vocabulary or Comprehension to substitute for Information or Similarities within the older age band's Full Scale IQ.

The test structures for each age band were supported within both sets of subtests (i.e., all subtests, core index subtests only), with statistically significant improvement of fit relative to less complex models and excellent fit indices (e.g., .97 Tucker-Lewis Index for all subtests on each battery). The fit indices were subsequently run for the selected model to confirm the older age band results within more narrow age groups (i.e., 4:0 to 4:11, 5:0 to 5:11, and 6:0 to 7:7). Each produced excellent fit indices (e.g., .98, .97, and .95 Tucker-Lewis Index for all subtests for each of the narrow age groups).

Relation to WPPSI-III

The WPPSI-IV represents a rather dramatic departure from its predecessor. As indicated in this chapter, a number of the traditional Wechsler subtests remain, others have been replaced, new subtests and composite scores have been added that measure constructs not previous measured, and the factor structure for both age bands is quite different as a result. Furthermore, as discussed in Chapter 2 of this book, a large proportion of items were replaced on many subtests, and the administration and scoring rules were revised. Additionally, as discussed in greater detail in Chapter 4 of this book, new comparison score approaches have been added to the test.

Evaluating the relation of the current test to the prior edition informs judgments about applicability of the research base on the prior edition to the current, and about how results may differ on the new test. This evaluation is particularly relevant for the WPPSI-IV due to the aforementioned changes.

For comparison purposes, Rapid Reference 1.10 lists the composition of the WPPSI-III and the WPPSI-IV Full Scale IQ by age band.

⚏ Rapid Reference 1.10

Comparison of the WPPSI-III and WPPSI-IV Full Scale IQ, by Age Band

Subtest	WPPSI-III 2:6–3:11	WPPSI-IV 2:6–3:11	WPPSI-III 4:0–7:3	WPPSI-IV 4:0–7:7
IN	✓	✓	✓	✓
SI				✓
RV	✓	✓		
VC			✓	
WR			✓	
BD	✓	✓	✓	✓
OA	✓	✓		
MR			✓	✓
PC			✓	
PM		✓		✓
BS				✓
CD			✓	

Note. Y = Core for ages 2:6–3:11, O = core for ages 4:0–7:7.
Abbreviations are IN = Information, SI = Similarities, RV = Receptive Vocabulary, VC = Vocabulary, WR = Word Reasoning, BD = Block Design, OA = Object Assembly, MR = Matrix Reasoning, PC = Picture Concepts, PM = Picture Memory, BS = Bug Search, CD = Coding.

For children aged 2:6 to 3:11, the Full Scale IQ is largely unchanged. The most important change is the inclusion of a Working Memory subtest in the score. The remaining subtests that contribute to the Full Scale IQ are the same as for the WPPSI-III. Hence, the contribution of Verbal Comprehension subtests to the Full Scale IQ is reduced from 50% to 40%, Visual Spatial from 50% to 40%, and Working Memory is changed from 0% to 20%. While an additional subtest contributes to the Full Scale IQ, the testing time necessary to obtain it is unchanged.

For ages 4:0 to 7:7, the changes relative to WPPSI-III are more extensive. The Full Scale IQ is derived using one fewer subtest (i.e., six) relative to the WPPSI-III, and the testing time to obtain the Full Scale IQ is shorter. The contribution of Verbal Comprehension subtests to the Full Scale IQ is decreased from 43% to 33%, and the contribution of Visual Spatial subtests to the Full Scale IQ is slightly higher (17% versus 14%), although Block Design remains the only contributing subtest from that domain. The contribution of Fluid Reasoning is also reduced (from 29% to 17%), as Picture Concepts is no longer core to the Full Scale IQ. As with younger children, one Working Memory subtest contributes to the Full Scale IQ, although the relative contribution of Working Memory is 17%. One Processing Speed subtest continues to contribute to the Full Scale IQ; however, the relative contribution of Processing Speed is slightly higher (17% versus 14%) because there are fewer subtests contributing to the Full Scale IQ. Three subtests (50% of the total) are shared across the WPPSI-III and WPPSI-IV Full Scale IQs due to different selections for core subtests (e.g., Similarities instead of Word Reasoning and Vocabulary) and replacements for dropped subtests (e.g., Bug Search instead of Coding).

There are other obvious changes to the test content and structure. New constructs are measured with the new Working Memory Index and subtests and the new Visual Spatial Index for ages 4:0 to 7:7, and the new Fluid Reasoning index for ages 4:0 to 7:7. The Verbal Comprehension subtests now all have initial picture items to ensure children with expressive issues and shy children who initially are hesitant to respond verbally can experience some success, and the new Processing Speed subtests are more developmentally appropriate.

The relation of the WPPSI-IV to the WPPSI-III was examined in 246 children aged 2:6 to 7:3 (mean age of 4.8). The tests were administered in counterbalanced order with a mean testing interval of 22 days and a range of 13 to 54 days (Wechsler, 2012). The sample contained representation from a variety of children from different races/ethnicities, parent education levels, and U.S. geographic regions, and roughly comprised half female and half male. Table 1.1 presents the mean composite score on each version, the standard difference, and the corrected correlation coefficients.

The overall correlation indicates that the Full Scale IQs for the two versions are the most highly correlated of all composite scores (.86), followed by the General Language Composite–Verbal Acquisition Index (.85), the Verbal Comprehension Index (.84), the Performance IQ–Fluid Reasoning Index (.76), and the Performance IQ–Visual Spatial Index (.71).

The Processing Speed Quotient–Processing Speed Index correlation was the lowest among the composite scores (.65), which is not an unexpected result due to the complete replacement of subtests across the two versions. Regardless of the extensive revisions to the test, the high correlation coefficient of .86 indicates the Full Scale IQ continues to measure the same construct.

As presented in Table 1.1, the average WPPSI-IV Full Scale IQ is 3.3 points lower than the WPPSI-III Full Scale IQ. The Verbal IQ–Verbal Comprehension

Table 1.1 Comparison of WPPSI-III and WPPSI-IV Scores

| | WPPSI-III | | WPPSI-IV | | | |
Score	Mean	SD	Mean	SD	Standard Difference	Corrected Correlation
VCI–VIQ	103.4	13.5	100.9	12.8	.19	.84
VSI–PIQ	104.9	13.7	102.6	13.3	.17	.71
FRI–PIQ	105.4	13.6	102.1	12.5	.25	.76
WMI			100.4	12.9		
PSI–PSQ	107.0	12.0	101.1	12.8	.48	.65
Full Scale IQ	105.0	13.5	101.7	13.0	.25	.86
VAI–GLC	104.6	13.4	101.7	12.8	.22	.85
NVI			102.1	12.9		
GAI			101.9	13.7		
CPI			100.4	11.7		

Source: Adapted from Table 5.5 of the *WPPSI-IV Technical and Interpretive Manual*.

Index, Performance IQ–Visual Spatial Index, and Performance IQ–Fluid Reasoning Index differences are similar to those observed for the Full Scale IQs, although the correlations are somewhat lower than those of the Full Scale IQ or the verbal composites. This likely occurs because the Performance IQ was split into two separate composites, so less construct overlap occurs across the two tests for these scores. These differences are in the direction and of the same size as expected according to the Flynn effect (Flynn, 2007), which predicts that observed scores on an older test become higher over time due to outdated norms. Hence, children score somewhat lower on the WPPSI-IV relative to the WPPSI-III, but the scores more accurately reflect the child's intellectual functioning because the norms are based on samples from the current population.

The largest standard difference was observed for the Processing Speed Quotient–Processing Speed Index (.48, with a difference of almost 6 points). This is not surprising, due to the new subtests that contribute to the WPPSI-IV Processing Speed Index and the relatively poorer floors of the WPPSI–III Processing Speed subtests. Children who could perform the tasks rather easily obtained higher scaled scores than on the corresponding WPPSI-IV subtests.

STANDARDIZATION AND PSYCHOMETRIC PROPERTIES

The WPPSI-IV normative information is based on a national sample of 1,700 children. It was collected from December 2010 through May 2012. Children were selected to match census proportions from 2010 U.S. Census data and the sample is stratified according to age, sex, race/ethnicity, parent education level, and U.S. geographic region. Nine age groups were created, with 200 children in each of eight age groups from 2:6 to 6:11 and 100 children in the 7:0 to 7:7 age group.

Reliability

The average reliability coefficient for the Full Scale IQ across the nine age groups was excellent, at .96 overall, with a range of .95 to .96 across the age groups. The primary index scores have overall reliability coefficients ranging from .86 for the Processing Speed Index to .94 for the Verbal Comprehension Index. The reliability coefficients ranged from .85 to .95 for the primary index scores at the individual age-group level. The subtest reliability coefficients ranged from .75 for Animal Coding to .93 for Similarities. At the age-group level, the subtest reliability coefficients ranged from .71 (for Animal Coding at the youngest ages) to .95 (for Similarities at the youngest age).

A subset of the normative sample ($N = 172$) provided retest reliability data, with an average of 23 days between the first and second testing. Results showed similar stability coefficients across the three age ranges in the study (2:6 to 3:11; 4:0 to 5:5, and 5:6 to 7:7). The average stability coefficients across all ages for composite scores ranged from .86 for the Processing Speed Index to .93 for the Full Scale IQ and the General Ability Index. The highest overall average subtest stability coefficient was .87 for Similarities, and the lowest was .75 for Zoo Locations and Animal Coding.

The average reliability coefficients for subtest, process, and composite scores, by age band and for all applicable ages, appear in Rapid Reference 1.11. Both internal consistency and test-retest stability coefficients are presented.

Loadings on the General Factor

General intelligence, or g (Spearman, 1927), can be derived by several methods. For the purposes of this book, g is calculated using the subtest factor loadings on the first unrotated factor in a principal components analysis. Factor loadings of .70 or greater are classified as good measures of g, loadings of .50 to .69 are classified as fair, and loadings below .50 are classified as poor. Squaring the subtest g loading provides the proportion of variance attributable to g.

≡ Rapid Reference 1.11

Average Reliability Coefficients of Subtest, Process, and Composite Scores

Subtest/ Composite Score	2:6–3:11 Internal Consistency	4:0–7:7 Internal Consistency	All Applicable Ages Internal Consistency	All Applicable Ages Test-Retest Stability
IN	.91	.88	.89	.83
SI	—	.93	.93	.87
VC	—	.89	.89	.84
CO	—	.91	.91	.84
RV	.91	.90	.90	.79
PN	.89	.88	.88	.83
BD	.85	.85	.85	.81
OA	.85	.85	.85	.77
MR	—	.90	.90	.82
PC	—	.89	.89	.79
PM	.91	.90	.91	.80
ZL	.90	.84	.86	.75
BS	—	—	—	.83
CA	—	—	—	.76
AC	—	—	—	.75
VCI	.94	.94	.94	.89
VSI	.89	.90	.89	.86
FRI	—	.93	.93	.88
WMI	.93	.91	.91	.87
PSI	—	—	—	.86
FSIQ	.96	.96	.96	.93
VAI	.94	.93	.93	.86
NVI	.94	.95	.95	.90
GAI	.95	.95	.95	.93
CPI	—	.92	.92	.89

Note. Abbreviations are IN = Information, SI = Similarities, VC = Vocabulary, CO = Comprehension, RV = Receptive Vocabulary, PN = Picture Naming, BD = Block Design, OA = Object Assembly, MR = Matrix Reasoning, PC = Picture Concepts, PM = Picture Memory, ZL = Zoo Locations, BS = Bug Search, CA = Cancellation, AC = Animal Coding, VCI = Verbal Comprehension Index, VSI = Visual Spatial Index, FRI = Fluid Reasoning Index, WMI = Working Memory Index, PSI = Processing Speed Index, FSIQ = Full Scale IQ, VAI = Vocabulary Acquisition Index, NVI = Nonverbal Index, GAI = General Ability Index, CPI = Cognitive Proficiency Index.
Source: Data are from the Technical and Interpretive Manual Tables 4.1 and 4.5.

Lichtenberger and Kaufman (2004) noted that the meaning of *g* loadings and of the concept of general intelligence has been the subject of much discussion and debate. That debate continues to the present day (S. B. Kaufman et al., 2012; Reynolds, 2013; te Nijenhius, van Vianen, & van der Flier, 2007). It therefore is important, as Lichtenberger and Kaufman state, not to interpret a subtest with a good *g* loading in isolation as representative of the child's general intellectual ability.

The subtest *g* loadings, strength of each subtest as a measure of *g*, and proportion of variance for each subtest attributed to *g*, by age band, is provided in Rapid Reference 1.12. The subtests are listed in descending order with respect to *g* loading.

Rapid Reference 1.12

Subtest *g* Loadings, Strength as Measures of *g*, and Proportions of Variance Attributed to *g*, by Age Band

Subtest	*g* Loading	Strength as Measure of *g*	Proportion of Variance Attributed to *g*
Ages 2:6–3:11			
IN	.80	good	.65
PN	.78	good	.62
RV	.77	good	.59
PM	.69	fair	.48
BD	.67	fair	.45
OA	.63	fair	.40
ZL	.55	fair	.30
Ages 4:0–7:7			
SI	.78	good	.60
IN	.77	good	.60
VC	.76	good	.58
CO	.73	good	.53
PN	.73	good	.53
RV	.71	good	.51
MR	.68	fair	.46
BD	.68	fair	.46
OA	.64	fair	.42

(continued)

Subtest	g Loading	Strength as Measure of g	Proportion of Variance Attributed to g
		Ages 4:0–7:7	
PM	.63	fair	.40
BS	.62	fair	.38
PC	.61	fair	.37
AC	.56	fair	.31
ZL	.55	fair	.30
CA	.51	fair	.26

Note. Abbreviations are IN = Information, SI = Similarities, VC = Vocabulary, CO = Comprehension, RV = Receptive Vocabulary, PN = Picture Naming, BD = Block Design, OA = Object Assembly, MR = Matrix Reasoning, PM = Picture Memory, ZL = Zoo Locations, BS = Bug Search, CA = Cancellation, AC = Animal Coding.
All g loadings of .70 or above are considered good, .50 to .69 are considered fair, and loadings below .50 are considered poor.

None of the WPPSI-IV subtests are poor measures of g; all are good or fair. For younger and older children, the strongest g loadings occur on the Verbal Comprehension subtests. All Verbal Comprehension subtests are good measures of g, and all other subtests are fair measures of g. This pattern is similar to that observed for the WPPSI-III (Lichtenberger & Kaufman, 2004).

For children aged 2:6 to 3:11, Information has the highest g loading (.80), followed by Picture Naming (.78) and Receptive Vocabulary (.77). For children aged 4:0 to 7:7, the core subtests for the Verbal Comprehension Index have the highest g loadings; Similarities is the highest (.78) by a slight margin (Information is .77). For both Information and Similarities, 60% of the variance is attributed to g. The next highest g loadings occur on the subtests that require verbal expression in at least some responses: Vocabulary (.76) and Comprehension (.73), and Picture Naming (.73). Among the Verbal Comprehension subtests, Receptive Vocabulary has the lowest g loading for this age band (.71).

For ages 2:6 to 3:11, the other three subtests that are core to the Full Scale IQ have the next-highest g loadings. Of these, Picture Memory has the highest g loading (.69), followed by Block Design (.67) and Object Assembly (.63). The lowest g loading occurs for Zoo Locations (.55), which attributes 30% of its variance to g.

For ages 4:0 to 7:7, the remaining subtests that are core to the Full Scale IQ, Matrix Reasoning, (.68), Block Design (.68), Picture Memory (.63), and Bug

Search (.62) occupy four of the subsequent five positions in descending order of g loading. Only Object Assembly (.64), which is core to the Visual Spatial Index, is present among those four core Full Scale IQ subtests. Picture Concepts (.61) has the next highest g loading, followed by two of the Processing Speed subtests, Animal Coding (.56) and Cancellation (.51), and Zoo Locations (.55). Zoo Locations produces the same relatively low g loading in both age bands. Of all WPPSI-IV subtests, Cancellation has the lowest g loading. However, its g loading is superior to other versions of Cancellation from WAIS-IV (.38; Lichtenberger & Kaufman, 2013) and WISC-IV (.25; Flanagan & Kaufman, 2009). From the beginning of WPPSI-IV development, we hypothesized that the Cancellation g loading would be higher for very young children relative to school-age children because classification of simple objects is a more challenging cognitive task at younger ages, and requires cognitive flexibility that not all young children have attained.

Subtest Specificities

The unique proportion of reliable variance of each subtest, or the proportion of subtest variance unrelated to measurement error and specific to that subtest (i.e., not shared with other subtests), is termed the *subtest specificity*. While interpretation at the subtest level is not recommended, the specificities are nevertheless useful when attempting to understand subtest performance. Lichtenberger and Kaufman (2004) suggest that if about 25% of a subtest's variance is specific, and the specific variance exceeds the subtest's error variance, the specificity associated with that subtest is sufficiently meaningful (ample). Lichtenberger and Kaufman's interpretive approach at that time involved grouping shared abilities, and only interpreting unique subtest abilities as a last resort. Their approach evolved subsequently, to focus much more on interpreting index-level strengths and weaknesses (Lichtenberger & Kaufman, 2013). Their more current work does not emphasize specificities for that reason.

We include the subtest specificities because we view them as another piece of information that facilitates a more complete understanding of the WPPSI-IV subtests. Evaluating their unique contribution to the battery and to the composite scores from which they are derived and understanding the relations of specific variance and error variance only adds richness and expertise to interpretation. Conceptually, we view the subtest specificities as an important aspect of battery selection: We believe specificity is an indicator of the lack of redundancy across selected measures. Flanagan and colleagues' cross-battery approach (Flanagan, Ortiz, & Alfonso, 2013) also conceptualizes lack of redundancy as important in evaluations. For example, their approach classifies measurement of a CHC broad ability as inadequate if at least two CHC narrow abilities are not represented.

To obtain the subtest specificity, the squared multiple correlation (from maximum-likelihood factor analysis with varimax rotation) is subtracted from the reliability for that subtest. To obtain the subtest's error variance, subtest's reliability is subtracted from 1. The subtest specificities for each age band, along with the error variance and strength of subtest specificity for each, are provided in Rapid Reference 1.13. The subtests are presented in descending order according to specificity value.

As seen in Rapid Reference 1.13, all subtests have ample specificity for both age bands. For children aged 2:6 to 3:11, the highest specificity value occurs for Zoo Locations, which does not contribute to Full Scale IQ. The highest subtest

≡ Rapid Reference 1.13

Subtest Specificities, by Age Band

Subtest	Squared Multiple Correlation*	Specificity	Error Variance	Strength of Subtest Specificity
Ages 2:6–3:11				
ZL	.19	.71	.10	ample
OA	.26	.59	.15	ample
PM	.34	.57	.09	ample
BD	.30	.55	.15	ample
RV	.44	.47	.09	ample
IN	.54	.37	.09	ample
PN	.52	.37	.11	ample
Ages 4:0–7:7				
PC	.32	.57	.11	ample
PM	.35	.55	.10	ample
ZL	.30	.54	.16	ample
MR	.41	.49	.10	ample
OA	.38	.47	.15	ample
CA	.29	.47	.24	ample
RV	.47	.43	.10	ample
BD	.42	.43	.15	ample
BS	.43	.40	.17	ample
AC	.37	.38	.25	ample

Subtest	Squared Multiple Correlation*	Specificity	Error Variance	Strength of Subtest Specificity
		Ages 4:0–7:7		
CO	.54	.37	.09	ample
PN	.54	.34	.12	ample
SI	.60	.33	.07	ample
VC	.58	.31	.11	ample
IN	.58	.30	.12	ample

*The squared multiple correlations are from maximum-likelihood factor analysis with varimax rotation.

Note. Abbreviations are IN = Information, SI = Similarities, VC = Vocabulary, CO = Comprehension, RV = Receptive Vocabulary, PN = Picture Naming, BD = Block Design, OA = Object Assembly, MR = Matrix Reasoning, PM = Picture Memory, ZL = Zoo Locations, BS = Bug Search, CA = Cancellation, AC = Animal Coding.

Ample specificity = specific variance that is at least 25% of total subtest variance, and greater than the subtest's error variance. Adequate specificity = specific variance that is 15%–24% of total subtest variance, and greater than the subtest's error variance. Inadequate specificity = specific variance less than 15% of total variance, or subtest's error variance exceeds specific variance.

To obtain the subtest specificity, the squared multiple correlation (from maximum-likelihood factor analysis with varimax rotation) is subtracted from the reliability for that subtest. To obtain the subtest's error variance, subtract the subtest's reliability from 1.

specificity for ages 4:0 to 7:7 is observed for Picture Concepts, followed by Picture Memory and Zoo Locations. In general, more highly *g*-loaded subtests tend to have lower subtest specificity values, and those with lower *g* loadings tend toward higher subtest specificity values. The Verbal Comprehension subtests, with the exception of Receptive Vocabulary in the older age band, tend to produce lower subtest specificities relative to other subtests. Subtests that rely on visual stimuli tend to show higher subtest specificities.

COMPREHENSIVE TEST REFERENCES

The *WPPSI-IV Administration and Scoring Manual* (Wechsler, 2012) and the *WPPSI-IV Technical and Interpretive Manual* (Wechsler, 2012) currently provide the most detailed information about the WPPSI-IV. These manuals review the scale's development, subtest descriptions, item- and subtest-level administration and scoring rules, standardization, and evidence of reliability and validity. Rapid Reference 1.14 provides basic information on the WPPSI-IV and the test publisher, Pearson.

Essentials of WPPSI-III Assessment (Lichtenberger & Kaufman, 2004) provides complete information about administration, scoring, and interpretation of the

⟰ Rapid Reference 1.14

- Wechsler Preschool and Primary Scale of Intelligence–Fourth Edition (WPPSI-IV)
- Author: David Wechsler
- Publication Date: 2012
- Age Range: 2:6 to 7:7
- What the Test Measures: verbal comprehension, visual spatial processing, fluid reasoning (for ages 4:0 to 7:7 only), working memory, processing speed (for ages 4:0 to 7:7 only), and general intellectual ability
- Administration Time: Full Scale IQ—24 to 29 minutes for younger children, 31 to 32 minutes for older children; Primary Index Subtests—29 to 35 minutes for younger children, 58 to 62 minutes for older children
- Qualification of Examiners: C level
- Publisher: Pearson
- 5601 Green Valley Drive
- Bloomington, MN 55437
- Customer Service: (800) 627-7271
- http://www.PsychCorp.com
- Product Number: 0158984900
- Price: WPPSI-IV Basic Kit: Includes (list materials) in a box. $1,120 (in box); $1,200 (in a rolling bag), $1,190 (in a hard case).

prior edition, the WPPSI-III (Wechsler, 2003). *Assessment of Children: Cognitive Foundations*, fifth edition, and its resource guide that accompanies the book (Sattler, 2008) provides an in-depth review of WPPSI-III administration and scoring, as well as relevant research on prior editions.

⚔ TEST YOURSELF ⚔

1. **Which of the following WPPSI-IV subtests is a core subtest that is used to compute FSIQ for ages 2:6 to 7:7?**

   (a) Cancellation
   (b) Picture Naming
   (c) Zoo Locations
   (d) Picture Concepts
   (e) Picture Memory

2. **What major structural change was implemented from the WPPSI-III to the WPPSI-IV?**

3. **For children aged 4:0 to 7:7, which two primary index scores replace the Performance IQ from WPPSI-III?**

4. **Which is a retained subtest from WPPSI-III?**

    (a) Picture Concepts

    (b) Picture Memory

    (c) Cancellation

    (d) Bug Search

    (e) Zoo Locations

5. **Which subtest is not a measure of Processing Speed?**

    (a) Cancellation

    (b) Animal Coding

    (c) Zoo Locations

    (d) Bug Search

6. **Which is not an Ancillary Index Score?**

    (a) General Ability Index

    (b) Vocabulary Acquisition Index

    (c) Cognitive Proficiency Index

    (d) Fluid Reasoning Index

    (e) Nonverbal Index

7. **Which is not a primary Index Score?**

    (a) Working Memory Index

    (b) Nonverbal Index

    (c) Visual Spatial Index

    (d) Fluid Reasoning Index

    (e) Verbal Comprehension Index

8. **Which primary index score includes the subtests that have the lowest subtest reliability coefficients for children ages 4:0 to 7:7?**

    (a) Visual Spatial Index

    (b) Working Memory Index

    (c) Processing Speed Index

    (d) Verbal Comprehension Index

    (e) Fluid Reasoning Index

9. **In general, more highly g-loaded subtests tend to have higher subtest specificity values, and those with lower g loadings tend toward lower subtest specificity values.**

    True or False?

    (continued)

10. **Which primary index contains the subtests that have the highest overall g loadings?**

Answers: 1. e; 2. Verbal IQ and Performance IQ are no longer in use, and PIQ has been replaced by the Visual Spatial Index and the Fluid Reasoning Index; 3. the Visual Spatial Index and the Fluid Reasoning Index; 4. a; 5. c; 6. d; 7. b; 8. c; 9. False; 10. Verbal Comprehension Index

REFERENCES

Albert, M. L. (1973). A simple test of visual neglect. *Neurology, 23,* 658–664.

Ammons, R. B., & Ammons, H. S. (1948). *The Full Range Vocabulary Test.* New Orleans, LA: Authors.

Binet, A. (1911). Nouvelles recherches sur la mesure du niveau intellectuel chez les enfants d'école. *L'Année Psychologique, 14,* 145–201.

Binet, A., & Simon, T. (1905). Méthods nouvelles pour le diagnostic du niveau intellectual des anormaux. *L'Année Psychologique, 11,* 191–244.

Binet, A., & Simon, T. (1908). Le développement de l'intelligence chez les enfants. *L'Année Psychologique, 14,* 1–90.

Boake, C. (2002). From the Binet-Simon to the Wechsler-Bellevue: Tracing the history of intelligence testing. *Journal of Clinical and Experimental Neuropsychology, 24,* 383–405.

Carlson, L., & Reynolds, C. R. (1981). Factor structure and specific variance of the WPPSI subtests at six age levels. *Psychology in the Schools, 18*(1), 48–54.

Carroll, J. B. (1993). *Human cognitive abilities: A survey of factor-analytic studies.* Cambridge, England: Cambridge University Press.

Carroll, J. B. (2012). The three-stratum theory of cognitive abilities. In D. P. Flanagan & P. L. Harrison (Eds.), *Contemporary intellectual assessment: Theories, tests, and issues* (3rd ed., pp. 883–890). New York, NY: Guilford Press.

Cattell, P. (1940). *The measurement of intelligence of infants and young children.* New York, NY: Psychological Corporation.

Coalson, D. L., Raiford, S. E., Saklofske, D. H., & Weiss, L. G. (2010). In L. G. Weiss, D. H. Saklofske, D. L. Coalson, & S. E. Raiford (Eds.), *WAIS-IV clinical use and interpretation: Scientist-practitioner perspectives* (pp. 3–23). Amsterdam, The Netherlands: Elsevier Academic Press.

Elliott, C. (2007). *Differential ability scales* (2nd ed.). San Antonio, TX: Pearson.

Flanagan, D. P., Alfonso, V. C., & Ortiz, S. O. (2012). The cross-battery assessment approach. In D. P. Flanagan & P. L. Harrison (Eds.), *Contemporary intellectual assessment: Theories, tests, and issues* (3rd ed., pp. 459–483). New York, NY: Guilford Press.

Flanagan, D. P., Alfonso, V. C., Ortiz, S. O., & Dynda, A. M. (2010). Integrating cognitive assessment in school neuropsychological evaluations. In D. C. Miller (Ed.), *Best practices in school neuropsychology: Guidelines for effective practice, assessment, and evidence-based intervention* (pp. 101–140). Hoboken, NJ: Wiley.

Flanagan, D. P., & Kaufman, A. S. (2009). *Essentials of WISC-IV assessment* (2nd ed.). Hoboken, NJ: Wiley.

Flanagan, D. P., Ortiz, S. O., & Alfonso, V. C. (2013). *Essentials of cross-battery assessment* (3rd ed.). Hoboken, NJ: Wiley.

Flynn, J. R. (2007). *What is intelligence? Beyond the Flynn effect.* Cambridge, England: Cambridge University Press.

Ford, L., Kozey, M. L., & Negreiros, J. (2012). Cognitive assessment in early childhood: Theoretical and practical perspectives. In D. P. Flanagan & P. L. Harrison (Eds.), *Contemporary intellectual assessment: Theories, tests, and issues* (3rd ed., pp. 585–622). New York, NY: Guilford Press.

Gesell, A., & Amatruda, C. S. (1941). *Developmental diagnosis: Normal and abnormal child development, clinical methods, and pediatric applications.* New York, NY: Hoeber.

Goddard, H. H. (1916). *The development of intelligence in children (the Binet-Simon Scale).* Baltimore, MD: Williams & Wilkins.

Goldstein, G., & Beers, S. R. (Eds.). (2003). *Comprehensive handbook of psychological assessment: Vol. 1. Intellectual and neuropsychological assessment.* Hoboken, NJ: Wiley.

Groth-Marnat, G. (2003). *Handbook of psychological assessment* (4th ed.). Hoboken, NJ: Wiley.

Gyurke, J. S., Stone, B. J., & Beyer, M. (1990). A confirmatory factor analysis of the WPPSI–R. *Journal of Psychoeducational Assessment, 8,* 15–21.

Horn, J. L., & Blankson, A. N. (2012). Foundations for better understanding of cognitive abilities. In D. P. Flanagan & P. L. Harrison (Eds.), *Contemporary intellectual assessment: Theories, tests, and issues* (3rd ed., pp. 73–98). New York, NY: Guilford Press.

Horn, J. L., & Noll, J. (1997). Human cognitive capabilities: Gf-Gc theory. In D. P. Flanagan, J. L. Genshaft, & P. L. Harrison (Eds.), *Contemporary intellectual assessment: Theories, tests, and issues* (pp. 53–91). New York, NY: Guilford Press.

Kaufman, A. S., & Kaufman, N. L. (2004). *Kaufman assessment battery for children* (2nd ed.). Bloomington, MN: Pearson.

Kaufman, S. B., Reynolds, M. R., Liu, X., Kaufman, A. S., & McGrew, K. S. (2012). Are cognitive *g* and academic achievement *g* one and the same *g?* An exploration on the Woodcock–Johnson and Kaufman tests. *Intelligence, 40,* 123–138. doi: 10.1016/j.intell.2012.01.009

Kelley M. F., & Surbeck, E. (2007). History of preschool assessment. In B. A. Bracken & R. J. Nagle (Eds.), *Psychoeducational assessment of preschool children* (pp. 3–28). Mahwah, NJ: Erlbaum.

Kirkpatrick, E. A. (1909). Studies in development and learning. *Archives of Psychology, 12,* 1–101.

Kohs, S. C. (1923). *Intelligence measurement: A psychological and statistical study based upon the block design tests.* New York, NY: Macmillan.

Kuhlmann, F. (1912). A revision of the Binet-Simon system for measuring the intelligence of children. *Journal of Psycho-Asthenics Monographs Supplement, 1*(1), 1–41.

Kuwajima, M., & Sawaguchi, T. (2010). Similar prefrontal cortical activities between general fluid intelligence and visuospatial working memory tasks in preschool children as revealed by optical topography. *Experimental Brain Research, 206,* 381–397.

Leiter, R.G. (1948). *International Performance Scale.* Chicago, IL: Stoelting.

Lichtenberger, E. O., & Kaufman, A. S. (2004). *Essentials of WPPSI®–III assessment.* Hoboken, NJ: Wiley.

Lichtenberger, E. O., & Kaufman, A. S. (2013). *Essentials of WAIS®–IV assessment* (2nd ed.). Hoboken, NJ: Wiley.

Locke, J. (1692). Some thoughts concerning education. In C. W. Eliot (Ed.), *Harvard Classics, 37*(1), New York, NY: Collier, 1909–1914; Bartleby.com, 2001. www.bartleby.com/37/1/

McCarthy, D. (1972). *The McCarthy Scales of Children's Abilities.* San Antonio, TX: Psychological Corporation.

Miller, D. C. (2010). School neuropsychological assessment and intervention. In D. C. Miller (Ed.), *Best practices in school neuropsychology: Guidelines for effective practice, assessment, and evidence-based intervention* (pp. 81–100). Hoboken, NJ: Wiley.

Miller, D. C. (2013). *Essentials of school neuropsychological assessment.* Hoboken, NJ: Wiley.

Morgan, K. E., Rothlisberg, B. A., McIntosh, D. E., & Hunt, M. S. (2009). Confirmatory factor analysis of the KABC–II in preschool children. *Psychology in the Schools, 46*(6), 515–525.

Piaget, J. (1952). *The origins of intelligence in children.* New York, NY: International University Press.

Pintner R. & Paterson, D. G. (1917). *A scale of performance tests.* New York, NY: Appleton.

Raven, J. C. (1941). Standardization of progressive matrices, 1938. *British Journal of Medical Psychology, 19,* 137–150.

Reynolds, M. R. (2013). Interpreting the *g* loadings of intelligence test composite scores in light of Spearman's law of diminishing returns. *School Psychology Quarterly, 28,* 63–76.

Reynolds, C. R., & Kamphaus, R. W. (2003). *Reynolds intellectual assessment scales.* Lutz, FL: Psychological Assessment Resources.

Roid, G. H. (2005). *Early Childhood Stanford-Binet intelligence scales* (5th ed). Austin, TX: Pro-Ed.

Rousseau, J. (1762 /1979). *Emile, or On education* (A. Bloom, Trans.). New York, NY: Basic Books.

Sattler, J. M. (2008). *Assessment of children: Cognitive foundations* (5th ed.). San Diego, CA: Author.

Schneider, B. H., & Gervais, M. D. (1991). Identifying gifted kindergarten students with brief screening measures and the WPPSI-R. *Journal of Psychoeducational Assessment, 9,* 201–208.

Schneider, W., Schumann-Hengsteler, R., & Sodian, B. (Eds.). (2005). *Young children's cognitive development: Interrelationships among executive functioning, working memory, verbal ability, and theory of mind.* Mahwah, NJ: Erlbaum.

Schneider, W., & Shiffrin, R. M. (1977). Controlled and automatic human information processing: I. Detection, search, and attention. *Psychological Review, 84*(1), 1–66.

Schneider, W. J., & McGrew, K. S. (2012). The Cattell-Horn-Carroll model of intelligence. In D. P. Flanagan & P. L. Harrison (Eds.), *Contemporary intellectual assessment: Theories, tests, and issues* (3rd ed., pp. 99–144). New York, NY: Guilford Press.

Silverstein, A. B. (1969). An alternative factor analytic solution for Wechsler's intelligence scales. *Educational and Psychological Measurement, 29,* 763–767.

Spearman, C. (1927). *The abilities of man.* London, England: MacMillan.

Sternberg, R. J. (Ed.). (2000). *Handbook of intelligence.* New York, NY: Cambridge University Press.

Sternberg, S. (1966). High-speed scanning in human memory. *Science, 153,* 652–654.

Stone, B. J., Gridley, B. E., & Gyurke, J. S. (1991). Confirmatory factor analysis of the WPPSI-R at the extreme of the age range. *Journal of Psychoeducational Assessment, 9,* 263–270.

te Nijenhuis, J., van Vianen, A. E. M., & van der Flier, H. (2007). Score gains on *g*-loaded tests: No *g. Intelligence, 35,* 283–300.

Terman, L. M. (1916). *The measurement of intelligence: An explanation of and a complete guide for the use of the Stanford revision and extension of the Binet-Simon Intelligence Scale.* Boston, MA: Houghton Mifflin.

Terman, L. M., & Merrill, M. A. (1937). *Measuring intelligence.* Boston, MA: Houghton Mifflin.

Ward, K. E., Rothlisberg, B. A., McIntosh, D. E., & Bradley, M. H. (2011). Assessing the SB–V factor structure in a sample of preschool children. *Psychology in the Schools, 48*(5), 454–463.

Wasserman, J. D. (2012). A history of intelligence assessment: The unfinished tapestry. In D. P. Flanagan & P. L. Harrison (Eds.), *Contemporary intellectual assessment: Theories, tests, and issues* (3rd ed., pp. 3–55). New York, NY: Guilford Press.

Wechsler, D. (1939). *Wechsler-Bellevue intelligence scale.* New York, NY: Psychological Corporation.

Wechsler, D. (1944). *The measurement of adult intelligence* (3rd ed.). Baltimore, MD: Williams & Wilkins.

Wechsler, D. (1949). *Wechsler intelligence scale for children.* New York, NY: Psychological Corporation.

Wechsler, D. (1950). Cognitive, conative, and non-intellective intelligence. *American Psychologist, 5*(3), 78–83.

Wechsler, D. (1955). *Wechsler adult intelligence scale.* New York, NY: Psychological Corporation.

Wechsler, D. (1967). *Wechsler preschool and primary scale of intelligence.* New York, NY: Pearson.

Wechsler, D. (1989). *Wechsler preschool and primary scale of intelligence* (revised). San Antonio, TX: Psychological Corporation.

Wechsler, D. (2002). *Wechsler preschool and primary scale of intelligence* (3rd ed.). San Antonio, TX: Pearson.

Wechsler, D. (2003). *Wechsler intelligence scale for children* (4th ed.). San Antonio, TX: Pearson.

Wechsler, D. (2008). *Wechsler adult intelligence scale* (4th ed.). San Antonio, TX: Pearson.

Wechsler, D. (2012). *Wechsler preschool and primary scale of intelligence* (4th ed.). Bloomington, MN: Pearson.

Woodcock, R. W., McGrew, K. S., & Mather, N. (2007). *Woodcock-Johnson tests of cognitive ability* (3rd ed.) *normative update.* Itasca, IL: Riverside.

Wortham, S. C. (2012). *Assessment in early childhood education* (6th ed.). New York, NY: Pearson.

Two

WPPSI-IV ADMINISTRATION

Susan Engi Raiford
Diane L. Coalson
Erik Gallemore

Adherence to the established administration procedures is critical when using a standardized, norm-referenced test such as the WPPSI-IV. Scores are used to understand the child's ability in relation to the normative group, for whom the same procedures were followed. Adherence to the standard procedures outlined in the *Administration and Scoring Manual* is necessary for interpreting the scores that are obtained using the norms tables. Following these procedures also helps to prevent data loss at the item and subtest level.

TEST MATERIALS

Become familiar with the WPPSI-IV test materials before beginning your first administration. Everything except the *Technical and Interpretive Manual* and the scoring keys and template is required for administration. If the kit is not new, ensure that all materials are present and in order well in advance of the testing session.

The materials necessary vary by age. Only the age-appropriate Record Form is necessary. For example, if you test a 4-year-old child, you do not need the Record Form for ages 2:6 to 3:11. For children aged 2:6 to 3:11, generally only Stimulus Books 1 and 2 are used. For children aged 4:0 to 7:7, only Stimulus Books 2 and 3 are used unless you administer Receptive Vocabulary and/or Picture Naming. For children aged 2:6 to 3:11, you do not need the Response Booklets or the ink dauber, but for children aged 4:0 to 7:7, you need the Response Booklets that

Table 2.1 WPPSI-IV Test Kit Materials

Administration and Scoring Manual	Zoo Locations Layouts (two)
Record Form for Ages 2:6–3:11	Zoo Locations Animal Card Set
Record Form for Ages 4:0–7:7	Object Assembly Puzzles
Stimulus Books 1–3	Bug Search Scoring Key
Response Booklets 1–3	Cancellation Scoring Template
Ink Dauber (two)	Animal Coding Scoring Key
Block Design Blocks (14, including 10 one-color blocks and 4 two-color blocks)	Technical and Interpretive Manual

correspond to the Processing Speed subtest(s) you will administer, and the ink dauber. The kit materials are listed in Table 2.1.

You should gather a few additional items prior to testing. A stopwatch and two pencils are essential. Use the stopwatch discreetly, and ensure the pencils are sharpened and have proper erasers. Moistened towelettes (e.g., baby wipes or individually prepackaged wipes) and a paper towel also are recommended for children aged 4:0 to 7:7 who use the ink dauber. A clipboard can be a useful addition, although the correct responses and notes on the Record Form can be concealed behind the *Administration and Scoring Manual* to ensure the child does not become distracted with attempts to see what you have written. The Don't Forget box lists materials to gather that are not in the kit.

The Stimulus Books should lie flat on the table. To administer a subtest, position the appropriate Stimulus Book faceup on the table with the binding toward the child. Grasp the tab and open the book toward the child. Turn the pages toward the child to advance through the items.

> **DON'T FORGET**
> ....
>
> *Materials Not in the WPPSI-IV Kit*
> - Stopwatch
> - Pencils with erasers (two)
> - Moistened towelettes
> - Paper towel
> - Clipboard

> **CAUTION**
> ....
>
> Correct responses appear on the Record Form and in the *Administration and Scoring Manual*. Shield the Record Form behind the free-standing *Administration and Scoring Manual*. Do not lay the *Administration and Scoring Manual* flat. Stand it upright by pushing back the bottom portion of the crackback hardcover until it bends along the crease to create a base.

The ink dauber used for the Processing Speed subtests is engaging and developmentally appropriate, but requires adult attention and care. Prior to the first use, test the dauber to ensure it contains and is adequately dispensing ink. Two daubers are included in each kit; if testing occurs in a location away from kit storage, it is essential to bring both daubers. If the dauber has dried out or is lost, a replacement may be purchased from Pearson or a similar one may be substituted. Ink daubers are readily available in many stores that carry toys and craft materials for children. It is recommended that the dauber be similar in circumference and weight to the daubers in the kit, but some variability is acceptable. In general, check to see that the child can grasp the dauber and use it comfortably. Ensure any replacement dauber is nontoxic. Do not leave the lid in reach of the child: If standard administration instructions are followed, this should not occur. Keep moistened towelettes nearby to wipe the child's hands and the table surface after administration and to prevent ink transfer to other components.

Dauber Practice, located on the back cover of Response Booklet 1, precedes administration of Bug Search. If Bug Search is not administered but Cancellation and/or Animal Shapes are, remember to administer Dauber Practice first. This ensures that the child has an opportunity to practice appropriate dauber use and that you are able to give the necessary feedback before the Processing Speed subtests begin. Overzealous children can use this time to become accustomed to the dauber and more readily focus on the task. A paper towel should be placed between the Response Booklet and the table surface after Dauber Practice if excessive ink is dispensed and still damp on the page.

PHYSICAL ENVIRONMENT

Before the testing session begins, identify a room well suited to administration. A room with adequate lighting that is most likely to remain quiet throughout the session is best. If necessary, place a sign on the door indicating that testing is taking place and that you should not be disturbed. Make attempts to accommodate the child's comfort, size, and developmental level. Find or (at least temporarily) create an uncluttered, clean testing area. Seek to remove or reposition potentially distracting extraneous items (e.g., mirrors, jackets, snacks, drinks, waste receptacles, books, toys, and papers) away from the child's view and reach.

Arrange the test materials and seating to optimize efficiency and minimize distractions. Place unnecessary test-kit items on a chair or on the floor. Plan the seating arrangement carefully. It is best if the child sits with his or her back to a window if one is present in the testing room. If child-sized furniture is not available in the testing room, a booster seat can be used for smaller children so that they will not slide low in the chair and be unable to see or reach the stimuli. Avoid using a chair with wheels, as some children easily can become distracted by or begin to play with and fidget in the chair. Sit directly across the table from the child. The WPPSI-IV does not utilize easel-based stimuli, and all of its test materials are designed to be used from across a table rather than at a 90-degree angle.

ESTABLISHING AND MAINTAINING RAPPORT WITH VERY YOUNG CHILDREN

There are numerous challenges inherent in assessment of very young children. The examiner's approach to establishing and maintaining rapport is a critical factor in keeping the child's interest and cooperation and obtaining maximum effort. Rapport is maximized if the examiner has received specialized training in early childhood assessment and is familiar with early childhood models of language, emotional, cognitive, and motor development, and can apply that knowledge to establish and maintain rapport (Ford, Kozey, & Negreiros, 2012; Kaufman & Kaufman, 1977).

Become familiar with all materials and administration procedures before the testing session so you can focus on the child, and he or she is not distracted by awkward fumbling or lapses in activity during or between subtests. Tailor your initial approach and continued interactions to the age, gender, language, observed behavior, level of discomfort, and other significant aspects of each child. Consider developmental level, the setting of the testing, the child's familiarity with you, and the child's attitude toward testing in general. Carefully monitor the child's attitude and effort throughout the testing session, so that you obtain the best estimate of the child's intellectual ability and not an underestimate as a result of lack of effort or discomfort with the testing environment.

Your initial approach to the child should focus on putting him or her at ease. Engaging the child in conversation about his or her interests can often accomplish this goal. If not, shift the child's focus to some feature of the present environment and encourage him or her to talk about it (e.g., a toy, the furnishings, a picture, the color of paint on the wall). When the child is sufficiently comfortable with you, shift your focus to the testing situation.

Introduce the test using the verbatim directions provided in the *Administration and Scoring Manual*. Vary your introduction to the test according to the child's developmental level. For younger children, you might describe the test as a series of special games for the child to play. For children in school who are familiar with testing or children who ask if they will be taking a test, it is acceptable to explain that it will not be like the tests at school. When the child is sufficiently comfortable with the testing situation, begin subtest administration.

The WPPSI-IV test materials, like those of the *McCarthy Scales of Children's Abilities* (McCarthy, 1972), are designed with the goal of establishing and maintaining rapport. The test materials include familiar objects (e.g., blocks and ink daubers), colorful pictures and puzzles, and game-like subtests (e.g., zoo cards and layouts). Attractive test materials can facilitate rapport (Kaufman & Kaufman, 1977). Indeed, the materials are similar to those of the McCarthy, which is noted for its ability to elicit engagement in very young children and shy, nonverbal children (Kaufman & Kaufman, 1977).

Feedback can help to maintain rapport and motivation. As you administer the items and subtests, praise the child's effort and thereby encourage the child to do his or her best. Do not give feedback about performance (e.g., "Good" or "Right") unless instructed to do so in the item administration directions. Record every item within a subtest in a similar manner. Recording only incorrect responses can cue the child to his or her performance, which is to be avoided unless prescribed. Sample items allow you to make an explicit statement about the child's response accuracy as well as to provide the correct response, but teaching items and items with two trials only permit you to provide the correct response. Other test items do not permit any feedback beyond praise of the child's effort. However, children sometimes still have a sense of poor performance. Monitor the child's awareness of his or her own successes and difficulties. If a child appears discouraged, reassure him or her that the other parts of the test may be easier, or remind him or her of a subtest that he or she appeared to enjoy.

The order of subtests within the WPPSI-IV was carefully designed with the knowledge that a carefully crafted order can help to maintain rapport (Kaufman & Kaufman, 1977). The child is not required to speak at all on the first three subtests for ages 2:6 to 3:11 (i.e., Receptive Vocabulary, Block Design, and Picture Memory). This is an excellent way to start for shy or very young children. Receptive Vocabulary uses an attractive set of pictures, along with auditory stimuli (i.e., words spoken by the examiner), that promote attention, and the child merely points at the pictures to indicate the response. Block Design, next in the sequence for very young children, requires simple imitation of the examiner's models. As with other subtests involving blocks, young children "feel almost compelled to join in the activity" as the examiner stacks the block models on the first few items while saying very little (Kaufman & Kaufman, 1977, p. 7). Picture Memory, the third subtest for younger children, involves colorful pictures of common and familiar objects, which may encourage verbalization; however, none is required.

Next in the sequence for 2:6 to 3:11, the Information subtest begins with items requiring only a pointing response. The subtest then provides a transition from mere visual stimuli and nonverbal responses through a few items that require the child to point or gesture to something other than the Stimulus Book (e.g., a facial body part), but can be answered without verbal responses. The first Information items that require verbal responses entail only brief and simple verbalizations. After Information, the child is given a respite from expressive requirements with Object Assembly and Zoo Locations. These two subtests both involve fun manipulatives (i.e., puzzles and a card game) that are very engaging. The last subtest in the standard order for younger children, Picture Naming, requires only single-word expressive responses. Hence, when administered in the standard order, the WPPSI-IV subtests provide varied stimuli and a gradual warm-up to expressive requirements, with some subtests interspersed that provide breaks from those demands.

Nevertheless, the child may become bored or restless. Monitor the child's effort level and engagement closely, and look for signs of cooperation. If the child responds "I don't know" excessively or states that he or she cannot complete a task, it may indicate he or she is discouraged, anxious, or does not wish to continue. Be careful to note such occurrences, as they can be relevant to interpretation of scores and performance on the current subtest. The converse can also occur: A child may not understand a task or may be unable to complete an item correctly, but hesitate to admit it and act out his or her frustration.

In these situations, it may be necessary to give breaks, to suspend a subtest and return to it, to vary subtest order, or to delay completion of testing for another session. Do not hesitate to allow a discouraged, tired, or fidgeting child to take breaks as needed. Multiple breaks are acceptable and may be necessary both for very young children and children with clinical or medical conditions that limit their ability to sit and concentrate for sustained time periods. If a child refuses to perform a particular task, you may temporarily suspend administration and move to the next subtest, returning later when the child appears engaged again. If necessary, mention an interesting component of the test that is yet to come and may pique the child's interest in continuing after a break or on another day (e.g., a zoo trip, some puzzles to solve).

Use your judgment to decide if testing should continue in another session. Multiple sessions are sometimes necessary and are acceptable. In this situation, test the child as soon as possible, preferably within a week. Note and evaluate the impact on test results of significant occurrences in the child's life and changes in mental status between sessions. The test date should reflect only the first date of testing, as this was the solution employed in the standardization samples when multiple test dates occurred.

STANDARD SUBTEST ADMINISTRATION ORDER

Subtest administration order varies by age band. Generally subtests are administered in an order that alternates selected subtests from originating scales (e.g., one from Verbal Comprehension, then one from Visual Spatial, then one from

Working Memory, and so on). First, the core FSIQ subtests are administered. Next, the remaining core subtests used to obtain all primary index scores are given. Last, supplemental and optional subtests are administered. Table 2.2 lists the standard subtest administration order by age band, along with the subtests' primary index scale memberships. When discussed in this chapter and in Chapter 3, the subtests always appear grouped by primary index scale membership, then in standard administration order within scales.

While some variation is acceptable based on the child's needs, subtests should be administered in the standard order whenever possible. If the standard order is not used, note the altered order on the Record Form and consider it when interpreting results. Table 2.2 provides subtests' primary index scale membership as a quick reference if flexibility in administration order becomes necessary. For example, suppose a child has a condition associated with weaknesses on tasks from a particular primary index scale, and appears discouraged or agitated immediately prior to a subtest from that scale. In this situation, it may be necessary to quickly select a different subtest to administer that may be less frustrating for the child.

SELECTION OF SUBTESTS

The WPPSI-IV offers a variety of composite scores and discrepancy analyses that can be used to address various referral questions. Not every subtest or composite score is relevant to every referral question. Before testing with the WPPSI-IV, consider which scores are most useful for the situation and plan to administer the

Table 2.2 Standard Subtest Administration Order and Scale Membership

Younger Age Band: Ages 2:6–3:11	
Subtest	Primary Index Scale Membership
1. Receptive Vocabulary	Verbal Comprehension
2. Block Design	Visual Spatial
3. Picture Memory	Working Memory
4. Information	Verbal Comprehension
5. Object Assembly	Visual Spatial
6. Zoo Locations	Working Memory
7. Picture Naming	Verbal Comprehension

(continued)

Table 2.2 Standard Subtest Administration Order and Scale Membership (continued)

Older Age Band: Ages 4:0–7:7

Subtest	Primary Index Scale Membership
1. Block Design	Visual Spatial
2. Information	Verbal Comprehension
3. Matrix Reasoning	Fluid Reasoning
4. Bug Search	Processing Speed
5. Picture Memory	Working Memory
6. Similarities	Verbal Comprehension
7. Picture Concepts	Fluid Reasoning
8. Cancellation	Processing Speed
9. Zoo Locations	Working Memory
10. Object Assembly	Visual Spatial
11. Vocabulary	Verbal Comprehension
12. Animal Coding	Processing Speed
13. Comprehension	Verbal Comprehension
14. Receptive Vocabulary	Verbal Comprehension
15. Picture Naming	Verbal Comprehension

appropriate subtests. If all core primary index subtests are administered, the FSIQ, all primary index scores, and all published ancillary index scores can be obtained, with the exception of the Verbal Acquisition Index (VAI). However, the additional index scores that appear only in this book often require administration of at least one additional subtest.

Norms and discrepancy analyses for additional index scores are provided in the appendixes and the WPPSI-IV Interpretive Assistant, both of which appear on the CD that accompanies this book. These index scores are provided for specific purposes. Some index scores are available for a CHC-theory based approach to interpretation. These index scores are theoretically consistent with various narrow abilities described for the CHC model (Carroll, 2012; Horn & Blankson, 2012; Lichtenberger & Kaufman, 2013). Other index scores are available for interpreting WPPSI-IV results or generating hypotheses from a neuro-psychological perspective. Other index scores are included that, in our clinical judgment, prove useful for new discrepancy analyses with the current WPPSI-IV composite scores. The additional index scores developed for readers of this book are discussed in Chapter 1 and in Chapter 4. Refer to Rapid Reference 1.8, Core Subtest Composition of Published Composite Scores, by Age Band, and Rapid Reference 1.9, Subtest Composition of Additional Index Scores, to plan subtest selection according to the scores most suited for your specific referral question.

SUITABILITY AND FAIRNESS

Due to the great and rapid cognitive and language development that takes place across the 2:6 to 7:7 age range, the WPPSI-IV provides separate batteries for two different age bands. Children aged 2:6 to 3:11 are administered subtests with relatively few expressive demands to reduce the impact of language development on scores. For these younger children, the number of subtests is reduced relative to children aged 4:0 to 7:7, to minimize attention requirements. The tasks are easily demonstrated to minimize demands on receptive vocabulary and attention. The battery for children aged 4:0 to 7:7 contains more subtests. Some of these subtests require more verbal expression (e.g., Vocabulary and Comprehension), or require the child to understand more complex instructions (e.g., Picture Concepts, Bug Search, Animal Coding) or advanced ideas such as the concept of speediness (e.g., Cancellation).

Assessing Children at the Extremes of the Age Range

Examiners testing children at the younger and older extremes of the WPPSI-IV age range (2:6 to 3:6 and 6:0 to 7:7, respectively) can select between the WPPSI-IV and alternate measures of intellectual ability. Although the WPPSI-IV items are unique, other tests contain tasks that are similar to those of the WPPSI-IV. Repeated administration effects (e.g., procedural learning) can impact scores on the second measure if both batteries are administered. Optimally, the selection between measures should be made based upon estimated ability level of the child, referral question, and the presence of special considerations. At times, a battery other than the WPPSI-IV may be preferable.

When testing children at the younger extreme of the age range, the *Bayley Scales of Infant and Toddler Development, Third Edition* (Bayley-III; Bayley, 2005) is one alternative measure. The Bayley-III provides estimates of the child's development in a number of domains, including cognitive, language, motor, behavioral, and emotional. The Bayley-III may provide more information about the very young child's strengths and needs if he or she is suspected of below average intellectual ability. The Bayley-III also might be selected if there are concerns about the child's expressive language (e.g., language disorders, autism spectrum disorder, English language learning). If intellectual ability is estimated as average or above average, the WPPSI-IV should be considered.

When testing children at the older extreme of the age range (6:0 to 7:7), the *Wechsler Intelligence Scale for Children–Fourth Edition* (WISC-IV; Wechsler, 2003) is a likely alternative. The WPPSI-IV is the more likely choice for an older child suspected of below average or average intellectual ability. If separate measures of visual spatial ability and fluid reasoning are relevant to the referral question (e.g., visual processing issues are suspected) or if there are concerns about the child's visual working memory, the WPPSI-IV might be selected. The WPPSI-IV may be a more appropriate choice for children with fine motor skill delays if the referral question involves processing speed. If intellectual ability is estimated as above average, the WISC-IV should be considered. The WISC-IV might also be selected if verbal working memory is of concern.

Regardless of the intellectual ability measure selected (i.e., WPPSI-IV or WISC-IV) for children aged 6:0 to 7:7, portions of the other measure may be administered following completion of the primary instrument to augment results and provide a multimodal assessment of working memory. For example, if the referral question involves low working memory ability or a clinical condition usually characterized by diffuse working memory deficits, the differences between the child's visual and verbal working memory can be evaluated using the WPPSI-IV Working Memory Index and the WISC-IV Working Memory Index to inform interventions targeted to meet the individual child's needs. Table 2.3 provides a summary of the intellectual ability battery to select for children at the extremes of the WPPSI-IV age range.

Table 2.3 Selecting Between the WPPSI-IV and Other Batteries When Testing Children at the Extremes of the Age Range

Age	Estimated Ability Level	Intellectual Ability Battery to Select
2:6–3:6	Below Average	Bayley-III or an appropriate alternative battery
	Average	WPPSI-IV
	Above Average	WPPSI-IV
6:0–7:7	Below Average	WPPSI-IV
	Average	WPPSI-IV
	Above Average	WISC-IV or an appropriate alternative battery

Assessing Children With Special Needs

Children with special physical, language, or sensory needs are often referred for intellectual ability testing. Caution must be exercised when interpreting intellectual ability test results in these situations, as low test scores may in fact be attributed to the special needs (Ford et al., 2012). For these children, it is especially important to supplement the WPPSI-IV with measures tailored to each child's special needs. It may be necessary to modify the WPPSI-IV procedures to gain the best understanding of the child, and these modifications or accommodations should be noted on the Record Form and considered when interpreting results. Although norms may be less applicable in some of these cases, individualized accommodations and testing of limits can help you to gain a wealth of information about the child's strengths, as well as areas that may benefit from intervention.

Prepare for testing a child with special needs through learning more about the accommodations in general and about the child specifically. Refer to comprehensive references on the subject of testing accommodations in these situations (Braden, 2003; Decker, Englund, & Roberts, 2012; Gordon, Stump, & Glaser, 1996). Also refer to Chapters 9 and 10 of the *Standards for Educational and Psychological Testing* (*Standards*; American Educational Research Association, American Psychological Association, & National Council on Measurement in Education, 1999) for guidelines pertaining to testing children in need of accommodation due to special needs. Gather information about the child's special needs and his or her preferred means of communicating. Review records from prior testing, if any. Interview parents/guardians, and obtain consent to speak with teachers or other professionals involved with the child as appropriate. Seek to learn more about how to obtain the best information and performance in light of his or her limitations. Consider extending testing over multiple sessions if quicker fatigue may be an associated feature of the child's needs. Use what you learn to plan accommodations or modifications to standard administration procedures, as well as to select subtests that are most appropriate.

Consider the following general recommendations for modifications, and their impact on the applicability of scaled and composite scores.

Limited motor skills:
- Do not administer Block Design, Object Assembly, or Zoo Locations.
- Administer the Verbal Comprehension and Fluid Reasoning subtests, and Picture Memory from the Working Memory scale. For children aged 6:0 to 7:7, consider augmenting the battery with the WISC-IV Working Memory Index, which is derived from subtests that require only verbal responses.

- Consider carefully if the Processing Speed subtests are appropriate. The ink dauber places relatively few demands on motor performance relative to subtests that use pencils, so these subtests could be used in some situations.

Serious language difficulties, children who are deaf or hard of hearing, and children who are English language learners:
- Administer the Visual Spatial, Fluid Reasoning, Working Memory, and Processing Speed subtests. If it is apparent that the child does not comprehend instructions for a specific task, discontinue administration of the subtest.
- Consider administering Receptive Vocabulary and Picture Naming to test the limits of the child's ability to communicate, but rely more heavily on the aforementioned subtests for information about the child's ability.
- For children who are English language learners, consider if the use of an interpreter or an adapted or translated version is appropriate.
- Use established procedures for intellectual assessment of children who are English language learners, such as those outlined by Ortiz, Ochoa, and Dynda (2012). Remember that assessment of children who are English language learners is a complex process that requires information about the child's English and native-language proficiency and facility with a number of models used to tailor evaluation of these children to the situation.
- Consider using the Nonverbal Index with children who are English language learners. Remember that the Nonverbal Index is not language-free; it is merely language reduced because the subtests from which it is derived require comprehension of instructions in English.
- For children who are deaf or hard of hearing, refer to the guidelines published in the previous edition for testing children who are deaf and hard of hearing. Similar guidelines are forthcoming in a technical report for the WPPSI-IV, which is not available at the time of this writing.

Children with visual impairment:
- Administer Information, Similarities, Vocabulary, and Comprehension. Do not administer the picture items for these subtests.
- Derive additional index scores available in this book (e.g., the Comprehensive Verbal Index and the Complex Expressive Index), if possible, in addition to the Verbal Comprehension Index (available in the published test).

For children aged 6 to 7, consider augmenting the battery with the WISC-IV Working Memory Index, which is derived from subtests involving verbally presented stimuli that require only verbal responses. Also consider administering Arithmetic without the picture items, because recent factor-analytic studies indicate it provides information about fluid reasoning (Benson, Hulac, & Kranzler, 2010; Keith, Fine, Taub, Reynolds, & Kranzler, 2006; Weiss, Keith, Zhu, & Chen, 2013a, 2013b).

START POINTS, REVERSE RULES, AND DISCONTINUE RULES

Start points, reverse rules, and discontinue rules are used to ensure the child is not administered unnecessary items. These administration guidelines are described in Chapters 3 and 4 of the *Administration and Scoring Manual*. Abbreviated descriptions also appear on each age-appropriate Record Form.

Start Points

Item administration generally begins at the start point and proceeds forward if the child receives perfect scores on the first two items administered. Start points are designated with arrows on the Record Forms and in the *Administration and Scoring Manual*, and often vary based on the child's age. Start-point items are set to ensure almost all children (i.e., 90% to 95% of the normative sample for a given age group) receive full credit on the first few items administered. The age-appropriate start point should be used in most situations. However, if any child is suspected of having intellectual disability or low cognitive ability, administration should begin with Item 1.

Some subtests contain demonstration and sample items that are administered prior to the start point. These items are not scored, nor are they included in the total raw score, although the child's responses for sample items should be recorded where appropriate.

Remember to award full credit for items prior to the start point if administration begins with Item 1 and the child then obtains perfect scores on the age-appropriate start-point item and subsequent item. Application of this rule thus overrides scores of 0 points on items prior to the start point. Refer to Figure 2.5 in the *Administration and Scoring Manual* for an illustrated example. Examiners commonly draw a slash mark through unadministered items (e.g., items prior to the start point) on the Record Form to indicate that those items were not administered. It is helpful to record the sum of credit for unadministered items next to the last item prior to the start point. Table 2.4 provides a summary of the subtest start points.

Table 2.4 Subtest Start Points

Subtest	Start Point by Age
Information	Ages 2:6–3:11: Item 1 Ages 4:0–5:11: Item 10 Ages 6:0–7:7: Item 16
Similarities	Ages 2:6–3:11: Do not administer Ages 4:0–5:11: Sample, then Item 1 Ages 6:0–7:7: Item 5
Vocabulary	Ages 2:6–3:11: Do not administer Ages 4:0–5:11: Item 1 Ages 6:0–7:7: Item 4
Comprehension	Ages 2:6–3:11: Do not administer Ages 4:0–5:11: Item 1 Ages 6:0–7:7: Item 5
Receptive Vocabulary	Ages 2:6–3:11: Item 1 Ages 4:0–5:11: Item 5 Ages 6:0–7:7: Item 13
Picture Naming	Ages 2:6–3:11: Item 1 Ages 4:0–5:11: Item 7 Ages 6:0–7:7: Item 9
Block Design	Ages 2:6–3:11: Item 1 Ages 4:0–5:11: Item 4 Ages 6:0–7:7: Samples A and B, then Item 9
Object Assembly	Ages 2:6–3:11: Item 1 Ages 4:0–5:11: Item 3 Ages 6:0–7:7: Item 7
Matrix Reasoning	Ages 2:6–3:11: Do not administer Age 4:0–4:11: Samples A–C, then Item 1 Age 5:0–5:11: Samples A–C, then Item 4 Ages 6:0–7:7: Samples A–C, then Item 7
Picture Concepts	Ages 2:6–3:11: Do not administer. Ages 4:0–5:11: Samples A and B, then Item 1 Ages 6:0–7:7: Samples A and B, then Item 8
Picture Memory	Ages 2:6–3:11: Sample A, then Item 1 Ages 4:0–7:7: Sample B, then Item 7
Zoo Locations	Ages 2:6–5:11: Sample, then Item I Ages 6:0–7:7: Sample, then Item 7
Bug Search	Ages 2:6–3:11: Do not administer Ages 4:0–7:7: Dauber Practice, Demonstration Items, Sample Items, then Test Items

Table 2.4 Subtest Start Points (*continued*)

Subtest	Start Point by Age
Cancellation	Ages 2:6–3:11: Do not administer Ages 4:0–7:7: Demonstration Item, Sample Item, then Item 1
Animal Coding	Ages 2:6–3:11: Do not administer Ages 4:0–7:7: Demonstration Items, Sample Items, then Test Items

Source: From the *Administration and Scoring Manual* of the *Wechsler Preschool and Primary Scale of Intelligence–Fourth Edition.* Copyright © 2012 Pearson. Adapted and reproduced by permission. All rights reserved.

Reverse Rules

Reverse rules are criteria for ages 4:0 to 7:7 that indicate when the items prior to the start point should be given if administration of a subtest did not begin at Item 1. If the child does not receive a perfect score (i.e., all possible points for a given item) on the first two items (i.e., the start point and subsequent item), reverse rules require a decision about which item should be administered next. The term *appropriate* is used in the administration instructions to cue examiners that item administration may proceed forward or backward in the order, depending on the child's performance.

It is important to note that for children aged 4:0 to 7:7, the Similarities and Picture Memory sample items are only administered if administration starts at Item 1. If administration begins at the age-appropriate start point, then the reverse rules for Picture Memory and Similarities should never result in the first sample item being administered. In this situation, do not administer those sample items even if administration continues in reverse to Item 1. Table 2.5 provides a summary of the subtest reverse rules.

Discontinue Rules

Discontinue rules provide criteria to indicate when subtest administration should stop, generally after scores of 0 on a certain number of consecutive items. Scores of 0 that the child earns while reversing count toward the discontinue rule. If the discontinue criterion is met while reversing, points are not awarded for items beyond the discontinue point, even if they were originally earned by the child. The discontinue rules are easily committed to memory. Subtests that involve unique manipulatives (i.e., blocks, cards, and puzzles) have discontinue rules of two consecutive scores of 0, subtests that involve use of the ink dauber have discontinue

Table 2.5 Subtest Reverse Rules

Subtest	Reverse Rule by Age
Information	Ages 4:0–7:7: Imperfect score on either of the first two items given, administer preceding items in reverse order until two consecutive perfect scores are obtained.
Similarities	Ages 6:0–7:7: Imperfect score on either of the first two items given, administer preceding items in reverse order until two consecutive perfect scores are obtained.
Vocabulary	Ages 6:0–7:7: Imperfect score on either of the first two items given, administer preceding items in reverse order until two consecutive perfect scores are obtained.
Comprehension	Ages 6:0–7:7: Imperfect score on either of the first two items given, administer preceding items in reverse order until two consecutive perfect scores are obtained.
Receptive Vocabulary	Ages 4:0–7:7: Imperfect score on either of the first two items given, administer preceding items in reverse order until two consecutive perfect scores are obtained.
Picture Naming	Ages 4:0–7:7: Imperfect score on either of the first two items given, administer preceding items in reverse order until two consecutive perfect scores are obtained.
Block Design	Ages 4:0–7:7: Imperfect score on either of the first two items given, administer preceding items in reverse order until two consecutive perfect scores are obtained.
Object Assembly	Ages 4:0–7:7: Imperfect score on either of the first two items given, administer preceding items in reverse order until two consecutive perfect scores are obtained.
Matrix Reasoning	Ages 5:0–7:7: Imperfect score on either of the first two items given, administer preceding items in reverse order until two consecutive perfect scores are obtained.
Picture Concepts	Ages 6:0–7:7: Imperfect score on either of the first two items given, administer preceding items in reverse order until two consecutive perfect scores are obtained.
Picture Memory	Ages 4:0–7:7: Imperfect score on either of the first two items given, administer preceding items in reverse order until two consecutive perfect scores are obtained.
Zoo Locations	Ages 6:0–7:7: Imperfect score on either of the first two items given, administer preceding items in reverse order until two consecutive perfect scores are obtained.

Table 2.5 Subtest Reverse Rules (*continued*)

Subtest		Reverse Rule by Age
Bug Search	None	
Cancellation	None	
Animal Coding	None	

Source: From the *Administration and Scoring Manual* of the *Wechsler Preschool and Primary Scale of Intelligence–Fourth Edition.* Copyright © 2012 Pearson. Adapted and reproduced by permission. All rights reserved.

rules that involve stopping administration after a specified amount of time has elapsed, and all other subtests have discontinue rules of three consecutive scores of 0. Table 2.6 provides a summary of the subtest discontinue rules. Rapid Reference 2.1 summarizes the discontinue rules across different types of subtests.

Table 2.6 Subtest Discontinue Rules

Subtest	Discontinue Rule
Information	After three consecutive scores of 0
Similarities	After three consecutive scores of 0
Vocabulary	After three consecutive scores of 0
Comprehension	After three consecutive scores of 0
Receptive Vocabulary	After three consecutive scores of 0
Picture Naming	After three consecutive scores of 0
Block Design	After two consecutive scores of 0
Object Assembly	After two consecutive scores of 0
Matrix Reasoning	After three consecutive scores of 0
Picture Concepts	After three consecutive scores of 0
Picture Memory	After three consecutive scores of 0
Zoo Locations	After two consecutive scores of 0
Bug Search	After 120 seconds
Cancellation	After 45 seconds for each item
Animal Coding	After 120 seconds

Source: From the *Administration and Scoring Manual* of the *Wechsler Preschool and Primary Scale of Intelligence–Fourth Edition.* Copyright © 2012 Pearson. Adapted and reproduced by permission. All rights reserved.

≡ Rapid Reference 2.1

Remembering Discontinue Rules

- Subtests with blocks, cards, and puzzles: Discontinue after two consecutive scores of 0.
- Subtests with an ink dauber: Discontinue after a specified amount of time has elapsed.
- All other subtests: Discontinue after three consecutive scores of 0.

TIMING

Some subtests have strict time limits, whereas others have no time limits and are merely subject to a 30-second guideline. Strict time limits are just that. If a subtest has a strict time limit, do not stop or pause the stopwatch for any reason. If administration is disrupted by extraneous noise or activity, note this on the Record Form but instruct the child to keep working. If repetition of instructions or items is permitted, or if prompts are given, do not stop timing.

The 30-second guideline is not strict and should not be rigidly applied, and a stopwatch should not be used to mark response time. Merely estimate the time that has passed. If the child's performance on a 30-second guideline subtest is waning, and he or she is spending an inordinate amount of time considering responses without benefit to performance, encourage the child to respond. This practice maintains administration pace, diminishes the potential for fatigue, and may result in the child being able to move to another task to experience more success. In this situation, if about 30 seconds have passed, you may ask the child if he or she has an answer. If he or she does not respond, initiate a transition to the next appropriate item. If a child is performing well and taking extra time to consider responses, be more generous with the time you allow before offering these prompts.

For some subtests, a stopwatch is required to mark the stimulus exposure time or to determine when the time limit has expired. Good stopwatch management and use ensures that standard administration procedures can be followed and prevents administration errors. For most subtests, timing starts immediately after the verbal instructions are completed. In general, for these subtests keep the stopwatch in your nondominant hand or on the table behind the *Administration and Scoring Manual*

DON'T FORGET

- Review Table 2.7 to become familiar with the subtests that require use of a stopwatch.
- The exposure of stimuli is timed on both Picture Memory and Zoo Locations.

Table 2.7 Subtest Timing Rules

Subtest	Stopwatch Required	Stimulus Exposure Timed	Strict Time Limits	30-Second Guideline
Information				X
Similarities				X
Vocabulary				X
Comprehension				X
Receptive Vocabulary				X
Picture Naming				X
Block Design	X		X	
Object Assembly	X		X	
Matrix Reasoning				X
Picture Concepts				X
Picture Memory	X	X		X
Zoo Locations	X	X		X
Bug Search	X		X	
Cancellation	X		X	
Animal Coding	X		X	

whenever possible as you give verbal instructions or present stimulus materials. Table 2.7 summarizes the timing rules by subtest.

DEMONSTRATION, SAMPLE, AND TEACHING ITEMS

Some subtests have demonstration, sample, and/or teaching items. These are included based on child need and research phase data indicating that they are necessary to ensure that lack of task understanding does not result in an underestimate of the child's ability. Proper administration of these items can improve understanding of a novel task or portion of a subtest.

Demonstration items allow you to demonstrate and explain how to respond to a task. Sample items allow the child to practice completion of an item before transitioning to test items.

Teaching items permit you to offer feedback about an incorrect response on initial items of a novel task, or about items that involve a change in response requirements as you proceed through a subtest. They are designated with a dagger symbol (†) in the *Administration and Scoring Manual* and on the Record Form. Remain aware that teaching sometimes occurs on items that are not the first ones administered. For example, because Picture Memory Items 7 and 8 are the first that require correct selection of two pictures (rather than only one) to receive credit, all children who take these items receive teaching for incorrect responses, even if teaching was previously provided on Items 1 and 2.

REPETITIONS, PROMPTS, AND QUERIES

Repetitions, prompts, and queries serve to facilitate comprehension of items, reinforce directions, redirect attention, and clarify responses. They are typically noted with **R**, **P**, and **Q** on the Record Form. It is important to familiarize yourself with their prescribed uses across subtests.

Repetitions

Subject to some restrictions, task- and item-level instructions generally can be repeated. Do not repeat instructions if the child is concentrating or still working. If permitted, a good practice is to repeat item instructions after 5 to 10 seconds if the child has not responded.

If the subtest does not require use of a stopwatch (see Table 2.7), repeat instructions upon request by the child and at your discretion, as many times as necessary. For these subtests, you may readminister items to which a child responded "I don't know" if later performance on the subtest indicates that the child might respond correctly to those items. Assign appropriate credit if the child's response is improved upon readministration.

If the subtest requires the use of a stopwatch, the following guidelines apply. You may not re-administer items. For those with strict response time limits (see Table 2.7), repeat instructions as many times as necessary, but do not stop timing during repetitions. For Block Design and Object Assembly, you may repeat verbal instructions, but do not model correct assembly a second time during the child's allotted time to respond. Whereas you may repeat verbal instructions on Picture Memory and Zoo Locations, do not reexpose the stimuli.

Prompts

Standard subtest-specific prompts are used as necessary to teach or remind the child of the task instructions. They are listed in the General Directions sections for each

---

Behind the Scenes

....

- The selection of sample responses for the manual is the result of accumulated evidence throughout all research phases. Every verbatim response is evaluated to determine final point values and whether additional query is necessary. If a **Q** follows a sample response, data suggests that additional inquiry often improves the item's ability to discriminate the child's ability.

---

subtest. During subtests that have strict time limits (see Table 2.7), do not stop timing to give necessary prompts. For your convenience, all subtest-specific prompts are reproduced in Appendix A on the CD that accompanies this book. The subtests are organized in administration order in Appendix A. You may print Appendix A and place it next to the *Administration and Scoring Manual* for use during administration until you commit the prompts to memory, so you do not need to turn the pages back to the General Directions sections during item administration.

Queries

Queries are used as necessary to gather additional information about the child's response if it is incomplete or unclear. In most cases, queries merely involve asking the child what he or she means, or to tell you more about it, or some other phrase that does not lead the child to any particular answer. Sample responses indicated with a **Q** in the *Administration and Scoring Manual* should be queried. Some specific sample responses to items require a special query; these are noted with an asterisk (*) in the *Administration and Scoring Manual*. For items that potentially require such a special query, an asterisk also appears next to the item number in the *Administration and Scoring Manual* and on the Record Form.

> **DON'T FORGET**
> ....
> - Don't query a response just to improve a low score or a clearly incorrect response.
> - An asterisk (*) next to an item number indicates a special query might be necessary.

RECORDING RESPONSES

Thorough recording of responses is in the best interest of the child for a number of reasons. Good records ensure more accurate scoring, facilitate interpretive observations and thus understanding of performance, and enhance communication with other professionals who may gain access to the test protocol in a transfer of records. Administered items should be distinguished from unadministered items with some notation that indicates as such. The Record Forms provide areas to circle or record verbatim responses, to indicate item- and/or subtest-level scores, and to note completion times or other subtest-specific information or behaviors. Repetitions, prompts, queries, nonverbal responses, and other behaviors should be noted. Examiners use commonly understood abbreviations to indicate their own test administration behaviors (e.g., queries, prompts) as well as to record various types of responses and behaviors by the child. A list of these common abbreviations appears in Rapid Reference 2.2.

≡ Rapid Reference 2.2

Commonly Used Recording Abbreviations

Abbreviation	Meaning
@	At
ABT	About
B	Be or both
BC	Because
C	See
DK	Child indicated he or she did not know the answer
-G	-Ing
INC	Response was incomplete at the time limit
LL	Looks like
NR	Child did not respond
P	Prompt administered
PC	Pointed correctly
PPL	People
PX	Pointed incorrectly
Q	Query administered
R	Repeated item
RR	Child requested repetition, item not repeated
SO	Someone
ST	Something
W/or c̄	With
W/O or s̄	Without
U	You
Y	Why

Source: Adapted from A. S. Kaufman and E. O. Lichtenberger, *Essentials of WISC-III and WPPSI-R Assessment.* Copyright © 2000 John Wiley & Sons, Inc., and J. E. Exner, Jr., *The Rorschach: A Comprehensive System, Volume 1: Basic Foundations, Third Edition.* Copyright © 1993 John Wiley & Sons, Inc. Expanded based on occurrence in WPPSI-IV standardization test protocols.

SUBTEST-BY-SUBTEST ADMINISTRATION

Verbal Comprehension Subtests

Information

Information is a Verbal Comprehension subtest. Picture items require the child to select among four pictured response options the one that best answers a verbally presented question about a general-knowledge topic. Verbal items require the child to answer verbally presented questions about a general-knowledge topic. Necessary materials include the *Administration and Scoring Manual*, the age-appropriate Record Form, and Stimulus Book 1 or 3.

Information start points vary by age, as follows. Children aged 2:6 to 3:11 start with Item 1. Children aged 4:0 to 5:11 start with Item 10, and children aged 6:0 to 7:7 start with Item 16. If a child aged 4:0 to 7:7 does not obtain a perfect score on *either* of the first two items administered, give the preceding items in reverse sequence until two consecutive perfect scores are obtained. The discontinue rule is three consecutive scores of 0. Be cautious not to discontinue too early. If you are unsure about a child's score on one of the items that may count toward the discontinue criterion, proceed by administering more items until you are confident a proper discontinue has been reached.

Items 1, 2, 5, 6, 10, 11, 16, and 17 are teaching items. The teaching items correspond with both the age-appropriate start points *and* the first few verbal items (Items 5 and 6) for children that were administered picture items. For teaching items, corrective feedback is given if the child does not receive a perfect score, even if the item in question is not one of the first items administered to a particular child.

You may repeat items as often as necessary, but do not reword the item. You may readminister items to which a child responded "I don't know" if later item performance on the subtest indicates correct responses to those items might be possible. If multiple pronunciation options exist for a word within an item, pronounce the word using the local pronunciation or the pronunciation you believe is most familiar to the child.

For picture items, the child must indicate a response option by pointing to or saying the number of the selection. If the child responds by naming a pictured option or with any other verbal response, ask the child to show you his or her selection.

Before administering the verbal items, become familiar with the sample responses, which are organized to facilitate accurate and quick scoring. Also, read the section on sample responses in Chapter 3 of this book. Clarify contradictory verbal and nonverbal responses (e.g., the child says "Two" but holds up three fingers) by asking the child which one he or she means.

Table 2.8 provides a comparison of Information administration procedures across WPPSI-III (Wechsler, 2002) and WPPSI-IV. The Don't Forget box lists behavioral observations that the examiner may wish to note during administration. Potential behavioral observations are listed for each subtest to assist the practitioner in understanding the child's approach to the task, identifying strengths and weaknesses, and planning interventions.

Table 2.8 Comparison of WPPSI-III and WPPSI-IV Information Administration

WPPSI-III	WPPSI-IV
Start points: 2:6–3:11: Item 1 4:0–5:11: Item 11 6:0–7:6: Item 17	Start points: Ages 2:6–3:11: Item 1 Ages 4:0–5:11: Item 10 Ages 6:0–7:7: Item 16
Discontinue after five consecutive scores of 0	Discontinue after three consecutive scores of 0
34 items	29 items
6 picture items	4 retained picture items
28 verbal items	25 verbal items: 13 new, 12 retained with little or no change in wording; revised scoring criteria and sample responses for all
34 total test items	29 total test items

DON'T FORGET

Behavioral Observations

For Information, note if the child

- Responds more readily to the picture items and Items 5 to 7 that require only nonverbal responses, then has more difficulty with items that require a verbal response. Because this is the first subtest with expressive requirements, it can provide important cues about the child's ability to respond verbally.
- Responds more readily to Items 1 to 4, which involve both pictorial and verbal stimuli, then has more difficulty with items that involve verbal stimuli only (Items 5 to 29).
- Appears to benefit from the feedback provided on teaching items, giving correct responses after learning the task.

- Provides complete responses or must be repeatedly queried as a cue to give all pertinent information about the response.
- Provides additional information about responses upon query, or tends to say he or she does not know any more.
- Continues to provide complete answers throughout the subtest, or if responses become briefer or vaguer as the subtest progresses.
- Provides multiple correct answers for items where this is appropriate (e.g., Items 8, 9, 12 to 15, 19, 22, 25, 28), versus only the single requisite answer.
- Does not know answers to items that might be more closely related to cultural opportunities, geographical location, and educational background (e.g., Items 4, 9, 13 to 15, 21, 23 to 29). Utilize this information in interpretation.

Similarities (Ages 4:0 to 7:7 Only)

Similarities is a Verbal Comprehension subtest. Picture items require the child to view two pictures at the top of the page and then choose one picture from four response options that is from the same category. Verbal items require the child to describe how two common objects or concepts are similar. Necessary materials include the *Administration and Scoring Manual*, the Record Form for ages 4:0 to 7:7, and Stimulus Book 3.

Similarities start points vary by age. Children aged 4:0 to 5:11 start with the picture items (i.e., Sample Item then Item 1). Children aged 6:0 to 7:7 start with the verbal items (i.e., Item 5). If a child aged 6:0 to 7:7 does not obtain a perfect score on *either* of the first two items administered, open the Stimulus Book and give the preceding picture items in reverse sequence until two consecutive perfect scores are obtained.

The discontinue rule is three consecutive scores of 0. Be careful not to discontinue too early. If you are unsure about a child's score on one of the items that may count toward the three consecutive scores of 0, administer more items until you are positive a proper discontinue has been reached.

Items 1, 2, 5, and 6 are teaching items. The teaching items correspond with both the age-appropriate start points *and* the first few verbal items (i.e., Items 5 and 6) for children who were administered picture items. As with Information, for teaching items, corrective feedback is given if the child does not receive a perfect score, even if the item in question is not one of the first items administered to a particular child.

You may repeat items as often as necessary. Do not use an alternate word or synonym, or attempt to explain. If multiple pronunciation options exist for a word, pronounce the word using the local pronunciation or the pronunciation you believe is most familiar to the child.

For picture items, remember to administer the sample item to all children who are starting with Item 1, but not to children who start with Item 5, even if they reverse all the way to Item 1. The child must indicate a response option by pointing to or saying the number of the selection. If the child responds by naming a pictured option or with any other verbal response, ask the child to show you his or her selection.

Before administering the verbal items, become familiar with the sample responses. Both the sample responses and the general scoring principles are used to determine item scores, so you must ensure you are familiar with the general scoring principles prior to administration. Review the section Using Sample Responses, General Scoring Principles, and General Concepts in Chapter 3 of this book for more information.

For some of the most difficult items, the two words represent opposite ends of a continuum, with the best responses describing them as extremes of the specified continuum dimension. However, some children are unable to describe the continuum's dimension and merely state how the two words are different. After all subtests have been administered, you may return to the item(s) and test the limits. At that time, point out that the child's previous response specified how the two objects or concepts were different, then ask the child to explain how they are *alike* or *the same*. Following this additional administration procedure, you may describe the additional support and explanation in the psychological report, but do not modify the score.

Table 2.9 provides a comparison of Similarities administration procedures across WPPSI-III and WPPSI-IV. The Don't Forget box lists behavioral observations that the examiner may note during administration.

Table 2.9 Comparison of WPPSI-III and WPPSI-IV Similarities Administration

WPPSI–III	WPPSI-IV
Start points: Age 4:0–7:6: Item 1	Start points: Age 4:0–5:11: Sample, then Item 1 Ages 6:0–7:7: Item 5
Discontinue after four consecutive scores of 0	Discontinue after three consecutive scores of 0
No sample item	New sample picture item
No picture items	4 new picture test items
24 verbal items	19 retained verbal items with revised scoring criteria and sample responses
24 total test items	23 total test items

DON'T FORGET

Behavioral Observations

For Similarities, note if the child:
- Initially appears to not understand the task and responds incorrectly to the sample item or a teaching item. Note whether the child appeared to benefit from the feedback provided.
- Responds more readily to the picture items, which involve both pictorial and verbal stimuli and can be responded to nonverbally, and then has more difficulty with the remaining items that involve only verbal stimuli and require a verbal response.
- Appears to benefit from the feedback provided on two trial items (Items 5 and 6) and teaching items, giving correct responses after learning the task.
- Provides complete responses or must be repeatedly queried as a cue to give all pertinent information.
- Provides additional information about responses upon query, or tends to say he or she does not know any more.
- Consistently states that the two objects or concepts are not alike, or are opposites.
- Demonstrates developing verbal reasoning abilities and prerequisite knowledge acquisition across Similarities and Information. First, examine the child's responses to Information items that provide a superordinate category and request an example (especially Items 8, 9, 12, 13, 14, 15, 19, and 22). Compare those responses to the child's responses on Similarities picture items, for which the child must recognize a pictorial example of a superordinate category when provided the category. Compare these to performance on Similarities verbal items, where the child must discover the superordinate category when provided two examples of the category.
- Performs better on Similarities than on Picture Concepts. This comparison can provide clues about the child's reasoning ability from the perspective of different stimulus modalities and response formats.

Vocabulary (Ages 4:0 to 7:7 Only)

Vocabulary is a Verbal Comprehension subtest. Picture items require the child to name a depicted object. Verbal items require the child to define words read by the examiner. Necessary materials include the *Administration and Scoring Manual*, the Record Form for ages 4:0 to 7:7, and Stimulus Book 3.

Vocabulary start points vary by age. Children aged 4:0 to 5:11 start with the picture items (i.e., Item 1). Children aged 6:0 to 7:7 start with the verbal items (i.e., Item 4). If a child aged 6:0 to 7:7 does not obtain a perfect score on *either* of the first two items administered, open the Stimulus Book and give the preceding picture items in reverse sequence until two consecutive perfect scores are obtained.

Notice that the Vocabulary picture items (i.e., Items 1, 2, and 3) are the same as Picture Naming Items 1, 3, and 7, respectively. Do not administer these items twice. If Picture Naming has already been administered, apply the scores the child received on Picture Naming Items 1, 3, and 7 to Vocabulary Items 1, 2, and 3, respectively.

The discontinue rule is three consecutive scores of 0. Carefully monitor item scores to prevent discontinuing too early. If you are unsure about a child's score on one of the items that may count toward the three consecutive scores of 0, administer more items until you know that a proper discontinue has been reached.

Items 1, 4, and 5 are teaching items. The teaching items correspond with both the age-appropriate start points *and* the first few verbal items (i.e., Items 4 and 5) for children who were administered picture items. As with the other Verbal Comprehension subtests, teaching items involve giving corrective feedback if the child does not receive a perfect score, even if the teaching item is not one of the first items administered to a particular child.

You may repeat items as often as necessary. Do not use a synonym or attempt to explain anything about the word. If multiple pronunciation options exist for a word, pronounce the word using the local pronunciation or the one you believe is most familiar to the child. Do not spell a word, either in an attempt to clarify or in response to a request from the child.

Unlike the other Verbal Comprehension subtests, for Vocabulary picture items a verbal response is required, and there are sample responses. Ensure you are familiar with these sample responses before administration begins. During picture item administration, four general response situations can arise in which the child's response is not incorrect, but fails to provide the common name of the pictured object. You should provide these queries as often as necessary. The verbatim queries are listed in the manual. For example, if the picture was of the "moon," the four types of responses for which queries should be provided are: marginal responses, too general responses, description of function, and the use of hand gestures. For a marginal but appropriate response (e.g., the child responds "Planet"), the examiner would agree, but ask the child what the picture is called. The same verbatim query is given if the child provides an appropriate function, such as responding "It shines," or uses appropriate hand gestures, such as holding up his or her hands and pantomiming holding up a spherical object. If a child gives an appropriate but too general response (e.g., the child responds "A thing in outer space"), ask him or her to clarify the response by asking what kind.

Before administering the verbal items, become familiar with the sample responses. Both the sample responses and the general scoring principles are used to determine item scores, so you must ensure you are familiar with both prior to administration. Read the section Using Sample Responses, General Scoring Principles, and General Concepts in Chapter 3 of this book for more information.

Table 2.10 provides a comparison of Vocabulary administration procedures across WPPSI-III and WPPSI-IV. The Don't Forget box lists behavioral observations that the examiner may note during administration.

Table 2.10 Comparison of WPPSI-III and WPPSI-IV Vocabulary Administration

WPPSI-III	WPPSI-IV
Start points: Ages 4:0–7:6: Item 6	Start points: Ages 4:0–5:11: Item 1 Ages 6:0–7:7: Item 4
Discontinue after five consecutive scores of 0	Discontinue after three consecutive scores of 0
5 picture items	3 picture items: 2 new, 1 retained
20 verbal items	20 verbal items: 11 new, 9 retained with revised scoring criteria and sample responses
25 total test items	23 total test items

DON'T FORGET

....

Behavioral Observations

For Vocabulary, note if the child
- Requires repeated use of the specific query on the picture items to encourage him or her to provide the name of the object rather than describe its function, or to clarify marginal responses. This pattern suggests word-retrieval difficulties or poor object recognition.
- Responds more readily to the picture items, which require only one-word verbal responses, then has more difficulty with Items 4 and 5, which require more lengthy verbal responses.
- Appears to benefit from the feedback provided on teaching items, giving correct responses after learning the task.
- Provides complete definitions or must be repeatedly queried as a cue to give all pertinent information.
- Provides additional information about responses upon query, or tends to say he or she does not know any more.
- Continues to provide complete answers throughout the subtest, or if responses become briefer or vaguer as the subtest progresses.
- Seems to not know answers to items that might be more closely related to cultural opportunities and educational background (e.g., Items 9, 12, 14, 19). Utilize this information in interpretation.

Comprehension (Ages 4:0 to 7:7 Only)

Comprehension is a Verbal Comprehension subtest. Picture items require the child to select among four pictured options the one that depicts the best reaction to a general principle or social situation. Verbal items require the child to respond to questions about general principles and social situations. Necessary materials include the *Administration and Scoring Manual*, the Record Form for ages 4:0 to 7:7, and Stimulus Book 3.

Comprehension start points vary by age. Children aged 4:0 to 5:11 start with the picture items (i.e., Item 1). Children aged 6:0 to 7:7 start with the verbal items (i.e., Item 5). If a child aged 6:0 to 7:7 does not obtain a perfect score on *either* of the first two items administered, open the Stimulus Book and give the preceding picture items in reverse sequence until two consecutive perfect scores are obtained.

The discontinue rule is three consecutive scores of 0. Carefully monitor item scores to prevent discontinuing too early. If you are not sure of a child's score on one of the items that may count toward the three consecutive scores of 0, administer more items until you know that a proper discontinue has been reached.

Items 1, 2, 5, and 6 are teaching items. The teaching items correspond with both the age-appropriate start points *and* the first few verbal items (Items 5 and 6) for children who were administered picture items. As with the other Verbal Comprehension subtests, teaching items involve giving corrective feedback if the child does not receive a perfect score, even if the teaching item is not one of the first items administered to a particular child.

You may repeat items as often as necessary. Do not reword items or expand upon them in any way. If multiple pronunciation options exist for a word, pronounce the word using the local pronunciation or the pronunciation you believe is most familiar to the child.

For picture items, the child must indicate a response option by pointing to or saying the number of the selection. If the child responds by describing a picture or with any other verbal response, ask the child to show you his or her response.

Before administering the verbal items, become familiar with the sample responses. Both the sample responses and the general scoring principles are used to determine item scores, so try to become familiar with the general scoring principles prior to administration as well. Review the section Using Sample Responses, General Scoring Principles, and General Concepts in Chapter 3 of this book for more information.

Table 2.11 provides a comparison of Comprehension administration procedures across WPPSI-III and WPPSI-IV. The Don't Forget box lists behavioral observations that the examiner may note during administration.

Table 2.11 Comparison of WPPSI-III and WPPSI-IV Comprehension Administration

WPPSI-III	WPPSI-IV
Start points: Ages 4:0–5:11: Item 1 Ages 6:0–7:6: Item 4	Start points: Ages 4:0–5:11: Item 1 Ages 6:0–7:7: Item 5
Discontinue after five consecutive scores of 0	Discontinue after three consecutive scores of 0
No picture items	4 new picture items
20 verbal items	18 verbal items: 1 new, 17 retained with revised scoring criteria and sample responses
20 total test items	22 total test items

DON'T FORGET
....
Behavioral Observations

For Comprehension, note if the child
- Responds more readily to the picture items, which require only a nonverbal response, and has more difficulty with Items 5 and 6, which require a verbal response.
- Appears to benefit from the feedback provided on teaching items, giving correct responses after learning the task.
- Provides complete responses for verbal items or must be repeatedly queried as a cue to give all pertinent information.
- Provides additional information about responses to verbal items upon query, or tends to say he or she does not know any more.
- Continues to provide complete answers throughout the verbal items on the subtest, or if responses become briefer or vaguer as the subtest progresses.
- Appears not to know answers to items that might be more closely related to cultural opportunities, geographical location, and educational background (e.g., Items 9, 12, 14, 17, 20, 21, 22). Utilize this information in interpretation.

Receptive Vocabulary

Receptive Vocabulary is a Verbal Comprehension subtest. The child selects among four visually presented response options the one that best represents a word read aloud. Necessary materials include the *Administration and Scoring Manual,* the age-appropriate Record Form, and Stimulus Book 1.

Receptive Vocabulary start points vary by age. Children aged 2:6 to 3:11 start with Item 1. Children aged 4:0 to 5:11 start with Item 5. Children aged 6:0 to 7:7 start with Item 13. If a child aged 4:0 to 7:7 does not obtain a perfect score on *either* of the first two test items administered, give the preceding items in reverse sequence until two consecutive perfect scores are obtained. The discontinue rule is three consecutive scores of 0.

Item 1 is a teaching item. As with the other Verbal Comprehension subtests, teaching items involve giving corrective feedback if the child does not receive a perfect score, even if the teaching item is not one of the first items administered to a particular child.

You may repeat items as often as necessary, but do not alter the wording. You may also readminister items to which a child responded "I don't know" if later item performance on the subtest indicates correct responses to those items might be possible. The child must indicate a response option by pointing to or saying the number of the selection. If the child responds by naming a pictured option or with any other verbal response, ask the child to show you his or her selection.

Table 2.12 provides a comparison of Receptive Vocabulary administration procedures across WPPSI-III and WPPSI-IV. The Don't Forget box lists behavioral observations that the examiner may note during administration.

Picture Naming

Picture Naming is a Verbal Comprehension subtest. The task requires the child to name a pictured object. Necessary materials include the *Administration and Scoring Manual*, the age-appropriate Record Form, and Stimulus Book 1.

Picture Naming start points vary by age. Children aged 2:6 to 3:11 start with Item 1. Children aged 4:0 to 5:11 start with Item 7, and children aged 6:0 to 7:7 start with Item 9. If a child aged 4:0 to 7:7 does not obtain a perfect score on *either*

Table 2.12 Comparison of WPPSI-III and WPPSI-IV Receptive Vocabulary Administration

WPPSI-III	WPPSI-IV
Start points:	Start points:
Ages 2:6–3:11: Item 1	Ages 2:6–3:11: Item 1
Ages 4:0–5:11: Item 6	Ages 4:0–5:11: Item 5
Ages 6:0–7:6: Item 16	Ages 6:0–7:7: Item 13
Discontinue after five consecutive scores of 0	Discontinue after three consecutive scores of 0
38 test items	31 test items: 8 new and 23 retained

DON'T FORGET

··

Behavioral Observations

For Receptive Vocabulary, note if the child

- Selects responses impulsively and misses important features that make his or her responses incorrect.
- Visually scans all response options before responding.
- Frequently self-corrects on items initially responded to correctly. This pattern of responding may indicate nervousness or anxiety.
- Appears to guess on more difficult items, or persists in studying them and appears determined to respond correctly.

Then, as appropriate or as desired, test the limits: Return to items with incorrect responses after all subtests have been administered. Point at each response option and ask the child to tell you the word he or she thinks is being depicted. This procedure can provide additional information about the child's verbal concept formation.

of the first two items administered, give the preceding items in reverse sequence until two consecutive perfect scores are obtained.

Notice that Picture Naming Items 1, 3, and 7 are the same as the Vocabulary picture items (i.e., Vocabulary Items 1, 2, and 3, respectively). Do not administer these items twice. If Vocabulary has already been administered, apply the scores the child received on Vocabulary Items 1, 2, and 3 to Picture Naming Items 1, 3, and 7, respectively. The discontinue rule is three consecutive scores of 0.

Item 1 is a teaching item. As with the other Verbal Comprehension subtests, teaching items involve giving corrective feedback if the child does not receive a perfect score, even if the teaching item is not one of the first items administered to a particular child.

You may repeat instructions as often as necessary. Do not attempt to explain anything about the picture. A verbal response is required, and there are sample responses for each item. Ensure you are familiar with these sample responses before administration begins. During item administration, four general response situations can arise that call for specific and further query. These situations, and specific queries, are the same as those of the picture items for Vocabulary. See the section of this chapter on Vocabulary for more information.

Table 2.13 provides a comparison of Picture Naming administration procedures across WPPSI-III and WPPSI-IV. The Don't Forget box lists behavioral observations that the examiner may note during administration.

Table 2.13 Comparison of WPPSI-III and WPPSI-IV Picture Naming Administration

WPPSI-III	WPPSI-IV
Start points:	Start points:
Ages 2:6–3:11: Item 1	Ages 2:6–3:11: Item 1
Ages 4:0–5:11: Item 7	Ages 4:0–5:11: Item 7
Ages 6:0–7:6: Item 11	Ages 6:0–7:7: Item 9
Discontinue after five consecutive scores of 0	Discontinue after three consecutive scores of 0
30 test items	24 test items: 4 new and 20 retained

DON'T FORGET

Behavioral Observations

For Picture Naming, note if the child
- Requires repeated use of the specific query to encourage him or her to provide the name of the object rather than describe its function, or to clarify marginal responses. This pattern may indicate word-retrieval difficulties or poor object recognition.
- Tends to provide more marginal, functional, gestural, or generalized responses to items as they become more difficult across the subtest, or if he or she merely answers "don't know" to more difficult items.

Then, as appropriate or as desired, test the limits: Return to items with incorrect responses at the end of the battery. Read another word along with the correct response and ask the child to tell you what is being depicted. Functionally similar responses are provided for each item in Table 2.14. Remember to vary the order in which you read the choices, so that the correct response is not always first. It may also be appropriate to use phonetically similar responses if you have observed word-finding difficulties.

Visual Spatial Subtests

Block Design

Block Design is a Visual Spatial subtest. For easier items, the child uses single-color blocks to re-create a model constructed by the examiner. For transitional items, the examiner constructs designs that match pictures and then disassembles the model for the child to try. More difficult items require the child to use only the picture in the Stimulus Book when constructing the block design. Necessary materials include the *Administration and Scoring Manual*, the age-appropriate Record Form, Stimulus

Table 2.14 Picture Naming Alternate Functionally Similar Responses for Testing the Limits

Item	Functionally Similar Alternate Response	Item	Functionally Similar Alternate Response
1.	Train	13.	Mop
2.	Lion	14.	Ant
3.	Apple	15.	Megaphone
4.	Feather	16.	Tangerine
5.	Moon	17.	Screw
6.	Picture	18.	Skillet
7.	Glue	19.	Map
8.	Comb	20.	Bongo
9.	Fly	21.	Scale
10.	Violin	22.	Saxophone
11.	Rabbit	23.	Headphones
12.	Sand	24.	Kickstand

Book 1 or 3, the full set of WPPSI-IV Block Design blocks, and a stopwatch. Ensure that the blocks are specific to the WPPSI-IV, because the necessary blocks differ from those of other Wechsler intelligence scales (e.g., the WISC-IV).

Block Design start points vary by age, as follows. Children aged 2:6 to 3:11 start with Item 1. Children aged 4:0 to 5:11 start with Item 4, and children aged 6:0 to 7:7 start with Sample Items A and B, then Item 9. If a child aged 4:0 to 7:7 does not obtain a perfect score on *either* of the first two items administered, give the preceding items in reverse sequence until two consecutive perfect scores are obtained. For children aged 6:0 to 7:7, a reversal requires switching block sets from two-color to one-color blocks; ensure you use the correct blocks. The discontinue rule is two consecutive scores of 0. Items 1 to 4 and Item 9 require administration of a second trial if the child does not receive a perfect score on the first trial. These items correspond with the first few items on the subtest and the first test item that uses two-color blocks.

Proper Block Design administration requires attention to a number of details. For items presented using a model, always verbally explain your construction, as outlined in the *Administration and Scoring Manual*. If the child attempts to match all sides of his construction to your model, tell the child only the tops need to match.

Although you may repeat verbal directions, do not reconstruct your model if it has been disassembled or reexpose stimulus pages of test items that are complete. If the child begins to build his or her construction on top of the Stimulus Book, point to the correct area specified in the diagram in the *Administration and Scoring Manual* and instruct the child to make it there. Correct rotation errors no more than once within Part A (the one-color block items) and once within Part B (two-color block items). However, for the one-color block items, do not count rotations as incorrect: This is an important point to note, to avoid prematurely discontinuing the subtest.

Table 2.15 provides a comparison of Block Design administration procedures across WPPSI-III and WPPSI-IV. The Don't Forget box lists behavioral observations that the examiner may note during administration.

Object Assembly

Object Assembly is a Visual Spatial subtest. The child assembles puzzle pieces within a time limit into a meaningful whole object that is named. Necessary materials include the *Administration and Scoring Manual*, the age-appropriate Record Form, 13 Object Assembly Puzzles, and a stopwatch.

Object Assembly start points vary by age. Children aged 2:6 to 3:11 start with Item 1. Children aged 4:0 to 5:11 start with Item 3. Children aged 6:0 to 7:7 start with Item 7. If a child aged 6:0 to 7:7 does not obtain a perfect score on *either* of the first two test items administered, give the preceding items in reverse sequence until two consecutive perfect scores are obtained. The discontinue rule is two consecutive scores of 0.

Proper Object Assembly administration requires attention to a number of details. The puzzle pieces should be stacked in your hand sequentially starting with

Table 2.15 Comparison of WPPSI-III and WPPSI-IV Block Design Administration

WPPSI-III	WPPSI-IV
Start points:	Start points:
Ages 2:6–3:11: Item 1	Ages 2:6–3:11: Item 1
Ages 4:0–7:6: Item 6	Ages 4:0–5:11: Item 4
	Ages 6:0–7:7: Samples A and B, then Item 9
Discontinue after three consecutive scores of 0	Discontinue after two consecutive scores of 0
2 sample items	2 sample items: 1 new, 1 retained
20 test items	17 test items: 4 new and 13 retained

DON'T FORGET

Behavioral Observations

For Block Design, note if the child

- Initially approaches the items by studying the model or picture or immediately begins working with the blocks. Note if the child reliably sets an initial anchor block (e.g., always works on the lower right corner first) then builds from it.
- Learns from trial and error on prior items, or if he or she approaches every item haphazardly.
- Finishes items relatively quickly or slowly, frequently and repeatedly studies the stimuli to confirm the construction, or rarely glances at the model or picture then checks after the construction to confirm. These observations can be informative about visual memory as well.
- Displays motor movements and skills that appear clumsy or skilled and smooth.
- Displays signs of nervousness or agitation such as trembling or shaking hands, or clutching the blocks tightly.
- Commits a break-in-configuration error at any time, or seems to understand that items are constrained within a predictable structural matrix. A break-in-configuration error occurs when the maximum dimension of the design is exceeded while assembling a construction. For example, if the child aligns three blocks in a row while constructing a 2 × 2 design, a break-in-configuration error has occurred.
- Commits an uncorrected rotation error on either part of the subtest, although rotation errors are penalized only on Part B.
- Performs better on items with model stimuli or items with pictorial stimuli.
- During Items 9 and 10, which use the model *and* the pictorial stimuli, displays a preference to use the model or picture as a guide.
- Is overly concerned about gaps between the blocks or aligning the design perfectly with the edge of the table or Stimulus Book.
- Attempts to rotate the Stimulus Book or model, or to change perspective on the stimulus by standing or twisting his or her head.
- Appears to recognize incorrect constructions upon comparison with the stimuli and attempts to correct them.

Note completion times on the Record Form. These are useful not only to determine if the child responded correctly within the time limit, but also to provide some information about speed of problem solving for more complex tasks, in contrast with the Processing Speed subtests, which involve simple perceptual speed.

the highest-numbered piece on the bottom, out of the child's view and face-down. The pieces are then laid out from your left to right with the number side faceup and readable from your perspective. Pieces with single-underlined numbers are placed in the row closest to the child, and those with double-underlined numbers are placed closest to you. Expose the pieces in order, beginning with the piece numbered 1. Flip the pieces from top to bottom rather than left to right.

You may repeat verbal directions, but do not re-model construction of the puzzle for the child on Item 1 after it has been disassembled, and do not re-administer items that are complete. If the child flips a piece over so that the number side is faceup during item administration, flip the piece back over. Monitor the child to ensure he or she is not merely playing with the pieces or being hesitant. If you believe this to be the case, encourage him or her to work as fast as he or she can. Item 1 has a second trial if the score on the first trial is not perfect. Ensure that you administer Trial 2 to any child who does not receive a perfect score for Trial 1.

Table 2.16 provides a comparison of Object Assembly administration procedures across WPPSI-III and WPPSI-IV. The Don't Forget box lists behavioral observations that the examiner may note during administration.

Fluid Reasoning Subtests

Matrix Reasoning (Ages 4:0 to 7:7 Only)

Matrix Reasoning is a Fluid Reasoning subtest. The child selects among visually presented response options the one that best completes a matrix. Necessary materials include the *Administration and Scoring Manual,* the Record Form for ages 4:0 to 7:7, and Stimulus Book 3.

Matrix Reasoning start points vary by age. Children aged 4:0 to 4:11 start with Sample Items A to C, then Item 1. Children aged 5:0 to 5:11 start with Sample Items A to C, then Item 4. Children aged 6:0 to 7:7 start with Sample Items A to C, then Item 7. If a child aged 5:0 to 7:7 does not obtain a perfect score on *either* of the first two test items administered, give the preceding items in reverse sequence until two consecutive perfect scores are obtained. The discontinue rule is three consecutive scores of 0.

Table 2.16 Comparison of WPPSI-III and WPPSI-IV Object Assembly Administration

WPPSI-III	WPPSI-IV
Start points:	Start points:
Ages 2:6–3:11: Item 1	Ages 2:6–3:11: Item 1
Ages 4:0–5:11: Item 3	Ages 4:0–5:11: Item 3
Ages 6:0–7:6: Item 8	Ages 6:0–7:7: Item 7
Discontinue after three consecutive scores of 0	Discontinue after two consecutive scores of 0
14 test items	13 test items: 2 new and 11 retained

DON'T FORGET

••

Behavioral Observations

For Object Assembly, note if the child
- Initially approaches the items by studying the pieces or immediately begins working with them.
- Displays motor movements and skills that appear clumsy or skilled and smooth. Note signs of nervousness or agitation such as trembling or shaking hands, or clutching the puzzle pieces tightly.
- Is overly concerned about gaps between the puzzle pieces or aligning the puzzle perfectly with the edge of the table or Stimulus Book.
- Turns puzzle pieces to be oriented at an angle or upside down.
- Appears to recognize incorrect junctures upon inspection and attempts to correct them.

Note completion times on the Record Form. These are useful not only to determine if the child responded correctly within the time limit, but also to provide some information about speed of problem solving for more complex tasks, in contrast with the Processing Speed subtests, which involve simple perceptual speed.

You may repeat item instructions as often as necessary. You may also readminister items to which a child responded "I don't know" if later item performance on the subtest indicates correct responses to those items might be possible. The child must indicate a response option by pointing to or saying the number of the selection. If the child responds by naming a pictured option or with any other verbal response, ask the child to show you his or her selection.

Table 2.17 provides a comparison of Matrix Reasoning administration procedures across WPPSI-III and WPPSI-IV. The Don't Forget box lists behavioral observations that the examiner may note during administration.

Picture Concepts (Ages 4:0 to 7:7 Only)

Picture Concepts is a Fluid Reasoning subtest. The child is required to form a group with a shared element by selecting one picture from each of either two or three rows. Necessary materials include the *Administration and Scoring Manual*, the Record Form for ages 4:0 to 7:7, and Stimulus Book 3.

Picture Concepts start points vary by age. Children aged 4:0 to 5:11 start with Sample Items A and B, then Item 1. Children aged 6:0 to 7:7 start with Sample Items A and B, then Item 8. If a child aged 6:0 to 7:7 does not obtain a perfect score on *either* of the first two test items administered, give the preceding items in

Table 2.17 Comparison of WPPSI-III and WPPSI-IV Matrix Reasoning Administration

WPPSI-III	WPPSI-IV
Start points:	Start points:
Age 4:0–4:11: Samples A–C, then Item 1	Age 4:0–4:11: Samples A–C, then Item 1
Age 5:0–5:11: Samples A–C, then Item 4	Age 5:0–5:11: Samples A–C, then Item 4
Ages 6:0–7:6: Samples A–C, then Item 6	Ages 6:0–7:7: Samples A–C, then Item 7
Discontinue after four consecutive scores or four scores of 0 on five consecutive items	Discontinue after three consecutive scores of 0
3 sample items	3 retained sample items
29 test items	26 test items: 5 new, 21 retained

DON'T FORGET

Behavioral Observations

For Matrix Reasoning, note if the child
- Initially approaches the items by studying the matrix or immediately begins searching the response options and comparing with the matrix.
- Selects response impulsively, based on color or shape, but misses other important features that make the response incorrect.
- Frequently self-corrects on items initially responded to correctly. This pattern of responding may indicate nervousness or anxiety.
- Finishes items relatively quickly or slowly. Note if the child frequently and repeatedly studies the matrix to confirm an answer, or rarely glances at the matrix then checks after selecting a response to confirm. These observations can be informative about visual memory.
- Gives up easily on more difficult items or persists in studying them and appears determined to understand the item and respond correctly.

Note completion times on the Record Form. These are useful to provide some information about speed of problem solving for more complex tasks, in contrast with the Processing Speed subtests, which involve simple perceptual speed.

reverse sequence until two consecutive perfect scores are obtained. The discontinue rule is three consecutive scores of 0.

You may repeat item instructions as often as necessary. You may also readminister items to which a child responded "I don't know" if later item performance on the subtest indicates correct responses to those items might be possible.

The child must indicate response options by pointing to or saying the number of the selections. If the child responds by naming a pictured option or with any other verbal response, ask the child to show you his or her selections.

Table 2.18 provides a comparison of Picture Concepts administration procedures across WPPSI-III and WPPSI-IV. The Don't Forget box lists behavioral observations that the examiner may note during administration.

Table 2.18 Comparison of WPPSI-III and WPPSI-IV Picture Concepts Administration

WPPSI-III	WPPSI-IV
Start points:	Start points:
Ages 4:0–5:11: Samples A and B, then Item 1	Ages 4:0–5:11: Samples A and B, then Item 1
Ages 6:0–7:6: Samples A and B, then Item 8	Ages 6:0–7:7: Samples A and B, then Item 8
Discontinue after four consecutive scores of 0	Discontinue after three consecutive scores of 0
2 sample items	2 retained sample items
28 test items	27 test items: 4 new, 3 revised, and 22 retained

DON'T FORGET

Behavioral Observations

For Picture Concepts, note if the child
- Frequently requests the names of objects.
- Selects responses impulsively but misses other important features that make his or her responses incorrect.
- Repeatedly selects options from a single row and does not appear to respond to the corrective feedback to choose one from each row.
- Frequently self-corrects on items initially responded to correctly. This pattern of responding may indicate nervousness or anxiety.
- Finishes items relatively quickly or slowly, frequently and repeatedly studies all options to confirm an answer, or glances at the rows initially then rechecks them after selecting a response to confirm.
- Gives up easily on more difficult items or persists in studying them and appears determined to understand the item and respond correctly.
- Compare performance on Picture Concepts and Similarities. This comparison can provide clues about the child's reasoning ability from the perspective of different stimulus modalities and response formats.

(continued)

Note completion times on the Record Form. These are useful to provide some information about speed of problem solving for more complex tasks, in contrast with the Processing Speed subtests, which involve simple perceptual speed.

Return to items with incorrect responses after all subtests have been administered, and query the child about the rationale for his or her selection by asking, "Why do they go together?" This procedure will permit observations about the sophistication of the child's reasoning ability. Frequently, responses of young children or children with low ability indicate that options on difficult items are related merely by color or location (e.g., "They are both red," or "They both can be outside.")

Behind the Scenes

• During research phases, examiners intentionally tested the limits to assist with item development by asking for the child's rationale for responses to administered items with scores of 0. This method can still be used following a standard administration of the test battery to determine if responses scored 0 were guesses or the child had a logical but uncreditable reason for the selections.

Working Memory Subtests

Picture Memory

Picture Memory is a Working Memory subtest. The child is shown stimulus picture(s) in the Stimulus Book, and then selects the stimulus picture(s) from a number of response options on a page. Necessary materials include the *Administration and Scoring Manual*, the age-appropriate Record Form, Stimulus Book 2, and a stopwatch.

Picture Memory start points vary by age. Children aged 2:6 to 3:11 start with items that require recognition of a single picture: Sample Item A, then Item 1. Sample Item A introduces the task of remembering the single picture and selecting it from among the array of response options. Children aged 4:0 to 7:7 start with items that require recognition of multiple pictures: Sample Item B, then Item 7. Sample Item B introduces the child to the task of remembering and selecting multiple pictures. If a child aged 4:0 to 7:7 does not obtain a perfect score on *either* of the first two test items administered, give the preceding items in reverse sequence until two consecutive perfect scores are obtained. Do not administer Sample Item A in this situation. The discontinue rule is three consecutive scores of 0.

Exposure of the stimulus pages is timed. For items that require recognition of a single picture (i.e., Sample Item A to Item 6), the stimulus page should be exposed for only 3 seconds. For items that require recognition of multiple pictures (i.e.,

DON'T FORGET

···

Behavioral Observations

For Picture Memory, note if the child

- Displays wandering attention during the brief stimulus exposure time, leading to a lower score.
- Gives up easily or responds impulsively on more difficult items, or appears determined to respond correctly.
- Hesitates to respond, resulting in decay of the encoded memory and increased errors. These are qualitatively different errors than those due to inattention during stimulus exposure.
- Selects the pictures in the same order they appeared on the stimulus page, and if this imposition of structure appears to be a successful strategy.
- Frequently self-corrects on items initially responded to correctly. This pattern of responding may indicate nervousness or anxiety.
- For items with multiple responses necessary to obtain credit, neglects to choose only one or a few responses. Look for clues as to why. For example, note if the child incorrectly selected pictures of objects that are similar phonemically or in appearance to the neglected correct answer(s).
- Has incorrect responses that correctly include some of the first or last pictures in the array but omit those in the middle of the array, or if the incorrect responses include mostly incorrect objects.
- Tends to respond incorrectly to the first item of a new span length or new number of response options, then experiences later success on similar items. This is in contrast to a child who responds correctly to sets of similar items, then discontinues quickly after reaching his or her maximum span length.

Note any interruptions or distractions that occur during a timed stimulus exposure. Check to see if the resulting change in raw score may have resulted in a higher subtest scaled score. For repeated interruptions, the subtest might be considered spoiled and uninterpretable.

Sample Item B to Item 35), the stimulus page is exposed for 5 seconds. You must use a stopwatch to ensure accurate exposure time. Do *not* shorten or eliminate the verbatim prompt that is given before you start the stopwatch to time the stimulus page exposure. Doing so will reduce the allotted exposure time.

You may repeat item instructions as often as necessary. However, do *not* re-administer items under any circumstances. Items 1, 2, 7, and 8 are teaching items. Only reexpose stimuli as instructed for sample and teaching items to provide the prescribed corrective feedback.

Behind the Scenes

- Picture Memory's previous name was *Picture Recognition*. The name was changed prior to final publication to distinguish the measure from other recognition memory tasks that do not place an emphasis on working memory. The controlled reuse of stimuli throughout the task and consequent proactive interference distinguishes it from such measures.
- Various attempts were made to require children to sequence their response to match the stimulus presentation for working memory tasks. Situations familiar to young children (e.g., a farmer feeding animals in line) did not facilitate sequencing.
- Picture Memory draws on the familiarize–recognize paradigm (Reznick, 2009) from infant working memory research to ensure that even children of very low ability can experience some success on the task. In this paradigm, children view a set of stimuli and later recognize them in response to a probe.
- Great care was taken to select objects that would fill reasonably well the dimensions of a square area allocated to each picture. This was done to prevent the child from using stimuli size to facilitate learning.

The child must indicate a response option by pointing to or saying the number of the selection. If the child responds by naming pictured options or with any other verbal response, ask the child to show you his or her selection. If the child asks if his or her response should follow a particular order (e.g., the order of presentation on the stimulus page), use the provided prompt to clarify that he or she does not need to say or point to them in order.

Zoo Locations

Zoo Locations is a Working Memory subtest. The child is shown animal cards that are placed on specified locations on a zoo layout for a brief time period, and then replaces each card in its recalled location. Necessary materials include the *Administration and Scoring Manual*, the age-appropriate Record Form, the Zoo Locations Layouts and Animal Cards, and a stopwatch.

The Zoo Locations start points vary by age. Children aged 2:6 to 5:11 start with items that require placement of a single card on a two-location layout: the sample item, then Item 1. A second trial should be administered for the sample item if the child does not place the card correctly on the first trial. Children aged 6:0 to 7:7 start with the sample item, but then proceed to Item 7, for which a single card is placed on a four-location layout.

If a child aged 4:0 to 7:7 does not obtain a perfect score on *either* of the first two test items administered, give the preceding items in reverse sequence until two consecutive perfect scores are obtained. The discontinue rule is two consecutive scores of 0.

Exposure of the cards in their specified locations is timed. For items that require use of the two- or three-location layouts, the cards should be exposed in their locations for only 3 seconds. For items that require use of other more complex layouts, the cards are exposed in their locations for 5 seconds. A red line on the Record Forms between Items 6 and 7 is intended to remind you of the exposure time change.

The timing does not begin until after all cards are laid out and the verbatim instruction to remember where the animals live is completed. You must use a stopwatch to ensure accurate exposure time. Do *not* shorten or eliminate the verbatim prompt that is given before you start the stopwatch to time the stimulus page exposure. Doing so will reduce the allotted exposure time.

You may repeat item instructions as often as necessary. However, do *not* readminister test items under any circumstances. Only replace the cards in their correct locations as instructed for the sample and teaching items to provide the prescribed corrective feedback.

Items 1, 2, 5, 6, 7, and 8 are teaching items. These correspond with the first few items for younger and for older children, as well as the first few items that require placement of multiple cards for younger children that begin with items that require placement of only one card. The teaching is provided in response to imperfect scores regardless as to which item the child started with.

Proper Zoo Locations administration requires practice. The cards should be stacked in alphabetical order, with the A card on the top of the stack and out of the child's view. Flip each card from top to bottom as you place it on the layout. Unlike Object Assembly, *do not* lay out the cards with their labeled side up prior to exposure: Each card is flipped as you are placing it on the layout so it is exposed upon placement. Place each card in its location as depicted on the item key in the manual. Lay out the cards in order, beginning with the card labeled *A*. You may repeat verbal directions, but do not replace cards on the layouts unless for the sample and teaching items as specified in the *Administration and Scoring Manual*, and do not re-administer items that are complete.

Monitor the child's performance and questions for each item to determine if a prompt is necessary. Prompts are provided if the child asks if the cards should be put down in a particular order that mirrors the presentation order, or if he or she places multiple animals in a single location or any animal in an unacceptable location (e.g., on a hedge). If the child flips a card over so that the animal picture side is facedown during item administration, flip the card back over.

DON'T FORGET

Behavioral Observations

For Zoo Locations, note if the child

- Displays wandering attention during the brief stimulus exposure time, leading to a lower score. Integrate this information into your interpretation of the score.
- Fumbles or drops cards, resulting in a potentially lowered score.
- Sorts or orders the cards before placing them on the layouts, and if this imposition of structure appears to be a successful or unsuccessful strategy.
- Hesitates to respond, resulting in decay of the encoded memory and more errors. These are qualitatively different errors than those due to inattention during stimulus exposure.
- Frequently self-corrects on items initially responded to correctly. This pattern of responding may indicate nervousness or anxiety.
- Neglects to place only one or a few cards correctly for items with multiple responses necessary to obtain credit. If this occurs, look for clues as to why. For example, did the child reverse only two pictures in their correct locations, or are the relative card positions correct, but shifted in another direction?
- Arranges responses that include correctly placed cards from the beginning or end of the placement sequence, but incorrectly places the cards presented in the middle of the sequence, or if the incorrect responses involve most or all cards placed incorrectly.
- Tends to respond incorrectly to the first item requiring a greater number of cards or to the first item associated with a new layout, then experiences later success on similar items. This is in contrast to a child who responds correctly to sets of similar items, then discontinues quickly after reaching his or her maximum span length.
- Gives up easily or responds impulsively on more difficult items, or appears determined to respond correctly.

Note any interruptions or distractions that occur during a timed stimulus exposure. Check to see if the resulting change in raw score may have resulted in a higher subtest scaled score. For repeated interruptions, the subtest might be considered spoiled and uninterpretable.

Processing Speed Subtests

Bug Search (Ages 4:0 to 7:7 Only)

Bug Search is a Processing Speed subtest. For each item, the child views a target bug, then marks a bug in the search group that matches it. The child works within a time limit of 120 seconds. Necessary materials include the *Administration and Scoring Manual*, the Record Form for ages 4:0 to 7:7, Response Booklet 1, the ink dauber, a stopwatch, and a paper towel to prevent ink transfer to the flat surface after the child practices use of the dauber. The Bug Search Scoring Key is necessary

---

Behind the Scenes

....

- Zoo Locations went through various titles as it evolved. When the task used farm animal magnets and a farm background in early research stages, we used titles such as *Farm Scene* and *Animal Magnetism*. The name changed to *Zoo Trip* when the setting changed to a zoo. The change to *Zoo Locations* was made prior to final publication to help practitioners more easily associate the task with spatial working memory.

- Zoo Locations draws on the observe–perform paradigm (Reznick, 2009) from infant working memory research to ensure that even children of very low ability can experience some success on the task. In this paradigm, children observe the examiner's actions and attempt to later reproduce them.

---

for scoring. Be careful to allow the Response Booklet to dry before scoring, to prevent ink transfer to the scoring key.

Be sure to administer Dauber Practice before Bug Search. Without this practice, children's responses to the Processing Speed subtests can vary considerably and detract from the final scores. Review the discussion of test materials early in this chapter that outlines use and care of the ink dauber and administration of Dauber Practice.

Children aged 4:0 to 7:7 start with the demonstration and sample items, then the test items. Administer all demonstration and sample items as described in the *Administration and Scoring Manual*. Practice the verbatim instructions for the subtest before administering it for the first time. Committing the instructions to memory ensures a smoother administration.

Do not permit the child to start early. Watch carefully during administration, because you must turn the pages for the child and prompt him or her to continue working as fast as possible. Some children mark the target bug instead of the search bug. If this occurs at any time, provide the necessary prompt. Ensure the child stamps the bug only once and stamps only one selection. Give the prompts in the *Administration and Scoring Manual* as necessary in response to multiple stamps. Do not allow the child to skip items; give the necessary prompt if this occurs.

Discontinue after 120 seconds. If a child is working on an item when the time limit expires, you may allow him or her to finish that item, indicate on the Response Booklet that the time limit had expired, and do not award credit (or penalize the score) for the response.

Cancellation (Ages 4:0 to 7:7 Only)

Cancellation is a Processing Speed subtest. The child views two 17 × 11 arrangements of clothing and other items, and marks all the clothing within

DON'T FORGET

••

Behavioral Observations

For Bug Search, note if the child

- Selects responses impulsively, based on shape, but misses important features that make his or her responses incorrect. Some stimuli (e.g., bee/fly) are more readily confused based on external shape by children with impulsive response styles.
- Displays wandering attention during the task, leading to a lower score due to loss of potential points. Integrate this information into your interpretation of the score. Consider also administering both other Processing Speed subtests if this occurs to provide additional information about performance.
- Displays trembling hands, keeps a tight grip on the ink dauber, or has sweaty palms, causing his or her hand to slip down or the dauber to slip out of his or her grip.
- Is overly concerned with the ink dauber's variability, marking bugs more than once if a mark is light.
- Loses time by checking and rechecking answers before marking them and moving on.
- Tends to scan the entire search group despite having identified the matching search group bug close to the target before marking the response. Items with the matching search group bug close to the target bug are usually responded to somewhat more quickly. This pattern may indicate the child becomes distracted by irrelevant information or detail at the expense of speed.
- Is able to ignore irrelevant bugs and quickly locate the correct bug, or lingers and examines the irrelevant bugs longer on items with the matching search group bug placed farther away from the target. These are usually responded to somewhat more slowly.

45 seconds. Materials include the *Administration and Scoring Manual,* the Record Form for ages 4:0 to 7:7, Response Booklet 2, the ink dauber, and a stopwatch. The Cancellation Scoring Template is necessary for scoring. Take caution to allow the Response Booklet to dry before scoring, to prevent ink transfer to the scoring template.

If Bug Search was not administered, be sure to give Dauber Practice before Cancellation. Refer to the discussion in this chapter about test materials that outlines use and care of the ink dauber and administration of Dauber Practice.

Children aged 4:0 to 7:7 start with the demonstration item, the sample item, then Item 1. The demonstration and sample items introduce the child to the

---

Behind the Scenes

• Before selecting the dauber, the research team tried various other solutions. Stamps, crayons, and markers all proved less durable and less effective than the ink dauber. The orange ink dauber was selected from among many colors because it was most visible yet did not obscure the marked stimuli.

• Bug Search's original name was *Bug Busters*. The name was changed prior to final publication to help practitioners more readily make the connection between this new task and its predecessor, Symbol Search.

• In early WPPSI-IV research stages, children tended to look for and mark matching bugs in incorrect rows. Every row is therefore a different color, to help the child search for the one matching search group bug on the page.

• WPPSI-III Symbol Search contained a "no match" condition for which, if no symbol matched, the child marked a question mark (?) on the far right column. In an attempt to improve the floor and to make Bug Search more intuitive and less language dependent, the "no match" condition was designated by a leaf (the bug was said to be hiding behind it). The youngest children could not understand the concept, so the "no match" condition was dropped. All items contain a bug that matches the target.

---

structured and random arrangements of objects, respectively, that he or she will see on Items 1 and 2. Be sure to administer the demonstration and sample items as described in the *Administration and Scoring Manual*. Provide all necessary feedback to teach the child to mark all clothing, to not mark anything else, and to mark targets only once as he or she completes the sample item.

Practice the verbatim instructions and prompts for the subtest before administering it for the first time. As with any Processing Speed subtest, committing the instructions to memory ensures a smoother administration.

Do not permit the child to begin either test item early. Watch carefully during administration, because you may need to prompt the child to mark targets only once or to continue working as fast as possible. Small lapses in your concentration can make big differences in scores on this subtest. Be careful to discontinue each test item after 45 seconds. Administer both Items 1 (Random) and 2 (Structured). Allow the pages to dry separately before reassembling the Response Booklet.

CAUTION

Do not allow the child to continue working on a Cancellation test item after 45 seconds. It is easy to forget that the time limit for each item is 45 seconds, not 120 seconds. This is the most commonly encountered Cancellation administration error.

DON'T FORGET

....

Behavioral Observations

For Cancellation, note if the child

- Selects responses impulsively but misses important features that make his or her responses incorrect. Distracter pictures were intentionally selected to pull for impulsive responses based on color.

- Displays wandering attention during the task, leading to a lower score due to loss of potential points. Integrate this information into your interpretation of the score. Consider also administering Animal Coding if this occurs to provide additional information about performance.

- Displays trembling hands, has a tight grip on the ink dauber, or has sweaty palms, causing his or her hand to slip down or the dauber to slip out of his or her grip.

- Is overly concerned with the ink dauber's variability, marking selections more than once if a mark is light.

- Loses time by checking and rechecking answers before marking them and moving on.

- Applies a strategy to the first item. If so, observe the effectiveness of the selected strategy. One common effective strategy is to mark every example of a single target on the page, then do the same for the next target, and so on. Another less effective strategy is to attempt to find all targets on a quadrant or quarter of a page, or to attempt to impose structure on the random arrangement by marking in rows or columns. Other children may search more haphazardly, quickly marking any clothing he or she sees as fast as possible and making a few errors along the way.

- Modifies his or her strategy from the first item based on the structured arrangement. Note any observed early reading behaviors, such as searching the rows from left to right and down the page.

- Completely neglects an entire side of the visual field. Follow up by gaining more information about the child's vision and medical history, including any neurological issues, if this is observed.

Behind the Scenes

....

- Cancellation was adapted from the WISC-IV subtest of the same name. Stimuli were selected for their relevance to young children.

- Some children did not understand the word clothing, so the instructions were reworded to direct the child to stamp things people wear.

- Attempts to adapt the Processing Speed subtests for very young children (ages 2:6 to 3:11) were unsuccessful. Although they understood the very basic concept

> (i.e., things you wear) upon which this subtest is based, they were unconcerned with their speed even during very brief tasks like Cancellation. While it was well within the motor skill abilities of 2-year-old children to use the ink dauber, they generally preferred to play with the dauber to make designs. Some 3-year-old children can perform the Processing Speed tasks.

Animal Coding (Ages 4:0 to 7:7 Only)

Animal Coding is a Processing Speed subtest. Using a key, the child marks shapes that are paired with depicted animals within a time limit of 120 seconds. Necessary materials include the *Administration and Scoring Manual*, the Record Form for ages 4:0 to 7:7, Response Booklet 3, the ink dauber, and a stopwatch. The Animal Coding Scoring Key is necessary for scoring. As with all of the Processing Speed subtests, be careful to allow the Response Booklet to dry before scoring, to prevent ink transfer to the scoring key.

If Bug Search and/or Cancellation were not administered, be sure to administer Dauber Practice before Animal Coding. Refer to the discussion in this chapter about test materials that outlines use and care of the ink dauber and administration of Dauber Practice.

Children aged 4:0 to 7:7 start with the demonstration and sample items, then the test items. Administer all demonstration and sample items as described in the *Administration and Scoring Manual*. Practice the verbatim instructions for the subtest before administering it for the first time. As with the other Processing Speed subtests, smooth administration is facilitated by committing the instructions to memory.

Do not permit the child to start early. Watch carefully during administration, because you must turn the pages for the child and prompt him or her to continue working as fast as possible.

Some children begin to stamp in the keys that appear at the top of each page or to stamp the animals. If this occurs at any time, give the necessary prompt.

Ensure the child stamps the selected shape only once and stamps only one selection for each test item. Provide the prompts in the *Administration and Scoring Manual* as necessary in response to multiple stamps. Do not allow the child to skip items; give the necessary prompt if this occurs.

Discontinue promptly after 120 seconds. If a child is working on an item when the time limit expires, you may allow him or her to finish that item, but note to yourself not to award credit (or penalize the score) for the item.

DON'T FORGET

....

Behavioral Observations

For Animal Coding, note if the child
- Selects responses impulsively, or misses items more frequently as they become more distant from the key at the top of the page.
- Displays wandering attention during the task, leading to a lower score due to loss of potential points. Integrate this information into your interpretation of the score. If this occurs, administer the other two Processing Speed subtests to obtain more information about performance.
- Displays trembling hands, has a tight grip on the ink dauber, or has sweaty palms, causing his or her hand to slip down or the dauber to slip out of his or her grip.
- Is overly concerned with the ink dauber's variability, marking shapes more than once if a mark is light.
- Loses time by checking and rechecking answers before marking them and moving on.
- Appears to benefit from ongoing experience with items and eventually memorizes one or more of the animal–shape pairs. After the subtest is complete, examine the impact of incidental learning on the child's performance. Ask the child if he or she can tell you without looking at the key which shape each animal liked. Mention each animal in turn. Then mention each shape in turn, and ask the child to tell you which animal liked that shape.

Behind the Scenes

....

- In very early pilot testing, an alternate version of Animal Coding called *Pet Pairing* required the child to pair pets with their owners (human stick figures). While more ecologically valid (true to life experiences), the task was too visually complex for young children.
- Animal Coding's original name was *Animal Shapes*. The name was changed prior to final publication to help practitioners more readily make the connection between this new task and its predecessor that also relied on associative memory (i.e., Coding).
- In early WPPSI-IV research stages, more animals and shapes appeared on this subtest. These proved too visually confusing and difficult, so the number of paired associates was reduced to three.

FREQUENTLY ASKED QUESTIONS: SUBTEST ADMINISTRATION

Pearson provides responses to frequently asked questions (FAQs) about the WPPSI-IV on the product website. One portion of the FAQs relates to subtest administration. The questions and responses are reproduced in Rapid Reference 2.3.

CAUTION

••

Common Errors in WPPSI-IV Subtest Administration

The most common errors observed on the WPPSI-IV subtests during research stages are listed below. The subtests are listed by primary index scale membership.

Verbal Comprehension Subtests

Information, Similarities, Comprehension, and Receptive Vocabulary:
- Failing to circle the selected response option where necessary. This is particularly important for items to which the child does not respond correctly.

Information, Similarities, Vocabulary, Comprehension, and Picture Naming:
- Neglecting to query sample responses followed by a Q. Query errors were the most frequent error noted in a recent study of Wechsler protocols (Mrazik, Janzen, Dombrowski, Barford, & Krawchuk, 2012).

Information, Similarities, Vocabulary, and Comprehension:
- Not providing the specific query for sample responses noted with an asterisk (*) in the *Administration and Scoring Manual.*
- Not providing corrective feedback on teaching items marked with a dagger (†) in response to an imperfect score.

Similarities, Vocabulary, and Comprehension:
- Where applicable, not administering the items prior to the start point in reverse sequence if the child obtains an imperfect score on either start-point item.

Similarities:
- For Items 5 and 6, failing to administer Trial 2 if the child does not provide a correct response to Trial 1.

Visual Spatial Subtests

Block Design and Object Assembly:
- Where applicable, not administering the items prior to the start point in reverse sequence if the child obtains an imperfect score on either start-point item.
- Forgetting to time the child, or forgetting to record completion time.
- Improper use of the stopwatch: allowing too little or too much time.

Block Design:
- Presenting the wrong blocks for a given item.
- Where applicable, failing to administer Trial 2 of an item if the child did not successfully complete Trial 1.
- Failing to record the correct design for every item using the grid.
- Penalizing rotation on Part A items and therefore discontinuing too early. For Part A, no degree of rotation is penalized. Even 180° rotations are acceptable.

(continued)

- Not penalizing rotation on Part B items and therefore discontinuing too late. For Part B, rotations of 30° or more are scored 0 points.
- Forgetting to correct the first rotation on Part A and the first rotation on Part B. The first rotation error on each Part is corrected.
- For Part B, forgetting to administer the sample items.
- For Part B, not following the guidelines about a variety of block faces being presented faceup (Moon, Blakey, Gorsuch, & Fantuzzo, 1991). The extant research does not examine the impact of this common error in clinical populations.

Object Assembly:
- Failing to circle the X corresponding to each correctly joined juncture.
- Forgetting to multiply the number of correctly joined junctures by one half to obtain the scores for Items 12 and 13, resulting in awarding too many raw score points for these items.

Fluid Reasoning Subtests

Matrix Reasoning and Picture Concepts:
- Failing to administer the sample items.
- Rigidly applying the 30 second guideline as a strict time limit, rather than granting more time to respond for a child who is benefitting from the additional time.

Matrix Reasoning:
- Failing to circle the selected response option. This is particularly important for items to which the child does not respond correctly.

Picture Concepts:
- Failing to prompt the child to select one response option from each row, if needed.
- Failing to circle all selected response options.

Working Memory Subtests

Picture Memory and Zoo Locations:
- Neglecting to use the stopwatch to track stimulus exposure time.

Picture Memory:
- Failing to circle all selected response options.
- Neglecting to administer Sample Items A or B.
- Administering Sample Item A to a child who does not start with Item 1.
- Forgetting to increase stimulus exposure time beginning with Sample Item B.

Zoo Locations:
- Neglecting to administer the sample item.
- Forgetting to administer the second trial of the sample item, if necessary.
- Forgetting to administer the second trial of Item 1, if necessary.

- Failing to record the child's placement of every animal card.
- Forgetting to switch from one zoo layout to the next for the appropriate item.
- Forgetting to increase exposure time for the cards beginning with Item 7.
- Neglecting to provide the appropriate corrective feedback on teaching items, if necessary.

Processing Speed Subtests

Bug Search, Cancellation, and Animal Shapes:
- Neglecting to watch the child during the tasks so that the appropriate prompt can be provided if the child stamps the same object multiple times.

Bug Search and Animal Shapes:
- Neglecting to watch the child during the tasks so that the appropriate prompts can be provided if the child is skipping items or stamping multiple stimuli for an item.
- Forgetting to turn the Response Booklet pages for the child.
- Stopping administration after 1 minute and 20 seconds rather than 120 seconds (2 minutes).

Cancellation:
- Ceasing administration at 120 seconds rather than 45 seconds for each item.
- Reassembling the Response Booklet before the pages have dried.

≡ *Rapid Reference 2.3 Frequently Asked Questions: Subtest Administration*

On the WPPSI-III, a pencil was used to draw forms in Coding (thus also assessing fine motor skills). It seems like it will be more difficult to assess fine motor skills when children are only using the ink dauber. Have you found this to be true?

In terms of the fine motor demands, yes, the ink dauber reduces the influence of fine motor demands on the measure of processing speed. Using the pencil was difficult for many 4-year-old children with developmental delays or other fine motor issues. Because the assessment of fine motor control was mainly qualitative in nature on the prior tasks, other measures such as the Beery VMI or portions of the NEPSY-II and consulting with an occupational therapist may be helpful if the referral question requires investigation of fine motor skills.

Have you found the ink dauber to be distracting to the children?

Children have found the ink dauber to be fun, but this does not result in unwillingness to complete the tasks. Similar daubers are quite commonly used in many daycare, preschool, and no-cost community recreational programs, so most children have encountered them. Dauber practice was built into the WPPSI-IV standard administration procedures; consequently, children are familiar with the

(continued)

dauber prior to completing any test items. Extra dauber use might also be used as a reinforcement technique following test completion.

How long do the ink daubers last? Are there replacement ink daubers available?

The ink dauber is approximately 4 inches long, with a standard amount of ink inside. The duration will be directly linked to how often it is used. Two daubers are provided in each WPPSI-IV test kit, and replacement ink daubers are available for purchase.

Can I replace an ink dauber with one I purchase at a craft store?

A similar ink dauber may be purchased from another source to use as a replacement; however, it is recommended that the replacement be as close to the original ink dauber as possible (e.g., color and size), and that it meet the necessary safety requirements for use with young children.

Is the ink in the dauber washable?

Yes, the ink is washable. It is also non-toxic. Product safety requirements to which all kit components adhere are discussed in the WPPSI-IV *Administration and Scoring Manual*.

Does the WPPSI-IV take longer to administer than the WPPSI-III?

Substantial efforts were made during development to achieve the briefest testing time possible and still offer greater construct coverage and flexibility, and even more composite scores. As a result, administration time is kept to a minimum and is comparable to the WPPSI-III. Because administration time is determined by which composite scores are desired, it varies based on the practitioner's choices. In some situations the administration time may be shorter than that of the WPPSI-III, but if more composite scores are desired, administration time may be slightly longer.

Why were the Processing Speed subtests changed?

In response to a review of current child development literature, a number of improvements were incorporated to improve the developmental appropriateness of processing speed measures. The new subtests are more play-like to ensure more valid assessment, because play is developmentally appropriate for young children. The new stimuli are familiar and engaging to young children, and the tasks are reminiscent of popular children's games. Because fine motor skills are still developing during the WPPSI-IV age range, all of the subtests employ an ink dauber rather than a pencil to indicate responses. In addition, the stimuli are larger and have more space separating them to reduce the likelihood of inadvertent stray marks. Also, to be more sensitive to language and cognitive development, the subtests now involve instructions that avoid using high-level vocabulary and concepts a young child cannot yet grasp.

What are the language requirements for the Working Memory subtest instructions?

The verbatim instructions for the Working Memory subtests are succinct, and active demonstration and practice are used to supplement verbal instructions because young children are unlikely to maintain attention and focus during lengthy verbal explanations. The instructions were tested repeatedly with children aged 2:0–2:5 (younger than the youngest children in the WPPSI-IV age range), as well as with children with intellectual disabilities, to ensure children with developmental delays or low intellectual ability would understand task demands. A WPPSI-IV study comparing the performance of English Language Learners and a matched control group showed no significant differences between the means on the Working Memory subtests for the two groups.

🖋 TEST YOURSELF 🖋

1. **Which of the following subtests have completion time limits that require the use of a stopwatch?**
   (a) Block Design, Picture Concepts, Zoo Locations, Animal Coding, Cancellation
   (b) Cancellation, Zoo Locations, Animal Coding, Matrix Reasoning, Picture Naming
   (c) Block Design, Picture Memory, Object Assembly, Receptive Vocabulary
   (d) Block Design, Bug Search, Cancellation, Object Assembly, Animal Coding

2. **A child aged 3:0 is administered fewer subtests than a child aged 4:0. Which of the following subtests is not administered to a 3-year-old child?**
   (a) Object Assembly
   (b) Zoo Locations
   (c) Bug Search
   (d) Picture Naming

3. **On a subtest with age-based start points, when the child does not receive a perfect score on either of the first two items given, the word *appropriate* is a cue that item administration may proceed forward or backward.**
   True or False?

4. **For a child aged 4:0 to 7:7, the sample items from _____ and _____ are not given if administration reverses.**
   (a) Similarities and Picture Memory
   (b) Picture Concepts and Matrix Reasoning
   (c) Picture Memory and Object Assembly
   (d) Vocabulary and Receptive Vocabulary

5. **Which of the following subtests requires the use of a Response Booklet?**
   (a) Picture Memory
   (b) Animal Coding

(continued)

(c) Zoo Locations

(d) Picture Naming

6. **Subtests that use blocks, cards, and puzzles have a discontinue rule of two consecutive scores of zero.**

   True or False?

7. **Teaching items are indicated with a dagger symbol (†) on the Record Form, and the instructions given for teaching items are only allowed on the first items administered on each subtest.**

   True or False?

8. **Sample responses noted with an asterisk (*) require the examiner to merely ask the child what he or she means.**

   True or False?

9. **Which Verbal Comprehension subtests are given to children aged 2:6 to 3:11?**

   (a) Similarities and Receptive Vocabulary

   (b) Information and Vocabulary

   (c) Receptive Vocabulary and Information

   (d) Picture Naming and Comprehension

10. **On Similarities, the best answers on items involving opposites involve describing which of the following?**

    (a) What each of the word pairs mean

    (b) What features the two words share

    (c) What specific property both words have in common

    (d) What continuum both share

11. **On Block Design, rotations are penalized on items with one-color blocks.**

    True or False?

12. **Proper administration of Object Assembly involves attention to detail. What is the proper way to display the puzzle pieces?**

    (a) The puzzle pieces should be stacked in your hand sequentially starting with the highest-numbered piece on the bottom. The pieces are then laid out from your left to right with the number side faceup. Pieces with single-underlined numbers are placed in the row closest to the child, and those with double-underlined numbers are placed closest to you. Expose the pieces in order, beginning with the piece numbered 1. Flip the pieces from top to bottom.

    (b) The puzzle pieces should be stacked in your hand sequentially starting with the highest-numbered piece on the bottom. The pieces are then laid out from your right to left with the number side faceup. Pieces with single-underlined numbers are placed in the row closest to the child, and those with double-underlined numbers are placed closest to you. Expose the pieces in order, beginning with the piece numbered 1. Flip the pieces from top to bottom.

    (c) The puzzle pieces should be stacked in your hand sequentially starting with the highest-numbered piece on the bottom. The pieces are then laid out from your left to right with the number side faceup. Pieces with single-underlined numbers are placed in the row closest to you, and those with double-underlined numbers are placed closest to the child. Expose the pieces in order, beginning with the piece numbered 1. Flip the pieces from top to bottom.

(d) The puzzle pieces should be stacked in your hand sequentially starting with the highest-numbered piece on the bottom. The pieces are then laid out from your left to right with the number side faceup. Pieces with single-underlined numbers are placed in the row closest to the child, and those with double-underlined numbers are placed closest to you. Expose the pieces in order, beginning with the piece numbered 1. Flip the pieces from left to right.

13. **Picture Memory and Zoo Locations have stimulus exposure time limits of 3 and 5 seconds.**

    True or False?

14. **When testing children with special needs or very young children, you may have to administer the WPPSI-IV in multiple sessions. What is the preferred maximum time interval?**

    (a) 1 day

    (b) 1 week

    (c) 1 month

    (d) Must be administered the same day

15. **Match the subtest with its Primary Index Scale.**

(a) Block Design	1. Verbal Comprehension
(b) Picture Naming	2. Fluid Reasoning
(c) Zoo Locations	3. Visual Spatial
(d) Picture Concepts	4. Processing Speed
(e) Animal Coding	5. Working Memory

Answers: 1. d; 2. c; 3. True; 4. a; 5. b; 6. True; 7. False; 8. False; 9. c; 10. d; 11. False; 12. a; 13. True; 14. b; 15. a–3, b–1, c–5, d–2, e–4

REFERENCES

American Educational Research Association, American Psychological Association, & National Council on Measurement in Education. (1999). *Standards for educational and psychological testing.* Washington, DC: Author.

Bayley, N. (2005). *Bayley scales of infant and toddler development* (3rd ed.). San Antonio, TX: Pearson.

Benson, N., Hulac, D., & Kranzler, J. H. (2010). Independent examination of the Wechsler Adult Intelligence Scale–Fourth Edition (WAIS-IV): What does the WAIS–IV measure? *Psychological Assessment, 22,* 121–130. doi: 10.1037/a0017767

Braden, J. P. (2003). Accommodating clients with disabilities on the WAIS–III and WMS. In D. S. Tulsky, D. H. Saklofske, G. J. Chelune, R. K. Heaton, R. J. Ivnik, R. Bornstein, & M. F. Ledbetter (Eds.), *Clinical interpretation of the WAIS–III and WMS–III* (pp. 451–486). San Diego, CA: Academic Press.

Carroll, J. B. (2012). The three-stratum theory of cognitive abilities. In D. P. Flanagan & P. L. Harrison (Eds.), *Contemporary intellectual assessment: Theories, tests, and issues* (3rd ed., pp. 883–890). New York, NY: Guilford Press.

Decker, S. L., Englund, J. A., & Roberts, A. M. (2012). Intellectual and neuropsychological assessment of individuals with sensory and physical disabilities and traumatic brain injury. In D. P. Flanagan & P. L. Harrison (Eds.), *Contemporary intellectual assessment: Theories, tests, and issues* (3rd ed., pp. 708–725). New York, NY: Guilford Press.

Ford, L., Kozey, M. L., & Negreiros, J. (2012). Cognitive assessment in early childhood: Theoretical and practice perspectives. In D. P. Flanagan & P. L. Harrison (Eds.), *Contemporary intellectual assessment: Theories, tests, and issues* (3rd ed., pp. 585–622). New York, NY: Guilford Press.

Gordon, R. P., Stump, K., & Glaser, B. A. (1996). Assessment of individuals with hearing impairments: Equity in testing procedures and accommodations. *Measurement and Evaluation in Counseling and Development, 29*, 111–118.

Horn, J. L., & Blankson, A. N. (2012). Foundations for better understanding of cognitive abilities. In D. P. Flanagan & P. L. Harrison (Eds.), *Contemporary intellectual assessment: Theories, tests, and issues* (3rd ed., pp. 73–98). New York, NY: Guilford Press.

Kaufman, A. S., & Kaufman, N. L. (1977). *Clinical evaluation of young children with the McCarthy Scales.* New York, NY: Grune & Stratton.

Keith, T. Z., Fine, J. G., Taub, G. E., Reynolds, M. R., & Kranzler, J. H. (2006). Higher order, multisample, confirmatory factor analysis of the Wechsler Intelligence Scale for Children—Fourth Edition: What does it measure? *School Psychology Review, 35*, 108–127.

Lichtenberger, E. O., & Kaufman, A. S. (2013). *Essentials of WAIS–IV assessment* (2nd ed). Hoboken, NJ: Wiley.

McCarthy, D. (1972). *The McCarthy Scales of Children's Abilities.* New York, NY: Psychological Corporation.

Moon, G. W., Blakey, W. A., Gorsuch, R. L., & Fantuzzo, J. W. (1991). Frequent WAIS-R administration errors: An ignored source of inaccurate measurement. *Professional Psychology: Research and Practice, 22*, 256–258.

Mrazik, M., Janzen, T. M., Dombrowski, S. C., Barford, S. W., & Krawchuk, L. L. (2012). Administration and scoring errors of graduate students learning the WISC-IV: Issues and controversies. *Canadian Journal of School Psychology, 27*, 279–290.

Ortiz, S. O., Ochoa, S. H., & Dynda, A. M. (2012). Testing with culturally and linguistically diverse populations: Moving beyond the verbal–performance dichotomy into evidence-based practice. In D. P. Flanagan & P. L. Harrison (Eds.), *Contemporary intellectual assessment: Theories, tests, and issues* (3rd ed., pp. 526–552). New York, NY: Guilford Press.

Reznick, J. S. (2009). Working memory in infants and toddlers. In M. L. Courage & N. Cowan (Eds.), *The development of memory in infancy and childhood* (pp. 343–365). New York, NY: Psychology Press.

Wechsler, D. (2002). *Wechsler preschool and primary scale of intelligence* (3rd ed.). San Antonio, TX: Pearson.

Wechsler, D. (2003). *Wechsler intelligence scale for children* (4th ed.). San Antonio, TX: Pearson.

Wechsler, D. (2012). *Wechsler preschool and primary scale of intelligence* (4th ed.). Bloomington, MN: Pearson.

Weiss, L. G., Keith, T. Z., Zhu, J., & Chen, H. (2013a). WAIS-IV and clinical validation of the four- and five-factor interpretive approaches. *Journal of Psychoeducational Assessment, 31*, 94–113.

Weiss, L. G., Keith, T. Z., Zhu, J., & Chen, H. (2013b). WISC-IV and clinical validation of the four- and five-factor interpretive approaches. *Journal of Psychoeducational Assessment, 31*, 114–131.

Three

WPPSI-IV SCORING

Susan Engi Raiford
Diane L. Coalson
Kathleen M. Rollins

This chapter begins with basic subtest scoring instructions and guidelines. A general description of WPPSI-IV score types and distributions is offered. An overview of the scoring process, from total raw scores to subtest scaled scores to composite scores, is accompanied by a discussion of more complex substitution, proration, and invalidation procedures. A primer on the scoring software is included.

SCORING SUBTESTS

The following sections offer scoring guidelines for the WPPSI-IV subtests. The subtests are organized by scale, and general information about scoring all subtests on the scale is presented, followed by subtest-specific information. Changes to scoring from the WPPSI-III to the WPPSI-IV are outlined.

In addition to the subtest total raw score, Cancellation permits the calculation of two process scores (i.e., Cancellation Random and Cancellation Structured). Process scores provide more detailed information relevant to subtest performance. The procedure used to calculate the Cancellation Random and Cancellation Structured process scores is discussed in the Cancellation subtest section.

Verbal Comprehension Subtests

With the exception of Picture Naming and the Picture Items on Vocabulary, picture items on the Verbal Comprehension subtests do not require an expressive response and therefore are relatively simple to score. The Information, Similarities, and Comprehension picture items, like all Receptive Vocabulary items, merely require a selection among four visually presented response options. If the child selects a correct response, he or she is awarded 1 point per item.

The verbal items on Information, Similarities, and Comprehension, and all items on Vocabulary and Picture Naming, require a verbal response. Of all items on the WPPSI-IV, these items involve the greatest need to apply judgment in scoring. You should record the child's response word-for-word, or *verbatim*. Failure to record the child's response verbatim is one of the most common recording errors seen in studies of Wechsler intelligence scale protocols (Alfonso, Johnson, Patinella, & Rader, 1998; Loe, Kadlubek, & Marks, 2007). Record verbatim responses, or scoring becomes more difficult, less accurate, and unverifiable. Many rich, qualitative observations are impossible without the verbatim responses.

Using Sample Responses, General Scoring Principles, and General Concepts

It is particularly critical to refer to the *Administration and Scoring Manual* when scoring verbatim responses. Increased scoring errors can occur if you assume you have learned the scoring rules or committed them to memory, and adherence to the scoring rules is strongly related to scoring accuracy (Erdodi, Richard, & Hopwood, 2009).

Matching the child's verbatim response to a sample response is the first and simplest choice when assigning a score. However, the sample responses are not an exhaustive list of every possible answer. The sample responses are distilled from among approximately 6,000 different responses obtained, read, and scored across various research phases. The most common answers are represented. Other sample responses appear because they illustrate important differences across point values or provide good exemplars of the scoring rules. Nevertheless, frequently at least one of a child's responses does not match any sample response exactly.

If a child's response does not match any sample response for an item, search for a sample response that is similar. The sample responses are organized to facilitate the process of searching for a similar response. Responses that appear together on a single line separated by semicolons typically are similar in meaning. More common responses and higher quality sample responses usually appear in higher positions in the lists for each point value. For responses that are not assigned perfect scores, those with a query also are positioned higher in the lists, because of their borderline quality. Responses that are similar in nature but differ in some way that distinguishes their quality often are positioned in analogous areas of the point-value sections. This organization makes scanning and visual comparison easier. For example, a 1-point response and a 0-point response that use the same word may both appear in the upper right-hand corner within their respective point-value sections.

Compare verbatim responses to all of the sample responses to ascertain if their quality is better than, similar to, or worse than those of a given point value, and score accordingly. Responses should be scored based on their content, not eloquence, lengthiness, grammar, pronunciation, or verbosity.

≡ Rapid Reference 3.1

Similarities Verbal Items General Scoring Principles

Award 2 points if the response:
- Provides a major classification that is relevant to both of the objects or concepts.

Award 1 point if the response:
- Describes a specific aspect that is common to both of the objects or concepts, describing a minor or less relevant commonality.
- Provides a major classification that is less relevant or more general for both of the objects or concepts.

Award 0 points if the response:
- Describes a property that is not relevant to both of the objects or concepts.
- Is too general.
- Describes differences between the objects or concepts.
- Is otherwise clearly incorrect.

Utilize the general scoring rules for guidance. If the response cannot be matched or easily compared to the sample responses, refer to the general scoring principles and general concepts to score the response. Strong familiarity with the general scoring principles on Similarities and Vocabulary and general concepts on Comprehension improves scoring accuracy and speed.

The general scoring principles for the Similarities and Vocabulary verbal items appear in Rapid References 3.1 and 3.2. Scoring keys for the Verbal Comprehension subtests appear in the Don't Forget box. A comparison of WPPSI-III and WPPSI-IV Verbal Comprehension subtest scoring appears in Table 3.1.

≡ Rapid Reference 3.2

Vocabulary Verbal Items General Scoring Principles

Award 2 points if the response indicates well-developed conceptualization of the word; for example, if the response:

- Contains a close synonym.
- Describes a major use of a noun.
- Provides a broad classification of the word.
- Offers primary or defining features of a noun.
- Offers a figurative use of the word that is correct.
- Provides several less defining or primary features that are correct, and when taken together indicate good concept formulation of the word.
- Describes a verb with a defining example of causation or action.

Award 1 point if the response indicates correct but incomplete understanding of the word; for example, if the response:

- Contains a less relevant synonym.
- Describes a minor use of a noun.
- Describes an aspect of the word that is correct but secondary, or not a defining feature.
- Provides an example using the word that is correct but not elaborated upon.
- Provides a common use of the word that is not elaborated upon.
- Correctly defines a closely related form of the word, but not the word itself.

Award 0 points if the response does not indicate any clear conceptualization of the word or is just incorrect; for example, if the response:

- Involves a demonstration or gesture(s) not verbally elaborated.
- Does not indicate any clear understanding of the word, even after query.
- Is not completely incorrect, but is vague, trivial, or weak, even after query.
- Is a regional use of the word or involves slang usage.
- Is a clearly incorrect definition.

DON'T FORGET

••

Verbal Comprehension Subtest Scoring Keys

Subtest	Item Score Range(s)	Scoring Tips
Information	0–1 points	*Picture Items:* • For each item, circle the number that corresponds to the child's response choice. The correct responses appear in color on the Record Form and are listed in the *Administration and Scoring Manual.* • Score 1 point if the child responds correctly; score 0 points if the child responds incorrectly, says he or she doesn't know the answer, or does not respond to the item. *Verbal Items:* • Use the sample responses that correspond to each item to score the child's response. • When multiple responses are provided, score the best response if none of the answers spoils the entire response. • If a 1-point answer is given along with a spoiled response, score the item as 0 points. • If the child makes a remark that is clearly not part of his or her response, it should not affect the score. • Award 1 point or 0 points for each item.
Similarities	Items 1–4: 0–1 points Items 5–23: 0–2 points	*Picture Items:* • For each item, circle the number that corresponds to the child's response choice. The correct responses appear in color on the Record Form and are listed in the *Administration and Scoring Manual.* • Score 1 point if the child responds correctly; score 0 points if the child responds incorrectly, says he or she doesn't know the answer, or does not respond to the item. *Verbal Items:* • First, use the sample responses that correspond to each item to score the child's response. • If necessary, refer to the General Scoring Principles in the *Administration and Scoring Manual* and in Rapid Reference 3.1.

(continued)

Subtest	Item Score Range(s)	Scoring Tips
		• When multiple responses are provided, score the best response if none of the answers spoils the entire response.
		• If a 2- or 1-point answer is given along with a spoiled response, score the item as 0 points.
		• If the child makes a remark that is clearly not part of his or her response, it should not affect the score.
		• Award 2, 1, or 0 points for each item.
Vocabulary	Items 1–3: 0–1 points Items 4–23: 0–2 points	*Picture Items:* • The Vocabulary Picture Items (Items 1–3) are the same as Picture Naming Items 1, 3, and 7, respectively. If the items were administered for Picture Naming, score the Vocabulary items based on that administration. If the child discontinued before reaching Item 7 on Picture Naming, administer Item 3 and score accordingly.
		• Use the sample responses that correspond to each item to score the child's response.
		• When multiple responses are provided, score the best response if none of the answers spoils the entire response.
		• Score 1 point if the child responds correctly; score 0 points if the child responds incorrectly, says he or she doesn't know the answer, or does not respond to the item.
		• Inappropriate marginal, functional, gestural, or generalized responses are scored 0 points.
		• Personalized responses are scored 0 points unless accompanied by a correct response.
		• If a 1-point answer is given along with a spoiled response, score the item as 0 points.
		• If the child makes a remark that is clearly not part of his or her response, it should not affect the score.
		• Award 1 point or 0 points for each item.

Subtest	Item Score Range(s)	Scoring Tips
		Verbal Items: • First, use the sample responses that correspond to each item to score the child's response. • If necessary, refer to the General Scoring Principles in the *Administration and Scoring Manual* and in Rapid Reference 3.2. • Award credit commensurate with the definition's quality for word meanings that appear in standard dictionaries. • Score 0 points for regional or slang word usages that are not improved upon query. • If a 2- or 1-point answer is given along with a spoiled response, score the item as 0 points. • If the child makes a remark that is clearly not part of his or her response, it should not affect the score. • Award 2, 1, or 0 points for each item.
Comprehension	Items 1–4: 0–1 points Items 5–22: 0–2 points	*Picture Items:* • For each item, circle the number that corresponds to the child's response choice. The correct responses appear in color on the Record Form and are listed in the *Administration and Scoring Manual*. • Score 1 point if the child responds correctly; score 0 points if the child responds incorrectly, says he or she doesn't know the answer, or does not respond to the item. *Verbal Items:* • Use the sample responses and general concepts that correspond to each item to score the child's response. • When multiple responses are provided, score the best response if none of the answers spoils the entire response. • If a 2- or 1-point answer is given along with a spoiled response, score the item as 0 points. • If the child makes a remark that is clearly not part of his or her response, it should not affect the score. • Award 2, 1, or 0 points for each item.

(continued)

Subtest	Item Score Range(s)	Scoring Tips
Receptive Vocabulary	0–1 points	• For each item, circle the number that corresponds to the child's response choice. The correct responses appear in color on the Record Form and are listed in the *Administration and Scoring Manual*.
		• Score 1 point if the child responds correctly; score 0 points if the child responds incorrectly, says he or she doesn't know the answer, or does not respond to the item.
Picture Naming	0–1 points	• Picture Naming Items 1, 3, and 7 are the same as the Vocabulary Picture Items (Items 1, 2, and 3, respectively). If the items were administered for Vocabulary, score the Picture Naming items based on that administration. If the child was not administered the Vocabulary Picture Items, administer Picture Naming Items 1, 3, and 7 if necessary, and score accordingly.
		• Score 1 point if the child responds correctly; score 0 points if the child responds incorrectly, says he or she doesn't know the answer, or does not respond to the item.
		• Use the sample responses that correspond to each item to score the child's response.
		• Inappropriate marginal, functional, gestural, or generalized responses are scored 0 points.
		• Personalized responses are scored 0 points unless accompanied by a correct response.
		• When multiple responses are provided, score the best response if none of the answers spoils the entire response.
		• If a 1-point answer is given along with a spoiled response, score the item as 0 points.
		• If the child makes a remark that is clearly not part of his or her response, it should not affect the score.
		• Award 1 point or 0 points for each item.

Table 3.1 Comparison of WPPSI-III and WPPSI-IV Verbal Comprehension Subtest Scoring

WPPSI-III	WPPSI-IV
Information	
Items 1–34: Score 0–1 points	Items 1–29: Score 0–1 points
Maximum Total Raw Score: 34 points	Maximum Total Raw Score: 29 points
	Sample responses for all verbal items revised or new
Similarities	
Items 1–2: Score 0–1 points	Items 1–6: Score 0–1 points
Items 3–24: Score 0–2 points	Items 7–23: Score 0–2 points
No multiple-choice items	Items 1–4: Picture items in a multiple-choice format with objective scoring
Maximum Total Raw Score: 46 points	Maximum Total Raw Score: 40 points
	Sample responses for all verbal items revised
Vocabulary	
Items 1–7: Score 0–1 points	Items 1–3: Score 0–1 points
Items 8–25: Score 0–2 points	Items 4–23: Score 0–2 points
Maximum Total Raw Score: 43 points	Maximum Total Raw Score: 43 points (no change)
	Sample responses for all items revised or new
Comprehension	
Items 1–2: Score 0–1 points	Items 1–4: Score 0–1 points
Items 3–20: Score 0–2 points	Items 5–23: Score 0–2 points
No multiple-choice items	Items 1–4: Picture items in a multiple-choice format with objective scoring
Items 1–2: verbal items scored 0–1 points	All verbal items scored 0–2 points
Maximum Total Raw Score: 38 points	Maximum Total Raw Score: 40 points
	Sample responses for all verbal items revised or new
Receptive Vocabulary	
Items 1–38: Score 0–1 points	Items 1–31: Score 0–1 points
Maximum Total Raw Score: 38 points	Maximum Total Raw Score: 31 points
Picture Naming	
Items 1–30: Score 0–1 points	Items 1–24: Score 0–1 points
Maximum Total Raw Score: 30 points	Maximum Total Raw Score: 24 points
	Sample responses for all items revised or new

Visual Spatial Subtests

The Visual Spatial subtests are relatively straightforward to score if performance and completion times are recorded accurately. Scoring keys for the Visual Spatial subtests appear in the Don't Forget box. A comparison of WPPSI-III and WPPSI-IV Visual Spatial subtest scoring appears in Table 3.2.

DON'T FORGET
....

Visual Spatial Subtest Scoring Keys

Subtest	Item Score Range(s)	Scoring Tips
Block Design	Items 1–4, 9: 0–2 Items 5–8, 10–17: 0 or 2	• For each item, record the completion time in seconds. • In the Constructed Design column, place a check mark on the grid for correct constructions. For incorrect constructions, shade the grid to indicate the construction that was present at the time limit. • In the Constructed Design column, indicate rotations by drawing an arrow to indicate the direction of the rotation and the number of degrees rotated. • Award credit for correct designs with gaps and/or misalignments of less than or equal to one-quarter inch. • For all items, a construction is not awarded any points if it is not complete at the time limit. *Items 1–4:* • Award 2 points for a correct construction on Trial 1. Do not penalize the child for a rotation. • Award 1 point for a correct construction on Trial 2. Do not penalize the child for a rotation. • Award 0 points for an incorrect construction on both trials. *Items 5–8:* • Award 2 points for a correct construction. Do not penalize the child for a rotation. • Award 0 points for an incorrect construction. *Item 9:* • Award 2 points for a correct construction without a rotation error (i.e., a rotation of 30 degrees or more) on Trial 1.

Subtest	Item Score Range(s)	Scoring Tips
		• Award 1 point for a correct construction without a rotation error on Trial 2.
		• Award 0 points for an incorrect construction or a correct construction with a rotation error on both trials.
		Items 10–17:
		• Award 2 points for a correct construction without a rotation error.
		• Award 0 points for an incorrect construction or a correct construction with a rotation error.
Object Assembly	Items 1–3: 0–1 points	• For each item, record the completion time in seconds.
	Items 5 and 9: 0–2 points	• Count and record the number of correct junctures. A juncture is defined as the plane
	Items 4, 7, 10, and 11: 0–3 points	where two adjoining pieces meet. A juncture is correct even if not integrated into the entire
	Item 6: 0–4 points	puzzle (i.e., joined in isolation of the rest of the picture).
	Item 8, 12, and 13: 0–5 points	• Award credit for correct junctures with gaps and/or misalignments of less than or equal to one-quarter inch.
		• Use the pictures on the Record Form to judge junctures as correct or incorrect.
		• *For all items, a juncture must be joined within the time limit to receive credit.*
		Item 1:
		• Award 1 point for a correctly joined juncture on either Trial 1 or Trial 2.
		• Award 0 points if the juncture is not correctly joined on either Trial 1 or Trial 2.
		Items 2–11:
		• Award 1 point for each correctly joined juncture.
		• Award 0 points for no junctures joined correctly.
		Items 12–13:
		• Award a half point for each correctly joined juncture.
		• Award 0 points for no junctures joined correctly.

Table 3.2 Comparison of WPPSI-III and WPPSI-IV Visual Spatial Subtest Scoring

WPPSI–III	WPPSI-IV
Block Design	
Items 1–6, 9: Score 0–2 points	Items 1–4, 9: Score 0–2 points
Items 7–20: Score 0 or 2 points	Items 5–8, 10–17: Score 0 or 2 points
Maximum Total Raw Score: 40 points	Maximum Total Raw Score: 34 points
Object Assembly	
Items 1–3: Score 0–1 points	Items 1–3: Score 0–1 points
Items 5, 6, and 8: Score 0–2 points	Items 5 and 9: Score 0–2 points
Items 4, 7, 9, and 11–13: Score 0–3 points	Items 4, 7, 10, and 11: Score 0–3 points
Items 10 and 14: Score 0–5 points	Item 6: Score 0–4 points
	Item 8, 12, and 12: Score 0–5 points
Items 13–14: Award a half point for each correctly joined juncture.	Items 12–13: Award a half point for each correctly joined juncture.
Maximum Total Raw Score: 37 points	Maximum Total Raw Score: 38 points

Fluid Reasoning Subtests

The Fluid Reasoning subtests are the simplest WPPSI-IV subtests to score. Scoring keys for the Fluid Reasoning subtests appear in the Don't Forget box. A comparison of WPPSI-III and WPPSI-IV Fluid Reasoning subtest scoring appears in Table 3.3.

DON'T FORGET
....

Fluid Reasoning Subtest Scoring Keys

Subtest	Item Score Range(s)	Scoring Tips
Matrix Reasoning	0–1 points	For each item, circle the number that corresponds to the child's response choice. The correct responses appear in color on the Record Form and are listed in the *Administration and Scoring Manual.*
		Score 1 point if the child responds correctly; score 0 points if the child responds incorrectly, says he or she doesn't know the answer, or does not respond to the item.
Picture Concepts	0–1 points	For each item, circle the numbers that correspond to the child's response choices. The correct responses appear in color on the Record Form and are listed in the *Administration and Scoring Manual.*

Subtest	Item Score Range(s)	Scoring Tips
		Score 1 point if the child chooses all of the correct responses (i.e., the correct response from each row); score 0 points if the child does not choose all of the correct responses, says he or she doesn't know the answer, or does not respond to the item.

Table 3.3 Comparison of WPPSI-III and WPPSI-IV Fluid Reasoning Subtest Scoring

WPPSI-III	WPPSI-IV
Matrix Reasoning	
Items 1–29: Score 0 or 1 points	Items 1–26: Score 0 or 1 points
Maximum Total Raw Score: 29 points	Maximum Total Raw Score: 26 points
Picture Concepts	
Items 1–28: Score 0 or 1 points	Items 1–27: Score 0 or 1 points
Maximum Total Raw Score: 28 points	Maximum Total Raw Score: 27 points

Working Memory Subtests

The Working Memory subtests are relatively straightforward to score if recording is accurate. Scoring keys for the Working Memory subtests appear in the Don't Forget box.

DON'T FORGET

Working Memory Subtest Scoring Keys

Subtest	Item Score Range(s)	Scoring Tips
Picture Memory	0–1 points	• For each item, circle the number(s) that correspond to the child's response choice(s). The correct responses appear in color on the Record Form and are listed in the *Administration and Scoring Manual*.

(continued)

Subtest	Item Score Range(s)	Scoring Tips
Zoo Locations	0–1 points	*Items 1–6:* • Score 1 point if the child responds correctly; score 0 points if the child responds incorrectly, says he or she doesn't know the answer, or does not respond to the item. *Items 7–35:* • Score 1 point if the child chooses all of the correct responses; score 0 points if the child does not choose all of the correct responses, chooses an incorrect response option in addition to all of the correct responses, says he or she doesn't know the answer, or does not respond to the item. • For each item, each Animal Card is pictured in its correct location in the response column of the Record Form. • A card placed in a rotated manner (e.g., animal appears upside down or turned to the right or left from the child's position) but in the correct location should be scored as correctly placed. • Place a check mark over the letter in the Response column for each correctly placed card. • Record the first initial of the animal's name in the location where it was placed, for each incorrectly placed card. *Items 1–4, 7:* • Score 1 point if the child places the card in the correct location; score 0 points if the child does not place the card in the correct location, says he or she doesn't know the answer, or does not respond to the item. *Items 5–6, 8–20:* • Score 1 point if the child places all cards in the correct locations; score 0 points if the child does not place all cards in the correct locations, says he or she doesn't know the answer, or does not respond to the item.

Processing Speed Subtests

It may be necessary to exercise some judgment when scoring the Processing Speed subtests. Judgment becomes necessary when the child makes a mark that is not made precisely and clearly on a single object. The child may make inadvertent or stray marks with the ink dauber due to motor imprecision or carelessness.

Self-corrections are permitted on all Processing Speed subtests. For this reason, it is important to attend to the child as he or she marks responses and note which response was the intended or final response when a self-correction is made. At times, what appears to be a self-correction actually may be a lapse in the child's attention to instructions.

Judge an object as marked if it is clear that the child meant to mark it. If a mark extends through an adjacent object, don't judge the object as marked unless the child clearly intended to mark it. If a child marks *more* than two responses on a Bug Search or Animal Coding test item, the entire item is scored as incorrect.

If the child marks on an area of white space between objects, judge the closest object to the mark as the intended selection. If you cannot determine which is closest, do not judge any object as marked.

Scoring keys with tips for the Processing Speed subtests appear in the Don't Forget box.

DON'T FORGET

Processing Speed Subtest Scoring Keys

Subtest	Item Score Range(s)	Scoring Tips
Bug Search	0–1 points	• Do not score items completed after the time limit expires.
		• The Bug Search Scoring Key is used to score all responses. The correct responses appear in bold. The pages of the key are double sided. Use Side A to score the responses for pages 5 and 7, Side B to score the responses for pages 9 and 11, and so on. Be careful to use the correct side of the key.
		• Place the key over the previous page in the Response Booklet, over the blue screening. Align the key with the items to be scored on the opposite page.
		• Count items with the correct bug and no other bug stamped as correct.
		• Count items with an incorrect bug stamped as incorrect.
		• Unless the child self-corrected, only one bug may be marked for an item to count as correct. Count any other item with more than one bug stamped as incorrect.
		• Items the child did not attempt do not count as correct or incorrect.

(continued)

Subtest	Item Score Range(s)	Scoring Tips
Cancellation	0–48 points	• Record the total number of correct and total number of incorrect responses at the bottom of each page attempted, including incomplete pages (e.g., a page with at least one of the items completed). • Sum the number of correct responses and incorrect responses across all pages. • Subtract the total of incorrect responses from the total of correct responses to obtain the total raw score. If the number of incorrect responses is greater than the number of correct responses, enter the total raw score for that item as 0. • Do not score objects that are stamped after the time limit expires. • The Cancellation Scoring Template is used to score all responses on both items. *Do not use the template until the ink is completely dry.* • Place the template over the Response Booklet. Line up the edges of the template and the Response Booklet. The target responses appear in outlined boxes when they are aligned. • Count marks on targets as correct, and count marks on other objects as incorrect even if a single mark passes through more than one object. • Record the total correct and total incorrect responses for each item on the Record Form. • For each item, subtract the total of incorrect responses from the total of correct responses to obtain the total raw score for that item. If the number of incorrect responses is greater than the number of correct responses, enter the total raw score for that item as 0. • The total raw score for Item 1 is the Cancellation Random total raw score. • The total raw score for Item 2 is the Cancellation Structured total raw score. • Sum the total raw scores for Items 1 and 2 to obtain the Cancellation total raw score.
Animal Coding	0–1 points	• Do not score items completed after the time limit expires. • The Animal Coding Scoring Key is used to score all responses. The correct responses appear in black print. Each side of the key depicts the correct responses for four pages of the Response Booklet. Use Side A to score the responses for pages 5, 7,

Subtest	Item Score Range(s)	Scoring Tips
		9, and 11; use Side B to score the responses for pages 13, 15, 17, and 19. Be careful to use the correct portion of the key.
		• Place the key next to the page you are scoring. Count items with the correct shape and no other shape stamped as correct. Count items with the incorrect shape stamped as incorrect.
		• Unless the child self-corrected, only one shape may be marked for an item to count as correct. Count any other item with more than one shape stamped as incorrect.
		• Items the child did not attempt do not count as correct or incorrect.
		• Record the total number of correct and total number of incorrect responses at the bottom of each page attempted, including incomplete pages (e.g., a page with at least one of the items completed).
		• Sum the number of correct responses and incorrect responses across all pages.
		• Subtract the total of incorrect responses from the total of correct responses to obtain the total raw score. If the number of incorrect responses is greater than the number of correct responses, enter the total raw score for that item as 0.

WPPSI-IV SCORES

The following section offers a general description of WPPSI-IV score types and distributions. Item scores, total raw scores, and standard scores (including scaled scores and composite scores) are described and explained.

Item Scores

An item score is equal to the total points that are awarded for aspects of the child's performance on a given item. The range of item scores varies across subtests, as well as within some subtests.

Points are awarded for correct responses. For some items, additional points are awarded for correct responses that are higher in quality (e.g., Verbal items on Similarities, Vocabulary, and Comprehension); relative completeness (e.g., Object Assembly); and attempts required to produce a correct response (e.g., Block Design items with two trials).

Total Raw Scores

In most cases, the total raw score is merely the sum of the item scores. For the Processing Speed subtests, the total raw score is calculated by subtracting total incorrect responses from total correct responses to reflect the contribution of both speed and accuracy to performance.

Total raw scores are converted to subtest scaled scores. Do not use total raw scores to make inferences about the child's intellectual ability relative to the general population. For this purpose, rely on the standard scores.

Standard Scores

The WPPSI-IV scaled scores (i.e., subtest scaled scores and the Cancellation Random and Cancellation Structured scaled process scores) and composite scores (i.e., index scores and the Full Scale IQ) are standard scores. Standard scores are scaled to various metrics listed in Rapid Reference 3.3.

Scaled Scores

Subtest scaled scores and scaled process scores are standard scores. They are scaled to a mean of 10, a standard deviation of 3, and a range of 1 to 19.

Composite Scores

Composite scores consist of the published index scores, the Full Scale IQ, and the additional index scores in this book. They are standard scores derived from various sums of subtest scaled scores.

Composite scores have a mean of 100 and a standard deviation (*SD*) of 15. The range of composite scores varies based on the number of subtests used to derive

≡ *Rapid Reference 3.3*

WPPSI-IV Standard Score Metrics

Standard Score Type	Mean	Standard Deviation	Range
Subtest scaled score and scaled process score	10	3	1–19
Composite scores derived from two or three subtests (e.g., primary index scores, Vocabulary Acquisition Index, Gc-VL)	100	15	45–155
Composite scores derived from more than three subtests (e.g., Full Scale IQ, Nonverbal Index, General Ability Index, and Cognitive Proficiency Index)	100	15	40–160

that composite score. For composite scores that are based on two to three subtests, the range is 45 to 155, and for composite scores that are based on more than three subtests, the range is 40 to 160.

Intellectual abilities are normally distributed in the general population. For composite scores, about 50% of children score within ±10 points of the mean (90 to 110), about 68% score within ±15 points (i.e., 1 SD) of the mean (85 to 115), and approximately 96% score within ±30 points (i.e., 2 SDs) of the mean (70 to 130). About 2% of children score higher than 130 (more than 2 SDs above the mean), and 2% of children score below 70 (more than 2 SDs below the mean).

STEP-BY-STEP: WPPSI-IV SUBTEST AND COMPOSITE SCORES

The following section provides an overview of the scoring process, from total raw scores to subtest scaled scores to composite scores. This information is accompanied by a discussion of substitution, proration, and invalidation procedures.

It is important to note that double-checking each step might reduce scoring errors. A recent study conducted on Wechsler protocols suggests that double-checking item-level scoring and each step in the scoring procedure reduces errors by 52.5% and reduces inaccurate Full Scale IQs by 67% (Kuentzel, Hetterscheidt, & Barnett, 2011).

Obtain Total Raw Scores

When calculating the sum of the item scores, remember to include points earned for reversal items and unadministered items prior to the start point, if applicable. After calculating the total raw score for each subtest and for the Cancellation Random and Cancellation Structured process scores, transfer them to the Total Raw Score to Scale Score Conversion table on the summary page of the Record Form. Cross-check the two numbers for consistency.

Of all errors on the Summary page, incorrect transfer of raw scores to the front page is one of the most common (Mrazik, Janzen, Dombrowski, Barford, & Krawchuk, 2012). Simple point-counting errors accounted for more than 60% of scoring errors on Wechsler protocols in a recent study (Kuentzel et al., 2011). The Caution box lists common errors in obtaining total raw scores.

Obtain Scaled Scores

Total raw scores are converted to scaled scores. Scaled scores are age based. The child's age on the date of testing in years, months, and days (i.e., test age; calculated in the upper right-hand corner of the summary page using the Calculation of Child's Age table) is used to select the proper portion of the normative table to use.

CAUTION

••

Common Errors in Obtaining Total Raw Scores
- Awarding points for sample items, which are not scored
- Not including points earned from unadministered items (e.g., prior to the start point, or prior to the first two items on which the child received full credit if the child reversed) in the total raw score
- Simple incorrect mental calculation when attempting to sum the item points
- Not awarding full credit for all items prior to the age-appropriate start point if the child receives full credit on both of the age-appropriate start point items but began with Item 1
- Neglecting to include points earned from items from the first page of a subtest section on the Record Form, when the subtest spreads across two pages (e.g., on the Record Form for ages 4:0 to 7:7, Block Design, Information, Similarities, Vocabulary, and Comprehension)
- Awarding credit to items that were mistakenly administered after a discontinue was established
- On subtests with items for which multiple points are possible (i.e., Block Design, Similarities, Object Assembly, Vocabulary, Comprehension), awarding only 1 point of credit for items on which 2 points or more were earned
- On subtests with a scoring key or template (i.e., Bug Search, Animal Coding, and Cancellation), forgoing use of the key or template and scoring incorrectly, resulting in an inaccurate total raw score
- Forgetting to subtract Number Incorrect from Number Correct to obtain the total raw score on subtests scored in this manner (i.e., Bug Search, Animal Coding, and Cancellation)
- On Object Assembly Items 12 to 13, forgetting to multiply the total junctures completed correctly by one half to obtain the item score

The age span for each page of the normative table is noted at the top of each page of Table A.1 of the *Administration and Scoring Manual*. For ages 2:6 to 3:11, each page includes two normative age groups. For ages 4:0 to 7:7, each page contains only one normative age group. The subtests appear in columns from left to right across Table A.1. For ages 4:0 to 7:7, the Cancellation Random and Cancellation Structured process scores appear in the last two columns on the far right, after the last subtest in standard administration order (Picture Naming).

Be very cautious to select the correct portion of the normative table. Using the incorrect area of the normative table represented 24% of Summary page scoring errors in a recent study of Wechsler protocols (Mrazik et al., 2012). Check the age span label to ensure you are on the page of Table A.1 that corresponds to the child's age. For ages 2:6 to 3:11, check the table header at the top of the panel to ensure you are using the appropriate panel of the page. A shaded column listing Scaled Score with a range from 1 to 19 separates the two panels. The left panel corresponds to the younger normative age group, and the right panel corresponds to the older normative age group, within the age span for that page.

Locate the appropriate column for the subtest in question, and read down the column until you locate the total raw score for that subtest. Read straight across the row to the shaded column that lists the scaled score corresponding to the child's raw score for that subtest. Transfer that value into all the unshaded boxes to the right of the raw score on the Total Raw Score to Scaled Score Conversion Table. Include unshaded boxes with parentheses, which indicate that a subtest is supplemental to a given composite score and the scaled score can be used in substitution (subject to some constraints).

If you plan to calculate any of the ancillary index scores or to examine the discrepancy between the Cancellation Random and Cancellation Structured scores, also fill in the appropriate unshaded boxes on the Sum of Scaled Scores table on the Ancillary Analysis page. The Ancillary Analysis page is located on the back side of the Summary page of the Record Form.

The Caution box lists common errors in obtaining scaled scores.

CAUTION

Common Errors in Obtaining Scaled Scores
- Transferring a total raw score from the subtest page to the wrong row of the Total Raw Score to Scaled Score Conversion table on the Record Form. For example, the examiner mistakenly transfers the total raw score for Information into the row that corresponds to Block Design.
- Using the wrong page of Table A.1.
- Using the wrong panel of a page from Table A.1 for ages 2:6 to 3:11. Typically the error involves using the left panel rather than the right.
- Reading down an incorrect column in Table A.1 that corresponds to a different subtest than the one being converted.
- If a *total raw score* is within the scaled score range (1 to 19), mistakenly reading down the *Scaled Score* column in Table A.1 to the number that corresponds to the *total raw score*, then reading across the row to the column that corresponds to the subtest's *total raw score* and entering that number as the scaled score on the Record Form.
- Recording the wrong scaled score in a given row. For example, the examiner mistakenly records the scaled score for Picture Naming in the row that corresponds to Receptive Vocabulary.

Obtain Sums of Scaled Scores

After obtaining scaled scores, the sums of scaled scores are calculated. On the Record Form Summary page in the Total Raw Score to Scaled Score Conversion table, and on the Ancillary Analysis page in the Sum of Scaled Scores table, the scaled scores of core subtests for each scale (column) appear in the unshaded boxes with no parentheses. The scaled scores of potential supplemental subtests corresponding to each scale appear in the unshaded boxes with parentheses.

Add the scaled scores for each column, subject to the restrictions outlined in the *Administration and Scoring Manual* and in this chapter. Enter the sums in the boxes at the bottom of the Total Raw Score to Scaled Score Conversion table (on the Summary page) in the row labeled *Sum of Scaled Scores*, as well as at the bottom of the Sum of Scaled Scores table in the row labeled *Sum of Scaled Scores* on the Ancillary Analysis page for any desired ancillary index scores.

Substitution

For the sums of scaled scores used to calculate many index scores, including the primary index scores and the Vocabulary Acquisition Index, there are only two core subtests and no supplemental subtests. This means that those sums of scaled scores do not allow for substitution of supplemental subtests in the sum if a core subtest is missing or invalid. If you do not have both core subtests for one of these sums of scaled scores, the corresponding index score cannot be calculated.

No substitution is permitted for any additional index score that appears in this book and on the accompanying CD. The Don't Forget box lists the core subtests for index scores in the published test with no substitution allowed, by age band.

DON'T FORGET

Core Subtests for Index Scores With No Substitution Allowed, by Age Band

Ages 2:6 to 3:11

Verbal Comprehension Index	Visual Spatial Index	Working Memory Index	Vocabulary Acquisition Index
Receptive Vocabulary	Block Design	Picture Memory	Receptive Vocabulary
Information	Object Assembly	Zoo Locations	Picture Naming

Ages 4:0 to 7:7

Verbal Comprehension Index	Visual Spatial Index	Fluid Reasoning Index	Working Memory Index	Processing Speed Index	Vocabulary Acquisition Index
Information	Block Design	Matrix Reasoning	Picture Memory	Bug Search	Receptive Vocabulary
Similarities	Object Assembly	Picture Concepts	Zoo Locations	Cancellation	Picture Naming

The sums of scaled scores used to calculate composite scores that are derived from more than two subtests (i.e., the Full Scale IQ, the Nonverbal Index, the General Ability Index, and the Cognitive Proficiency Index) permit substitution of *only one* supplemental subtest if one of the core subtests is missing or invalid. Only one supplemental subtest can be substituted, even though for some composite scores there are multiple supplemental subtests available. The Don't Forget box lists the core subtests for composite scores with one supplemental subtest substitution allowed, by age band. The substitutions for these core subtests are restricted to certain supplemental subtests that are similar to the core subtest in terms of construct measured. These acceptable substitutions are listed by age band in Rapid Reference 3.4.

DON'T FORGET
. . . .

Core Subtests for Composite Scores With One Substitution Allowed, by Age Band

Ages 2:6 to 3:11

Full Scale IQ	Nonverbal Index	General Ability Index
Receptive Vocabulary	Block Design	Receptive Vocabulary
Information	Object Assembly	Information
Block Design	Picture Memory	Block Design
Object Assembly	Zoo Locations	Object Assembly
Picture Memory		

(continued)

Ages 4:0 to 7:7			
Full Scale IQ	**Nonverbal Index**	**General Ability Index**	**Cognitive Proficiency Index**
Information	Block Design	Information	Picture Memory
Similarities	Matrix Reasoning	Similarities	Zoo Locations
Block Design	Picture Concepts	Block Design	Bug Search
Matrix Reasoning	Picture Memory	Matrix Reasoning	Cancellation
Picture Memory	Bug Search		
Bug Search			

Proration of the Full Scale Sum of Scaled Scores

Subtests can be rendered invalid due to unexpected occurrences during administration. For example, administration errors, low effort on the part of the child, or interruptions during a subtest may render a subtest invalid. In this situation, subtest substitution is the preferred option where available because it provides an additional measure of a similar aspect of the child's cognitive ability (i.e., subtest performance on a subtest from the same scale).

Proration of a sum of scaled scores permits a composite score to be derived if a suitable substitution is unavailable. For the WPPSI-IV, proration is permitted only for deriving the Full Scale IQ. Proration is not permitted when deriving any primary or ancillary index score. Proration when deriving the Full Scale IQ should be limited to rare situations, because it is likely to increase measurement error. Interpret the Full Scale IQ with great caution if proration is used, particularly if the score will be used to make decisions about diagnosis, services, or placement.

If only one core subtest is missing, proration may be used to derive the sum of scaled scores for either age band's Full Scale IQ score. Because the two age bands' Full Scale IQ scores are based on a different number of core subtests, the number of necessary core subtest scaled scores differs by age band. Ages 2:6 to 3:11 must have four valid core subtest scores for the Full Scale and ages 4:0 to 7:7 must have five valid core subtest scores for the Full Scale, in order to obtain the prorated sum of scaled scores for the Full Scale. For this reason, Table A.12 in the *Administration and Scoring Manual* has two sections corresponding to the two age bands. Ensure

≡ Rapid Reference 3.4

Acceptable Substitutions for Core Subtests by Age Band for Composite Scores

Ages 2:6 to 3:11

Substitution for Core Subtest	Full Scale IQ	Nonverbal Index	General Ability Index
Receptive Vocabulary (Picture Naming)	X		X
Picture Memory (Zoo Locations)	X		

Ages 4:0 to 7:7

Substitution for Core Subtest	Full Scale IQ	Nonverbal Index	General Ability Index	Cognitive Proficiency Index
Information (Vocabulary or Comprehension)	X		X	
Similarities (Vocabulary or Comprehension)	X		X	
Block Design (Object Assembly)	X	X	X	
Matrix Reasoning (Picture Concepts)	X		X	
Picture Memory (Zoo Locations)	X	X		
Bug Search (Cancellation or Animal Coding)	X	X		
Bug Search (Animal Coding)				X
Cancellation (Animal Coding)				X

Note. Each acceptable substitution appears in parentheses after the core subtest for which it can substitute.

CAUTION

Limits on Substitution and Proration

- No supplemental subtests can be substituted for a core subtest if the index score has only two core subtests (i.e., the Verbal Comprehension Index, Visual Spatial Index, Fluid Reasoning Index, Working Memory Index, Processing Speed Index, and Vocabulary Acquisition Index).

- Only *one* supplemental subtest can be substituted for a core subtest if the composite score is based on more than two subtests (i.e., the Full Scale IQ, Nonverbal Index for ages 4:0 to 7:7, General Ability Index, and Cognitive Proficiency Index.

- Proration is allowed for the sum of scaled scores that corresponds to the Full Scale IQ, but only one core subtest's scaled score can be missing.

- Proration and substitution cannot be combined. If a substitution is made for a core subtest on the Full Scale, proration cannot be used. If proration is used, a substitution cannot be made for core subtests.

- Proration cannot be used for the sum of scaled scores that corresponds to any index score.

you are in the portion of the table that corresponds to the correct age band when looking up the prorated sum of scaled scores. Record the value on the Summary page in the Sum of Scaled Scores to Composite Score Conversion table, in the box corresponding to the Full Scale. Note *PRO* next to that value to indicate the sum of scaled scores was based on proration.

Limits on Substitution and Proration

The use of substitution and proration is limited to reduce the occurrence of measurement error. The limits on substitution and proration are listed in the Caution box.

Substitution, Proration, or . . . Retest?

When deriving composite scores, the most difficult decisions arise when a core subtest's score is missing because the subtest was not administered or was spoiled. For example, a subtest's score may be missing due to task interruption during a subtest with a time limit, or due to the child being unable to complete a task such as Block Design due to physical limitations. For whatever reason, when a core subtest's score that contributes to the Full Scale IQ is missing, the published test indicates you must decide if you will substitute using an acceptable supplemental subtest or prorate the Full Scale sum of scaled scores. Additional measurement error is introduced in either case.

One recent investigation conducted on the WPPSI-IV standardization normative sample, the combined special group samples, and the retest sample investigated the impact of three methods of replacing missing subtests (Zhu & Cayton, 2013). The three methods were

1. Substitution
2. Proration
3. Retest (i.e., retesting the child on the same subtest, then using the subtest score from the second testing to calculate the Full Scale IQ)

Results indicated that substitution and proration tend to result in slightly more frequent underestimation of the Full Scale IQ, whereas retest tends to result in slightly more frequent overestimation. Substitution, proration, and retest appear to increase the measurement error in the Full Scale IQ by 20% to 64%, depending on the particular subtest and the method used.

Of the three methods, retest resulted in the least additional measurement error. For retest, only 2.9% to 5.8% of Full Scale IQs in the retest sample changed by at least 6 points, depending on the subtest that was retested.

Substitution and proration introduced amounts of measurement error that were similar to one another, but the specific results (i.e., which method introduced more measurement error) varied according to which subtest was substituted. For substitution, between 6.6% and 15.1% of Full Scale IQs in the normative sample changed by at least 6 points, depending on the subtest that was substituted. For proration, between 9.7% and 14.0% of Full Scale IQs in the normative sample changed by at least 6 points, depending on the subtest that was missing.

Measurement error introduced by substitution and proration was similar across the nonclinical and clinical samples. Because no retest study was conducted with special group studies, retest could not be compared with substitution and proration among clinical samples.

There are important limitations to the aforementioned investigation that give us pause about recommending retest as best practice, despite its apparent reduction in measurement error. These include the testing interval in the retest study, the size of the retest sample, and the child's initial score. With respect to the testing interval, the test–retest interval ranged from 7 to 48 days, with a mean interval of 23 days. The impact of retesting immediately after an interrupted or spoiled subtest, or at the end of the testing session, to obtain a retest score is unknown. One might speculate that immediate retest could result in a larger score increase on some subtests where procedural learning is more likely (e.g., Bug Search), and a smaller score increase on subtests where children do not have an intervening 23 days to learn additional words and information (e.g., Information).

The size of the retest sample was relatively small ($N = 115$). Furthermore, the retest results seem very likely to vary by the child's initial score due to regression to the mean; children with higher scores may have lower scores upon retest, and children with lower scores may have higher scores upon retest.

Invalidation of Composite Scores

A composite score is considered invalid if there are too many subtest total raw scores of 0 on subtests that contribute to its sum of scaled scores. A score of 0 does not indicate that the child does not have the abilities measured by the subtest; it merely indicates that the items on the subtest did not permit the child's ability in that area to be determined. The limits on the number of total raw scores of 0 for each composite score vary based on the number of subtests that contribute to that composite score. For index scores based on only two subtests, one may have a total raw score of 0. For index scores based on four contributing subtests, two may have total raw scores of 0. For composite scores based on five or six subtests, three may have total raw scores of 0. Rapid Reference 3.5 lists the acceptable number of total raw scores of 0 for each composite score, by age band.

≡ Rapid Reference 3.5

Acceptable Number of Total Raw Scores of 0 for Each Composite Score, by Age Band

Ages 2:6 to 3:11

Composite Score

VCI	VSI	WMI	FSIQ	VAI	NVI	GAI
1	1	1	3	1	2	2

Ages 4:0 to 7:7

Composite Score

VCI	VSI	FRI	WMI	PSI	FSIQ	VAI	NVI	GAI	CPI
1	1	1	1	1	3	1	3	2	2

Note. If for a given composite score the number of total raw scores of 0 is greater than acceptable, that composite score is considered invalid.

Abbreviations are VCI = Verbal Comprehension Index, VSI = Visual Spatial Index, WMI = Working Memory Index, FSIQ = Full Scale IQ, VAI = Vocabulary Acquisition Index, NVI = Nonverbal Index, GAI = General Ability Index, FRI = Fluid Reasoning Index, PSI = Processing Speed Index, CPI = Cognitive Proficiency Index.

Obtain Composite Scores

After the sums of scaled scores are calculated, the primary index scores and Full Scale IQ are derived. Copy the sum of scaled scores for each desired composite into the Sum of Scaled Scores column in the Sum of Scaled Scores to Composite Score Conversion table on the Summary page. Refer to the age-appropriate tables to convert the sums of scaled scores to composite scores. For this step, you will need the Sums of Scaled Scores as well as your selection for the confidence level (90% or 95%).

For ages 2:6 to 3:11, use Tables A.2 to A.5 of the *Administration and Scoring Manual* to derive the primary index scores (Verbal Comprehension Index, Visual Spatial Index, and Working Memory Index) and the Full Scale IQ and to look up the percentile ranks and confidence intervals that pertain to each composite score. For ages 4:0 to 7:7, use Tables A.6 to A.11 of the *Administration and Scoring Manual* to derive the primary index scores (Verbal Comprehension Index, Visual Spatial Index, Fluid Reasoning Index, Working Memory Index, and Processing Speed Index) and the Full Scale IQ.

For each composite score, read down the Sum of Scaled Scores column until you locate the appropriate value from your calculated sum of scaled scores. Read across the row to the composite score, the percentile rank, and the confidence interval. Record these values in the appropriate columns to the right of the Sums of Scaled Scores column.

If you have selected any of the ancillary index scores, use the Sum of Scaled Scores to Index Score Conversion table on the Ancillary Analysis page. For ages 2:6 to 3:11, use Tables C.1, C.2, and D.1 of the *Technical and Interpretive Manual* to derive the Vocabulary Acquisition Index, Nonverbal Index, and General Ability Index, respectively. For ages 4:0 to 7:7, use Tables C.1, C.3, D.2, and D.3 of the *Technical and Interpretive Manual* to derive the Vocabulary Acquisition Index, Nonverbal Index, General Ability Index, and Cognitive Proficiency Index, respectively. Follow the same procedure outlined earlier for the primary index scores.

CAUTION

The Full Scale IQ is not the average of the primary index scores. It is derived from the sum of scaled scores for its own core subtests (or all but one of its core subtests and an acceptable substitution).

You cannot add the primary index scores sums of scaled scores together and obtain the WPPSI-IV Full Scale sum of scaled scores.

USING THE WPPSI-IV SCORING ASSISTANT

The WPPSI-IV scoring assistant is available on Q-global™, Pearson's web-based scoring and reporting platform. It can be accessed from any computer with Internet access. You must use a standard browser (e.g., relatively current versions of Microsoft® Internet Explorer®, Firefox®, Chrome®, or Safari®). You must also have a relatively current operating system.

At this time, Q-global does not facilitate WPPSI-IV data entry access from tablets or handheld devices. However, the reports can be produced in a PDF format or in a document format, which permits you to read them on a device.

In addition to access to the scoring assistant on the Q-global platform, you will need the child's test age and total raw scores. With this information, the scoring assistant outputs every viable and desired subtest and score, and the strengths and weaknesses and discrepancy comparisons, in the published test.

Figure 3.1 depicts the demographics entry page within the WPPSI-IV scoring assistant on Q-global. Figure 3.2 depicts the total raw score entry page within the scoring assistant.

Substitution is facilitated within the scoring software by accessing various drop-down menus. Selecting a substitution for one composite score restricts you to the same substitution on all other applicable composite scores. *If you make a substitution for a core subtest, the index scores that are derived using that core subtest and that do not permit substitution are not calculated by the scoring assistant.* As a result, some discrepancy and score comparisons are not available for some substitutions. If you wish to use the core subtest to obtain the corresponding index score(s) that are based in part on that subtest, the report can be rerun without the substitution at no additional charge.

Ensure you have a good clinical rationale for subtest substitution. Be careful to describe the rationale, the correct results, and any interpretive implications in your report. Figure 3.3 depicts the report configuration page, which utilizes drop-down menus to facilitate substitution selections for the composite scores.

Note in Figure 3.3 that the interface specifies that if Object Assembly is substituted for Block Design, the same substitution will be applied to the Full Scale IQ, General Ability Index, and Nonverbal Index. A second substitution option, Animal Coding for Cancellation, may be made for the Cognitive Proficiency Index, because Object Assembly does not contribute to that index so no prior substitution has been made.

The Full Scale IQ is automatically prorated by the scoring software if one core subtest is missing and a substitution is not selected. No more than one core subtest may be missing. As outlined in this chapter, proration is not permitted in combination with substitution within the software. Proration is not available for any index score.

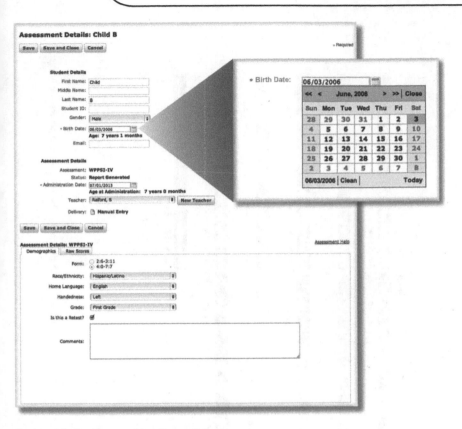

Figure 3.1 Demographics Entry Page

Wechsler Preschool and Primary Scale of Intelligence–Fourth Edition (WPPSI-IV). Copyright © 2012 NCS Pearson, Inc. Reproduced with permission. All rights reserved.

"Wechsler Preschool and Primary Scale of Intelligence" and "WPPSI" are trademarks, in the United States and/or other countries, of Pearson Education, Inc., or its affiliates.

Use of the WPPSI-IV scoring assistant is recommended. If you calculate more than the Full Scale IQ and one or two primary index scores, using the scoring assistant saves a significant amount of time. With the increased number of index scores relative to WPPSI-III, consequent greater number of potential discrepancy comparisons, and the inclusion of strengths and weaknesses at the index level, a meticulous examiner easily can spend 45 to 60 minutes double-checking basic arithmetic, transferring total raw scores, looking up and recording standard scores, and performing strengths and weaknesses and discrepancy analyses. Furthermore, using the scoring assistant prevents needless computation errors.

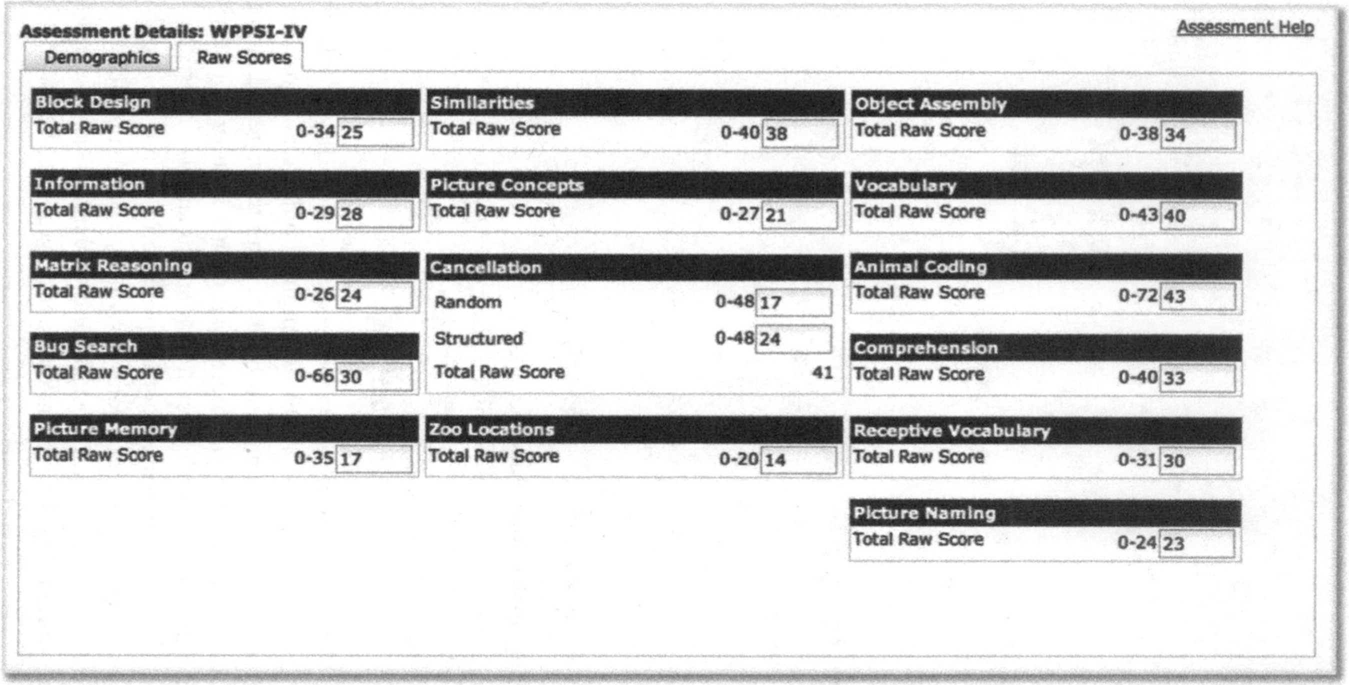

Figure 3.2 Total Raw Score Entry Page

Wechsler Preschool and Primary Scale of Intelligence–Fourth Edition (WPPSI-IV). Copyright © 2012 NCS Pearson, Inc. Reproduced with permission. All rights reserved.

"Wechsler Preschool and Primary Scale of Intelligence" and "WPPSI" are trademarks, in the United States and/or other countries, of Pearson Education, Inc, or its affiliates.

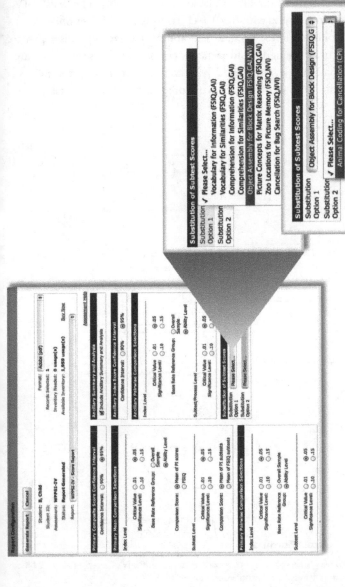

Figure 3.3 Report Configuration Entry Page

Wechsler Preschool and Primary Scale of Intelligence–Fourth Edition (WPPSI-IV). Copyright © 2012 NCS Pearson, Inc. Reproduced with permission. All rights reserved.

"Wechsler Preschool and Primary Scale of Intelligence" and "WPPSI" are trademarks, in the United States and/or other countries, of Pearson Education, Inc, or its affiliates.

Sample outputs from the scoring assistant to illustrate its functionalities appear in Figures 3.4 to 3.6.

A combination WPPSI-IV and Wechsler Individual Achievement Test–Third Edition (WIAT-III) report is additionally available within Q-global. The WPPSI-IV provides two types of joint analyses with the WIAT-III to assist with identification of specific learning disabilities. These include the ability–achievement discrepancy analysis and the pattern of strengths and weaknesses analysis. These methods are described in Chapter 6 of the *Technical and Interpretive Manual*. Briefly, the ability–achievement discrepancy analysis involves the use of an ability score to establish an

PRIMARY SUMMARY

Scaled Score Summary

Subtest Name		Total Raw Score	Scaled Score	Percentile Rank	Age Equivalent	SEM
Information	IN	28	17	99	>7:7	1.04
Similarities	SI	38	18	99.6	>7:7	0.85
(Vocabulary)	VC	40	18	99.6	>7:7	1.04
(Comprehension)	CO	33	14	91	>7:7	0.99
Block Design	BD	25	10	50	7:0	1.12
Object Assembly	OA	34	13	84	>7:7	1.27
Matrix Reasoning	MR	24	16	98	>7:7	1.04
Picture Concepts	PC	21	13	84	>7:7	1.04
Picture Memory	PM	17	9	37	6:4	0.85
Zoo Locations	ZL	14	13	84	>7:7	1.12
Bug Search	BS	30	7	16	5:9	1.31
Cancellation	CA	41	9	37	6:1	1.41
(Animal Coding)	AC	43	12	75	>7:7	1.41

Subtests used to derive the FSIQ are bolded. Subtests not typically core for any composite score are in parentheses.

Subtest Scaled Score Profile

Figure 3.4 Primary Subtest Summary

Composite Score Summary

Composite		Sum of Scaled Scores	Composite Score	Percentile Rank	95% Confidence Interval	Qualitative Description	SEM
Verbal Comprehension	VCI	35	143	99.8	134-147	Very Superior	3.67
Visual Spatial	VSI	23	109	73	99-117	Average	4.97
Fluid Reasoning	FRI	29	127	96	118-132	Superior	4.24
Working Memory	WMI	22	107	68	98-114	Average	4.24
Processing Speed	PSI	16	89	23	81-100	Low Average	5.81
Full Scale IQ	FSIQ	77	121	92	115-126	Superior	3.00

Confidence intervals are calculated using the Standard Error of Estimation.

Composite Score Profile

Note. Vertical bars represent the Confidence Intervals.

Figure 3.5 Composite Score Summary

Wechsler Preschool and Primary Scale of Intelligence–Fourth Edition (WPPSI-IV). Copyright © 2012 NCS Pearson, Inc. Reproduced with permission. All rights reserved.

"Wechsler Preschool and Primary Scale of Intelligence" and "WPPSI" are trademarks, in the United States and/or other countries, of Pearson Education, Inc., or its affiliates.

expectation for achievement scores. The pattern of strengths and weaknesses analysis utilizes the primary index scores to establish cognitive strengths and weaknesses. The cognitive strength is compared with the cognitive weakness and the achievement weakness. Sample outputs from the joint scoring assistants for each of these analyses appears in Figures 3.7 and 3.8.

FREQUENTLY ASKED QUESTIONS: SCORING

Pearson provides responses to FAQs about the WPPSI-IV on the product website. One portion of the FAQs relates to subtest scoring and use of the scoring assistant. The questions and responses are reproduced in Rapid Reference 3.6.

ANCILLARY SUMMARY

Scaled Score Summary

Subtest Name		Total Raw Score	Scaled Score	Percentile Rank	Age Equivalent	SEM
Receptive Vocabulary	RV	30	17	99	>7:7	0.95
Picture Naming	PN	23	16	98	>7:7	1.24
Cancellation Random	CAR	17	8	25	5:3	1.41
Cancellation Structured	CAS	24	10	50	7:0	1.67

Index Score Summary

Composite		Sum of Scaled Scores	Standard Score	Percentile Rank	95% Confidence Interval	Qualitative Description	SEM
Vocabulary Acquisition	VAI	33	136	99	126-141	Very Superior	4.24
Nonverbal	NVI	55	107	68	100-113	Average	3.35
General Ability	GAI	61	133	99	125-138	Very Superior	3.35
Cognitive Proficiency	CPI	38	96	39	89-104	Average	4.24

Figure 3.6 Ancillary Summary

Wechsler Preschool and Primary Scale of Intelligence–Fourth Edition (WPPSI-IV). Copyright © 2012 NCS Pearson, Inc. Reproduced with permission. All rights reserved.

"Wechsler Preschool and Primary Scale of Intelligence" and "WPPSI" are trademarks, in the United States and/or other countries, of Pearson Education, Inc., or its affiliates.

ABILITY-ACHIEVEMENT DISCREPANCY ANALYSIS

Ability Score Type: WPPSI-IV FSIQ   Ability Score: 94

Predicted Difference Method

	Predicted WIAT-III Score	Actual WIAT-III Score	Difference	Critical Value .05	Significant Difference Y/N	Base Rate	Standard Deviation Discrepancy ≥ 1.5 SD
WIAT-III Subtest							
Early Reading Skills	96	88	8	10.01	N	<=25%	N
Reading Comprehension	96	88	8	9.41	N	<=25%	N
Word Reading	96	90	6	5.65	Y	>25%	N
Pseudoword Decoding	96	89	7	6.16	Y	>25%	N
Oral Reading Fluency	97	75	22	8.97	Y	<=4%	N
WIAT-III Composite							
Total Reading	96	82	14	5.85	Y	<=10%	N
Basic Reading	96	89	7	4.68	Y	>25%	N

Note. Base rates and standard deviation discrepancies are not reported when the achievement score equals or exceeds the ability score.

*Indicates that the achievement score exceeds the ability score.

Figure 3.7 Ability-Achievement Discrepancy Analysis

Wechsler Preschool and Primary Scale of Intelligence–Fourth Edition (WPPSI-IV). Copyright © 2012 NCS Pearson, Inc. Reproduced with permission. All rights reserved.

"Wechsler Preschool and Primary Scale of Intelligence" and "WPPSI" are trademarks, in the United States and/or other countries, of Pearson Education, Inc., or its affiliates.

Pattern of Strengths and Weaknesses Analysis

Area of Achievement Weakness	WIAT-III	Oral Reading Fluency: 75
Area of Processing Weakness	WPPSI-IV	WMI: 84
Area of Processing Strength	WPPSI-IV	FRI: 117

Comparison	Relative Strength Score	Relative Weakness Score	Difference	Critical Value .05	Significant Difference Y/N	Supports SLD hypothesis? Yes/No
A Processing Strength/ Achievement Weakness	117	75	42	11.76	Y	Yes
B Processing Strength/ Processing Weakness	117	84	33	11.75	Y	Yes

The PSW model is intended to help practitioners generate hypotheses regarding clinical diagnoses. The analysis should always be used within a comprehensive evaluation that incorporates multiple sources of information.

Pattern of Strengths and Weaknesses Model

Figure 3.8 Pattern of Strengths and Weaknesses Analysis

Wechsler Preschool and Primary Scale of Intelligence–Fourth Edition (WPPSI-IV). Copyright © 2012 NCS Pearson, Inc. Reproduced with permission. All rights reserved.

"Wechsler Preschool and Primary Scale of Intelligence" and "WPPSI" are trademarks, in the United States and/or other countries, of Pearson Education, Inc., or its affiliates.

≡ Rapid Reference 3.6

Frequently Asked Questions: Subtest Scoring

On the WPPSI–III, a pencil was used to draw forms in Coding (thus also assessing fine motor skills). It seems like it will be more difficult to assess fine motor skills when children are only using the ink dauber. Have you found this to be true?

In terms of the fine motor demands, yes, the ink dauber reduces the influence of fine motor demands on the measure of processing speed. Using the pencil was difficult for many 4-year-old children with developmental delays or other fine motor issues. Because the assessment of fine motor control was mainly

(continued)

qualitative in nature on the prior tasks, other measures such as the Beery VMI or portions of the NEPSY–II and consulting with an occupational therapist may be helpful if the referral question requires investigation of fine motor skills.

Did you consider removing the time limit for Object Assembly, or providing a table to use for scoring that considers completion outside of the time requirement—in essence, a process score for speed and for accuracy?

Removing the time limit on this subtest would result in a loss of the ceiling, greatly reduced reliability, and a much lower correlation with general intelligence. Removing the time limit results in children completing correctly who do not have commensurate intellectual ability. These issues greatly reduce the meaningfulness of scores that could be derived from the results. The additional puzzles that would be required to ensure a ceiling without a time requirement would substantially raise the kit cost and kit weight and greatly increase administration time. There is nothing that precludes a practitioner from returning to Object Assembly after WPPSI-IV administration to test the child's limits of performance.

If I substitute a supplemental subtest for a core subtest to derive a composite score, is it considered a standard administration?

No. Because this procedure estimates performance on a core subtest using a supplemental subtest, the results should be interpreted with caution and considered non-standard.

How was it decided that one subtest score could or could not be substituted for another?

Because substituted subtests are being used as an estimate of performance on another subtest, only supplemental subtests within the same cognitive domain that are sufficiently highly related to the core subtest can be substituted.

Can I substitute the supplemental subtests for a core subtest?

For composite scores that are derived from more than two subtests (i.e., Full Scale IQ, Nonverbal Index, General Ability Index, and Cognitive Proficiency Index), a maximum of one substitution may be made. However, the supplemental subtest must be from the same cognitive domain as the core subtest.

Can I administer all of the core and supplemental subtests and choose to use the highest subtest scaled scores when computing composite scores?

No. When deriving composite scores, you can only substitute supplemental subtests for core subtests that are spoiled or invalidated, or for a specific clinical purpose. Supplemental subtests can also provide additional information on cognitive functioning. If you need to substitute a supplemental subtest in place of a core subtest, it is best practice to decide this before you administer the subtest—not after you have derived scaled scores. Supplemental subtests are also useful when the scores within a primary index score are widely discrepant. In this situation, additional information from supplemental subtests can help to shed light on factors that may contribute to such disparate results.

Why isn't supplemental subtest substitution allowed on the Verbal Comprehension Index, Visual Spatial Index, Fluid Reasoning Index, Working Memory Index, or Processing Speed Index?

Because the use of supplemental subtest substitution for core subtests may introduce measurement error into derived composite scores, substitution is limited. The primary index scores are derived from only two subtests, and the risk of such error therefore is greater for these composite scores. Furthermore, if a supplemental subtest substitutes for a core subtest for the Full Scale IQ or an ancillary index score that permits substitution, the Q-global™ scoring software will not allow calculation of the primary index score to which the substituted subtest contributes.

Is score proration still available?

Under specific guidelines and circumstances, prorating is available for the Full Scale IQ only. Substitution, if available, is preferred over proration.

Q-global Scoring and Reporting
What is Q-global?

Q-global is a web-based scoring and reporting platform that offers accessibility from any computer connected to the Internet and allows for quick and automatic organization of examinee information and the ability to generate scores and produce accurate and detailed results. Reports are available in a PDF or Word document format.

When will the WPPSI-IV scoring assistant and WPPSI-IV writer be available?

WPPSI-IV scoring and reporting is available on Q-global. The score report is available now. The interpretive report generally becomes available approximately 6 months following the publication of a test.

Can I reprint a scoring report at no charge?

Yes. You can reprint a report at no charge if you change any demographic or report options. However, if you alter raw data, a new record is created and a new report usage is required to print the output.

How do you use supplemental subtest substitution and proration when scoring WPPSI-IV in Q-global?

Two dropdown menus within the WPPSI-IV Q-global scoring software facilitate supplemental subtest substitution. Choose your substitution in the first dropdown menu. The second dropdown menu will become activated if additional substitutions are allowed. A table within the Q-global Resource Library section explains which subtest substitutions are allowed together in the Q-global scoring software.

On rare occasions, an inadequate number of valid subtest scores are obtained to derive the Full Scale IQ, despite the availability of supplemental subtests. Q-global automatically prorates the Full Scale IQ if a core subtest that contributes to it is missing and a supplemental subtest is not selected for substitution. If more than one core subtest is missing, the Full Scale IQ is not calculated. Proration is only available for the Full Scale IQ, and only when the prorated sum of scaled scores is based on core subtests. You cannot combine supplemental subtest substitution and proration when deriving the Full Scale IQ.

(continued)

Are the allowable substitutions for core subtests different on Q-global compared to hand scoring?

The rules governing allowable substitutions for core subtests for Q-global and hand scoring (i.e., in the WPPSI-IV *Administration and Scoring Manual*) are the same. Substitution should only be used when the core subtest is invalid or in certain clinical situations when it is determined that a supplemental subtest is a better estimate of the cognitive ability than the core subtest (e.g., when a child's physical condition interferes with performance). Any substitution selected within Q-global is made on all applicable composites, and any score comparisons that utilize the substituted subtest are impacted.

Why are some score comparisons not available on the Q-global platform if I substitute a supplemental subtest for a core subtest?

The score comparisons are not available because the data they are based on require the missing subtest. For example, pairwise index-level difference comparisons that include the Verbal Comprehension Index are not provided in Q-global if Vocabulary is substituted for Information when deriving the Full Scale IQ, because the Verbal Comprehension Index is not calculated.

Some other comparisons may also be unavailable if substitution is used. For example, index-level strengths and weaknesses comparisons require calculation of the mean primary index score or the Full Scale IQ. If the Verbal Comprehension Index is unavailable, the MIS cannot be calculated. In this situation, the Full Scale IQ becomes the comparison score, and the other available primary index scores are compared with the Full Scale IQ rather than the MIS.

Are score comparisons with the WIAT-III available on Q-global?

Yes. It is possible to either manually enter the WPPSI-IV scores when creating a WIAT-III score report or to create a combination report for the WPPSI-IV and WIAT-III using Q-global.

What is included in the WPPSI-IV/WIAT-III Combination Report on Q-global?

In addition to the WPPSI-IV Score Report and the WIAT-III Score Report, the combination report includes two analyses to aid in the identification of specific learning disabilities: the traditional ability-achievement discrepancy analysis and the pattern of strengths and weaknesses discrepancy analysis.

🪶 TEST YOURSELF 🪶

1. **Recording the child's verbatim responses is necessary for accurate scoring on the Verbal Comprehension subtests. What are the item scores based on?**

   (a) Grammar

   (b) Content

   (c) Eloquence

   (d) Verbosity

2. **Personalized responses on the Verbal Comprehension subtests are always scored as 0 points even if accompanied by a correct response.**
   True or False?

3. **The Working Memory subtests were not available on the WPPSI-III.**
   True or False?

4. **For which subtests can a 6-year-old child earn additional points for correct responses that are higher in quality?**
   (a) Similarities, Receptive Vocabulary, Information
   (b) Vocabulary, Zoo Locations, Picture Memory
   (c) Similarities, Vocabulary, Comprehension
   (d) Information, Vocabulary, Animal Coding

5. **Total raw scores are the sum of item scores, and are used to compare the child's intellectual ability to the normal population.**
   True or False?

6. **Composite scores based on two to three subtests have what range?**
   (a) 45–155
   (b) 50–155
   (c) 40–160
   (d) 45–160

7. **One common scoring error on Object Assembly is not multiplying the total junctures completed correctly on Items 12 and 13 by one half to obtain the item score.**
   True or False?

8. **Which composite scores that are derived from more than two subtests permit substitution of *only one* supplemental subtest if one of the core subtests is missing or invalid?**
   (a) Vocabulary Acquisition Index, Full Scale IQ, General Ability Index, Visual Spatial Index
   (b) Full Scale IQ, Nonverbal Index, General Ability Index, Cognitive Proficiency Index
   (c) Fluid Reasoning Index, Cognitive Proficiency Index, Working Memory Index
   (d) Processing Speed Index, Full Scale IQ, Nonverbal Index, Verbal Comprehension Index

9. **For children aged 4:0 to 7:7, which of the following is an acceptable substitution for a core subtest in the Full Scale IQ?**
   (a) Animal Coding for Picture Memory
   (b) Picture Concepts for Block Design
   (c) Picture Naming for Comprehension
   (d) Zoo Locations for Picture Memory

10. **Proration and substitution cannot be combined.**
    True or False?

11. **If a child aged 5:0 has only four valid core subtest scores for the Full Scale, a prorated sum of scaled scores for the Full Scale IQ can be obtained.**
    True or False?

12. A 3-year-old child may have two scores of 0 on which of the following composite scores?

(a) General Ability Index

(b) Verbal Comprehension Index

(c) Visual Spatial Index

(d) Working Memory Index

13. You cannot add primary index sums of scaled scores together to obtain the sum of scaled scores for the Full Scale.

True or False?

14. You must use the *WPPSI-IV Technical and Interpretive Manual* to derive which index score?

(a) Visual Spatial Index

(b) Working Memory Index

(c) Nonverbal Index

(d) Fluid Reasoning Index

15. A combination WPPSI-IV and WIAT-III ability-achievement discrepancy analysis available within Q-global involves the use of an ability score to establish an expectation for achievement scores.

True or False?

Answers: 1. b; 2. False; 3. True; 4. c; 5. False; 6. a; 7. True; 8. b; 9. d; 10. True; 11. False; 12. a; 13. True; 14. c; 15. True

REFERENCES

Alfonso, V. C., Johnson, A., Patinella, L., & Rader, D. E. (1998). Common WISC-III examiner errors: Evidence from graduate students in training. *Psychology in the Schools, 35,* 119–125.

Erdodi, L. A., Richard, D. C. S., & Hopwood, C. (2009). The importance of relying on the manual: Scoring error variance in the WISC-IV Vocabulary subtest. *Journal of Psychoeducational Assessment, 27,* 374–385.

Kuentzel, J. G., Hetterscheidt, L. A., & Barnett, D. (2011). Testing intelligently includes double-checking Wechsler IQ scores. *Journal of Psychoeducational Assessment, 29,* 39–46.

Loe, S. A., Kadlubek, R. M., & Marks, W. J. (2007). Administration and scoring errors on the WISC-IV among graduate student examiners. *Journal of Psychoeducational Assessment, 25,* 237–247.

Mrazik, M., Janzen, T. M., Dombrowski, S. C., Barford, S. W., & Krawchuk, L. L. (2012). Administration and scoring errors of graduate students learning the WISC-IV: Issues and controversies. *Canadian Journal of School Psychology, 27,* 279–290.

Wechsler, D. (2012). *Wechsler preschool and primary scale of intelligence* (4th ed.). Bloomington, MN: Pearson.

Zhu, J. J., & Cayton, T. (2013). *Substitution, proration, or retest: The best strategy when a core subtest score is missing.* Symposium presented at the annual meeting of the American Psychological Association, Honolulu, Hawaii.

Four

WPPSI-IV SCORE ANALYSIS AND INTERPRETATION

This chapter offers information relevant to WPPSI-IV score analysis and interpretation. The published composite scores and a number of additional index scores are described. A step-by-step approach to score analysis is detailed.

UNDERSTANDING THE COMPOSITE SCORES

Between those that appear on the published test and this book, there are a greater number of composite scores available for the WPPSI-IV than any prior Wechsler intelligence scale. The large complement of scores provides more flexibility for interpretation, and challenges the practitioner to employ careful consideration in selecting the appropriate scores for a particular child. Not all of these scores will necessarily be useful or meaningful when describing a particular child.

There are two types of composite scores: global composite scores (i.e., useful to describe or summarize overall intellectual ability) and specific composite scores (i.e., useful to provide information about a specific cognitive domain, as opposed to overall intellectual ability). Interpretation requires a clear understanding of the global scores so that you may select which is most useful for describing overall intellectual ability given the presenting issues and the purpose of the evaluation. Interpretation also involves selection of the appropriate specific scores to provide targeted information about the child's cognitive abilities, strengths, and weaknesses, and according to your theoretical orientation. As with the global scores, not all specific scores will be useful in every situation. Descriptions of the global and specific scores follow in the subsequent sections of this chapter.

Global Composite Scores

There are three global composite scores available within the published test: the Full Scale IQ, the Nonverbal Index, and the General Ability Index. These are described in turn in the following sections.

Full Scale IQ

The Full Scale IQ is the most reliable of the composite scores. It is derived from the sum of five subtest scaled scores for ages 2:6 to 3:11 and from the sum of six subtest scaled scores for ages 4:0 to 7:7. Of all composite scores, the Full Scale IQ most closely represents general intellectual ability (g).

Full Scale IQ interpretation is best approached through understanding the primary index scores, because they represent constructs that contribute vital information to general intellectual ability. Comparing the available primary index scores to an estimate of overall performance (e.g., the mean of all primary index scores [MIS] or the Full Scale IQ) and to one another (e.g., the Verbal Comprehension Index and the Visual Spatial Index) therefore informs Full Scale IQ interpretation. We consider this step so fundamental that additional estimates of overall performance are provided for these purposes if the mean of all primary index scores cannot be calculated because one of the primary index scores is unavailable (see Step 5). Comparing the subtest scaled scores to an indicator of overall subtest-level performance (e.g., the mean scaled score of the primary index subtests [abbreviated *MSS-I* in the published test] or the mean scaled score of the Full Scale IQ subtests [abbreviated *MSS-F*]) can inform Full Scale IQ interpretation in a similar manner.

Some interpretive approaches indicate that composite scores are less valid or less reliable if their component parts are discrepant. In these interpretive approaches, the Full Scale IQ is described as valid, reliable, and interpretable *only* if no significant discrepancy exists between the highest and lowest primary index scores. Similarly, the index scores are only described as valid and reliable if their contributing subtests are not significantly discrepant. We do not find sufficient evidence that there is a discrepancy or index score scatter beyond which the Full Scale IQ becomes invalid, unreliable, and uninterpretable. We do believe, however, that when great variability or discrepancy characterizes the primary index scores or the subtest scaled scores, the Full Scale IQ *alone* is insufficient to describe a child's intellectual abilities. However, reliance on *any* single score is never recommended for describing a child's intellectual abilities or identifying his or her strengths and needs.

Recent research indicates that the Full Scale IQ has equal construct validity regardless of primary index score discrepancies. The construct and predictive validity of the Full Scale IQ is independent of the discrepancy (Daniel, 2007). Similarly, the construct and predictive validity of the primary index scores is independent of the amount of discrepancy between subtests (Daniel, 2009). We believe the same to be true of other composite scores, such as the Nonverbal Index and the General Ability Index. Furthermore, it is quite typical to have a discrepancy of greater than 1.5 *SD*s (24 points or more) between two primary index scores. In fact, 40% of the WPPSI-IV normative sample (that is, 675 of the 1,700 children in the normative sample) had such a discrepancy. Given the vast evidence in support of the predictive validity of *g* and Full Scale IQ (Daniel, 2007; Deary & Johnson, 2010; Deary, Strand, Smith, & Fernandes, 2007; Johnson, Deary, & Iacono, 2009; Kaufman, Reynolds, Liu, Kaufman, & McGrew, 2012), it seems counterintuitive to assume that for 40% of children the Full Scale IQ is not valid. Moreover, because more specific domains of intellectual ability do not show the same *broad* degree of predictive validity as does *g* (Gottfredson, 2008; Hartmann, Larsen, & Nyborg, 2009; Kotz, Watkins, & McDermott, 2008; Reeve & Charles, 2008), the Full Scale IQ provides essential, clinically rich information when attempting to understand the expression of intelligent behavior in real world settings (Jacobson, Delis, Hamilton, Bondi, & Salmon, 2004).

With respect to the Full Scale IQ's reliability in the presence of relatively large discrepancies among primary index scores, we do not find evidence that the Full Scale IQ becomes unreliable in these circumstances. Table 4.2 of the *WPPSI-IV Technical and Interpretive Manual* (*Technical and Interpretive Manual*) lists the subtest reliability coefficients for special groups. For the WPPSI-IV special groups with larger scatter among primary index scores, such as English language learner and Asperger's disorder, the subtest reliabilities are comparable with those of other special groups with smaller scatter among primary index scores (e.g., intellectual disability—mild). Because these coefficients are comparable with those of the normative sample, it is more likely that the Full Scale IQ reliability for special samples would be similar to that of the normative sample.

Nonverbal Index
The Nonverbal Index is available for ages 2:6 to 7:7. It offers an estimate of overall ability for children who have expressive issues (e.g., language disorder, autism spectrum disorder, English language learner). The Nonverbal Index provides a more comprehensive choice for estimating overall ability than the Visual Spatial Index or (for children aged 4:0 to 7:7) the Fluid Reasoning Index in these situations, because it includes subtests from every scale available for the given age band, other than Verbal Comprehension.

Behind the Scenes

• •

The subtests that contribute to the Full Scale IQ, and the relative contributions of subtests drawn from the primary index scales, are carefully selected. A wide range of considerations are weighed, including:

- Reliability
- Subtest g loadings
- Factor (representing the primary index scales) g loadings
- Construct coverage and subtest redundancy
- Consistency across the two age bands
- Other measures and common practice
- Expert input
- Internal stakeholder input
- Administration time
- Relations with achievement
- Consistency with the prior edition
- Relations with the Full Scale IQ of the prior edition
- Consistency with related Wechsler intelligence scales

Chapter 4 of the *Technical and Interpretive Manual* indicates the Nonverbal Index possesses reliability similar to that of the Full Scale IQ. Evidence in Chapter 5 of the *Technical and Interpretive Manual* indicates the Nonverbal Index demonstrates similar classification accuracy as that of the Full Scale IQ for children with intellectual disabilities (see also Chapter 7 of this book), and appears promising for use with children identified with conditions (e.g., language disorder, autism spectrum disorder) or situations (e.g., English language learner) that raise concerns about expressive language.

The Nonverbal Index can be interpreted as an estimate of general intellectual ability that minimizes expressive demands for children with such conditions or in these special situations. It is not a "language free" measure, but should be described as "language reduced" (Ortiz, Ochoa, & Dynda, 2012) because it still requires the child to comprehend English subtest instructions. See Chapter 7 of this book for more detailed information about use of the Nonverbal Index with various frequent referral questions in early childhood.

General Ability Index

The General Ability Index is available for ages 2:6 to 7:7. Relative to the Full Scale IQ, the General Ability Index offers an estimate of intellectual ability that is less influenced by working memory and processing speed. Chapter 4 of the *Technical and Interpretive Manual* indicates that it possesses reliability similar to that of the Full Scale IQ.

The General Ability Index can be interpreted as an estimate of general intellectual ability that minimizes working memory and processing speed demands in situations when neurodevelopmental disorders are present that are associated with difficulties in these areas. Children with such issues can obtain relatively lower Full Scale IQ scores than children without these issues, because subtests from the Working Memory and/or Processing Speed scales contribute to the Full Scale IQ. For example, working memory displays sensitivity to specific learning disorders, attention-deficit/hyperactivity disorder (ADHD), language disorders, and autism spectrum disorder (Archibald & Gathercole, 2006a, 2006b; Belleville, Ménard, Mottron, & Ménard, 2006; Passolunghi, 2006; Pickering, 2006; Roodenrys, 2006; Swanson, 2006); and processing speed is sensitive to specific learning disorders, ADHD, and autism spectrum disorder (Compton, Fuchs, Fuchs, Lambert, & Hamlett, 2012; Mayes & Calhoun, 2007, 2008). In these situations, the General Ability Index may reveal meaningful differences between intellectual ability and other cognitive functions (e.g., achievement, memory, or executive functions) that are obscured when the Full Scale IQ is used as a comparison score.

We believe the General Ability Index is most informative when reported with the Full Scale IQ and the Cognitive Proficiency Index, as well as the other primary index scores. Working memory and processing speed have proven again and again to be critical components of overall intellectual ability (Blalock & McCabe, 2011; Bunting, 2006; Dodonova & Dodonov, 2012), and excluding them generally results in a less comprehensive score with reduced construct coverage and predictive validity (Rowe, Kingsley, & Thompson, 2010).

In most cases, the main utility of the General Ability Index is as a comparison score, not a stand-alone measure of intellectual ability. See Chapter 7 of this book for more detailed information about use of the General Ability Index with various frequent referral questions in early childhood.

Specific Composite Scores

There are a variety of specific composite scores available for the WPPSI-IV within the published test, described and discussed in the sections that follow. New index scores were created to complement the published index scores. These additional index scores are available in this book and on the accompanying CD. They were developed based upon specific theoretical approaches and practical considerations.

WPPSI-IV Published Index Scores

The primary index scores are included in the published test. They are derived based on the factor analysis that specifies the latent traits measured by the test. A vast amount of other evidence supports their validity and clinical utility. They permit descriptiveness of discrete cognitive abilities that cannot be achieved by reporting a global composite score.

Verbal Comprehension Index The Verbal Comprehension Index is the index score that best represents acquired knowledge, verbal reasoning, and verbal concept formation. Experts in CHC theory classify the subtests that contribute to the Verbal Comprehension Index as measures of Gc, especially the narrow abilities of general information (K0), lexical knowledge (VL), and language development (LD); and one of the subtests for ages 4:0 to 7:7 (i.e., Similarities) as a secondary measure of the broad ability of Gf, especially the narrow ability of induction (I) (Flanagan, Alfonso, & Ortiz, 2012; Flanagan, Alfonso, Ortiz, & Dynda, 2010; Lichtenberger & Kaufman, 2013; Schneider & McGrew, 2012).

From a neuropsychological perspective, the Verbal Comprehension Index provides a mixed measure of Lurian Blocks 2 and 3 (i.e., simultaneous processing and planning and metacognition). It taps neuropsychological constructs including memory and learning, language (receptive language for ages 2:6 to 3:11), and executive function (concept recognition and generation for ages 4:0 to 7:7; Flanagan et al., 2010; Miller, 2010, 2013; Miller & Maricle, 2012).

Visual Spatial Index The Visual Spatial Index is the index score that measures visual–spatial processing, part–whole relationship integration and synthesis, and visual–motor integration. Experts in CHC theory classify the subtests that contribute to the Visual Spatial Index as measures of Gv, especially the narrow abilities of speeded rotation (SR), visualization (Vz), and closure speed (CS) (Flanagan et al., 2010; Flanagan et al., 2012; Lichtenberger & Kaufman, 2013; Schneider & McGrew, 2012).

From a neuropsychological perspective, the Visual Spatial Index provides a mixed measure of Lurian Blocks 2 and 3 (i.e., simultaneous processing and planning and metacognition). It measures neuropsychological constructs including visual–spatial processing (visual–motor construction), and executive function (problem solving, cognitive flexibility, reasoning, and planning; Flanagan et al., 2010; Miller, 2010, 2013; Miller & Maricle, 2012).

Fluid Reasoning Index (Ages 4:0 to 7:7 Only) The Fluid Reasoning Index is the index score that best represents inductive and fluid reasoning, broad visual intelligence, conceptual thinking, simultaneous processing, and classification ability.

Experts in CHC theory classify the Fluid Reasoning Index as a measure of Gf (fluid reasoning), especially the narrow abilities of induction (I) and general sequential reasoning (RG), and one of the subtests (i.e., Picture Concepts) as a secondary measure of the broad ability Gc (Flanagan et al., 2010; Flanagan et al., 2012; Lichtenberger & Kaufman, 2013; Schneider & McGrew, 2012).

From a neuropsychological perspective, the Fluid Reasoning Index provides a mixed measure of Lurian Blocks 2 and 3 (i.e., successive processing and planning and metacognition). It measures neuropsychological constructs within the executive function domain (concept recognition and generation; problem solving, cognitive flexibility, reasoning, and planning) (Flanagan et al., 2010; Miller, 2010, 2013; Miller & Maricle, 2012).

Working Memory Index   The Working Memory Index is the index score that measures visual and visual–spatial working memory, and ability to withstand proactive interference. A large body of literature supports working memory as an essential part of other higher order cognitive abilities (Chuderski & Necka, 2012; Conway & Kovacs, 2013; Hornung, Brunner, Reuter, & Martin, 2011; Martínez et al., 2011). Experts in CHC theory classify subtests similar to those that contribute to the Working Memory Index as good measures of Gsm (short-term memory), especially the narrow abilities of working memory capacity (MW) and memory span (MS), and as secondary measures of Gv, especially visual memory (MV) (Flanagan et al., 2010; Lichtenberger & Kaufman, 2013; Schneider & McGrew, 2012).

From a neuropsychological perspective, the Working Memory Index provides a mixed measure of Lurian Blocks 1, 2, and 3 (i.e., attention, simultaneous and successive processing, and planning and metacognition). It measures neuropsychological constructs including attention (attentional capacity), visual–spatial processing (visual–motor construction), learning and memory (visual immediate memory for pictures and for spatial locations, visual working memory), and executive functions (response inhibition) domains (Flanagan et al., 2010; Miller, 2010, 2013; Miller & Maricle, 2012).

Processing Speed Index (Ages 4:0 to 7:7 Only)   The Processing Speed Index is the index score that best represents processing speed, especially quick scanning and discrimination of simple visual information. It also may be related to short-term memory, visual–motor coordination, and rate of test taking (Lichtenberger & Kaufman, 2004; Sattler, 2008). Experts in CHC theory classify subtests similar to those that contribute to the Processing Speed Index as good measures of Gs, especially the narrow abilities of perceptual speed (P) and rate of test taking (R9) (Flanagan et al., 2010; Lichtenberger & Kaufman, 2013; Schneider & McGrew, 2012).

From a neuropsychological perspective, the Processing Speed Index provides a mixed measure of Lurian Blocks 1, 2, and 3 (i.e., attention, simultaneous processing, and planning and metacognition). It measures neuropsychological constructs including speed and efficiency, attention (selective and sustained attention), visual–spatial processing (visual scanning/tracking), learning and memory (visual immediate memory for objects and for pictures), and executive function (response inhibition) (Flanagan et al., 2010; Miller, 2010, 2013; Miller & Maricle, 2012).

Vocabulary Acquisition Index The Vocabulary Acquisition Index is available in the published test for ages 2:6 to 7:7. It offers a closer examination of a child's receptive and expressive vocabulary acquisition. For children with expressive issues, the Vocabulary Acquisition Index can be used as a measure of verbal ability, as it requires less expression than does the Verbal Comprehension Index. It is based on Receptive Vocabulary and Picture Naming, which rely on vocabulary recognition rather than more expressive or advanced conceptual processes. Receptive Vocabulary has no expressive demands, and Picture Naming requires only single-word responses. The consistent loading of these two subtests on the Verbal Comprehension factor for all ages provides theoretical support for this application of the Vocabulary Acquisition Index. The Vocabulary Acquisition Index (i.e., the Receptive Vocabulary and Picture Naming subtests) additionally emerged as a nested subfactor within the Verbal Comprehension factor in the 4:0 to 7:7 confirmatory factor analysis. The remainder of the Verbal Comprehension subtests loaded on the other nested subfactor, providing construct evidence for the Vocabulary Acquisition Index as a focused, simple measure of verbal abilities.

Additional Index Scores in This Book

There are a number of additional index scores provided in this book and on the accompanying CD. The additional index scores were developed based upon specific theoretical approaches and practical considerations. The norms for these additional index scores are available on the CD that accompanies this book, which contains appendix matter and the WPPSI-IV Interpretive Assistant 1.0.

Rapid Reference 1.7 provides a summary of the subtest composition of the additional index scores. Table 4.1 presents the reliability coefficients of the additional index scores by age group and for the 4:0 to 7:7 age band. The average reliability coefficients were calculated using the same procedures described in Chapter 4 of the *Technical and Interpretive Manual.* Similarly, Table 4.2 provides the standard errors of measurement (*SEMs*) of the additional index scores by age

Table 4.1 Reliability Coefficients of Additional Index Scores for Ages 4:0 to 7:7

Index Score	4:0–4:5	4:6–4:11	5:0–5:5	5:6–5:11	6:0–6:5	6:6–6:11	7:0–7:7	4:0–7:7 (overall)[a]
Gc-K0	0.94	0.93	0.94	0.93	0.92	0.92	0.93	0.94
Gc-VL	0.95	0.95	0.95	0.95	0.93	0.94	0.95	0.95
Gf-Verbal	0.96	0.95	0.95	0.95	0.94	0.94	0.95	0.96
WKI	0.93	0.93	0.93	0.93	0.92	0.91	0.93	0.93
CRGI	0.94	0.95	0.94	0.94	0.92	0.93	0.94	0.94
CVI	0.97	0.97	0.97	0.97	0.96	0.96	0.97	0.97
CEI	0.94	0.94	0.95	0.94	0.93	0.93	0.94	0.94

Note. WKI = Word Knowledge Index, CRGI = Concept Recognition and Generation Index, CVI = Comprehensive Verbal Index, CEI = Complex Expressive Index.
[a] Average reliability coefficients were calculated with Fisher's z transformation.

Table 4.2 Standard Errors of Measurement of Additional Index Scores for Ages 4:0 to 7:7

Index Score	4:0–4:5	4:6–4:11	5:0–5:5	5:6–5:11	6:0–6:5	6:6–6:11	7:0–7:7	4:0–7:7 (overall)
Gc-K0	3.67	3.97	3.67	3.97	4.24	4.24	3.97	3.67
Gc-VL	3.35	3.35	3.35	3.35	3.97	3.67	3.51	3.35
Gf-Verbal	3.00	3.35	3.35	3.35	3.67	3.67	3.41	3.00
WKI	3.97	3.97	3.97	3.97	4.24	4.50	4.11	3.97
CRGI	3.67	3.35	3.67	3.67	4.24	3.97	3.77	3.67
CVI	2.60	2.60	2.60	2.60	3.00	3.00	2.74	2.60
CEI	3.67	3.67	3.35	3.67	3.97	3.97	3.72	3.67

Note. WKI = Word Knowledge Index, CRGI = Concept Recognition and Generation Index, CVI = Comprehensive Verbal Index, CEI = Complex Expressive Index.

group and for the 4:0 to 7:7 age band. Each additional index score is then described in turn.

CHC-Based Additional Index Scores (Ages 4:0 to 7:7 only) Based upon expert classification of the WPPSI-IV subtests, development of prior index scores designed to measure CHC-based narrow abilities, and our own clinical judgment, three additional index scores were created as measures of CHC-based narrow abilities. The CHC-based index scores are designed to provide measures of narrow abilities within

Gc that are not captured in the purer sense by the primary index scores. The CHC-based index scores include Gc-K0, Gc-VL, and Gf-Verbal.

Gc-K0 is available for ages 4:0 to 7:7. It is derived from Information and Comprehension. It is based on two subtests that primarily measure the broad Gc ability, and the narrow Gc ability of general information, defined as the range of general knowledge. It is based on the Gc-K0 clinical cluster score developed by Flanagan and Kaufman (2009).

Gc-VL is available for ages 4:0 to 7:7. It is derived from Vocabulary, Receptive Vocabulary, and Picture Naming. It is based on three subtests that primarily measure the broad Gc ability, and the narrow Gc ability of lexical knowledge. Lexical knowledge is defined as knowledge of word meanings.

Gf-Verbal is available for ages 4:0 to 7:7. It is derived from Similarities and Comprehension. It is based on two subtests that primarily measure the broad Gc ability. However, they also require use of the narrow Gf ability of induction, or inductive reasoning, with verbal stimuli. It is based on the Gf-Verbal clinical cluster score developed by Flanagan and Kaufman (2009).

Neuropsychologically Based Additional Index Scores (Ages 4:0 to 7:7 Only) Based upon a review of neuropsychological literature, additional index scores were created as measures of processes of interest in typical neuropsychological evaluations. The neuropsychologically based index scores are designed to provide measures of neuropsychological processes that are not summarized by the index scores available on the published test. These index scores include the Word Knowledge Index and the Concept Recognition and Generation Index.

Within the domain of language functions, we created the *Word Knowledge Index*, an index score designed to summarize word knowledge. It is available for ages 4:0 to 7:7. It is derived from Vocabulary and Picture Naming. Word knowledge is defined as the ability to know the meaning of words (Miller & Maricle, 2012). We did not include Receptive Vocabulary in the Word Knowledge Index, as it is best classified as a measure of receptive language rather than oral expression.

Within the domain of executive functions, the *Concept Recognition and Generation Index* was created to summarize concept recognition and generation. It is available for ages 4:0 to 7:7. It is derived from Similarities and Picture Concepts. Concept recognition and generation is defined as the process of classifying objects or pictures into groups that share a common attribute (Miller & Maricle, 2012).

Practically Based Index Scores (Ages 4:0 to 7:7 Only) Based upon a review of the WPPSI-IV test model and factor analysis results, additional practically based index scores were created to meet specific clinical needs and complement the published index scores. These index scores are the Comprehensive Verbal Index and the Complex Expressive Index.

The *Comprehensive Verbal Index* is an index score designed to provide a counterpart to the Nonverbal Index for ages 4:0 to 7:7. The Nonverbal Index is new to the Wechsler scales, and no counterpart index derived from tasks that involve expressive demands is available within the WPPSI-IV complement of scores. The Verbal Comprehension Index and the Vocabulary Acquisition Index are based on two subtests and have different clinical purposes. Hence, no difference comparisons are available with the Nonverbal Index in the published WPPSI-IV manuals. The Comprehensive Verbal Index was created to provide a comprehensive measure of a wide variety of abilities primarily requiring verbal expression, including crystallized knowledge; verbal expression, concept formation, and conceptualization; abstract reasoning; categorical and associative thinking; word/lexical knowledge; vocabulary development; learning; and practical knowledge and judgment.

The Comprehensive Verbal Index is derived from Information, Similarities, Vocabulary, and Comprehension. These four subtests emerged on a nested subfactor within the Verbal Comprehension factor in the ages 4:0 to 7:7 confirmatory factor analysis. The remainder of the Verbal Comprehension subtests (i.e., Receptive Vocabulary and Picture Naming) loaded on the other nested subfactor, providing construct evidence for the Comprehensive Verbal Index as a broad, complex measure of verbal abilities. The Comprehensive Verbal Index may be useful for children with moderate to severe motor delays or impairments, as many other choices among the composite scores that are relatively broad with respect to content (e.g., the Full Scale IQ, the Nonverbal Index, and the General Ability Index) require motor responses. The Comprehensive Verbal Index additionally may have some applications for children with visual impairment, although the picture items for each subtest are problematic if they are included in the items administered.

The *Complex Expressive Index* is an index score designed to provide a measure of complex verbal expression. It is available for ages 4:0 to 7:7 and is derived from Vocabulary and Comprehension. The subtests that contribute to the Verbal Comprehension Index, Information and Similarities, require simpler and briefer expressive responses relative to Vocabulary and Comprehension. The Complex Expressive Index can be compared with the Verbal Comprehension Index to provide information about the child's development of relatively more complex oral expression skills.

STEP-BY-STEP WPPSI-IV SCORE ANALYSIS TO INFORM INTERPRETATION

The score analysis approach in this book is grounded in five principles:

1. Interpretation relies on both normative-based and intrapersonal-based understanding of intellectual ability.
2. Composite scores are the primary level of analysis, because they are the most reliable and comprehensive representatives of the child's performance.
3. Examination of the composing parts helps to clarify the meaning of the whole. Just as understanding item-level performance clarifies subtest-level results, understanding subtest-level performance clarifies index-level results.
4. Interpretation should be flexible to the real constraints and problems in testing situations. For example, if one composite score cannot be obtained, other information remains that can shed light on the child's intellectual abilities.
5. A single score never should be used alone to make decisions about a child. Test results should be used to generate hypotheses about the child's intellectual abilities and should be integrated with information obtained from a variety of other sources, including the referral question; psychosocial, medical, and educational background and history; cultural and linguistic background; testing session behaviors and observations; and other results drawn from an appropriate battery of instruments. It is recommended that other sources of information be used to corroborate test results when making inferences about the child's abilities, strengths, and needs.

The approach facilitates interpretive case formulations from varied theoretical and clinical perspectives. In this book and the accompanying CD, we offer additional scores or data according to the primary theoretical orientation used by the practitioner, and according to the referral question. We agree with Kamphaus and colleagues' thesis (Kamphaus, Winsor, Rowe, & Kim, 2012) that test design should occur based on a strong theoretical foundation. Development of the WPPSI–IV was not guided by a single theory, because such an approach could limit the measure for a number of reasons. Intellectual theories are in the process of evolving, so they are by definition incomplete and imperfect in their conceptualization. As an example, CHC theory and terminology has evolved considerably over its existence, and its development is projected to continue (Schneider & McGrew, 2012). In addition to theory, clinical and practical utility is another important consideration that guides test development and should also guide interpretation. At the genesis of the Wechsler intelligence scales, David

Wechsler provided scores for both verbal and nonverbal ability, in addition to the Full Scale IQ. He observed that both scores were clinically and practically useful and essential. This approach was contrary to the predominant thinking of the day, as it went beyond the provision of a single score to describe general intellectual ability. Excluding clinical and practical utility from consideration during development may lead to missing key aspects of the child's ability, and to measuring aspects that are less relevant to the child's everyday functioning. This step-by-step approach to score analysis was developed with these guiding principles in mind.

Step 1a. Select the Appropriate Global Composite Score to Describe Overall Intellectual Ability

Three global composite scores are available for the WPPSI-IV: the Full Scale IQ, the Nonverbal Index, and the General Ability Index. Each may be appropriate to describe overall intellectual ability, depending on the clinical situation and the purpose of the evaluation.

The Full Scale IQ is the most comprehensive and reliable of all of the global scores. A large body of research accrued across 75 years supports its predictive validity and clinical utility. Unless there is a compelling reason to deviate, the Full Scale IQ is the default global score of choice.

The Nonverbal Index is appropriate and informative in a number of situations. If the child is an English language learner and can comprehend subtest instructions in English, the Nonverbal Index is the global score of choice. It is important to note that the Nonverbal Index is not language free but should be described as language reduced because it still requires the child to comprehend English subtest instructions. A good evaluation of children from diverse linguistic backgrounds incorporates the methods described by Ortiz et al. (2012) rather than relying on the Nonverbal Index alone.

The Nonverbal Index is the most informative global composite if a diagnosis of intellectual disability is already established, but a diagnosis of language disorder is under consideration. The *Diagnostic and Statistical Manual of Mental Disorders*, fifth edition (*DSM-5*; American Psychiatric Association, 2013) recommends that a nonverbal ability score be compared with language scores to establish that the language impairments are in excess of the child's intellectual limitations to establish a diagnosis of language disorder.

The Nonverbal Index might also be selected when conducting intellectual ability assessment of a child with language impairment when seeking to establish a diagnosis of intellectual disability or to identify a cognitive developmental delay. If total raw scores of 0 are obtained on both of the Verbal Comprehension subtests that contribute to the Full Scale IQ due to receptive and expressive language impairments, the Full Scale IQ cannot be computed. In this situation, the Nonverbal Index might be used to determine presence of intellectual disability or cognitive developmental delay. The classification accuracy of the Nonverbal Index is similar to that of the Full Scale IQ, making it a viable option for such purposes (see Chapter 7 of this book).

Other situations are less clear-cut. Initial evaluations where both intellectual disability and language disorder are possibilities might be best conducted through reporting the Full Scale IQ *and* the Nonverbal Index. A number of conditions in the *DSM-5* require use of a score that summarizes nonverbal ability. Becoming familiar with the diagnostic criteria of all disorders under consideration will help you to select accordingly.

Evaluations of children with autism spectrum disorder present a number of situations where selection of the global composite score may be challenging. Depending on the referral question and degree of language impairment, the Full Scale IQ, the Nonverbal Index, or the General Ability Index may be most descriptive and useful. Several examples follow.

When evaluating for specific learning disorder in a child with an established diagnosis of autism spectrum disorder with significant accompanying language impairment, the language impairment can result in decreased differences between the Full Scale IQ and the achievement scores. In this situation, the Nonverbal Index may be useful if an ability–achievement discrepancy is required by the local education agency and the use of the Nonverbal Index is permitted. On the other hand, if significant language impairment is not present and the primary index scores are relatively consistent, perhaps with weaknesses in Fluid Reasoning and Working Memory, the Full Scale IQ may be more appropriate because the weaknesses are less characteristic of the disorder in general and more specific to the child. However, for many of these children, the Processing Speed Index is a significant intrapersonal weakness. The General Ability Index may be the most appropriate choice for an ability–achievement discrepancy in this situation.

Some gifted advocates assert that the General Ability Index, an estimate of overall ability with reduced emphasis on working memory and processing speed, is an acceptable score to use in gifted program evaluations (National Association for Gifted Children, 2010; Rimm, Gilman, & Silverman, 2008). There are indications that this is reasonable when using the WPPSI-IV. In particular, recent research suggests that processing speed can improve when children who are intellectually gifted receive proper gifted education (Duan, Shi, & Zhou, 2010; see the section on Children With Intellectual Giftedness in Chapter 7 of this book for more discussion). For this reason, the General Ability Index may better represent intellectual ability in the application process for gifted education programs if the Processing Speed Index is lower than the mean of the primary index scores (MIS) at a significant and unusual level, or if Bug Search (or the subtest being substituted for Bug Search) is lower than the mean scaled score of the primary index subtests (MSS-I) at a significant and unusual level. The Full Scale IQ is also informative in this situation if the evaluation serves other purposes, such as appropriateness of placement in accelerated educational programs (e.g., honors, enriched, or advanced placement), because it has been found to be more predictive of academic achievement than has the General Ability Index (Rowe et al., 2010).

The General Ability Index is also recommended as the global score for comparison with other cognitive functions (e.g., achievement, memory, or executive functions) for children with a variety of other neurodevelopmental disorders characterized by working memory and/or processing speed deficits. The deficits associated with these disorders (e.g., specific learning disorders, ADHD, language disorders, and autism spectrum disorder) could obscure important differences between ability and those other areas. In these situations, the General Ability Index may reveal meaningful differences that are obscured when the Full Scale IQ is used as the global comparison score.

Rapid References 4.1 and 4.2 list several examples of appropriate uses of the Nonverbal Index and the General Ability Index.

≡ Rapid Reference 4.1

Examples of Appropriate Uses of the Nonverbal Index

- Intellectual ability assessment of a child with low cognitive ability *and* expressive language issues. In this situation, use the Nonverbal Index to determine presence of intellectual disability or cognitive developmental delay.
- Differential diagnosis of language disorder that is in excess of intellectual limitations: Compare the Nonverbal Index with Language Scores.
- Establishing comorbidity of intellectual disability and language disorder.
- Intellectual ability assessment of a child who is an English language learner and can comprehend spoken instructions in English.
- Differential diagnosis between autism spectrum disorder and intellectual disability.
- Establishing comorbidity of autism spectrum disorder and intellectual disability.
- Establishing diagnosis of a specific learning disorder in a child with autism spectrum disorder and significant accompanying language impairment, if an ability–achievement discrepancy is required by the local education agency. Also consider using the Visual Spatial Index or the Fluid Reasoning Index if more pervasive intellectual deficits are present across primary index scores other than the Verbal Comprehension Index.

≡ Rapid Reference 4.2

Examples of Appropriate Uses of the General Ability Index

- Intellectual ability assessment of a child for gifted program admissions evaluations. May also report with the Full Scale IQ if admission to accelerated (e.g., honors, advance placement, enriched) educational programs is also under consideration.
- If an ability–achievement discrepancy is required by a local education agency, and working memory and processing speed are lowered due to the likely presence of a specific learning disorder.
- If an ability–achievement discrepancy is required by a local education agency to establish specific learning disability classification, and working memory and processing speed are lowered due to comorbid ADHD or autism spectrum disorder (without significant accompanying language impairments).

Step 1b. Report and Describe the Global Composite Score

Qualitative descriptors characterize the level of performance relative to the child's same-aged peers. The traditional qualitative descriptions appear in Table 6.3 of the *Technical and Interpretive Manual* and are listed in Rapid Reference 4.3.

Varied other classification systems for the composite scores exist. All of these systems attempt to place the scores in context relative to the normative sample. We propose an alternate system in Rapid Reference 4.4 that contains structure that is more parallel, and eliminates descriptors that are easily confused with other terms.

≡ Rapid Reference 4.3

Traditional Descriptors of Composite Scores

Composite Score Range	Descriptor
130 and higher	Very Superior
120–129	Superior
110–119	High Average
90–119	Average
80–89	Low Average
70–79	Borderline
69 and lower	Extremely Low

Source: Adapted from Table 6.3 of the WPPSI-IV *Technical and Interpretive Manual.*

≋ Rapid Reference 4.4

Proposed Alternate Composite Score Descriptors

Composite Score Range	Qualitative Descriptor
130 and higher	Extremely High
120–129	Very High
110–119	High
90–109	Average
80–89	Low
70–79	Very Low
69 and lower	Extremely Low

This alternate system is reflected on the WPPSI-IV tab of the *WPPSI-IV Interpretive Assistant 1.0.*

Create a table to report the selected measure of overall intellectual ability. This table will also be used to report the selected index scores at Step 2. Appendix A on the CD that accompanies this book includes a sample table for this purpose. The table should contain columns for the composite score name, standard score, percentile rank, confidence interval, and qualitative descriptive classification.

Transfer the values for the standard score, percentile rank, and confidence interval from the Record Form summary page, being sure to note below the table the confidence level (i.e., 90% or 95%) upon which the confidence intervals were based. The scoring assistant on Q-global can also be used to generate this information.

If you enter the selected global composite score in the WPPSI-IV Interpretive Assistant 1.0 on the WPPSI-IV tab, the program provides the percentile ranks based on the theoretical normal curve, and the qualitative descriptors from the alternate system proposed in this book (see Rapid Reference 4.5). All selected composite scores from Steps 2 and 3 may be entered on this tab to generate similar information.

After you have listed the selected score(s) in the table, you will need to provide paragraphs that describe the score(s). If you are reporting both the Full Scale IQ and the General Ability Index, provide the descriptions of both scores. The necessary descriptions of each global composite score appear in the first sections of this chapter.

Step 2a. Report and Describe the Cognitive Proficiency Index for Ages 4:0 to 7:7 (Perform Step 2 Only If the General Ability Index Was Selected as the Global Score; Otherwise, Proceed to Step 3)

The Cognitive Proficiency Index is available for ages 4:0 to 7:7 only. It provides an estimate of cognitive information processing efficiency. Working memory and processing speed subtests contribute to the Cognitive Proficiency Index. These abilities are related because quick processing speed facilitates information processing before decay from working memory occurs (Wechsler, 2012). On the other hand, slow processing speed ability results in slower information processing and additional opportunity for decay of that information from memory. The Cognitive Proficiency Index is most useful in the context of a pairwise difference comparison with the General Ability Index.

If you are reporting the Cognitive Proficiency Index, transfer the appropriate information from the Record Form Ancillary Analysis page into the table you created to report composite scores, using the same procedure as was used for the global composite scores. The scoring assistant on Q-global can also be used to generate this information. If you enter the Cognitive Proficiency Index on the WPPSI-IV tab of the WPPSI-IV Interpretive Assistant 1.0, the program provides analogous information to that given for the global composite scores.

Step 2b. If the General Ability Index Was Selected as the Global Score, Evaluate Pairwise Discrepancy Comparisons With the Full Scale IQ (2:6 to 7:7) and the Cognitive Proficiency Index (4:0 to 7:7 Only)

The General Ability Index–Full Scale IQ comparison is available for ages 2:6 to 7:7, and the General Ability Index–Cognitive Proficiency Index comparison is available for ages 4:0 to 7:7. To evaluate the differences between the General Ability Index and the Full Scale IQ, and the General Ability Index and the Cognitive Proficiency Index, use the Ancillary Analysis page of the Record Form or the WPPSI-IV scoring assistant on Q-global.

Copy the composite scores from the Sum of Scaled Scores to Index Score Conversion table (about halfway down the page) into the Pairwise Difference Comparisons table, in the appropriate boxes within the columns labeled *Score 1* and *Score 2*. Subtract Score 2 from Score 1 and record the difference with its appropriate sign (+ or −) in the Difference column.

Examine the differences for statistical significance and frequency of occurrence in the normative sample. The critical values and base rates for pairwise difference comparisons are provided in Tables D.4 and D.5 of the *Technical and Interpretive Manual*. Table D.4 provides the relevant critical values for both comparisons at the .01, .05, .10, and .15 significance levels, by age group and age band. We recommend using the age group rather than the age band, to allow the child's results to be compared with his or her same-age peers and to avoid unnecessary aggregation of data that may obscure focal age-related differences. Table D.5 provides the base rate information, by overall sample and by General Ability Index ability level.

In Table D.4, locate the age group or age band of the child and the selected significance level for the critical value. Read across the row to the columns that correspond to the score comparisons, and record these values in the column labeled *Critical Value*. If the absolute value of the difference is greater than or equal to the critical value, the difference is statistically significant. For each value, circle *Y* or *N* in the column labeled Significant Difference. Statistically significant differences occur frequently in both normative samples and in clinical populations (Lichtenberger & Kaufman, 2004; Sattler, 2008).

For each value that is statistically significant, report the base rate of the difference. Use Table D.5 to determine how rare the child's difference scores are within the normative sample. First, select the reference group (i.e., Overall Sample or Ability Level), then turn to the appropriate page of the table according to that selection. Ensure that if you are using Ability Level as the reference group, you refer to the General Ability Index and not the Full Scale IQ. Note the columns are separated into − and + columns, based on the direction of the difference. Record the appropriate base rate value in the *Base Rate* column.

Hypotheses: If the General Ability Index–Full Scale IQ difference is statistically significant and unusual, the influence of working memory and processing speed on intellectual ability may have resulted in a difference in the child's overall performance. If the General Ability Index–Cognitive Proficiency Index difference is statistically significant and unusual, general ability and cognitive proficiency may not be commensurate (Wechsler, 2012).

Step 3a. Select the Index Scores (Specific Composite Scores)

We strongly recommend reporting all available primary index scores, because they are derived based on the factor analysis that specifies the latent traits measured by the test. A vast array of other evidence supports their validity and clinical utility. They permit description of discrete cognitive abilities that cannot be differentiated by reporting a global composite score.

Primary index score interpretation is shaped by your theoretical orientation. The descriptions of the primary index scores that appear in previous sections of this chapter facilitate conceptualization of performance from the perspective of CHC, Lurian, or school neuropsychology perspectives. For example, if your theoretical orientation is CHC theory, you might describe the Visual Spatial Index as a measure of Gf, especially visualization and closure speed, but if you are using a neuropsychological approach, you may conceptualize it as measuring neuro-psychological constructs including visual–motor construction, problem solving, cognitive flexibility, reasoning, and planning.

Your theoretical orientation may also support the use of some of the additional index scores in this book and on the accompanying CD. For example, if you conceptualize performance using CHC theory, you may wish to administer the additional index scores described in prior sections of this chapter that provide measures of the CHC constructs.

Finally, the referral question and clinical situation may call for use of other index scores. For example, if you are using the WPPSI-IV within a battery to establish the presence of a language disorder in a child with low cognitive ability, you may wish to administer the subtests necessary to obtain the Vocabulary Acquisition Index to obtain a measure of verbal ability with fewer expressive requirements than those of the Verbal Comprehension Index. The Complex Expressive Index may also be of interest in this situation, to provide a measure of verbal ability with comparably greater expressive requirements so that a contin-uum of index scores involving verbal ability can be examined. All selected index scores are reported and described in Step 3b.

Step 3b. Report and Describe the Index Scores

In the same table you created to report the global composite score for overall intellectual ability, include the selected index scores. List the index score name, standard score, percentile rank, confidence interval, and qualitative descriptive classification. Transfer the figures for the standard score, percentile rank, and confidence interval from the Record Form summary page. Use the qualitative descriptors listed in Step 1b.

If you select any of the additional index scores in this book, use the WPPSI-IV Interpretive Assistant 1.0 to enter the appropriate subtest scaled scores on the WPPSI-IV tab. Tab 3b automatically calculates each additional index score for which all of the necessary subtest scaled scores are present.

After you have listed the selected score(s) in the table for your report, provide paragraphs that describe the index score(s). This chapter provides the necessary descriptions of each index score in the Understanding the Composite Scores section. A thorough interpretation may also involve investigation of the relations between the building blocks of the index scores (i.e., the subtest scaled scores; see Step 8).

An extreme discrepancy between the two subtests that contribute to an index score indicates that the score is a summary of diverse abilities. It does not indicate the index score is invalid, unreliable, or should not be interpreted. Describe the index score as a summary of diverse abilities, understand the subtest scaled scores that contribute to that index score, and interpret discrepancies based on that index score with caution. Details about pairwise subtest comparisons are provided in Step 8.

Step 4. Report and Describe the Subtest Scaled Scores

The subtest scaled scores are essential because they are the basic building blocks that constitute all other scores. Interpretation of composite score performance is enhanced by understanding those basic building blocks. Furthermore, subtest scaled scores should be reported because they are scaled by age, and therefore have the same meaning for any subtest at any age, on any Wechsler intelligence scale. Most practitioners list the subtest scaled scores before the index scores and the Full Scale IQ in their intellectual ability reports for this reason.

Qualitative descriptors for subtests are not included in our score analysis approach. The range of subtest scaled scores (1 to 19) does not allow for fine discrimination between scores when they are converted to percentile ranks. For those practitioners who wish to include qualitative descriptors for subtests, examples of subtest qualitative descriptor systems appear in Sattler (2008).

Create a table to report and describe the subtest scaled scores. Appendix A on the CD that accompanies this book includes a sample table for this purpose. The table should contain columns for the subtest name, subtest scaled score, and percentile rank in a theoretical normal distribution. If you enter the subtest scaled scores on the WPPSI-IV tab of the WPPSI-IV Interpretive Assistant 1.0, the program provides the percentile ranks based on the theoretical normal distribution.

You may also use Table 6.1 in the *Technical and Interpretive Manual* to look up the percentile ranks that correspond to each scaled score. For each subtest, read down the first column to locate the scaled score, then read across the row to the percentile rank equivalent column to locate the corresponding percentile rank equivalent. Record this value in the table. The scoring assistant on Q-global also can be used to generate this information automatically.

Step 5a. Select the Index-Level Strengths and Weaknesses Comparison Score

Intraindividual strengths and weaknesses comparisons provide useful information and minimize the likelihood of Type I error relative to several pairwise comparisons (Grégoire, Coalson, & Zhu, 2011; Longman, 2004; Naglieri & Paolitto, 2005). Strengths and weaknesses are identified by comparing the index scores with some indicator of overall index-level performance.

Ideally, the indicator of overall index-level performance (i.e., comparison score) should involve each of the cognitive ability domains represented by the selected measure of overall intellectual ability. If a primary index score is significantly greater than the comparison score it may represent an intrapersonal cognitive strength, and if it is significantly less it may represent an intrapersonal cognitive weakness.

Comparison Score Options When the Full Scale IQ Is Selected as the Global Measure of Performance

You generally should select the most comprehensive and relevant score as your basis for comparison when determining intrapersonal strengths and weaknesses. Your comparison score typically should be the mean of all primary index scores provided in the published test (abbreviated *MIS*) if all primary index scores are present. The selection of the Full Scale IQ as the comparison score is not recommended when all primary index scores are available, because the mean of all primary index scores is based on more subtests and therefore offers a broader sample of index-level performance.

In some situations, the mean of the primary index scores is not available and another comparison score must be selected. For example, you may choose not to administer all primary index subtests, a subtest could be invalid due to administration errors, or the child may have motor difficulties that preclude administration of some subtests (e.g., Block Design). Because substitution and proration are not possible for the primary index scores, a missing score for any of the primary index score subtests precludes use of the mean primary index score as the basis for comparison.

The Full Scale IQ is provided as an alternate comparison score in the published test, in the event that not all primary index scores are calculated. The Full Scale IQ is a good alternative to the mean of the three primary index scores for ages 2:6 to 3:11, because only one subtest differentiates it from the full set of primary index subtests. If a child aged 4:0 to 7:7 is missing a primary index score, more options are available. The Full Scale IQ also is available in the published test as an alternate comparison score for ages 4:0 to 7:7. In some situations, a mean of four primary index scores may be preferable to the Full Scale IQ as a comparison score. For example, if the Verbal Comprehension Index and Full Scale IQ cannot be derived in an evaluation of a 5-year-old child who is an English language learner, the mean of the other four primary index scores could be selected as the comparison score. This would allow for comparisons between the Visual Spatial Index, Fluid Reasoning Index, Working Memory Index, and Processing Speed Index to the mean of those four primary index scores.

The WPPSI-IV Interpretive Assistant 1.0 recommends the comparison score that is based on the largest sample of performance on Step 5a2-3. The program automatically calculates the mean of all primary index scores when all are entered on the WPPSI-IV tab for ages 2:6 to 7:7. If one of the primary index scores is missing for ages 4:0 to 7:7, the program allows you to compare the remaining four primary index score to their corresponding mean. Five different mean comparison scores based on four of the five primary index scores (abbreviated *MIS-4A*, *B*, *C*, *D*, and *E*; see Rapid Reference 4.5) are available on the CD that accompanies this book. They differ only based on which one of the five primary index scores is missing. Step 5a4-7 of the WPPSI-IV Interpretive Assistant 1.0 calculates the appropriate mean of four primary index scores as an alternate comparison score to serve as a basis for evaluating intrapersonal strengths and weaknesses. If the Full Scale IQ is available and desired as a comparison score, an evaluation of intrapersonal strengths and weaknesses at the index level is performed using

≡ *Rapid Reference 4.5*

Abbreviations and Composition of Comparison Scores Based on the Mean of Four Primary Index Scores for Ages 4:0 to 7:7

Comparison Score Abbreviation	Missing Primary Index Score	Primary Index Scores Included in the Mean for Comparison Score
MIS-4A	VCI	VSI, FRI, WMI, and PSI
MIS-4B	VSI	VCI, FRI, WMI, and PSI
MIS-4C	FRI	VCI, VSI, WMI, and PSI
MIS-4D	WMI	VCI, VSI, FRI, and PSI
MIS-4E	PSI	VCI, VSI, FRI, and WMI

Note. MIS-4 = Mean of four primary index scores; VCI = Verbal Comprehension Index; VSI = Visual Spatial Index; FRI = Fluid Reasoning Index; WMI = Working Memory Index; PSI = Processing Speed Index.

relevant sections of the Record Form and corresponding tables in appendices of the *Administration and Scoring Manual*.

Rapid Reference 4.5 lists the missing primary index score associated with the practical need to use a different comparison score, as well as the four primary scores included in the calculation of each of the mean of four primary index scores.

Comparison Score Options If the Nonverbal Index Is Selected as the Global Measure of Performance (Ages 4:0 to 7:7 Only)

For ages 2:6 to 3:11, if you selected the Nonverbal Index as the global measure, the only possible pairwise primary index-level comparison to clarify interpretation of intrapersonal strengths and weaknesses is the comparison of the Visual Spatial Index and the Working Memory Index. If you selected the Nonverbal Index as the global intelligence score for a child aged 4:0 to 7:7, additional comparisons may be available. If the four primary index scores represented in the Nonverbal Index (i.e., Visual Spatial Index, Fluid Reasoning Index, Working Memory Index, and Processing Speed Index) are available, consider using the mean of those four primary index scores, labeled *MIS-4A*, as the comparison score. It is automatically calculated, when recommended, on Step 5a4-7 of the WPPSI-IV Interpretive Assistant 1.0. These comparisons may be especially helpful for referrals with probable language issues that interfere with performance, such as children who are English language learners or are diagnosed with an autism spectrum disorder with language impairment.

Comparison Score Option If the General Ability Index Is Selected as the Global Measure of Performance (Ages 4:0 to 7:7 Only)

For ages 2:6 to 3:11, if you selected the General Ability Index as the global measure, the only possible pairwise primary index-level comparison to clarify interpretation of the global score is the comparison of the Verbal Comprehension Index and the Visual Spatial Index. However, if you selected the General Ability Index for a child aged 4:0 to 7:7 and its contributing primary index scores (i.e., Verbal Comprehension Index, Visual Spatial Index, and Fluid Reasoning Index) are available, consider using the mean of those three primary index scores (MIS-G) as the comparison score to clarify General Ability Index interpretation and to provide additional information about the child's intrapersonal cognitive strengths and weaknesses. It is automatically calculated, when recommended, on Step 5a4-7 of the WPPSI-IV Interpretive Assistant 1.0.

Step 5b. Evaluate Index-Level Strengths and Weaknesses Comparisons

It is crucial to ground interpretation of the index-level strengths and weaknesses in the context of Step 3, where the ranges in which the index scores fell were described in relation to the normative sample as extremely high, very high, high, average, low, very low, and extremely low. At this step, use interpretive statements that refer to both the normative performance and the intrapersonal strengths and weaknesses analysis to avoid confusing those who read your report. For example, if the Verbal Comprehension Index is described as falling in the average range relative to the normative sample at Step 3b, but is an intrapersonal strength relative to the comparison score, use a statement such as, "Lisa's Verbal Comprehension ability is average compared to other children her age, but it is one of her personal areas of cognitive strength."

It is typical to have some areas of strength and weakness across intellectual ability domains. A significant strength or weakness relative to an overall indicator of performance is a normal occurrence and should not be taken as a sign of pathology or abnormality. In fact, 69.5% of children in the WPPSI-IV normative sample (i.e., $N = 1,182$ of 1,700) have at least one primary index score that is different than the mean of all primary index scores at the .05 significance level. This percentage is nearly identical among children in the WPPSI-IV special group study samples, 71.7% (i.e., $N = 499$ of 696). (These analyses were conducted for this book by the authors.)

The source materials used to evaluate the index-level strengths and weaknesses vary depending on the selected comparison score. If you selected the mean of all primary index scores (MIS) or the Full Scale IQ, you will use the Record Form and the tables in the *Administration and Scoring Manual* or the scoring assistant on Q-global.

Comparison Score Selected Is the Mean of All Primary Index Scores (MIS) or Full Scale IQ

If you selected the mean of all primary index scores (MIS) or the Full Scale IQ as the comparison score, use the scoring assistant on Q-global or the Primary Analysis page of the Record Form to examine the differences for statistical significance and frequency of occurrence in the normative sample. Copy the primary index scores from the Summary page to the upper panel of the Strengths and Weaknesses table that is labeled *Index-Level*, in the appropriate boxes within the column labeled *Score*. Then, copy the comparison score to the Strengths and Weaknesses table column labeled *Comparison Score*. Subtract the Comparison Score from the Score and record the difference with its appropriate sign (+ or −) in the Difference column.

The critical values and base rates for comparisons of each primary index score with two indicators of overall performance, the mean of all primary index scores and the Full Scale IQ, are provided in Tables B.1 and B.2 of the *Administration and Scoring Manual*. Table B.1 provides the values at the .01, .05, .10, and .15 significance levels. Use the appropriate table, locate the age group or age band of the child, and find the selected significance level for the critical value. Read across the row to the columns that correspond to the score comparisons, and record these values in the column labeled *Critical Value*. If the absolute value of the difference is greater than or equal to the critical value, the difference is statistically significant. For each significant value, use the sign of the difference to determine if the primary index score represents an intrapersonal strength or weakness, and circle *S* or *W* in the column labeled *Strength or Weakness*.

For each value that is statistically significant, you should also report the base rate of the difference. Use Table B.2 to determine how rare the child's difference scores are within the normative sample. Note the columns are separated into − and + columns, based on the sign of the difference. Not every value appears in the table; only the values corresponding with 1%, 2%, 5%, 10%, or 25%. If the child's difference score appears in the appropriate column of the table, record the corresponding percentage. If the child's difference score does not appear in the table, record a range of percentages corresponding to the two closest scores that are reported in the table. The scoring assistant on Q-global can be used to provide similar values automatically.

Comparison Score Selected Is a Mean of Four Primary Index Scores (an MIS-4) or Three Primary Index Scores (the MIS-G)

Use the Step5b4-7 tab of the WPPSI-IV Interpretive Assistant 1.0 if the mean of four index scores is selected as a global comparison score for a child aged 4:0 to 7:7. This tab is also used for score comparisons between primary index scores that contribute to the General Ability Index and their corresponding mean (MIS-G). The program permits you to select between the .01 or .05 significance levels. Differences between the primary index scores and the comparison scores are calculated automatically, using the selected critical values. The worksheet indicates if the obtained score differences are statistically significant strengths or weaknesses in the S or W column.

The program also provides the base rate information for differences between the relevant primary index scores and the comparison score. The base rate data is calculated bidirectionally. Using the base rate provided, you can determine how rare that difference was in the normative sample. Practitioners commonly describe 10% to 15% as rare levels of occurrence.

Step 6a. Select the Subtest-Level Strengths and Weaknesses Comparison Score(s)

Subtest-level performance may be examined for intra-individual strengths and weaknesses to clarify interpretation of a composite or of a specific ability. In this procedure, the subtest scaled scores are compared to an indicator of overall subtest-level performance (i.e., comparison score). As at the index level, these comparisons provide useful information and minimize the likelihood of Type I error relative to multiple pairwise comparisons, and can assist with understanding and explaining composite-level performance. It is typical to have some areas of strength and weakness across subtest performance. The result obtained from a single subtest should not be used as the sole criteria for a clinical decision.

The comparison score you select for subtest-level strengths and weaknesses comparisons will vary based on the clinical and practical situation. If the purpose is to clarify interpretation of the global composite score you selected, your choice may be influenced by that selection. It can also be affected by the number of subtests that are available in a given clinical situation.

If all primary index subtests are available, you should use the mean of all primary index subtests (abbreviated *MSS-I* in the published test) as the comparison score, because it is based on the broadest sample of performance. If one or more of the primary index subtests are missing, however, you may wish to use the mean of all Full Scale IQ subtests in the published test (MSS-F).

Other comparison scores are available in this book and the accompanying CD. These comparison scores were derived based on practical needs stemming from global score selection, missing or invalid subtests, or questions about strengths and weaknesses within a particular scale. For example, if the Nonverbal Index or the General Ability Index were selected as the global composite score, you may need to compare subtests that contribute to those composite scores to a mean of the respective subtests' scaled scores. In addition, the need for alternative comparisons may arise due to missing or invalid subtests and the restrictions on subtest substitution for primary index scores. It could be possible to have three valid Verbal Comprehension subtest scores but be unable to derive the Verbal Comprehension Index. In this situation, you might consider using one of the subsets of three verbal comprehension subtests (i.e., MSS-V3A or MSS-V3B) to learn more about performance within that scale.

The clinical situations in which these various comparison scores and strengths and weaknesses analyses may be useful within groups of three or more subtests are listed in Rapid Reference 4.6, by age band. Rapid Reference 4.6 also provides the appropriate tables in the *Administration and Scoring Manual* or tabs of the WPPSI-IV Interpretive Assistant 1.0 to use to obtain the relevant comparison score.

≡ Rapid Reference 4.6

Subtest-Level Strengths and Weaknesses Analysis, by Age Band

Clinical Situation	Available Subtests for Analysis	2:6–3:11 Subtests	4:0–7:7 Subtests	Comparison Score	Comparison Score Abbreviation	Location
Reported the Full Scale IQ, and all primary index subtests are available	All primary index subtests	IN, RV, BD, OA, PM, ZL	IN, SI, BD, OA, MR, PC, PM, ZL, BS, CA	The mean scaled score for all primary index subtests	MSS-I	*Administration and Scoring Manual* Tables B.3 and B.4
Reported the Full Scale IQ, and all primary index subtests are not available	All subtests that contribute to the Full Scale IQ	IN, RV, BD, OA, PM	IN, SI, BD, MR, PM, BS	The mean scaled score for the Full Scale IQ subtests	MSS-F	*Administration and Scoring Manual* Tables B.3 and B.4
Reported the Nonverbal Index	All subtests that contribute to the Nonverbal Index	BD, OA, PM, ZL	BD, MR, PC, PM, BS	The mean scaled score for the Nonverbal Index subtests	MSS-N	WPPSI-IV Interpretive Assistant 1.0 Step 6a and b tabs
Reported the General Ability Index	All subtests that contribute to the General Ability Index	IN, RV, BD, OA	IN, SI, BD, MR	The mean scaled score for the General Ability Index subtests	MSS-G	WPPSI-IV Interpretive Assistant 1.0 Step 6a and b tabs

(continued)

Need an in-depth assessment of Verbal Comprehension skills, and all three subtests are available in the Younger Battery	All Verbal Comprehension subtests in Younger Battery	IN, RV, PN	n/a	The mean scaled score for the three Verbal Comprehension subtests that can contribute to Full Scale IQ	MSS-V3Y	WPPSI-IV Interpretive Assistant 1.0 Step 6a and b2-3 tabs
Need an in-depth assessment of Verbal Comprehension skills, and all four subtests are available in the Older Battery	All Verbal Comprehension subtests that can contribute to the Full Scale IQ in Older Battery	n/a	IN, SI, VC, CO	The mean scaled score for the four Verbal Comprehension subtests that can contribute to Full Scale IQ	MSS-V4	WPPSI-IV Interpretive Assistant 1.0 Step 6a and b4-7 tabs
Gave three Verbal Comprehension subtests to a child aged 4:0–7:7, but missing the Verbal Comprehension Index and need an in-depth assessment of Verbal Comprehension skills	Subset A of Verbal Comprehension subtests in Older Battery	n/a	SI, VC, CO (Subset A)	The mean scaled score for three Verbal Comprehension subtests, subset A	MSS-V3A	WPPSI-IV Interpretive Assistant 1.0 Step 6a and b4-7 tabs
Gave three Verbal Comprehension subtests to a child aged 4:0–7:7, but missing the Verbal Comprehension Index and need an in-depth assessment of Verbal Comprehension skills	Subset B of Verbal Comprehension subtests in Older Battery	n/a	IN, VC, CO (Subset B)	The mean scaled score for three Verbal Comprehension subtests, subset B	MSS-V3B	WPPSI-IV Interpretive Assistant 1.0 Step 6a and b4-7 tabs

(continued)

Clinical Situation	Available Subtests for Analysis	2:6–3:11 Subtests	4:0–7:7 Subtests	Comparison Score	Comparison Score Abbreviation	Location
Reported the Gc-VL	All subtests that contribute to the Gc-VL in Older Battery	n/a	VC, RV, PN	The mean scaled score for the three Gc-VL subtests	MSS-VL	WPPSI-IV Interpretive Assistant 1.0 Step 6a and b4-7 tabs
Gave all Processing Speed subtests to a child aged 4:0–7:7 and need an in-depth assessment of Processing Speed skills	All subtests from the Processing Speed scale	n/a	BS, CA, AC	The mean scaled score for the three Processing Speed subtests	MSS-P	WPPSI-IV Interpretive Assistant 1.0 Step 6a and b4-7 tabs

Abbreviations are IN = Information, SI = Similarities, VC = Vocabulary, CO = Comprehension, RV = Receptive Vocabulary, PN = Picture Naming BD = Block Design, OA = Object Assembly, MR = Matrix Reasoning, PC = Picture Concepts, PM = Picture Memory, ZL = Zoo Locations, BS = Bug Search, CA = Cancellation, AC = Animal Coding.

Step 6b. Evaluate Subtest-Level Strengths and Weaknesses

Comparison Scores in the Published Test
If you selected the mean scaled score for all primary index subtests (MSS-I) or the mean scaled score for the Full Scale IQ subtests (MSS-F), the strengths and weaknesses analysis can be performed using the *Administration and Scoring Manual* and the Primary Analysis page of the Record Form. Use the lower panel (Subtest-Level) of the Strengths and Weaknesses table on the Record Form to examine the differences for statistical significance and frequency of the score difference in the normative sample.

Follow the same procedures you followed for the index-level strengths and weaknesses for the scores in the published test. The critical values and base rates for comparisons of each subtest scaled score with the mean scaled score for all primary index subtests and the mean scaled score for the Full Scale IQ subtests are provided in Tables B.3 and B.4 of the *Administration and Scoring Manual*. Table B.3 provides the values at the .01, .05, .10, and .15 significance levels. For each value that is statistically significant, you should also report the base rate of the difference. Use Table B.4 to determine how rare the child's difference scores are within the normative sample, being careful to use the side of the column that reflects the direction of the difference.

Comparison Scores in This Book and on the Accompanying CD
If you selected one of the other comparison scores, use the age-appropriate tab of the WPPSI-IV Interpretive Assistant 1.0 (see Rapid Reference 4.7) to perform the analysis. Follow the same procedures you followed for the index-level strengths and weaknesses for the comparison scores in this book. The program automatically outputs the statistical significance and rarity of the score differences if all required subtests are available.

Step 7. Evaluate Index-Level Pairwise Comparisons

A pairwise comparison between two index scores may be useful to determine if a given area of intellectual functioning is significantly different from that in another area. As with other comparisons, statistically significant differences occur frequently in both normative samples and in clinical populations (Lichtenberger & Kaufman, 2004; Sattler, 2008).

With rare exceptions, it is unnecessary and inappropriate to conduct every pairwise index score comparison that is possible, particularly with children aged 4:0 to 7:7, who have available 10 pairwise comparisons among the five primary index scores. As the number of score comparisons increases, so does the possibility of finding a significant difference that is due to chance, rather than a true difference in performance (Grégoire et al., 2011). If you conduct pairwise comparisons, having a sound and planned rationale for doing so will ease interpretation and decrease the chances of this family-wise Type I error. For example, if assessing a child suspected of preliteracy concerns related to visual–spatial issues, you may wish to compare the Visual Spatial Index and the Working Memory Index with the other primary index scores to understand visual–spatial cognitive ability and visual–spatial working memory in an intrapersonal context with other cognitive domains, and to facilitate treatment/intervention planning.

Exercise good judgment in selecting the significance level for these comparisons, depending on the situation. If you are examining one or two discrepancies that are predictable or not surprising based on the referral question and reported issues, you may wish to select a relatively more lenient significance level. If you are conducting post-hoc comparisons or a greater number of pairwise comparisons, you might select a relatively more stringent significance level. Of course, more stringent levels of significance are typically required for referrals involving high-stakes decision making.

Comparing Index Scores in the Published Test

For comparisons between two published index scores, use the Primary Analysis page to examine the differences between index scores that are of interest. Using this table, examine the differences for statistical significance and frequency of occurrence in the normative sample. Copy the index scores from the Summary page to the upper panel (i.e., Index Level) of the Pairwise Difference Comparisons table, in the appropriate boxes within the columns labeled *Score 1* and *Score 2*. Subtract Score 2 from Score 1 and record the difference with its appropriate sign (+ or −) in the Difference column.

The critical values and base rates for primary index level pairwise difference comparisons are provided in Tables B.5 and B.6 of the *Administration and Scoring Manual*. Table B.5 provides the values at the .01, .05, .10, and .15 significance levels. Using the appropriate table, locate the age group or age band of the child and the selected significance level for the critical value. Read across the row to the columns that correspond to the score comparisons, and record these values in the column labeled *Critical Value*. If the absolute value of the difference is greater than or equal to the critical value, the difference is statistically significant. For each value, circle *Y* or *N* in the column labeled *Significant Difference*.

For each value that is statistically significant, report the base rate of the difference. Use Table B.6 to determine how rare the child's difference scores are within the normative sample. First, select the reference group (i.e., Overall Sample or Ability Level), then turn to the appropriate page of the table according to that selection. Note the columns are separated into − and + columns, based on the direction of the difference. Record the appropriate base rate value in the Base Rate column.

Five specific pairwise comparisons from the published test that are of particular interest are discussed here.

Visual Spatial Index Versus Fluid Reasoning Index (Ages 4:0 to 7:7 Only)   The Visual Spatial Index can be compared with the Fluid Reasoning Index for ages 4:0 to 7:7 to provide information about the child's visual processing compared with his or her fluid reasoning as assessed using primarily visual stimuli. This pairwise difference comparison is available on the Record Form.

Hypothesis: If the Visual Spatial Index is less than the Fluid Reasoning Index, the child may overcome visual-spatial processing limitations on his or her visual problem-solving ability by using verbal mediation (assuming the child has relatively high scores on Gf-Verbal or the Comprehensive Expressive Index) and translating the visual information into verbal information (e.g., mentally or verbally rehearsing the changes across rows of a matrix, such as "Blue square turns to red square, blue circle turns to red circle") or quantitative strategies (e.g., counting the stimuli). If the Visual Spatial Index is greater than the Fluid Reasoning Index, the child may have good concrete visual processing skills, but lower relative ability to utilize them to engage in higher order problem solving (Lichtenberger & Kaufman, 2013), and may benefit from learning visualization or imagery for problem solving.

Visual Spatial Index Versus Working Memory Index   The Visual Spatial Index can be compared with the Working Memory Index to provide information about the child's visual–spatial processing compared with his or her visual and visual–spatial working memory. This pairwise difference comparison is available on the Record Form.

Hypothesis: If the Visual Spatial Index is less than the Working Memory Index, the child may overcome visual–spatial processing limitations when performing visual working memory tasks by using verbal mediation and translating the visual informa-tion into verbal information (e.g., verbally rehearsing an array of objects). If the Visual Spatial Index is greater than the Working Memory Index, the child may have good concrete visual processing skills, but lower relative ability to utilize them in situations where they must maintain distinctions between current and previous information to determine which response is appropriate or relevant at the present time.

Fluid Reasoning Index Versus Working Memory Index (Ages 4:0 to 7:7 Only)   The Fluid Reasoning Index can be compared with the Working Memory Index to provide information about the child's fluid reasoning and working memory abilities, both measured using visual modes of administration. This pairwise difference comparison is available on the Record Form.

Hypothesis: If the Fluid Reasoning Index is less than the Working Memory Index, the child may have relatively weaker visual–spatial problem-solving skills compared with his or her ability to remember distinctions between current and previously presented visual and visual–spatial information. He or she may maintain these distinctions well, but be less able to leverage the information to engage in planful higher order problem solving. If the Fluid Reasoning Index is greater than the Working Memory Index, the child may have good problem-solving abilities, but need greater support maintaining distinctions between current and previously presented visual and visual–spatial information.

Working Memory Index Versus Processing Speed Index (Ages 4:0 to 7:7 Only) The Working Memory Index can be compared with the Processing Speed Index to provide information about the child's visual and visual–spatial working memory compared with his or her processing speed. This pairwise difference comparison is available on the Record Form.

Hypothesis: If the Working Memory Index is less than the Processing Speed Index, the child may have relatively weaker ability to remember distinctions between current and previously presented visual and visual–spatial information, and how it is temporally related, compared with his or her simple perceptual speed where the relevant stimuli remains in the visual field. He or she may process simple information quickly, but be less able to capitalize on that speediness to maintain distinctions between relevant and irrelevant stimuli. If the Working Memory Index is greater than the Processing Speed Index, the child may have stronger ability to maintain distinctions between current and previously presented visual and visual–spatial information to determine which response is appropriate or relevant at the present time, but may be more concerned with accuracy than with speedy response production.

Comparing Index Scores From This Book and the Accompanying CD
Some index-level pairwise comparisons suggested from different theoretical perspectives and for practical purposes can be made using the published index scores and the additional index scores in this book. For these comparisons, use the CD that accompanies this book.

Each pairwise comparison is discussed in turn in the sections that follow. If a comparison involves an index score from this book, it is made using the Step7 tab of the WPPSI-IV Interpretive Assistant 1.0.

Verbal Comprehension Index Versus Complex Expressive Index (Ages 4:0 to 7:7 Only) The Verbal Comprehension Index for ages 4:0 to 7:7 can be compared with the Complex Expressive Index to compare the child's verbal comprehension ability on tasks with different levels of expressive demands, providing a deeper evaluation of the child's oral expression performance on more complex tasks. The WPPSI-IV Interpretive Assistant 1.0 performs the pairwise difference comparisons between these index scores based upon the child's age group and the selected significance level for the critical value. For each statistically significant difference, the program provides the base rate for the score difference in the overall sample.

Hypothesis: If the Verbal Comprehension Index–Complex Expressive Index difference is statistically significant and unusual, performance on tasks with more complex expressive demands may lead to an underestimation of the child's intellectual ability. Depending upon the severity of the difference and the level of the scores (e.g., scores that are significantly different and below average), additional evaluation of speech and language abilities may be warranted.

Nonverbal Index Versus Comprehensive Verbal Index (Ages 4:0 to 7:7 only) The Nonverbal Index (a comprehensive measure of a wide variety of abilities assessed with no expressive demands) can be compared with the Comprehensive Verbal Index (a comprehensive measure of a wide variety of abilities primarily assessed verbally) for ages 4:0 to 7:7. The WPPSI-IV Interpretive Assistant 1.0 performs the pairwise difference comparisons between these index scores based upon the child's age group and the selected significance level for the critical value. For each statistically significant difference, the program provides the base rate for the score difference in the overall sample.

Hypothesis: If the Nonverbal Index–Comprehensive Verbal Index difference is statistically significant and unusual, and the Nonverbal Index is greater than the Comprehensive Verbal Index, the child's ability to fully demonstrate his or her cognitive potential may be limited if measures are limited to those with verbal comprehension or expressive demands. If the Nonverbal Index is less than the Comprehensive Verbal Index, the child's intellectual ability may be stronger on primarily verbal tasks than on tasks with no expressive requirements.

CHC Based: Gc-K0 Versus Gc-VL (Ages 4:0 to 7:7 Only) Gc-K0 can be compared with Gc-VL for ages 4:0 to 7:7 to provide information about the child's factual information knowledge relative to his or her lexical (word) knowledge. The WPPSI-IV Interpretive Assistant 1.0 performs the pairwise difference comparisons between these index scores based upon the child's age group and the selected significance level for the critical value. For each statistically significant difference, the program provides the base rate for the score difference in the overall sample.

Hypothesis: If the Gc-K0–Gc-VL difference is statistically significant and unusual, it may provide insight into emerging difficulties with reading or writing. If Gc-K0 is less than Gc-VL, the child might display poverty of content in writing assignments despite adequate vocabulary, or might have difficulty placing what he or she reads into context, despite adequate decoding and comprehension skills (Lichtenberger & Kaufman, 2013). If Gc-K0 is greater than Gc-VL, the child might have good information and knowledge but difficulty expressing ideas in written assignments due to the constraints of word knowledge. He or she might comprehend when reading about familiar topics, but have difficulty comprehending new or unfamiliar information (Lichtenberger & Kaufman, 2013).

CHC Based: Gf-Verbal Versus Fluid Reasoning Index (Ages 4:0 to 7:7 Only) The Gf-Verbal can be compared with the Fluid Reasoning Index for ages 4:0 to 7:7 to provide information about the child's fluid reasoning as assessed using primarily verbal stimuli relative to primarily visual stimuli. The WPPSI-IV Interpretive Assistant 1.0 performs the pairwise difference comparisons between these index scores based upon the child's age group and the selected significance level for the critical value. For each statistically significant difference, the program provides the base rate for the score difference in the overall sample.

Hypothesis: If Gf-Verbal is less than the Fluid Reasoning Index, the child may reason and learn better with visually presented material than verbally presented material. If Gf-Verbal is greater than the Fluid Reasoning Index, the reverse may be true (Lichtenberger & Kaufman, 2013).

Step 8. Evaluate Subtest- and Process-Level Pairwise Comparisons

Pairwise comparisons between the two subtest scaled scores that contribute to an index score are useful to understand how to interpret that index score. Because only two subtests contribute to most of the index scores, be sure to examine the difference between the subtests to facilitate the index score's interpretation. For example, comparing performance on Block Design and Object Assembly can help with interpretation of the Visual Spatial Index and provide useful information relevant to hypotheses about the child's relative analysis and synthesis abilities with abstract, uniform stimuli and meaningful, varied stimuli.

The Primary Analysis page and the Ancillary Analysis page Pairwise Difference Comparison tables on the Record Form provide space to examine the pairwise differences between every pair of subtests that contribute to a primary index score, as well as between the Cancellation Random and Cancellation Structured process scores. Table B.7 of the *Administration and Scoring Manual* provides the critical values for every pair of scores at the .01, .05, .10, and .15 significance levels. As for the index level pairwise comparisons, exercise good judgment when selecting the significance level for these comparisons, depending on the number of comparisons and the implications of any decisions that may be made based on the scores as part of a high-stakes assessment. Use the appropriate portion and page of the table according to the selected significance level. If the absolute value of the difference is greater than or equal to the critical value, the difference is statistically significant. For each value, circle *Y* or *N* in the column labeled *Significant Difference*. For each value that is statistically significant, report the base rate of the score difference in the normative sample.

Base Rates for Subtest- and Process-Level Pairwise Comparisons in the Published Test

The base rates for a limited number of subtest-level pairwise comparisons and for the process-level pairwise comparison are available in Table B.8. The available comparisons are limited to pairs of subtests that are used to derive the two-subtest index scores, including the primary index scores. For example, a base rate for the comparison between Block Design and Object Assembly is available, because those two subtests compose the Visual Spatial Index. Use Table B.8 to determine how rare the child's difference scores are within the normative sample, being careful to use the side of the column that reflects the direction of the difference.

Base Rates for Subtest-Level Pairwise Comparisons in This Book

The base rates for additional subtest-level pairwise comparisons are available on the Step8 tab of the WPPSI-IV Interpretive Assistant 1.0. These comparisons include additional pairs of subtests that are used to derive the two-subtest index scores that appear in this book. For example, a base rate for the comparison between Similarities and Picture Concepts is available, because those two subtests compose the Concept Recognition and Generation Index. The program provides the relevant base rates for score differences in the overall normative sample. Rapid Reference 4.7 lists the additional subtest-level pairwise comparison base rates available in the WPPSI-IV Interpretive Assistant 1.0.

≡ *Rapid Reference 4.7*

Additional Index Scores and Subtest-Level Pairwise Difference Comparisons

Additional Index Score	Subtest Comparison
Gc-K0	Information vs. Comprehension
Gf-Verbal	Similarities vs. Comprehension
Word Knowledge Index	Vocabulary vs. Picture Naming
Concept Recognition and Generation Index	Similarities vs. Picture Concepts
Complex Expressive Index	Vocabulary vs. Comprehension

🔖 TEST YOURSELF 🔖

1. **Which of the following is *not* one of the three global composite scores available with the WPPSI-IV?**
   (a) Global Composite Score
   (b) Full Scale IQ
   (c) General Ability Index
   (d) Nonverbal Index

2. **When great variability or discrepancy characterizes the primary index scores, the Full Scale IQ**
   (a) Is sufficient when used alone to describe ability.
   (b) Is insufficient when used alone to describe ability.
   (c) Cannot be used to diagnose intellectual disability.
   (d) Can be used as an estimate of intellectual ability that is less influenced by working memory.

3. **The General Ability Index**
   (a) Is available for ages 4:0 to 7:7 only.
   (b) Cannot be used to represent intellectual ability.
   (c) Is less influenced by fluid reasoning than is the Full Scale IQ.
   (d) Minimizes working memory and processing speed demands.

4. **The following statement is true when comparing the Verbal Comprehension Index to the Vocabulary Acquisition Index:**
   (a) The Verbal Comprehension Index best represents acquired knowledge, while the Vocabulary Acquisition Index best represents verbal reasoning.
   (b) The Verbal Comprehension Index is available in the published test for ages 2:6 to 4:0, while the Vocabulary Acquisition Index is available for ages 4:0 to 7:7 only.

    (c) The Verbal Comprehension Index requires more verbal expression, while the Vocabulary Acquisition Index requires less verbal expression.

    (d) The Verbal Comprehension Index primarily measures vocabulary acquisition and recognition, while the Vocabulary Acquisition Index primarily measures verbal concept formation.

5. **Which of the following is an index score included in the published test?**

    (a) Visual Spatial Index

    (b) Word Knowledge Index

    (c) Gf-Verbal

    (d) Concept Recognition and Generation Index

6. **The Comprehensive Verbal Index, while not in the published test, is**

    (a) Added in this book as an index score designed to provide a measure of complex oral expression especially useful for children with motor delays.

    (b) Added in this book as a broad measure of verbal ability especially useful for children with visual impairment.

    (c) Derived from the Vocabulary and Comprehension subtests only.

    (d) Derived from the Information and Similarities subtests only.

7. **The Nonverbal Index is the global score of choice if**

    (a) The child is an English language learner and can comprehend subtest instructions in English.

    (b) A diagnosis of intellectual disability is established, but a diagnosis of language disorder is under consideration.

    (c) The examinee has expressive language issues and a "language reduced" measure is needed.

    (d) All of the above are true statements regarding the Nonverbal Index.

8. **An extreme discrepancy between two subtests that contribute to an index score indicates that**

    (a) The index score is invalid and unreliable.

    (b) The index score is a summary of diverse abilities.

    (c) The index score should *not* be interpreted.

    (d) The discrepancy is most likely due to administration error.

9. **The subtest scaled scores are essential because**

    (a) They are the basic building blocks that constitute all other scores.

    (b) Interpretation of composite scores is enhanced by understanding subtest-level performance.

    (c) Both of the above statements are true.

    (d) Neither of the above statements is true.

10. **The final step in the step-by-step score analysis is to**

    (a) Report and describe the global composite score.

    (b) Report and describe the index scores.

    (c) Evaluate subtest- and process-level pairwise comparisons.

    (d) Evaluate subtest-level strengths and weaknesses.

(continued)

11. **The normative data for the additional index scores provided in this book are available on the accompanying CD, which also contains appendix matter and the WPPSI-IV Interpretive Assistant 1.0.**
    True or False?

12. **The traditional qualitative composite score descriptors are referenced in this book; however, no alternate composite score descriptors are proposed.**
    True or False?

Answers: 1. a; 2. b; 3. d; 4. c; 5. a; 6. b; 7. d; 8. b; 9. c; 10. c; 11. True; 12. False

REFERENCES

American Psychiatric Association. (2013). *Diagnostic and statistical manual of mental disorders* (5th ed.). Arlington, VA: American Psychiatric Publishing.

Archibald, L. M. D., & Gathercole, S. E. (2006a). Short-term memory and working memory in specific language impairment. In T. P. Alloway & S. E. Gathercole (Eds.), *Working memory and neurodevelopmental disorders* (pp. 139–160). New York, NY: Psychology Press.

Archibald, L. M. D., & Gathercole, S. E. (2006b). Visuospatial immediate memory in specific language impairment. *Journal of Speech, Language, and Hearing Research, 49*, 265–277. doi: 10.1044/1092-4388(2006/022)

Belleville, S., Ménard, É., Mottron, L., & Ménard, M.-C. (2006). Working memory in autism. In T. P. Alloway & S. E. Gathercole (Eds.), *Working memory and neurodevelopmental disorders* (pp. 213–238). New York, NY: Psychology Press.

Blalock, L. D., & McCabe, D. P. (2011). Proactive interference and practice effects in visuospatial working memory span task performance. *Memory, 19*, 83–91. doi: 10.1080/09658211.2010.537035

Bunting, M. (2006). Proactive interference and item similarity in working memory. *Journal of Experimental Psychology: Learning, Memory, and Cognition, 32*, 183–196. doi: 10.1037/0278-7393.32.2.183

Chuderski, A., & Necka, E. (2012). The contribution of working memory to fluid reasoning: Capacity, control, or both? *Journal of Experimental Psychology. Learning, Memory, and Cognition, 38*, 1689–1710. doi: 10.1037/a0028465

Compton, D. L., Fuchs, L. S., Fuchs, D., Lambert, W., & Hamlett, C. (2012). The cognitive and academic profiles of reading and mathematics learning disabilities. *Journal of Learning Disabilities, 45*, 79–95. doi: 10.1177/0022219410393012

Conway, A. A., & Kovacs, K. (2013). Individual differences in intelligence and working memory: A review of latent variable models. In B. H. Ross (Ed.), *The psychology of learning and motivation* (Vol. 58, pp. 233–270). San Diego, CA: Elsevier Academic Press.

Daniel, M. H. (2007). "Scatter" and the construct validity of FSIQ: Comment on Fiorello et al. (2007). *Applied Neuropsychology, 14*, 291–295.

Daniel, M. H. (2009). *Subtest variability and the validity of WISC–IV composite scores*. Blue ribbon paper presented at the annual meeting of the American Psychological Association, Toronto, Canada.

Deary, I. J., & Johnson, W. (2010). Intelligence and education: Causal perceptions drive analytic processes and therefore conclusions. *International Journal of Epidemiology, 39*, 1362–1369. doi: 10.1093/ije/dyq072

Deary, I. J., Strand, S., Smith, P., & Fernandes, C. (2007). Intelligence and educational achievement. *Intelligence, 35*, 13–21.

Dodonova, Y. A., & Dodonov, Y. S. (2012). Processing speed and intelligence as predictors of school achievement: Mediation or unique contribution? *Intelligence, 40,* 163–171. doi: 10.1016/j.intell. 2012.01.003

Duan, X., Shi, J., & Zhou, D. (2010). Developmental changes in processing speed: Influence of accelerated education for gifted children. *Gifted Child Quarterly, 54,* 85–91.

Flanagan, D. P., Alfonso, V. C., & Ortiz, S. O. (2012). The cross-battery assessment approach. In D. P. Flanagan & P. L. Harrison (Eds.), *Contemporary intellectual assessment: Theories, tests, and issues* (3rd ed., pp. 459–483). New York, NY: Guilford Press.

Flanagan, D. P., Alfonso, V. C., Ortiz, S. O., & Dynda, A. M. (2010). Integrating cognitive assessment in school neuropsychological evaluations. In D. C. Miller (Ed.), *Best practices in school neuropsychology: Guidelines for effective practice, assessment, and evidence-based intervention* (pp. 101–140). Hoboken, NJ: Wiley.

Flanagan, D. P., & Kaufman, A. S. (2009). *Essentials of WISC®-IV assessment* (2nd ed.). Hoboken, NJ: Wiley.

Gottfredson, L. S. (2008). Of what value is intelligence? In A. Prifitera, D. Saklofske, & L. G. Weiss (Eds.), *WISC–IV clinical assessment and intervention* (2nd ed., pp. 545–564). Amsterdam: Elsevier Academic Press.

Grégoire, J., Coalson, D. L., & Zhu, J. (2011). Analysis of WAIS-IV index score scatter using significant deviation from the mean index score. *Assessment, 18,* 168–177. doi: 10.1177/1073191110386343

Hartmann, P., Larsen, L., & Nyborg, H. (2009). Personality as a predictor of achievement. *Journal of Individual Differences, 30,* 65–74. doi: 10.1027/1614-0001.30.2.65

Hornung, C., Brunner, M., Reuter, R. A. P., & Martin, R. (2011). Children's working memory: Its structure and relationship to fluid intelligence. *Intelligence, 39,* 210–221.

Jacobson, M. W., Delis, D. C., Hamilton, J. M., Bondi, M. W., & Salmon, D. P. (2004). How do neuropsychologists define cognitive constructs? Further thoughts on limitations of factor analysis used with normal or mixed clinical populations [Letter to the editor]. *Journal of the International Neuropsychological Society, 10,* 1020–1021. doi: 10.1017/S1355617704107121

Johnson, W., Deary, I. J., & Iacono, W. G. (2009). Genetic and environmental transactions underlying educational attainment. *Intelligence, 37,* 466–478. doi: 10.1016/j.intell.2009.05.006

Kamphaus, R. W., Winsor, A. P., Rowe, E. W., & Kim, S. (2012). A history of intelligence test interpretation. In D. P. Flanagan & P. L. Harrison (Eds.), *Contemporary intellectual assessment: Theories, tests, and issues* (3rd ed., pp. 56–70). New York, NY: Guilford Press.

Kaufman, S. B., Reynolds, M. R., Liu, X., Kaufman, A. S., & McGrew, K. S. (2012). Are cognitive *g* and academic *g* one and the same *g*? An exploration on the Woodcock–Johnson and Kaufman tests. *Intelligence, 40,* 123–138. doi: 10.1016/j.intell.2012.01.009

Kotz, K. M., Watkins, M. W., & McDermott, P. A. (2008). Validity of the general conceptual ability score from the Differential Ability Scales as a function of significant and rare interfactor variability. *School Psychology Review, 37,* 261–278.

Lichtenberger, E. O., & Kaufman, A. S. (2004). *Essentials of WPPSI®-III assessment.* Hoboken, NJ: Wiley.

Lichtenberger, E. O., & Kaufman, A. S. (2013). *Essentials of WAIS®-IV assessment* (2nd ed.). Hoboken, NJ: Wiley.

Longman, R. S. (2004). Values for comparison of WAIS-III index scores with overall means. *Psychological Assessment, 16,* 323–325. doi: 10.1037/1040-3590.16.3.323

Martínez, K., Burgaleta, M., Román, F. J., Escorial, S., Shih, P. C., Quiroga, M. A., & Colom, R. (2011). Can fluid intelligence be reduced to "simple" short term storage? *Intelligence, 39,* 473–480. doi: 10.1016/j.intell.2011.09.001

Mayes, S. D., & Calhoun, S. L. (2007). Learning, attention, writing, and processing speed in typical children and children with ADHD, autism, anxiety, depression, and oppositional-defiant disorder. *Child Neuropsychology, 13*, 469–193. doi: 10.1080/09297040601112773

Mayes, S. D., & Calhoun, S. L. (2008). WISC-IV and WIAT-II profiles in children with high-functioning autism. *Journal of Autism and Developmental Disorders, 38*, 429–439. doi: 10.1007/s10803-007-0410-4

Miller, D. C. (2010). School neuropsychological assessment and intervention. In D. C. Miller (Ed.), *Best practices in school neuropsychology: Guidelines for effective practice, assessment, and evidence-based intervention* (pp. 81–100). Hoboken, NJ: Wiley.

Miller, D. C. (2013). *Essentials of school neuropsychological assessment*. Hoboken, NJ: Wiley.

Miller, D. C., & Maricle, D. E. (2012). The emergence of neuropsychological constructs into tests of intelligence and cognitive abilities. In D. P. Flanagan & P. L. Harrison (Eds.), *Contemporary intellectual assessment: Theories, tests, and issues* (3rd ed., pp. 800–819). New York, NY: Guilford Press.

Naglieri, J. A., & Paolitto, A. W. (2005). Ipsative comparisons of WISC–IV index scores. *Applied Neuropsychology, 12*, 208–211.

National Association for Gifted Children. (2010, March). *Use of the WISC–IV for gifted identification* [NAGC Position Statement]. Retrieved from http://www.nagc.org/uploaded-Files/WISC%20IV%20Position%20Paper.pdf

Ortiz, S. O., Ochoa, S. H., & Dynda, A. M. (2012). Testing with culturally and linguistically diverse populations: Moving beyond the verbal–performance dichotomy into evidence-based practice. In D. P. Flanagan & P. L. Harrison (Eds.), *Contemporary intellectual assessment: Theories, tests, and issues* (3rd ed., pp. 526–552). New York, NY: Guilford Press.

Passolunghi, M. C. (2006). Working memory and arithmetic learning disability. In T. P. Alloway & S. E. Gathercole, (Eds.), *Working memory and neurodevelopmental disorders* (pp. 113–138). New York, NY: Psychology Press.

Pickering, S. J. (2006). Working memory in dyslexia. In T. P. Alloway & S. E. Gathercole (Eds.), *Working memory and neurodevelopmental disorders* (pp. 7–40). New York, NY: Psychology Press.

Reeve, C. L., & Charles, J. E. (2008). Survey of opinions on the primacy of *g* and social consequences of ability testing. A comparison of expert and non-expert views. *Intelligence, 36*, 681–688.

Rimm, S., Gilman, B., & Silverman, L. (2008). Alternative assessments with gifted and talented students. In J. L. VanTassel-Baska (Ed.), *Nontraditional applications of traditional testing* (pp. 175–202). Waco, TX: Prufrock Press.

Roodenrys, S. (2006). Working memory function in attention deficit hyperactivity disorder. In T. P. Alloway & S. E. Gathercole (Eds.), *Working memory and neurodevelopmental disorders* (pp. 187–211). New York, NY: Psychology Press.

Rowe, E. W., Kingsley, J. M., & Thompson, D. F. (2010). Predictive ability of the General Ability Index (GAI) versus the Full Scale IQ among gifted referrals. *School Psychology Quarterly, 25*, 119–128. doi: 10.1037/a0020148

Sattler, J. M. (2008). *Assessment of children: Cognitive foundations* (5th ed.). San Diego, CA: Author.

Schneider, W. J., & McGrew, K. S. (2012). The Cattell–Horn–Carroll model of intelligence. In D. P. Flanagan & P. L. Harrison (Eds.), *Contemporary intellectual assessment: Theories, tests, and issues* (3rd ed., pp. 99–144). New York, NY: Guilford Press.

Swanson, H. L. (2006). Working memory and reading disabilities: Both phonological and executive processing deficits are important. In T. P. Alloway & S. E. Gathercole (Eds.), *Working memory and neurodevelopmental disorders* (pp. 59–88). New York, NY: Psychology Press.

Wechsler, D. (2012). *Wechsler preschool and primary scale of intelligence* (4th ed.). Bloomington, MN: Pearson.

Five

STRENGTHS AND WEAKNESSES OF THE WPPSI-IV

Ron Dumont
John O. Willis

After a careful review, the authors of this chapter believe that the WPPSI-IV (Wechsler, 2012a) is overall a very good instrument, good enough for us to use in our own practices, to teach to our captive audiences of graduate students, and to write this chapter. For comparison, we have had extensive experience with many other cognitive assessment instruments back to the WISC (Wechsler, 1949) and the Stanford-Binet L-M (Terman & Merrill, 1960). Because the WPPSI-IV has only recently been released, there is little published information regarding how the new test has been accepted by practitioners. We had the opportunity to extensively review all of the materials used during the standardization of the test and then again reviewed the final, published version. We have each used the WPPSI-IV several times in real assessment cases and have developed opinions, both positive and negative, about the test. Although we find the test to be a significant improvement over the prior edition and have welcomed most of the changes in the update, we still find a few aspects of the test annoying or problematic. Admittedly, we have been told we are very easily annoyed.

The WPPSI-IV provides an efficient, flexible, thorough, reasonable, and statistically reliable and valid assessment of cognitive abilities. Attention has been given to designing features to enhance useful interpretation. We have found the test to be much more child friendly than prior editions. The materials used are stimulating and colorful and consequently make the testing session more enjoyable for children.

ASSETS OF THE WPPSI-IV

Fairly Easy Administration

The WPPSI-IV is not effortless to administer, but it is not unduly or unnecessarily difficult. Only Block Design, Object Assembly, Zoo Locations, and Processing Speed subtests require anything other than the *Administration and Scoring Manual* (Wechsler, 2012b), Record Form, and Stimulus Books for administration. However, there is much back-and-forth maneuvering between Stimulus Books. Some examiners would prefer easels to Stimulus Books. For older students, the books are not used in numerical (sequential) order. You do need to use the *Administration and Scoring Manual* (which stands independently with its crack-back design), Record Form, Response Booklets, the ink dauber (for Bug Search, Cancellation, and Animal Coding), and the Stimulus Book along with a stopwatch for some subtests, especially Block Design and Object Assembly, but this divided-attention task is not difficult to master. Spreading out the materials may be difficult if the assessment location is small since some of the student Response Booklets require somewhere to air dry after use and the multiple Stimulus Books, manipulatives, and Zoo Locations landscapes take up space—one more reason for evaluators to demand adequate testing conditions. As with any preschool assessment, use of the WPPSI-IV requires careful preparation of materials.

Better Alignment With Current Wechsler Scales

One major improvement to the WPPSI-IV is its use of a common terminology for the composite scores produced by the several Wechsler scales. The WPPSI (Wechsler, 1967), WPPSI-R (Wechsler 1989), and WPPSI-III (Wechsler, 2002) each used the terms *Verbal* and *Performance IQ* to describe the composites obtained on those tests. With the advances in understanding of human cognitive abilities, the WPPSI-IV now incorporates terminology that more accurately reflects the configuration of the subtests and their contributions to specific cognitive abilities. This new version aligns itself well with the WISC-IV (Wechsler, 2003) and WAIS-IV (Wechsler, 2008) in terms of its scale arrangement (except for the highly desirable separation of Visual Spatial and Fluid Reasoning scores). As with the other modern Wechsler scales, the WPPSI-IV has dropped the use of the terms *Verbal* and *Performance IQ* for more descriptive terms for the factor-based composite scores, using the term *Index* rather than *IQ* or *Quotient*. *IQ* lives on in *Full Scale IQ* and *FSIQ*, but *Quotient* has apparently been put to rest. The inclusion of these more accurate and descriptive composite terms enhances the user's ability to clearly communicate the test results and will clarify comparisons with future evaluations of the same child with the WISC or WAIS. Especially welcome are the separation of the Perceptual Reasoning Index (included in the WISC-IV and WAIS-IV) into the Visual Spatial (Gv in Cattell-Horn-Carroll, or CHC, terminology) (Flanagan, Ortiz, & Alfonso, 2013; Schneider & McGrew, 2012) and Fluid Reasoning (Gf), the inclusion of General Ability Index (GAI) and Cognitive Proficiency Index (CPI) scores, and the welcome renaming of *General Language Composite* as *Vocabulary Acquisition Index.*

Limitations to Subtest Substitution

We agree that it is better to allow subtest substitutions and prorating rather than to invalidate an entire test, be unable to compute a FSIQ, or have to report results that are obviously biased against an examinee's disability, but we applaud the strong admonitions against the use of unnecessary substitutions and the strict guidelines provided for their use. Since the normative information for all composite scores is based upon the administration of the core subtests, and because there does not appear to be any evidence provided for the comparability of scores obtained with the use of substitutions, examiners are cautioned to use substitutions sparingly. Thankfully, the rules for the WPPSI-IV limit the index substitutions to the Nonverbal Index (NVI), GAI, and CPI. The *Administration and Scoring Manual* (Wechsler, 2012b, pp. 28–29 and 51–53) discusses substitutions and limits them to no more than one substitution when computing the FSIQ, NVI (for ages 4:0 to 7:7), GAI, and CPI. Those rules greatly limit the number of possible different versions of the WPPSI-IV composed of different subtests with varying reliabilities and different correlations with their Index Scales and the FSIQ, or "IQ roulette" (Zuccaro, 2012). Examiners have the option to prorate the sum of scaled scores only for the FSIQ (*Administration and Scoring Manual*, Wechsler, 2012b, pp. 51–52, and 294–295). Zhu and Cayton (2013) found that "substitution, proration and retesting to replace 1 missing core subtest may increase measurement error in the WPPSI-IV FSIQ by 20–64% . . . and lead to as much as 22% misclassification" (slide 15). They concluded that "retesting a subtest to replace a missing subtest generally introduces less error than substitution and proration" (slide 15). (The authors of this text note that additional research is needed to determine if results could be replicated in samples with shorter test intervals and are consistent across different overall cognitive ability levels.)

Clearer Distinction Between the Perceptual Reasoning Subtests—Split Between Visual Spatial and Fluid Reasoning

The WPPSI-IV is the first of the Wechsler Scales to clearly endorse the Fluid Reasoning composite. Although both the WISC-IV (Wechsler, 2003) and WAIS-IV (Wechsler, 2008) included subtests that were designed to tap fluid reasoning abilities (e.g., Matrix Reasoning, Figure Weights), these scales did not include or allow for the computation of a Fluid Reasoning score (index). In both cases the Fluid Reasoning subtests were subsumed within the Perceptual Reasoning Index, and even then, the PRI contained only one unequivocal fluid reasoning task (Matrix Reasoning). We applaud the creation of the Fluid Reasoning Index for ages 4:0 to 7:7, given the importance that fluid reasoning abilities have in certain areas of development and applications to the school setting and the important differences found in some children between Fluid Reasoning and Visual Spatial abilities.

Inclusion of Ancillary Index Scales

The Ancillary Index Scales are a valuable addition to the test. Although these scales are primarily theoretical in nature, their addition allows evaluators several extremely useful options. Clearly, the comparison between the General Ability (verbal and nonverbal tasks) and the Cognitive Proficiency (working memory and processing speed tasks) can often be very useful, especially for children suspected of giftedness or intellectual disabilities as well as for assessment of specific learning disabilities and neuropsychological assessment. These scales have proved useful with the WISC-IV and WAIS-IV, but the WPPSI-IV is the first Wechsler scale to include norms for both scales in the test manual, a tremendous boon to evaluators.

A particular strength of the WPPSI-IV is the Nonverbal Index (NVI), composed of four subtests from two of the three indexes for ages 2:6 to 3:11, and five subtests from four of the five indexes for ages 4:0 to 7:7. At all ages, this index excludes the Verbal Comprehension subtests. It provides examiners with a very useful index score conceptually similar to the Special Nonverbal Composite score on the DAS-II (Elliott, 2007) and the Nonverbal IQ of the Stanford-Binet 5 (Roid, 2003). Since the NVI excludes any subtest that requires any expressive verbal response, it may be especially useful with children for whom subtests with verbal content or those that require oral responses may not be appropriate. The WPPSI-IV Nonverbal Index may provide a more appropriate estimate of overall ability for children who are not fluent in English, who are deaf or hard of hearing, or who have speech and language impairments.

Future research investigating the utility of this index will certainly be welcomed. The *Technical and Interpretive Manual* (Wechsler, 2012c, Chapter 5) does provide a glimpse at how certain clinical samples performed on this specific index relative to other indexes as well as in comparison to matched controls. For one example (pp. 128–129), for a small sample of children with expressive language disorders ($N = 25$), the mean NVI score was approximately 7 points higher than the VCI. The effect size difference between the matched controls and the expressive language group was reduced almost in half, from 1.30 for VCI to .67 for NVI. Even more striking differences were found for the English language learners, for whom the mean difference between the VCI and the NVI was approximately 13 points and the NVI very closely approximated that of the primary English language population as a whole. Research with children who were deaf and hard of hearing would have been valuable.

More Developmentally Appropriate Processing Speed Tests (Bug Search and Animal Coding)

Because young children may have a difficult time conceptually understanding the use of a question mark to indicate the absence of a target figure in a search group, the Bug Search subtest was modified to exclude any "no match" option. In an effort to reduce the impact of fine-motor skill development, the examiner is responsible for turning the pages of the Response Booklets. However, this may interfere with the administration if the examiner has weak hand skills and the pages do not separate or fold flat easily. Folding back and creasing each page before the examination or use of rubber finger tips might help some examiners. The examiner should take care to not cover the items or move the booklet while preparing to turn the pages. Again, preparation and practice are essential as with most preschool tests.

New Working Memory Tasks (Picture Memory and Zoo Locations)

The WPPSI-IV now provides strong measures of visual short-term memory appropriate for this age group. Picture Memory and Zoo Locations are both new subtests for the WPPSI scales but seem similar to tasks on other tests. For example, Picture Memory has the same general format as Face Recognition on the Kaufman Assessment Battery for Children, Second Edition (Kaufman & Kaufman, 2004) and Picture Recognition on the Differential Abilities Scale-II (Elliott, 2007) among others, and the Zoo Locations format is similar to the Spatial Memory subtests of the Kaufman Assessment Battery for Children

(Kaufman & Kaufman, 1983), the Leiter International Performance Scale–Revised (Roid & Miller, 1997), and the Universal Nonverbal Intelligence Test (Bracken & McCallum, 1998). Those similarities mean that there is a history of demonstrated utility and useful interpretation of such measures even though the WPPSI-IV subtests are newly developed, unique tasks. Both of these tasks are typically identified in CHC theory (e.g., Flanagan et al., 2013) as measures of visual–spatial ability (Gv) and specifically the narrow ability of visual memory—or the ability to form and store a mental representation or image of a visual stimulus and then recognize or recall it later. When both working memory subtests are given (Zoo Locations is a supplemental subtest at all ages), they can be combined to form the Working Memory Index. Pages 22 and 23 in the *Technical and Interpretive Manual* (Wechsler, 2012c) provide a strong justification for, and explanation of, Working Memory models. The WPPSI-IV is not intended to be a CHC test, although CHC theory helped guide its development and can enhance interpretation.

Efficient Testing Time

The WPPSI-IV offers the user a very time-efficient way to obtain a multifaceted Full Scale IQ. Practitioners need to administer only five subtests at ages 2:6 to 3:11 or six subtests at ages 4:0 to 7:7 to obtain a Full Scale IQ. At the younger ages, the extra time it takes to obtain the additional Primary Indexes is only about five minutes, while at the upper ages that difference jumps to almost 30 minutes. At the lower ages, administering the five core subtests takes approximately 24 minutes and allows for the computation of the FSIQ as well as both Verbal Comprehension and Visual Spatial scales. At the upper ages, the administration of the six core subtests takes approximately 31 minutes but produces only the Full Scale IQ and the Verbal Comprehension scale. This arrangement strikes us as a good balance between efficiency and comprehensiveness.

Something's Lost and Something's Gained

We believe that, in addition to the inclusion of new subtests, the WPPSI-IV is enhanced by the loss of Word Reasoning and Picture Completion. Although we have heard Word Reasoning commended by a few psychologists and speech/language pathologists and specialists, we have always been puzzled by its scoring system and have never found much use for this subtest. We admit to nostalgia for Picture Completion, but the subtest was a confusing mixture of visual and verbal abilities and cultural knowledge with weak psychometric properties.

It is a relief that Object Assembly, long at risk in Wechsler revisions and omitted from the first WPPSI (Wechsler, 1967), is still with us, contributing to the Visual Spatial Index at all ages and the FSIQ at ages 2:6 to 3:11. We have found Object Assembly, especially observations of the child's approach to the puzzles, to be a fruitful subtest. We were pleased by the return of the WPPSI and WPPSI-R (Wechsler, 1967, 1989) Animal House/Pegs in a paper-and-dauber format that reduces the finger dexterity demands of the old versions.

Generally Easy Scoring

Difficult judgments and subjectivity in scoring rules cause interexaminer variation and errors in scores. Some mistakes are frequent and some result in serious errors in subtest and total test scores (e.g., Alfonso & Pratt, 1997; Belk, LoBello, Ray, & Zachar, 2002; Kuentzel, Hetterscheidt, & Barnett, 2011; LoBello & Holley, 1999; Loe, Kadlubek, & Marks, 2007; Willis, 2001). With the exception of three Verbal subtests (Similarities, Vocabulary, and Comprehension), in which responses can earn 0, 1, or 2 points, the scoring rules for all other subtest items strike us as generally clear and unequivocal. Those three Verbal subtests do require thoughtful judgment, and even careful examiners will occasionally disagree about scores for certain marginal responses. Careless examiners will simply be careless and should be hounded out of the field. However, we found only a few items on the WPPSI-IV on which we seriously questioned the application of the scoring criteria to certain possible responses, which is unusually few for us on such tests. We were glad to see the traditional Wechsler acceptance of correct responses not listed in the *Administration and Scoring Manual*: "All word meanings recognized by standard dictionaries are acceptable and are scored according to the quality of the definition. Regionalisms or slang that are not found in standard dictionaries should be scored 0 points. If such a response is given or you are unsure about the acceptability of a response, query the child" (Wechsler, 2012b, p. 210). For the record, the informal and mildly offensive, two-word, phrasal verb synonym for Item 18 is listed as "vulgar slang" in the *American Heritage Dictionary* (2011), so it would qualify. This valuable rule contrasts with the unduly restrictive rule on many vocabulary tests that only answers listed in the test manual are acceptable.

Additional Interpretive Information

As with the WISC-IV (Wechsler, 2003), the WPPSI-IV provides valuable tables of critical values for statistically significant differences between scores, base rates of examinees obtaining various differences between scores, and intersubtest scatter (Wechsler, 2012b, pp. 300–327). Critical values are now given for four different significance levels (.15, .10, .05, and .01). Examiners should take the time to review the charts to ensure the same and intended levels are consistently selected. Tables for comparing WPPSI-IV and WIAT-III (Wechsler, 2009) scores are provided in Wechsler (2012c, Appendix B, pp. 168–207). There is a table (5.6, p. 88) of "Ranges of Expected WPPSI-IV Composite Scores for Selected WPPSI-III Composite Scores," which should be very helpful when a child who has taken the WPPSI-III is retested with the WPPSI-IV. In addition to the tables in both manuals, Chapter 6 of the *Technical and Interpretive Manual* (Wechsler, 2012c, pp. 139–155) provides 17 pages of interpretive guidance. The WPPSI-IV (unlike the WIAT-III; Pearson, 2009) has maintained the traditional Wechsler score ranges for qualitative descriptions of index scores and FSIQ, with Average still 90 to 109. As always, no descriptive classifications are provided for scaled scores.

Normative Sample

Normative samples are important for tests, just as for opinion polls. If the normative sample does not resemble the population to whom examinees will be compared, scores can be misleading. The normative sample of the WPPSI-IV is described in Chapter 3 of the *Technical and Interpretive Manual* (Wechsler, 2012c), and we consider it to meet or exceed good current practice and to provide a trustworthy basis for an individual's scores.

Examinee candidates for the normative sample were extensively screened for potentially confounding issues that presumably might impact the validity of test performance. A complete list of the exclusionary criteria for the normative sample is presented in Table 3.1 (p. 38) of the *Technical and Interpretive Manual* (Wechsler, 2012c). Procedures were established to evaluate such variables as an individual's language ability, recent testing, upper extremity dexterity, and medication use, particularly those medications that could potentially affect cognitive test performance. We need to observe here that exclusion of a group of people from the norming sample does not make a test somehow unfair to that group (any more than simply including them would make it fair). The appropriateness and fairness of a test depend on the content, format, and necessary capacities (such as vision or finger movement) of the test and are assessed by measures of validity. For example, children with a history of central nervous system radiation treatment were excluded from the norming, but the WPPSI-IV might be very useful in the evaluation of a child with that history. As noted later, special studies were done with 13 selected groups of children.

Reliability

The WPPSI-IV composite scores, index scores, and subtests generally have strong reliability. This topic is discussed at length in Chapter 4 of the *Technical and Interpretive Manual* (Wechsler, 2012c). Test scores cannot be trusted unless the tests are internally consistent and likely to yield very similar scores for the same person under similar circumstances, so reliability is an essential foundation for any responsible use of test scores. Reliability is a necessary, but not sufficient, basis for application of test scores. A test can be reliable, but still not valid for a particular purpose, but without reliability, it cannot be valid for any purpose.

Internal consistency (corrected split-half except for test–retest stability for Cancellation, Animal Coding, and Bug Search) reliability for all subtests and composite scores ranged from acceptable to excellent. Only two subtests (Cancellation and Animal Coding) and the two process scores (Cancellation Random and Cancellation Structured) had lower reliabilities and even these appear acceptable.

It is still too early to be able to measure long-term stability of WPPSI-IV scores, and long-term stability statistics are depressed by genuine changes in the abilities of the persons being retested. Short-term stability coefficients for all subtests (including process scores) at all tested ages (Wechsler, 2012c, pp. 56–59), ranged from .67 (acceptable) to .93 (excellent). For the core subtests, short-term stability coefficients across all ages were .79 to .87, with a median of .82. The tables provide the means and *SD*s for both scores, the uncorrected and corrected correlations, and—importantly—the standard differences (difference divided by the square root of the pooled variance) (Cohen, 1988).

Evidence of Validity

Validity data for the WPPSI-IV are discussed in the WPPSI-IV *Technical and Interpretive Manual* (Wechsler, 2012c, pp. 65–138). Validity evidence from comparisons with tests of cognitive abilities and tests of academic achievement supports the use of the WPPSI-IV for cognitive assessment and prediction of achievement.

We find that the WPPSI-IV has adequate top for all subtests at all ages and adequate bottom for almost all subtests at almost all ages. The full range of scaled scores (1 to 19) is available for all applicable ages (2:6 to 7:7 or 4:0 to 7:7) for Information, Matrix Reasoning, Bug Search, Similarities, Picture Concepts, Cancellation (total, Random, and Structured), and Vocabulary. Among the subtests that begin at age 2:6, the full range of scaled scores is available for

Receptive Vocabulary at ages 2:9 to 7:7, Picture Naming at 3:3 to 6:11, Block Design at 2:6 to 6:7, Picture Memory at 3:3 to 7:7, Object Assembly at 3:3 to 5:11, and Zoo Locations at 3:6 to 7:7. For subtests that begin at age 4:0, the full range of scaled scores is available for Animal Coding at ages 5:3 to 7:7 and for Comprehension at ages 4:3 to 7:7. The lowest possible scaled score at the starting age is 1 for all subtests except Receptive Vocabulary, Picture Naming, Object Assembly, and Comprehension (2); Animal Coding (3); and Picture Memory and Zoo Locations (4). At age 7:7, scaled scores of 19 are available for all subtests except for tops of 18 for Block Design, Object Assembly, and Picture Naming. The range of available scaled scores at the youngest and oldest ages on the WPPSI-IV is equal or superior to most tests.

Evidence of Validity With Special Groups

While the WPPSI-IV is not normed on individuals with severe disabilities or disabilities likely to invalidate test scores, special studies were done with 13 special groups (Wechsler, 2012c, pp. 110–138). When you are assessing individuals with special characteristics, the information in the *Technical and Interpretive Manual* (Wechsler, 2012c) is extremely helpful.

The *Administration and Scoring Manual* (Wechsler, 2012b, pp. 12–15) provides some brief, helpful considerations for testing individuals at the extremes of the ability and age ranges, for testing for reevaluation purposes, and for testing children with special needs. Unfortunately no specific or detailed recommendations are provided for testing examinees who are deaf or hard of hearing or who have visual impairments. *Extensive information about testing children who are deaf and hard of hearing and who have other special needs can be found in* Chapter 2 *of this book. The Comprehensive Verbal Index, which is available in this book and on the accompanying CD and discussed in* Chapters 1 and 4 *of this book, provides a global intellectual ability score for testing children who have visual impairments.*

Start Points

For ages 2:6 to 3:11, all subtests start with Item 1. For ages 4:0 to 7:11, six subtests (Block Design, Information, Picture Memory, Object Assembly, Receptive Vocabulary, and Picture Naming) have starting points (after any sample items) higher than Item 1. Six subtests (Matrix Reasoning, Similarities, Picture Concepts, Zoo Locations, Vocabulary, and Comprehension) have multiple starting points depending upon the child's age. Bug Search, Cancellation, and Animal Coding are all administered as complete items with no starting point distinction made for the child's age. There are clear rules for dropping back from the starting item when necessary and examinees who are believed to have intellectual disabilities or "general intellectual deficiency" should always begin with Item 1. It has always been thus, but we wish that rule mentioned other disabilities, such as severe language impairment, that might require an Item 1 start for some subtests. These rules should minimize both boredom and frustration.

Update of Materials, Artwork, and Record Form

The materials for the WPPSI-IV have been updated to include new artwork, revised Record Forms, and large Bug Search, Cancellation, and Animal Coding Response Booklets. We are especially happy with the revised Record Form as there is now much more room for writing an examinee's responses. As an example, the sections of the Record Form for recording the responses to the Information, Vocabulary, Similarities, Comprehension, and Picture Naming subtests have been enlarged so that the examiner can now record verbatim the entire response given by the child. The extra space is especially important for testing young children because their responses are sometimes circuitous, the precise wording of the responses is especially important for scoring (although examiners always should record all examinees' responses verbatim), and the examiner cannot devote as much time to the Record Form as with older examinees. On the WPPSI-III, there was very little room to fit the actual responses in the space provided.

We found the pages for Primary Analysis of Strengths and Weaknesses and Pairwise Difference Comparisons to be clear and easy to use. The examiner may compare the subtest scores to the mean of all 6 or 10 index subtests or to the mean of the 5 or 6 FSIQ subtests. There is no provision for comparing Receptive Vocabulary, Picture Naming, or the two Cancellation tasks.

The Bug Search response form (new for the WPPSI-IV) is colorful and seems large enough for the youngest children. The black-and-white response form for Animal Coding (nostalgically resurrecting the WPPSI-R Animal House/Pegs) seems a little crowded and might benefit from darker dividing lines between items, but these may be issues more for an aging reviewer than for young children.

The three 17 × 11 Cancellation sheets are colorful and appealing. The randomness of the Random form is minimal compared to the Structured form. Cancellation uses three sheets, including the prudently provided Sample and Demonstration page. Only the Structured sheet has spaces to record the child's name and the date (as well as the examiner's name and the child's age). Examiners should also write the child's name and the date on the other two sheets in case later inspection proves necessary.

Block Design is consistent with previous Wechsler scales and is suitable for young children. The Object Assembly puzzles are colorful and each has a narrow white margin when assembled, which provides an additional clue for the child. Several strategies are possible for assembling the puzzles, so examiners may gain information about the child's thinking by observing carefully during this subtest. The largest puzzle is about 9.5×8 when assembled so, again, adequate working space is essential. The materials for Zoo Locations are large, colorful, and appealing to children. The Object Assembly storage box is easy to use and appears to be durable. Administration of Zoo Locations will be discussed later.

Streamlining of Discontinue Rules, Start Points

The administration of the WPPSI-IV seems to flow a bit more efficiently than the WPPSI–III (Wechsler, 2002). One reason for this may be the revised discontinue rules, which have been shortened. Many subtest discontinuations have been reduced by at least one item. Five subtests (Vocabulary, Comprehension, Information, Receptive Vocabulary, and Picture Naming) have been reduced from five to three consecutive failures, three from four consecutive failures (or four out of five) to three, and two (Block Design and Object Assembly) from three to two. Although shortened discontinue rules may occasionally prevent erratically scoring children from demonstrating their best abilities, the new rules will probably make the assessment process less frustrating for most children. Entry points and other essential information are generally clear and user friendly on the Record Form. The Wechsler Giveth and Wechsler Taketh Away rules apply to the WPPSI-IV: "*Regardless of the child's performance on items preceding the start point, full credit is awarded for preceding items if perfect scores are obtained on the age-appropriate start point and subsequent item*" (emphasis in original) (Wechsler, 2012b, p. 35) and, when reversing from the age-appropriate start point, "*do not award points for those items beyond the correct discontinue point, even if the child's responses ordinarily would have earned credit*" (Wechsler, 2012b, p. 36). These rules protect the child and interexaminer reliability from examiners' flawed judgment in selecting starting points.

WEAKNESSES

We have mentioned a few minor quibbles in the preceding. Our significant concerns (none of which is fatal) are listed here.

Sum of Scaled Scores for Determination of FSIQ

For both the WISC-IV (Wechsler, 2003) and WAIS-IV (Wechsler, 2008), the Full Scale score is the sum of the Verbal Comprehension, Perceptual Reasoning,

Working Memory, and Processing Speed scaled scores. Because of this, when calculating the FSIQ, examiners typically calculate the sums of scaled scores for each of the indexes and then simply add those sums together to arrive at the sum of scaled scores for the FSIQ (even though it is best practice always to double-check by adding all of the subtest scores). For each of the Wechsler tests (WPPSI-IV included), the Record Form provides a convenient set of boxes into which the examiner places the "sum of scaled scores" for each index and then the FSIQ. Now with the WPPSI-IV, and its core and supplemental subtest configuration, the FSIQ is not the sum of the scaled scores from the three or five indexes computed. As with the WAIS-III (Wechsler, 1997), some of the subtests used in the index scores are not included in the FSIQ, but the complicated WAIS-III Record Form made it difficult to include the wrong subtests in the FSIQ.

Our concern is that if examiners are familiar with the WISC-IV and WAIS-IV, and they are used to adding together the sums of scaled scores for each index to obtain the sum of scaled score for the FSIQ, they will inadvertently be adding in supplemental subset scores. Although the WPPSI-IV *Administration and Scoring Manual* (Wechsler, 2012b, p. 50) clearly describes the procedure used to calculate the FSIQ and the Record Form has parentheses in the FSIQ column boxes for subtests not included in the FSIQ, we have already seen examiners new to the WPPSI-IV make this type of calculation error. Adding to the potential for error is the fact that the Record Form for the WPPSI-IV provides a column in which to place the five (ages 2:6 to 3:11) or six (ages 4:0 to 7:7) subtest scaled scores used in calculating the FSIQ. Unfortunately, this column also includes space for the supplemental subtests, which would only be relevant to the FSIQ calculation if used as a substitution (and by the rules, only one may be used when calculating a FSIQ). We feel it would have been better and less prone to calculation error if the supplemental subtest scaled scores were recorded in a column other than the FSIQ column. The parentheses do not dissuade examiners determined to make this error on the Record Form, and there is a warning in Chapter 3 of this book that emphasizes the same point. Several subtest scaled scores (Receptive Vocabulary, Picture Naming, and the two Cancellation subtests) are entered on the Record Form in a separate column for ages 4:0 to 7:7.

Lack of Full Cattell-Horn-Carroll Coverage

With the inclusion of Matrix Reasoning and Picture Concepts, the WPPSI-IV has extended and clearly delineated the addition of a Fluid Reasoning domain, which brings the test into closer alignment with CHC theory, although the WPPSI-IV is not intended primarily to be a CHC instrument.

Unfortunately, the WPPSI-IV has missed the chance to include a comprehensive assessment of all of the commonly accepted CHC cognitive abilities. Using the CHC terminology, the WPPSI-IV appears to measure, and in some cases over-measure, several abilities. There appear to be six subtests for Gc, two for Gf, two for Gv, three for Gs, and two for Working Memory:

Gc: Information, Similarities, Vocabulary, Comprehension, Receptive
  Vocabulary, and Picture Naming
Gv: Block Design and Object Assembly
Gf: Matrix Reasoning and Picture Concepts
Gs: Bug Search, Cancellation, and Animal Coding
Working Memory (Gv-MV): Picture Memory and Zoo Locations

In the end, these 15 subtests assess four or five of the traditional CHC domains at the expense of not measuring two domains at all (Auditory Processing [Ga] and Long-Term Storage and Retrieval [Glr]). The Wechsler scales are not based on CHC theory, but given the importance of these two cognitive domains in understanding young children's success or failure in academics, the exclusion of these measures in the WPPSI-IV is, in our opinion, a missed opportunity to place the WPPSI-IV squarely in the realm of the Woodcock-Johnson III (Woodcock, McGrew, Schrank, & Mather, 2007) or the DAS–II (Elliott, 2007), each of which provides examiners with adequate measures of all seven of the traditional CHC cognitive domains (although there are now as many as 16 broad abilities [Flanagan, Ortiz, & Alfonso, 2013; Schneider & McGrew, 2012]).

Core Versus Supplemental Subtests

As noted earlier, at the lower ages, administering the five core subtests allows for the computation of the FSIQ as well as both Verbal Comprehension and Visual Spatial scales. However, at the upper ages, the administration of the six core subtests produces only the Full Scale IQ and the Verbal Comprehension scale. Unfortunately, we predict that the complete WPPSI-IV will be underutilized, particularly at the upper ages. Since each of the subtests that measure processing speed abilities (Bug Search, Cancellation, and Animal Coding) requires the use of separate Response Booklets, we believe that these tasks will often simply not be administered because of the additional costs in both time and money. That would be a significant loss of potential information from a well-designed, multifaceted instrument.

Possible Interpretive Confusion Because of Index Name (Working Memory)

Short-term memory is often defined as the ability to apprehend and hold information in immediate awareness and then use it within a few seconds. Within the short-term memory domain, a distinction is typically made in CHC theory (e.g., Flanagan et al., 2013; Schneider & McGrew, 2012) between tasks that assess Memory Span (Gsm MS) versus those that assess Working Memory (Gsm MW). Memory Span is defined as the ability to attend to and immediately recall temporally ordered elements in the correct sequence after a single presentation, while Working Memory is the ability to temporarily store data while performing on the information a set of cognitive operations that requires divided attention and the management of the limited capacity of short-term memory. Aside from the question of verbal or visual content, the subtests of the WPPSI-IV Working Memory Index appear to be much more specifically related to measures of Memory Span rather than to a strict CHC definition of Working Memory.

This issue is similar to that of the Working Memory Index of the WISC-IV and WAIS-IV. On both of these tests, Digit Span is included in the Working Memory Index. Because Digit Span includes both Digits Forward and Digits Backward, and on the WAIS-IV an additional Digit Sequencing task, there is often the need to carefully examine any differences between the Digits Forward, a measure of Memory Span, and Digits Backward and Digit Sequencing, both measures of Working Memory (Hale, Hoeppner, & Fiorello, 2002; Reynolds, 1997). We have found it important for examiners to explain in their reports precisely how they are using such terms as *Working Memory*, *Memory Span*, and *Short-Term Memory*. Otherwise, the potential for misunderstanding is significant.

Use of the term *Working Memory* (which conforms to a common usage in some of the neuropsychological literature) for the WPPSI-IV Index may confuse evaluators and readers who are used to thinking in terms of CHC theory. While the tasks are referred to as Working Memory, they would be measures of visual–spatial ability (Gv) and visual memory (MV) in CHC theory (e.g., Flanagan et al. 2013). Pages 22 and 23 in the *Technical and Interpretive Manual* (Wechsler, 2012c) provide an explanation of working memory models that merge phonological and visual memory processes (e.g., Baddeley, 2012; Scheller, 2013) and the rationale for the WPPSI-IV Index. The WPPSI-IV is not a CHC test, but examiners who apply CHC theory as their primary means of test interpretation need to be careful and not be misled (and not confuse CHC-oriented readers) by the name *Working Memory*.

Inclusion of Ancillary Scales

The tables needed for the calculation of the ancillary scales are not included in the WPPSI-IV *Administration and Scoring Manual* (Wechsler, 2012b). Examiners who wish to calculate these additional scores must use appendixes of the WPPSI-IV *Technical and Interpretive Manual* (Wechsler, 2012c). Nonetheless, we are pleased to see the ancillary scales included anywhere in the test kit rather than in separate publications.

One other point about the ancillary indexes is that they are not all uniformly equal. For example, the Nonverbal Index for ages 2:6 to 3:11 is composed of four core subtests (two Visual Spatial and two Working Memory tests). For ages 4:0 to 7:7, the Nonverbal Index is made up of four core subtests and one supplemental subtest. The resulting index is therefore made up of one Visual Spatial, one Working Memory, one Processing Speed subtest, and two Fluid Reasoning subtests. There does not appear to be any rationale provided in the manual to explain these varied subtest compositions. Why, at ages 4 and above, does the Nonverbal Index require the administration of a second Fluid Reasoning subtest? Does Fluid Reasoning therefore carry more importance in the calculation of the NVI than do the other abilities? Will comparisons of Nonverbal Reasoning abilities assessed at age 3:6 differ substantially when reassessed at age 4:6? Will the differences, if any, be in the result of the change in subtest composition rather than any real differences in the child's nonverbal abilities? Could this lead to misunderstanding and/or misinterpretation?

More Cumbersome Administration With Inclusion of Zoo Locations and Object Assembly

The administration instructions for Zoo Locations are probably the most complex and require special preparation by the test administrator. The animal cards must be stacked and placed in the correct order before the test, and the layouts also need to be stacked in order, which is easier. The stacking will require foresight by the administrator to make sure this is done before the testing session. Without a screen, placement of Object Assembly pieces must be done carefully according to detailed but clear rules on pp. 102–103 of the *Administration and Scoring Manual*. This is another subtest that examiners should practice to mastery. Most of the other subtests do not require significant preparation of materials. Object Assembly Item 13 has 10 possible junctures. The score for this item (as well as Item 12) is the number of correct junctures divided by two and rounded up if necessary. Two of the pieces are connected to the rest of the puzzle by only one juncture each, so either of those pieces could be completely omitted without lowering the score ($9 \div 2 = 4.5$ rounded up to 5).

Dauber and Template Issues

The inclusion of the ink dauber rather than the traditional lead pencil for use with the WPPSI-IV Processing Speed subtests is a welcomed innovative idea for how to engage and thus assess younger children and diminish demands for fingertip dexterity and experience with pencils.

No estimate is given for how long a dauber might last (10 administrations versus 100 administrations). Given the cost of the dauber ($3.00 plus a minimum shipping and handling cost of $10.00), examiners are allowed to provide their own. Does a different size or color make any difference? What should an examiner do if the dauber appears to run out during an administration of a subtest (discontinue, use supplemental subtest, swiftly supply a new dauber, restart with new dauber)? Similarly, though the *Administration and Scoring Manual* (Wechsler, 2012b) does explain the scoring rules for self-corrections, there is no physical way for a child to mark a self-identified error. Without a verbal or gestural comment, it could be difficult to differentiate between an attempted revision and a supplemental response to an individual item.

Another more practical dauber issue relates to messiness. The manual suggests bringing cleaning supplies, and in our experience this is necessary. Not only does the ink tend to get on the child's (and administrator's) hands, but on the table and many other objects as well. We found that children do like the dauber, but particularly younger children liked to experiment and play with it outside of the test materials. Also if the child pushes too hard the dauber may get a little leaky. The test administrator needs to pay close attention; otherwise examiner and child may get very dirty (and parents might not be happy at the next Individualized Education Program (IEP) meeting if their child's clothes were marked in ink after the testing session). Nonetheless, the dauber is appealing to children, makes more visible marks than do pencils in the hands of many children, and probably diminishes potential unfairness toward children with limited experience using pencils.

Anytime the dauber is used, the manual recommends that the Response Booklets dry completely before attempting to score them. This requires that the testing environment have sufficient space to accommodate the spread-out, drying Response Booklets along with all the other testing materials. If the Response Booklets are folded before the ink is completely dry, it is very likely that they will smudge and print on the opposite side, making it nearly impossible to interpret the results.

The scoring template for Cancellation is translucent and a little flimsy. Judith Newcomb (personal communication, May 16, 2003) recommends copying each half of the 17 × 11 template (with a sheet of white paper between the halves) onto overhead transparencies on a plain paper copier. The resulting transparent templates are easier to use and the original can be carefully preserved.

Issues With Subtest Administration and Instructions

Color

Although we approve of the liberal use of color in the WPPSI-IV test materials, the colors could put children with various kinds and degrees of color blindness at a disadvantage. Examiners should be cautioned to find out everything they can about the child's hearing and vision, especially color vision and (because color blindness is often diagnosed late) to be alert to any indications that the child has difficulty discriminating any of the colors. It might have been helpful to specifically mention color vision on the Behavioral Observations pages of the Record Forms, along with current prescription, nonprescription, and alternative medications being taken by the child. There is, however, the risk that the examiner will simply assume color vision is adequate if no report has been made of difficulty.

Receptive Vocabulary

The 31 items in the subtest require the child to select the response item that best represents the word read aloud by the examiner. On the Record Form and in the *Administration and Scoring Manual* (Wechsler, 2012b), each item is presented, not as a single word, but in a full sentence (e.g., "Show me the **dog**," or "Show me the toy **under** the bed") with the target word printed in bold. Each item is read verbatim to the child and repeated as often as necessary. The administrative directions note that aside from the corrective feedback given only to Item 1, no further assistance is given on this subtest.

Some confusion may arise because of the bolded word in each of the item sentences. Some examiners may believe that when reading the sentences verbatim they should emphasize the target word, perhaps by raising their voice when saying the specific word. It should be noted that there is no explicit directive to do so; in fact the directions seem to imply that this is not the case. This issue should be clarified by the test company so that all examiners are administering the items in the same fashion. (This issue arose with the directions on the Listening Comprehension subtest of the WIAT [The Psychological Corporation, 1992]. In the stories to be read aloud to the examinee, several target words in three of the stories were printed in bold capitals or italicized bold capitals for no apparent reason.

Because of the bold capitals, many examiners believed that they should strongly emphasize the words during the initial readings of the stories. The test company later clarified that this was not the case and that the stories should be read in a natural voice, with no emphasis on any of the words printed in bold capitals. We assume the same to be true for the Receptive Vocabulary subtest.)

Picture Naming

On this subtest, the child is presented with a picture on a page and is asked, "What is this?" In the General Directions section for this subtest, it is noted that there are four general response types that require further querying of the child. There are marginal responses, generalized responses, functional descriptions, and hand gestures. Later in the manual, under the section describing how to score the subtest, it becomes clear that each of these response types is further delineated as either an "appropriate" or an "inappropriate" response. If a child does respond with any one of these four types of responses, *and* they are judged to be appropriate, the examiner is instructed to give specific queries. However, if the response is judged to be an inappropriate response, apparently no queries are given. Under the rules for scoring responses, the direction notes that "inappropriate marginal responses, generalized responses, functional descriptions, and hand gestures are scored as 0 points." Examiners must pay close attention to the subtle distinction with these directives. Querying is appropriate and required for the four types of general responses only if they are first deemed to be appropriate responses. No querying is given and the response is scored as 0 if the examiner deems the initial response to be inappropriate. Some confusion may arise if the examiner does not make the distinction between appropriate and inappropriate initial responses. (Note that this issue also applies to Items 1 to 3 of the Vocabulary subtest.)

One minor error involving the Picture Naming subtest is in the *Administration and Scoring Manual* (Wechsler, 2012b, p. 27). Table 2.5 shows the subtests combinations that make up the Primary scales. For ages 2:6 to 3:11, under the heading for VCI, there is a check mark next to Picture Naming. This check mark should actually be next to Information. (The authors of this text have noted this error, which is corrected for the next and subsequent printings.)

Vocabulary

One minor problem with the instructions for the Vocabulary subtest is the explanation of how to score responses in which the child uses the target word in a sentence. The instructions note that a child should be awarded 1 point if his or her response is "an example using the word itself, not elaborated." Examiners must be aware that this does not mean that any use of the target word in a sentence results in a score of 1 point. It is applied only when the use of the word in the sentence conveys some correct approximation of the word's meaning, although with a poverty of content. For example, for the word *train*, the response, "I rode a train once" would receive 1 point. "I'd like a train" would not.

Picture Memory

If the child selects more response options than are required or self corrects a response, the *Administration and Scoring Manual* (Wechsler, 2012b, p. 161) provides specific instructions for how to proceed. Unfortunately, the *Administration and Scoring Manual* provides no information about what to do if the child points to only one object when two or more objects are shown. Should the examiner query for the remaining response options or simply mark the item incorrect and move on to the next item? (The authors of this text note that a query is not provided if the child omits [does not identify] a target picture in response to an item.)

Zoo Locations

The general directions in the *Administration and Scoring Manual* (Wechsler, 2012b, p. 191) say, "The cards are removed from the layout, randomly stacked, and then presented to the child." However, the Item Administration instructions for items with multiple cards (5, 6, and 8–20, pp. 198–201), say, "Collect the cards, hand them to the child, and say, 'Put each animal where it lives.'" They should say, "Collect the cards, *randomly stack them*, hand them to the child, and say, 'Put each animal where it lives.'" Skeptical about our own attention and long-term storage and recall, we have inserted "randomize," before "hand them to the child" in the instructions in our manuals for Items 5, 6, 8, 9–10, 11–13, 14–15, and 16–20. (All of our test manuals are heavily annotated, highlighted, and index-tabbed.) In addition to always having the cards and layouts correctly arranged before each evaluation, the examiner must practice administering Zoo Locations as often as necessary to achieve effortless fluency with minimum allocation of attentional resources. Some children may protest the animals' moving from one location to another. On Item 1, the examiner tells the child, "The [*animal*] lives here [on the child's right]. Remember where the [*animal*] lives." If the child incorrectly replaces the animal card on the left, the examiner says, "The [*animal*] lives here [on the child's right], so you should put it here. Let's try again." The examiner collects the card and administers a second trial, saying, "The [*animal*] lives here [child's right]. Remember where the [*animal*] lives." Then, the examiner moves on to the second item, placing the same animal card on the child's left side, and saying, "Now the [*animal*] lives here. Remember where the [*animal*] lives." It is essential to ensure that the child clearly hears the "Now." Even so, the examiner may have to deal with an objection to the apparent self-contradiction about the animal's domicile. For older children starting with the Sample and Item 7, the same issue may arise when the another animal card placement switches position from the child's far left on Item 7 to near left on Item 9 and another animal card switches position from far left on Item 8 to far right on Item 9.

Picture Concepts
The correct answers for both samples and for Items 1, 2, and 4 are from the same superordinate category. Examiners should be alert to the possibility of a child beginning to look for the superordinate category rather than for related pictures.

Language in Subtest Instructions
Younger children, children with language delays or disorders, and children with limited or nonmainstream English language may have difficulty with some of the vocabulary in the instructions for some of the subtests. For the most part, vocabulary and basic concepts in subtest instructions have been kept admirably clear and simple, and demonstrations, pointing, and sample items with feedback help clarify the tasks. Nonetheless, examiners need to be alert to potential misunderstanding of concepts such as *skip* or *in order*.

Divergent Responses
It would be helpful on Information and Comprehension to provide examiners with instructions for dealing with children's divergent responses based on family beliefs and values (e.g., Comprehension Item 17 and Item 18). Experienced examiners can attempt to elicit an explanation of why misguided people do something the child firmly believes is wrong, but novice examiners need some guidance.

Additional Interpretive Information
Tables for comparing WPPSI-IV and WIAT-III (Pearson, 2009) scores are provided in Wechsler (2012c, Appendix B, pp. 168–207). These WIAT-III comparisons appear to be based on correlational data from 222 children between the ages of 4:0 and 7:6 administered both tests with a mean test interval of 13 days. It should be noted that, given the age restriction of the tests, 9 of the 16 WIAT-III subtests and three of the six Composites had fewer than 60 children in the comparative sample, which may suggest the need for cautious interpretation.

The Record Form does not contain any area related to WPPSI-IV/WIAT-III comparisons. Also, of the 10 Composite/Index scores available on the WPPSI-IV, WIAT-III predicted scores are provided for only six WPPSI-IV scores (i.e., FSIQ, VCI, VSI, FRI, NVI, and GAI). No predicted scores are available when utilizing the WMI, PSI, VAI, or CPI. These omissions are probably intentional.

Determining S and W Based on Only the Core Subtests

The *Administration and Scoring Manual* (Wechsler, 2012b, pp. 305–308, Table B.3) provides examiners with critical values that can be used to determine if a subtest differs significantly from the overall mean of Primary Indexes or the FSIQ. Unfortunately, this information, typically used to determine strengths and weaknesses, is incomplete. If an examiner administers the supplemental subtests (administering all 15 subtests) to gain additional information about the person, the manual provides no way of determining if those additional subtests differ significantly from the person's mean subtest score. This information could easily have been provided.

FINAL COMMENT

Although we have identified some concerns with the new WPPSI-IV (and each concern takes longer to explain than each commendation), our concerns are fewer than we have with many popular tests. We definitely consider the WPPSI-IV a significant improvement over the WPPSI-III and, on balance, find it to be a child-friendly, engaging, valuable instrument with significant strengths. We will use and teach it.

TEST YOURSELF

1. **The WPPSI-IV** *Technical and Interpretive Manual* **provides evidence of:**
   (a) Generally strong reliability but weak validity for assessing intelligence.
   (b) Generally strong reliability and validity for assessing intelligence.
   (c) Weak reliability but generally strong validity for assessing intelligence.
   (d) Weak reliability and validity for assessing intelligence.

2. **WPPSI-IV discontinue rules for subtests:**
   (a) Facilitate administration by requiring fewer consecutive failures than the rules for most of the same WPPSI-III subtests.
   (b) Facilitate administration by requiring fewer consecutive failures than the rules for all of the same WPPSI-III subtests.
   (c) Are the same as the rules for the same WPPSI-III subtests.
   (d) Provide additional data by requiring more consecutive failures than the rules for all of the same WPPSI-III subtests.
   (e) Improve WPPSI-III procedures by no longer requiring consecutive failures to discontinue any subtests.

3. **A notable improvement of the WPPSI-IV over previous Wechsler intelligence scales is that it provides separate Index scores for**
   (a) Verbal Reasoning and Verbal Knowledge
   (b) Auditory Working Memory and Visual Spatial Working Memory

(c) Visual Spatial and Fluid Reasoning

(d) Verbal Comprehension and Processing Speed

(e) Working Memory and Processing Speed

4. **A strength of the WPPSI-IV is the addition of this new Index:**

(a) Verbal Comprehension

(b) Processing Speed

(c) Perceptual Reasoning

(d) Working Memory

(e) Full Scale IQ

5. **A strength of the WPPSI-IV is that it includes a General Ability Index, a Cognitive Proficiency Index, a Vocabulary Acquisition Index, and a Nonverbal Index. However, norms are not included in the WPPSI-IV manuals and must be found on the Pearson website for**

(a) General Ability Index and Cognitive Proficiency Index

(b) Vocabulary Acquisition Index and Nonverbal Index

(c) Nonverbal Index

(d) All of the above

(e) None of the above

6. **Compared to the WPPSI-III, the Processing Speed subtests on the WPPSI-IV**

(a) Are more developmentally appropriate

(b) Require more finger dexterity

(c) Require finer visual discriminations

(d) Have less appealing artwork

(e) All of the above

7. **The limitation of subtest substitution to only composite scores with more than two subtests, to only one substitution for each composite score, and to only supplemental subtests in the same cognitive domain is a weakness because it limits examiner flexibility.**

True or False?

8. **A weakness of the WPPSI-IV is**

(a) The need to use multiple Stimulus Books

(b) The lack of easels for test administration

(c) The change in sequence of Stimulus Books for older children

(d) Possible problems with dauber ink smearing or running out during a test

(e) All of the above

9. **The normative sample for the WPPSI-IV is**

(a) A strength because of the size and representativeness of the sample

(b) A strength because large numbers of children with severe disabilities were included

(c) A weakness because only English-speaking children were included

(continued)

(d) A weakness because children whose parents had less than 9 years of formal education were included

(e) A weakness because four different geographic regions were represented

Answers: I. b; 2. b; 3. c; 4. d; 5. e; 6. a; 7. False; 8. e; 9. a

REFERENCES

Alfonso, V. C., & Pratt, S. I. (1997). Issues and suggestions for training professionals in assessing intelligence. In D. P. Flanagan, J. L. Genshaft, & P. L. Harrison (Eds.), *Contemporary intellectual assessment: Theories, tests, and issues* (pp. 326–344). New York, NY: Guilford Press.

The American Heritage Dictionary of the English Language (5th ed.). (2011). Boston, MA: Houghton Mifflin Harcourt.

Baddeley, A. (2012). Working memory: Theories, models, and controversies. *Annual Review of Psychology, 63,* 1–29. doi: 10.1146annurev-psych-120710-100422

Belk, M. S., LoBello, S. G., Ray, G. E., & Zachar, P. (2002). WISC–III administration, clerical, and scoring errors make by student examiners. *Journal of Psychoeducational Assessment, 20*(3), 290–300.

Bracken, B. A., & McCallum, R. S. (1998). *Universal Nonverbal Intelligence Test.* Austin, TX: Pro Ed.

Cohen, J. (1988). *Statistical power analysis for the behavioral sciences* (2nd ed.) Hillsdale, NJ: Erlbaum.

Elliott, C. D. (2007). *Differential Ability Scales—Second Edition administration and scoring manual.* San Antonio, TX: Psychological Corporation.

Flanagan, D. P., Ortiz, S. O., & Alfonso, V. C. (2013). *Essentials of cross-battery assessment.* Hoboken, NJ: Wiley.

Hale, J. B., Hoeppner, J. B., & Fiorello, C. A. (2002). Analyzing Digit Span components to assessment of attention processes. *Journal of Psychoeducational Assessment, 20*(2), 128–143.

Kaufman, A. S., & Kaufman, N. L. (1983). *Kaufman Assessment Battery for Children.* Circle Pines, MN: American Guidance Service.

Kaufman, A. S., & Kaufman, N. L. (2004). *Kaufman Assessment Battery for Children, Second Edition.* Circle Pines, MN: American Guidance Service.

Kuentzel, J. G., Hetterscheidt, L. A., & Barnett, D. (2011). Testing intelligently includes double-checking Wechsler IQ scores. *Journal of Psychoeducational Assessment, 29*(1), 39–46. doi: 10.1177/0734282910362048.

LoBello, S. G., & Holley, G. (1999). WPPSI-R administration, clerical, and scoring errors by student examiners. *Journal of Psychoeducational Assessment, 17*(1), 15–23. doi: 10.1177/073428299901700102

Loe, S. A., Kadlubek, R. M., & Marks, W. J. (2007). Administration and scoring errors on the WISC-IV among graduate student examiners. *Journal of Psychoeducational Assessment, 25* (3), 237–247. doi: 10.1177/0734282906296505

Pearson. (2009). *Wechsler Individual Achievement Test* (3rd ed.). San Antonio, TX: Author.

The Psychological Corporation. (1992). *Wechsler Individual Achievement Test.* San Antonio, TX: Author.

Reynolds, C. R. (1997). Forward and backward memory span should not be combined for clinical analysis. *Archives of Clinical Neuropsychology, 12,* 29–40.

Roid, G. H. (2003). *Stanford-Binet Intelligence Scales, Fifth Edition.* Itasca, IL: Riverside Publishing. (SB 5)

Roid, G. H., & Miller, L. J. (1997). *Leiter International Performance Scale—Revised.* Wood Dale, IL: Stoelting. (Leiter-R)

Scheller, A. (2013). *WPPSI-IV: Working memory.* WPPSI-IV Introductory Training Session. San Antonio, TX: Pearson. Retrieved from https://www.brainshark.com/pearsonassessments/WPPSI-IV_WorkingMemory/zGpz8jaatz4FEHz0?intk=2097410

Schneider, W. J., & McGrew, K. S. (2012). The Cattell-Horn-Carroll model of intelligence. In D. P. Flanagan & P. L. Harrison (Eds.), *Contemporary intellectual assessment: Theories, tests, and issues* (3rd ed., pp. 99–144). New York, NY: Guilford Press.

Terman, L. M., & Merrill, M. A. (1960). *Stanford-Binet Intelligence Scale, Form L-M.* Boston, MA: Houghton Mifflin.

Wechsler, D. (1949). *Wechsler Intelligence Scale for Children.* New York, NY: Psychological Corporation.

Wechsler, D. (1967). *Wechsler Preschool and Primary Scale of Intelligence Scale.* New York, NY: Psychological Corporation.

Wechsler, D. (1989). *Wechsler Preschool and Primary Scale of Intelligence Scale—Revised.* San Antonio, TX: Psychological Corporation.

Wechsler, D. (1997). *Wechsler Adult Intelligence Scale—Third Edition.* San Antonio, TX: Psychological Corporation.

Wechsler, D. (2002). *Wechsler Preschool and Primary Scale of Intelligence Scale—Third Edition.* San Antonio, TX: Psychological Corporation.

Wechsler, D. (2003). *Wechsler intelligence scale for children* (4th ed.). San Antonio, TX: Pearson.

Wechsler, D. (2008). *Wechsler adult intelligence scale* (4th ed.). San Antonio, TX: Pearson.

Wechsler, D. (2012a). *Wechsler preschool and primary scale of intelligence* (4th ed.). San Antonio, TX: Pearson.

Wechsler, D. (2012b). *Wechsler preschool and primary scale of intelligence (4th ed.): Administration and scoring manual.* San Antonio, TX: Pearson.

Wechsler, D. (2012c). *Wechsler preschool and primary scale of intelligence (4th ed.): Technical and interpretive manual.* San Antonio, TX: Pearson.

Willis, J. O. (2001). Scoring errors necessitate double-checking protocols. *Today's School Psychologist, 4*(5), 7.

Woodcock, R. W., McGrew, K. S., & Mather, N. (2007). *Woodcock-Johnson tests of cognitive ability (3rd ed.) normative update.* Itasca, IL: Riverside.

Zhu, J., & Cayton, T. (2013, July). *Substitution, proration, or retest: The best strategy when a score subtest is missing.* Paper presented at the Annual Convention of the American Psychological Association, Honolulu, HI.

Zuccaro, C. A. (2012). Subtest substitution in the VCI and PSI and its effects on the WISC-IV full scale IQ: Sound assessment or IQ roulette? (Doctoral dissertation). Retrieved from ProQuest (3521151), http://search.proquest.com//docview/1033587381

Six

WPPSI-IV SCORE DIFFERENCES ACROSS DEMOGRAPHIC GROUPS

Susan Engi Raiford
Diane L. Coalson
Mark D. Engi

INTRODUCTION

Cognitive ability test scores commonly show mean differences across children grouped according to sex, parent education level, and race/ethnicity. For this reason, each age band of the WPPSI-IV normative sample was matched to the 2010 U.S. census proportions for these variables, so that scores derived from performance of the normative sample are representative of performance in the U.S. population.

Group differences in mean scores do not necessarily indicate that a test is biased. Item bias, or differential item functioning based on group membership, is a separate but related validity issue. Item bias indicates that the same item functions differently (i.e., the item is more difficult for one segment than another) within two segments of a sample (e.g., White compared with African American) that are matched based on other important characteristics (e.g., age, sex, parent education, geographic region). Item bias was examined statistically during WPPSI-IV development phases. Oversamples of children from different racial/ethnicity categories were tested during development, and results were compared across groups to determine if any items functioned differently based on categorical membership. Biased items were removed before publication (Wechsler, 2012). This chapter examines results at the composite score level *after* that process was completed. Group differences at this stage are often shown to be related to variation on *other* important characteristics.

DON'T FORGET
....

Racial/ethnic groups vary greatly in the distribution of other important variables related to socioeconomic status and their home environment.

For example, children's cognitive ability varies with parent education attainment, and parent education in turn differs across racial/ethnic groups (as do a great number of other variables related to socioeconomic status; see Weiss, Chen, Harris, Holdnack, & Saklofske, 2010, and Weiss, Harris, et al., 2006 for reviews of these factors). To illustrate, Table 6.1 provides the percentage of adults from selected racial/ethnic groups in the United States completing various levels of education (U.S. Bureau of the Census, 2012).

As seen in Table 6.1, the proportion of adults who attain less than a high school diploma or its equivalent varies across racial/ethnic groups. Notably, the percentage of individuals in this category who are Hispanic is approximately tenfold the analogous percentages of White individuals. The proportion of individuals who are African American and attain less than a high school education is more than twice that of White individuals. Similar proportions of White, Hispanic, and African American individuals obtain a high school diploma or equivalent. The percentage of White individuals who obtain a bachelor's degree is more than double that of Hispanic individuals who obtain bachelor's degrees, and 50% higher than that of African American individuals. Hence, racial/ethnic group means on WPPSI-IV composite scores are expected to show differences that are partially related to group differences in parent education level or other factors related to socioeconomic status.

Table 6.1 Percentage of Adults From Selected Racial/Ethnic Groups Completing Various Levels of Education

Years of Education	White (Non-Hispanic)	Hispanic (Any Race)	African American	Asian
≤ 8 Years	2.1	20.4	3.9	6.3
9–11 Years	5.4	14.6	11.2	4.8
High School Diploma or Equivalent	30.5	29.9	34.0	20.6
Some College or Associate's Degree	21.7	16.7	24.1	12.7
Bachelor's Degree or Higher	40.3	18.3	26.8	55.5

Source: U.S. Bureau of the Census (2012).

Therefore, this chapter compares means and standard deviations of the composite scores from the published test for children from the normative sample of WPPSI-IV segmented by sex, parent education level, and race/ethnicity. As parent education level is closely related to the composite scores on measures of intellectual ability, the race/ethnicity means are reported with and without controlling for parent education and sex.

DON'T FORGET

....

U.S. Census Bureau data from 2012 indicate that, relative to White individuals, 10 times as many Hispanic individuals attain less than a high school diploma, and that the percentage of White individuals who obtain a bachelor's degree is more than double that of Hispanic.

SCORES BY SEX

An array of research supports the general finding that males and females perform differently on measures of cognitive ability. The performance differences between the sexes vary by age. While the mechanisms of these differences are not known definitively and substantial controversy characterizes theoretical explanations (Keith, Reynolds, Roberts, Winter, & Austin, 2011), research suggests sex-related brain architecture, connectivity, development, and volume may be related to the distinctions in performance (Burgaleta et al., 2012; Rushton & Ankney, 2009; Schmithorst, 2009).

Whereas in many studies the differences across very young males and females are statistically significant, they are slight and may not be practically meaningful. Among young children, females tend to slightly outperform males on formal measures of general intellectual ability (Kaufman & Kaufman, 1973, 2004) as well as some specific cognitive abilities (Kaufman & Kaufman, 1973, 2004; Keith et al., 2011). *Gc*, which is related to the WPPSI-IV Verbal Comprehension Index, is found to show no sex difference in young children, however (Kaufman & Kaufman, 2004; Keith et al., 2011).

The picture appears to change a few years after children enter formal schooling. The pattern of females outscoring males is no longer present around age 7, when male and female children perform roughly the same on composite scores (Kaufman & Kaufman, 2004). In fact, some results suggest a reversal of the pattern observed in young children: By age 10, there are indications that groups of males outscore groups of females on general intellectual ability measures (Dykiert, Gale, & Deary, 2009).

Sex-related advantages for specific cognitive abilities are also evident. School-age males have been shown to outscore females on factors related to visual–spatial ability (Kaufman & Kaufman, 2004; Keith et al., 2011), which is analogous to the WPPSI-IV Visual Spatial Index. School-age females appear to show an advantage on the processing speed factor (Keith et al., 2011).

For adolescents and adults, results indicate that males usually outscore females on measures of both overall intellectual ability (Lynn & Irwing, 2008; Nyborg, 2005; Rushton & Ankney, 2009) and most specific cognitive domains. For example, on the Wechsler Adult Intelligence Scale–Fourth Edition (WAIS-IV; Wechsler, 2008), males score higher on general intellectual ability, represented by the Full Scale IQ, and higher on verbal comprehension, perceptual reasoning, and working memory; but females maintain their school-age advantage on processing speed (Lichtenberger & Kaufman, 2013; Salthouse & Saklofske, 2010).

Each of the nine age bands in the WPPSI-IV normative sample is equally composed of males and females. Table 6.2 presents the mean WPPSI-IV composite scores of male and female children in the normative sample. The values presented are not controlled for differences across parent education levels, races/ethnicities, or other variables that may importantly contribute to the discrepancies. (All analyses in this chapter were conducted for this book by the authors.)

All WPPSI-IV composite scores are significantly higher in female than in male children. These results are consistent with prior results that indicate young females display general intellectual ability and specific cognitive ability scores that are

Table 6.2 WPPSI-IV Normative Sample Composite Score Means and Standard Deviations, by Sex

Sex		VCI	VSI	FRI	WMI	PSI	FSIQ	VAI	NVI	GAI	CPI
Female	Mean	101.6	100.7	100.9	101.6	102.3	101.7	101.6	101.6	101.4	102.1
	SD	14.6	14.7	14.6	14.9	15.0	14.7	14.7	14.9	14.6	14.7
	N	850	850	550	850	550	850	850	850	850	550
Male	Mean	98.4	99.2	99.0	98.4	97.7	98.3	98.4	98.4	98.5	97.9
	SD	15.2	15.3	15.4	14.9	14.8	15.2	15.2	14.9	15.3	15.1
	N	850	850	550	850	550	850	850	850	850	550
Mean Difference (F-M)		3.2**	1.5*	1.8*	3.3**	4.6**	3.5**	3.2**	3.2**	2.9**	4.2**

*$p < .05$
**$p < .001$
Note. VCI = Verbal Comprehension Index, VSI = Visual Spatial Index, FRI = Fluid Reasoning Index, WMI = Working Memory Index, PSI = Processing Speed Index, FSIQ = Full Scale IQ, VAI = Vocabulary Acquisition Index, NVI = Nonverbal Index, GAI = General Ability Index, CPI = Cognitive Proficiency Index.

≡ *Rapid Reference 6.1*

Sex Differences on the WPPSI-IV and as Developmental Trends

- On average, female children scored higher than male children on all composite scores. The difference was statistically significant for all scores.
- Female children outscored male children on the WPPSI-IV Full Scale IQ by an average of 3.5 points.
- By around age 7 to 10, the average Full Scale IQ scores of females and males are close to equivalent.
- By adolescence and adulthood, the trend begins to reverse, with male children outscoring female children on the Full Scale IQ.
- The largest sex difference was observed on the WPPSI-IV Processing Speed Index (close to a 5-point advantage), followed by the Cognitive Proficiency Index. For both comparisons, females obtained the higher score.
- The processing speed advantage is consistently observed in females across all age ranges, including school-age children, adolescents, and adults.

slightly higher than their same-age male peers. Contrary to some prior results, however, the mean difference for the Verbal Comprehension Index is significant and one of the largest male-female differences among the composite scores. Consistent with findings at other ages, the largest female advantage was observed on the Processing Speed Index.

Rapid Reference 6.1 summarizes the key results in the WPPSI-IV analysis for differences between female and male children, and the developmental trends in sex differences on intellectual ability tests.

SCORES BY PARENT EDUCATION LEVEL

Socioeconomic status is strongly associated with children's intellectual ability test scores. It is often represented in intelligence test research by parent education level. However, a rich body of studies published early in the last century until the present day documents the strong relations of various other proxies for socioeconomic status (e.g., parent occupation level, family income) with intellectual ability.

In early studies examining the association of parent education and child intellectual ability, Goodenough (1927) found significant associations between the Kuhlmann-Binet IQs of preschool children and the number of years of formal schooling for each parent. These associations were greater than other proxies for socioeconomic status, such as parent occupation. In a study utilizing developmental scales and the Stanford-Binet with children aged 0 to 6, Bayley and Jones (1937) found similar results beginning at age 2. Parent education was noted as superior to other proxy representations for socioeconomic status in this study. Honzik (1940) obtained similar results with children aged 3 to 8 years. Mother's education was more closely related to child cognitive ability than were a host of other proxy socioeconomic status variables. Furthermore, results suggested the influence of parent education on children's cognitive ability scores continued to increase throughout the 5-year span.

Kaufman (1973b) segmented portions of the WPPSI (Wechsler, 1967) normative sample according to father's occupation, which is closely related to education, and compared their performance on the three IQ scores. Results indicated a significant relation between father's occupation and mean Verbal, Performance, and Full Scale IQ, and that all IQ scores of children with fathers from professional and technical occupations differed significantly from those of children with fathers from other employment segments. On the extreme ends of the father occupation spectrum, the Verbal IQ differences were 17 points, Performance IQ varied by around 15 points, and the Full Scale IQ differences were 18 points. Hence, the largest difference was noted on the Full Scale IQ, followed by the Verbal IQ, and then the Performance IQ. Father's occupation was more predictive of performance than was grouping by rural versus urban domicile or U.S. geographic region.

Among preschool children aged 2:6 to 4:11 on the Kaufman Assessment Battery for Children (KABC; Kaufman & Kaufman, 1983), the influence of parent education was strongest on the Simultaneous Processing and Nonverbal scales and the Mental Processing Composite. For these three scales, the approximate differences between extreme segments of parent education were 14 to 15 standard-score points, whereas the difference was least on the Sequential Processing Scale (12).

An investigation with the WPPSI-R (Wechsler, 1989) normative sample demonstrated that parent education was more predictive of Verbal, Performance, and Full Scale IQs than was race/ethnicity, parent occupation, and geographic region (Sellers, Burns, & Guyrke, 1996). The strongest relations with parent education were noted on the Full Scale IQ and the Verbal IQ, although the correlation with Performance IQ was also significant.

For preschool children aged 3 to 6 on the KABC-II (Kaufman & Kaufman, 2004), the influence of parent education was most clear on the Gc scale, which is conceptually similar to the WPPSI-IV Verbal Comprehension Index, and the Fluid-Crystallized Index (FCI), which is analogous to the WPPSI-IV Full Scale IQ. Differences for all composite scores and subtests were statistically significant. The approximate differences between extreme segments of parent education ranged from 15 (Gsm and Glr) to 22 points (Gc). These results are indicative of the importance of the home environment (and potentially, genetic variability) in cognitive development among younger children.

Among school-age children aged 7 to 18, the mean KABC-II score differences by parent education level were less divergent, albeit all significant. The greatest difference continued to occur on the Gc scale and the FCI, with smaller differences on the remainder of the composite scores. Hence, parent education remained a significant predictor of performance among school-age children. Weiss, Harris, et al. (2006) found a similar result for school-age children at the Full Scale IQ level when examining the WISC-IV (Wechsler, 2003) normative sample (aged 6 to 16), segmented by parent education level. The average Full Scale IQ was more than 20 points lower in children of parents with an eighth-grade education or less relative to children of parents with a bachelor's degree. The results for composite scores other than the Full Scale IQ were not reported.

Table 6.3 presents the mean WPPSI-IV composite scores of children in the normative sample segmented into five parent education levels. The sample is matched within each age band to census proportions for parent education level. If the child lives with only one parent or guardian, the education level of that individual is used. If the child lives with two parents or guardians, the education level of those individuals is averaged. Partial levels are rounded up to the next level.

The N count in Table 6.3 for each parent education level varies by composite score, because children aged 2:6 to 3:11 do not take the Fluid Reasoning or Processing Speed subtests. Hence, fewer children have scores on composite scores that are derived using those subtests. The lowermost row presents the percentage of score variance accounted for by parent education level.

As with other cognitive ability tests, parent education level is strongly related to WPPSI-IV performance. The variance in performance explained by parent education level suggests it has the greatest influence on the Vocabulary Acquisition Index, followed by the General Ability Index, the Full Scale IQ, and the Verbal Comprehension Index. The influence is least for the Working Memory Index and Processing Speed Index.

These results are consistent with those of prior studies that indicate verbal and crystallized abilities, as well as general intellectual ability, are more highly correlated with parent education level relative to visual–spatial, fluid reasoning, working memory, and processing speed abilities. The strong association between parent education and the verbal skills of young children is observed consistently in prior research. The association between parent education and the General Ability Index, which has reduced working memory and processing speed demands relative to the Full Scale IQ, also reflects the weaker association between parent education and measures of working memory and processing speed.

Table 6.3 WPPSI-IV Normative Sample Composite Score Means and Standard Deviations, by Parent Education Level

Parent Education Level	Value	VCI	VSI	FRI	WMI	PSI	FSIQ	VAI	NVI	GAI	CPI
8 years or less	Mean	87.8	91.5	92.7	94.4	99.1	89.9	86.7	91.4	88.3	99.1
	SD	12.3	12.0	12.6	13.9	15.4	12.0	11.0	13.0	10.8	14.2
	N	40	40	25	40	25	40	40	40	40	25
9–11 years	Mean	89.8	92.5	91.8	94.5	93.8	89.6	88.5	91.6	89.7	92.8
	SD	12.7	12.2	12.3	12.6	12.8	11.4	11.5	11.7	11.1	12.6
	N	170	170	106	170	106	170	170	170	170	106
12 years (high school diploma or equivalent)	Mean	95.4	94.8	94.9	97.3	95.4	94.9	95.1	95.2	94.7	95.4
	SD	14.8	14.6	15.3	16.2	16.8	15.1	14.8	15.6	14.7	16.8
	N	392	392	254	392	254	392	392	392	392	254
13–15 years (some college)	Mean	100.0	100.6	100.5	99.8	101.4	100.2	100.8	100.4	100.2	100.9
	SD	13.5	13.9	14.0	13.9	15.1	13.5	13.6	13.7	13.5	14.4
	N	544	544	352	544	352	544	544	544	544	352
16 years or more (college graduate)	Mean	107.3	105.9	105.9	104.2	103.7	107.4	107.2	106.3	107.5	104.6
	SD	13.6	14.9	14.3	14.9	12.9	13.8	13.7	14.1	14.0	13.3
	N	554	554	363	554	363	554	554	554	554	363
% of variance explained*		15.7	10.6	10.5	4.7	4.8	15.8	17.5	11.7	16.7	6.3

*All statistically significant ($p < .001$)

Note. VCI = Verbal Comprehension Index, VSI = Visual Spatial Index, FRI = Fluid Reasoning Index, WMI = Working Memory Index, PSI = Processing Speed Index, FSIQ = Full Scale IQ, VAI = Vocabulary Acquisition Index, NVI = Nonverbal Index, GAI = General Ability Index, CPI = Cognitive Proficiency

≡ *Rapid Reference 6.2*

....

Parent Education Level Differences on the WPPSI-IV

- Among the WPPSI-IV index scores, parent education level explains the most variance in scores involving verbal ability (i.e., the Vocabulary Acquisition Index and the Verbal Comprehension Index).
- Parent education level explains more variance in the Full Scale IQ and the General Ability Index than in the Nonverbal Index. This difference likely reflects their reliance on verbal ability.
- The average Full Scale IQ of children with a parent education level of eighth grade or less is about 18 points lower than the average Full Scale IQ of children with a parent education level of a bachelor's degree or higher.
- The WPPSI-IV Working Memory Index and the Processing Speed Index are relatively less affected by parent education level. Parent education level only explains about 5% of the variance in these composite scores.

Rapid Reference 6.2 lists the key results in the WPPSI-IV analysis for differences across parent education levels.

SCORES BY RACE/ETHNICITY

Comparing the mean score differences of groups of White children to groups of African American children and groups of Hispanic children has been a goal of many investigations. An investigation by Kaufman (1973a) created groups of White and African American children aged 4 to 6 matched on age, sex, region, father's occupation, and urban–rural residence from the WPPSI normative sample, and compared their performance on the Verbal IQ, Performance IQ, and Full Scale IQ. The mean difference was greatest on Full Scale IQ (10.8 standard-score points), followed by Verbal IQ (10.5) and Performance IQ (8.9). When the results were examined by single-year increments, the differences on Performance IQ and on Full Scale IQ decreased for each year the child aged.

Kaufman and Kaufman (1973) examined 148 pairs of African American and White children matched on age, sex, and father's occupation on the General Cognitive Index (GCI) of the McCarthy Scales of Children's Abilities (McCarthy Scales; McCarthy, 1972). They found no significant racial/ethnic differences on the cognitive scales among children aged 2:6 to 5:5, but a significant difference for ages 6:5 to 8:6.

Arinoldo (1981) administered the McCarthy Scales and either the WPPSI or the WISC-R (Wechsler, 1974) in counterbalanced order to 40 children aged 4:0

to 5:6 and 7:0 to 8:6, then compared the mean McCarthy GCI and WPPSI/ WISC-R Full Scale IQ scores across groups of White and African American children. He found smaller differences for preschool than school-age children, and smaller differences overall on the McCarthy GCI than on the Wechsler Full Scale IQs. In the preschool group, the White group outscored the African American group on the McCarthy GCI by 3.8 points and on the WPPSI Full Scale IQ by 4.2 points. For school-age children, the White group outscored the African American group on the McCarthy GCI by 15.5 points and on the Wechsler Full Scale IQ by 21.3 points. All differences were significant ($p < .05$ for preschool, and $p < .001$ for school-age). Hence, the pattern observed by Arinoldo was similar to that observed in the Kaufmans' (1973) investigation: Differences between African American and White groups were relatively larger in the older group.

An investigation with the WPPSI-R normative sample (Sellers et al., 1996) split children by race/ethnicity into Black Hispanic, Black, White Hispanic, Native American, Other Ethnicity, White, and Asian groups, and examined contribution to the three IQ scores of race/ethnicity, parent education, parent occupation, geographic region, and sex. The strongest predictor was parent education, followed by race/ethnicity (all $p < .001$), for the three IQ scores. Beyond parent education, race/ethnicity accounted for 5.9% of the variance for the Full Scale IQ, 4.6% for the Verbal IQ, and 4.9% for the Performance IQ. Unfortunately, group means were not reported, and the results were not reported by age.

For children aged 3 to 6 in the KABC-II normative sample, the percentage of score variance accounted for by race/ethnicity after controlling for sex and mother's education level was greatest for the Gc scale (6%). The least variance was accounted for within Glr (0.2%) and Gsm (1.3%) (Kaufman & Kaufman, 2004).

The largest adjusted differences between White and African American children occurred on the Gc scale (almost 7 standard-score points in favor of Whites) and the Gv scale (4.3 points). The smallest differences were present on the Gsm scale (African American outscored White by 0.4 points), analogous to the WPPSI-IV Working Memory Index, and the Glr scale, which showed only a 0.4 point advantage for Whites. For the FCI, analogous to the WPPSI-IV Full Scale IQ, the adjusted mean difference in favor of Whites was 3.6 points (Kaufman & Kaufman, 2004). Between White and Hispanic children, the largest adjusted composite score differences were present on Gc (9.1), FCI (5.0), and Gsm (4.3). In contrast, Gv (0.6), Glr (0.8), and NVI (1.1) showed almost no difference.

The authors noted that adjusting for parent education among ethnic groups was appropriate because the distribution of parent education differs across racial/ ethnic groups (as seen in Table 1.1 of this chapter), but that it does not thoroughly account for the socioeconomic differences across racial/ethnic groups. Parent education, they indicated, is objectively measured, typically accurately reported by the parents (which is not the case with many socioeconomic status variables such as income), and is plausibly related to child cognitive development. Thus, parent education merely serves as a *proxy variable* for many other aspects of socioeconomic status that vary by race/ethnicity, and therefore *only provides a partial estimate of the impact of socioeconomic status on racial/ethnic score differences* (Kaufman & Kaufman, 2004).

These differences persist into adolescence and adulthood. For example, among adolescents and adults aged 11 to 24, a White group outscored an African American and a Hispanic group on the Crystallized, Fluid, and Composite IQ scores of the Kaufman Adolescent and Adult Intelligence Test (KAIT; Kaufman & Kaufman, 1993). The differences between the White and African American groups varied from approximately 10 (Crystallized) to 12 standard-score points (Fluid and Composite). The White and Hispanic group means were discrepant by approximately 9 (Fluid) to 13 points (Crystallized).

Table 6.4 presents the mean WPPSI-IV composite scores of children in the normative sample segmented into five racial/ethnicity groups. The WPPSI-IV normative sample is matched within each age band to census proportions for these five groups. Because the percentages of children of parents with the five education levels differ across racial/ethnic groups, the scores are reported unadjusted *and* adjusted for parent education level and sex.

The summary rows at the bottom of Table 6.4 present the percentage of score variance accounted for by sex, parent education level, and race/ethnicity combined; sex and parent education level combined; and the residual percentage accounted for by race/ethnicity alone. The Vocabulary Acquisition Index and the Verbal Comprehension Index have the greatest residual variance attributable to race/ethnicity (2.5% and 2.3%, respectively), followed by the General Ability Index (2.0%) and the Full Scale IQ (1.6%). The Processing Speed Index (0.1%), Cognitive Proficiency Index (0.2%), and Working Memory Index (0.5%) show the smallest residual percentage of variance accounted for by race/ethnicity.

Because the mean differences of White children compared with African American children and with Hispanic children are greatest, they are here discussed in turn.

African American Children

The largest unadjusted differences between White and African American children appear on the General Ability Index (8.8 standard-score points), the Full Scale IQ

Table 6.4 WPPSI-IV Normative Sample Composite Score Means and Standard Deviations, by Race/Ethnicity, Adjusted for Sex and Parent Education Level

Race/Ethnicity		VCI	VSI	FRI	WMI	PSI	FSIQ	VAI	NVI	GAI	CPI
Asian	Unadjusted Mean	105.4	104.2	104.0	105.2	105.6	106.1	102.8	105.4	105.7	106.2
	Adjusted Mean	**102.0**	**101.4**	**101.6**	**103.0**	**103.5**	**102.5**	**99.1**	**102.1**	**102.2**	**103.9**
	SD	14.5	16.0	16.3	15.2	16.6	14.8	16.2	14.7	15.3	16.5
	N	52	52	37	52	37	52	52	52	52	37
African American	Unadjusted Mean	95.5	94.8	95.0	96.8	95.8	94.6	95.8	95.0	94.6	95.4
	Adjusted Mean	**96.6**	**95.8**	**96.3**	**97.5**	**96.7**	**95.7**	**97.0**	**96.1**	**95.8**	**96.4**
	SD	13.7	13.5	14.8	14.9	13.7	13.9	13.2	14.3	13.0	14.3
	N	250	250	163	250	163	250	250	250	250	163
Hispanic	Unadjusted Mean	94.0	97.0	98.0	97.9	98.9	95.3	93.7	97.0	94.8	98.5
	Adjusted Mean	**96.8**	**99.5**	**100.7**	**99.7**	**100.8**	**98.3**	**96.8**	**99.7**	**97.9**	**100.7**
	SD	12.2	13.4	14.1	13.1	14.8	12.5	12.6	13.1	12.3	13.5
	N	413	413	254	413	254	413	413	413	413	254
Other	Unadjusted Mean	100.9	99.4	99.9	100.7	102.6	101.2	100.8	101.2	100.5	101.9
	Adjusted Mean	**100.8**	**99.3**	**99.1**	**100.6**	**101.8**	**101.1**	**100.6**	**101.1**	**100.4**	**101.1**
	SD	16.0	14.6	15.4	15.5	16.6	16.1	14.4	15.8	15.7	15.5

White

	N									
	77	77	47	77	47	77	77	77	77	47
Unadjusted Mean	103.6	102.6	101.9	101.5	101.0	103.2	103.7	102.4	103.4	101.4
Adjusted Mean	**102.2**	**101.4**	**100.6**	**100.6**	**100.2**	**101.7**	**102.2**	**101.1**	**101.9**	**100.4**
SD	15.2	15.4	15.0	15.6	15.1	15.3	15.3	15.4	15.5	15.4
N	908	908	599	908	599	908	908	908	908	599
% of variance accounted for by sex, parent education, and race/ethnicity	19.3	12.1	11.6	6.2	7.8	19.0	20.9	13.8	19.8	9.1
% of variance for sex and parent education	17.0	11.1	10.8	5.7	7.7	17.4	18.4	13.0	17.8	8.9
[a] residual % of variance for race/ethnicity	2.3	1.0	0.8	0.5	0.1	1.6	2.5	0.8	2.0	0.2

[a] % of variance accounted for by race/ethnicity, above that accounted for by parent education level and sex

Note. VCI = Verbal Comprehension Index, VSI = Visual Spatial Index, FRI = Fluid Reasoning Index, WMI = Working Memory Index, PSI = Processing Speed Index, FSIQ = Full Scale IQ, VAI = Vocabulary Acquisition Index, NVI = Nonverbal Index, GAI = General Ability Index, CPI = Cognitive Proficiency Index.

(8.6), the Verbal Comprehension Index (8.1), the Vocabulary Acquisition Index (7.9), and the Visual Spatial Index (7.8). For the unadjusted and adjusted means, the smallest differences between White and African American children are present on the Working Memory Index (unadjusted 4.7 standard-score points and adjusted 3.1, respectively) and the Processing Speed Index (5.2 unadjusted, 3.5 adjusted).

After adjustment for sex and parent education level, the mean group differences shrink to around 5 to 6 points for each of these composite scores. The Full Scale IQ difference remains at 5.2 points, or about a third of a standard deviation. Adjusting for sex and parent education level has the greatest impact on the differences for the General Ability Index (a decrease in the difference of 2.7 standard-score points), Vocabulary Acquisition Index (decrease of 2.7), Full Scale IQ (decrease of 2.6), and Fluid Reasoning Index (decrease of 2.6), although all differences drop at least 1.6 standard-score points with the adjustment.

These results are similar to those previously observed. The White group composite score means remain significantly higher than the African American group means. The differences are noticeably larger on scores that include measures of crystallized ability and acquired knowledge. As noted by Kaufman and Kaufman (2004), adjustment for parent education alone cannot compensate entirely for the differences in socio-economic status across these two population segments. It provides only a crude and incomplete estimate of the impact of socioeconomic differences across the groups. For example, Weiss, Harris, et al. (2006) demonstrated that living in a home with more than one parent/guardian or with parents who have high expectations of the child's eventual achievement also has an impact on mediating these differences. As these aspects of the home environment can also vary by race/ethnicity, they could provide additional explanation of the remaining differences.

Hispanic Children

The most substantial unadjusted and adjusted differences between White and Hispanic children are present on the Vocabulary Acquisition Index (10.0 and 5.4, respectively), Verbal Comprehension Index (9.6, 5.4), General Ability Index (8.6, 4.0), and Full Scale IQ (7.9, 3.4). After adjustment for sex and parent education level, the Full Scale IQ difference remains at only 3.4 standard-score points (only about a fifth of a standard deviation) and the Nonverbal Index difference at only 1.4.

Adjustment for sex and parent education level has the largest impact on the Vocabulary Acquisition Index (a decrease in the difference of 4.6 standard-score points), General Ability Index (decrease of 4.6), Full Scale IQ (decrease of 4.5), and Verbal Comprehension Index (decrease of 4.2). For the unadjusted means, the smallest differences between White children and Hispanic children are present on the Processing Speed Index (2.1), the Cognitive Proficiency Index (2.9), the Working Memory Index (3.6), and the Fluid Reasoning Index (3.9).

Following adjustment, the differences between White and Hispanic children decrease substantially for composite scores that are not derived from Verbal Comprehension subtests. In fact, the Hispanic group has adjusted average scores slightly higher than the White group on the Processing Speed Index (0.6 points), Cognitive Proficiency Index (0.3), and Fluid Reasoning Index (0.1), and the Working Memory Index mean difference decreases to less than 1 point.

The White and Hispanic score differences are substantially smaller after adjustment, with the Hispanic group outscoring the White group on three composite scores. Even the largest difference is probably not practically meaningful. Weiss, Harris, et al. (2006) demonstrated that when additional socioeconomic factors such as household income are accounted for among school-age children, the White–Hispanic score differences vanish.

Rapid Reference 6.3 summarizes the average WPPSI-IV racial/ethnic score differences before and after adjustment for sex and parent education level.

≡ Rapid Reference 6.3

Racial/Ethnic Differences on the WPPSI-IV

- Race/ethnicity, sex, and parent education level together account for 19% of the variance in the Full Scale IQ. After adjustment for sex and parent education level, however, race/ethnicity only accounts for 1.6% of the variance.

- Following adjustment for sex and parent education level, race/ethnicity accounts for 1% or less of the variance in most composite scores.

- For composite scores that do not rely much on acquired knowledge, such as the Working Memory Index and Processing Speed Index, race/ethnicity accounts for almost no variance following adjustment for sex and parent education level.

- Following adjustment for sex and parent education level, the mean Full Scale IQ difference between Hispanic and White children drops from 7.9 points to only 3.4 points. The Nonverbal Index drops to only 1.4 points.

- The unadjusted Full Scale IQ and General Ability Index differences between White and African American children are close to 9 points. A similar discrepancy is observed on many intellectual ability measures.

- After adjustment for sex and parent education level, the mean White and African American group differences shrink to around 5 to 6 points for the WPPSI-IV Full Scale IQ and the General Ability Index.

- These results are similar to those previously observed. The unadjusted and adjusted White group composite score means remain significantly higher than the African American group means. The differences are noticeably larger on scores that include measures of crystallized ability and acquired knowledge.

CAUTION

Adjustment for parent education alone cannot compensate entirely for the differences in socioeconomic status (SES) across White and African American groups, because it provides only a crude and incomplete estimate of the SES impact across groups. However, it is one of the few SES variables that are most often reported accurately by research participants.

SUMMARY OF FINDINGS

To summarize, WPPSI-IV score differences are evident across sex, parent education level, and race/ethnicity. Additional research is needed to more closely examine the impact of other indicators of socioeconomic status and home environment variables on racial/ethnic differences, particularly for White compared with African American children. It is critical to examine the results for all composite scores to more fully understand how these differences manifest across specific cognitive abilities. Furthermore, examining patterns of these differences across infants and toddlers, as well as preschool and school-age children, may provide insight into their genesis and reveal more about their developmental progression.

CLINICAL APPLICATIONS OF SCORE DIFFERENCES

Risk factors and protective factors are likely to exert a great deal of influence on cognitive development during early childhood (Brassard & Boehm, 2007). Assessing those factors and utilizing them to design appropriate intervention and treatment plans is important for comprehensive evaluations.

Although parent education level represented socioeconomic status and roughly accounts for home environment influences in the analyses for this chapter, it is not malleable in many cases and is merely a proxy for a host of other important variables. It is selected within this chapter because, as noted, it is objective, easy to obtain, and more readily reported accurately in research settings. Hence, the results of these analyses and of the studies reviewed in this chapter reaffirm the importance of the practitioner's responsibility to consider the role of contextual variables in test interpretation. This is not new information, and is emphasized in many early childhood assessment, development, and intervention models (Avan & Kirkwood, 2010; Brassard & Boehm, 2007; D. Ford, 2012; L. Ford, Kozey, & Negreiros, 2012; Vig & Sanders, 2007).

Most early childhood assessment models emphasize the importance of a number of key influences on child cognitive development related to family and the home environment. Brassard and Boehm (2012), for example, list key influences to include poverty, parental substance abuse, work constraints and childcare, parental expectations, early intervention programs, developmental risk factors, exposure to maltreatment or violence, developmental protective factors, resilience, community context, and sociocultural considerations (Brassard & Boehm, 2012).

Risk and protective factors are rich areas to discover in the assessment process, and many are amenable to intervention. Some particularly relevant risk and protective factors that can be associated with preschool cognitive development ability and are fertile recommendation targets are listed in Rapid Reference 6.4. Refer to Brassard and Boehm (2007) for a more complete list of protective and risk factors, including those that are relatively static and thus more relevant to conceptualization rather than intervention.

≡ Rapid Reference 6.4

Malleable Risk and Protective Factors for Preschool Assessment and Intervention

Protective Factors
Child:
- Good nutrition
- Skills to elicit positive attention from others
- Communication behaviors
- Self-help skills
- Independence
- Good peer relationships

Family:
- Time with caring, interested adults
- Affection and strong bonds
- Family support
- Routines and consistency
- Monitored TV time

(continued)

- Reading together
- High parental expectation of child educational attainment
- Parental school involvement

Community:

- Support from friends and religious groups
- Parent training

Risk Factors
Family:

- Child abuse
- Maternal anxiety or depression
- Extreme poverty
- Unlimited TV viewing

Source: Adapted from Brassard and Boehm, 2007.

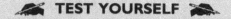

🐟 TEST YOURSELF 🐟

1. **Item bias indicates that the same item**
   (a) Functions exactly the same within two different segments of a matched sample.
   (b) Functions differently within two different segments of a matched sample.
   (c) Functions exactly the same across two different unmatched samples.
   (d) Functions differently across two different unmatched samples.

2. **As parent education level is closely related to the composite scores on measures of intellectual ability, the race/ethnicity means are reported**
   (a) With and without controlling for parent education level and sex.
   (b) Only without controlling for parent education level.
   (c) Only without controlling for sex.
   (d) Controlling for *either* parent education level *or* sex.

3. **Which of the following statements is *true* regarding ability scores by sex?**
   (a) School-age females show higher general intellectual ability than males; however, school-age males outscore females on factors related to visual–spatial ability.
   (b) School-age females show higher general intellectual ability than males; however, school-age males outscore females on the processing speed factor.
   (c) School-age males show higher general intellectual ability than females; however, school-age females outscore males on factors related to visual–spatial ability.

(d) School-age males show higher general intellectual ability than females; however, school-age females outscore males on the processing speed factor.

4. **Key results in the WPPSI-IV analysis for differences between female and male children indicate that**

   (a) On average, females scored higher than males on all composite scores; however, males outscored females on the Full Scale IQ.

   (b) On average, males scored higher than females on all composite scores; however, females outscored males on the Full Scale IQ.

   (c) On average, females scored higher than males on all composite scores, as well as the Full Scale IQ.

   (d) On average, males scored higher than females on all composite scores, as well as the Full Scale IQ.

5. **A study with the WPPSI-R normative sample (Sellers et al., 1996) demonstrated that**

   (a) Parent education level was more predictive of the Full Scale IQ than was race/ethnicity, parent occupation, or geographic region.

   (b) Parent occupation was more predictive of the Full Scale IQ than was race/ethnicity, parent education level, or geographic region.

   (c) Parent education level was less predictive of the Full Scale IQ than was parent occupation.

   (d) Parent education level was less predictive of the Full Scale IQ than was race/ethnicity.

6. **The variance accounted for in WPPSI-IV performance suggests that parent education level has**

   (a) The greatest influence on the Verbal Comprehension Index, followed by the Full Scale IQ.

   (b) The greatest influence on the Vocabulary Acquisition Index, followed by the General Ability Index.

   (c) The greatest influence on the General Ability Index, followed by the Full Scale IQ.

   (d) Equal influence on both the Working Memory Index and Processing Speed Index.

7. **Overall, the White group composite score means remain significantly**

   (a) Higher than the Asian group means, with differences noticeably larger on scores that include measures of working memory and processing speed.

   (b) Higher than the Asian group means, with differences noticeably larger on scores that include measures of crystallized ability and acquired knowledge.

   (c) Higher than the African American group means, with differences noticeably larger on scores that include measures of working memory and processing speed.

   (d) Higher than the African American group means, with differences noticeably larger on scores that include measures of crystallized ability and acquired knowledge.

(continued)

8. **Which of the following variables related to socioeconomic status is reported most accurately in research?**

    (a) Household income

    (b) Parent education level

    (c) Father's occupation

    (d) Urban–rural residence

9. **Which of the following is *not* a risk factor for preschool cognitive development?**

    (a) Parent and child reading together

    (b) Extreme poverty

    (c) Maternal depression

    (d) Unlimited TV viewing

10. **Socioeconomic status is only weakly associated with children's ability scores.**
    True or False?

11. **Parent education level serves as a proxy variable and therefore provides only a partial estimate of the impact of socioeconomic status on racial/ ethnic score differences.**
    True or False?

Answers: 1. b; 2. a; 3. d; 4. c; 5. a; 6. b; 7. d; 8. b; 9. a; 10. False; 11. True

REFERENCES

Arinoldo, C. G. (1981). Black–white differences in the general cognitive index of the McCarthy Scales and in the Full Scale IQs of Wechsler's scales. *Journal of Clinical Psychology, 37*, 630–638.

Avan, B., & Kirkwood, B. (2010). Review of the theoretical frameworks for the study of child development within public health and epidemiology. *Journal of Epidemiology and Community Health, 64*, 388–393. doi: 10.1136/jech.2008.084046

Bayley, N., & Jones, H. E. (1937). Environmental correlates of mental and motor development: A cumulative study from infancy to six years. *Child Development, 8*, 329–341.

Brassard, M. R., & Boehm, A. E. (Eds.). (2007). *Preschool assessment: Principles and practices.* New York, NY: Guilford Press.

Burgaleta, M., Head, K., Alvarez-Linera, J., Martinez, K., Escorial, S., Haier, R., & Colom, R. (2012). Sex differences in brain volume are related to specific skills, not to general intelligence. *Intelligence, 40*, 60–68.

Dykiert, D., Gale, C. R., & Deary, I. J. (2009). Are apparent sex differences in mean IQ scores created in part by sample restriction and increased male variance? *Intelligence, 37*, 42–47.

Ford, D. (2012). Culturally different students in special education: Looking backward to move forward. *Exceptional Children, 78*, 391–405.

Ford, L., Kozey, M. L., & Negreiros, J. (2012). Cognitive assessment in early childhood: Theoretical and practice perspectives. In D. P. Flanagan & P. L. Harrison (Eds.), *Contemporary intellectual assessment: Theories, tests, and issues* (3rd ed., pp. 585–622). New York, NY: Guilford Press.

Goodenough, F. L. (1927). The relation of intelligence of pre-school children to the education of their parents. *School and Society, 26*, 54–56.

Honzik, M. P. (1940). Age changes in the relationship between certain environmental variables and children's intelligence. *Yearbook of the National Society for the Study of Education, 39*, 185–205.

Kaufman, A. S. (1973a). Comparison of the performance of matched groups of Black children and White children on the Wechsler Preschool and Primary Scale of Intelligence. *Journal of Consulting and Clinical Psychology, 41*, 186–191.

Kaufman, A. S. (1973b). The relationship of WPPSI IQs to SES and other background variables. *Journal of Clinical Psychology, 39*, 354–357.

Kaufman, A. S., & Kaufman, N. L. (1973). Sex differences on the McCarthy Scales of Children's Abilities. *Journal of Clinical Psychology, 29*, 362–365.

Kaufman, A. S., & Kaufman, N. L. (1983). *Kaufman assessment battery for children*. Circle Pines, MN: American Guidance Service.

Kaufman, A. S., & Kaufman, N. L. (1993). *Kaufman adolescent and adult intelligence test*. Circle Pines, MN: American Guidance Service.

Kaufman, A. S., & Kaufman, N. L. (2004). *Kaufman assessment battery for children* (2nd ed.). Bloomington, MN: Pearson.

Keith, T. Z., Reynolds, M. R., Roberts, L. G., Winter, A. L., & Austin, C. A. (2011). Sex differences in latent cognitive abilities ages 5 to 17: Evidence from the Differential Ability Scales–Second Edition. *Intelligence, 39*, 389–404.

Lichtenberger, E. O., & Kaufman, A. S. (2013). *Essentials of WAIS®-IV assessment* (2nd ed.). Hoboken, NJ: Wiley.

Lynn, R., & Irwing, P. (2008). Sex differences in mental arithmetic, digit span, and *g* defined as working memory capacity. *Intelligence, 36*, 226–235.

McCarthy, D. (1972). *The McCarthy Scales of Children's Abilities*. New York, NY: The Psychological Corporation.

Nyborg, H. (2005). Sex-related differences in general intelligence g, brain size, and social status. *Personality and Individual Differences, 39*, 497–509.

Rushton, J. P., & Ankney, C. D. (2009). Whole brain size and general mental ability: A review. *International Journal of Neuroscience, 119*(5), 692–732.

Salthouse, T. A., & Saklofske, D. H. (2010). Do the WAIS-IV tests measure the same aspects of cognitive functioning in adults under and over 65? In L. G. Weiss, D. H. Saklofske, D. Coalson, & S. E. Raiford (Eds.), *WAIS-IV clinical use and interpretation: Scientist-practitioner perspectives* (pp. 217–235). Amsterdam, The Netherlands: Elsevier Academic Press.

Schmithorst, V. J. (2009). Developmental sex differences in the relation of neuroanatomical connectivity to intelligence. *Intelligence, 37*, 164–173.

Sellers, A. H., Burns, W. J., & Guyrke, J. S. (1996). Prediction of premorbid intellectual functioning of young children using demographic information. *Applied Neuropsychology, 3*, 21–27.

Vig, S., & Sanders, M. (2007). Cognitive assessment. In M. R. Brassard & A. E. Boehm (Eds.), *Preschool assessment: Principles and practices* (pp. 383–419). New York, NY: Guilford Press.

U.S. Bureau of the Census (2012). *Educational attainment*. Retrieved from http://www.census.gov/hhes/socdemo/education/data/cps/2012/tables.html

Wechsler, D. (1967). *Wechsler preschool and primary scale of intelligence*. New York, NY: Psychological Corporation.

Wechsler, D. (1974). *Wechsler intelligence scale for children–revised*. New York, NY: Psychological Corporation.

Wechsler, D. (1989). *Wechsler preschool and primary scale of intelligence–revised*. San Antonio, TX: Psychological Corporation.

Wechsler, D. (2003). *Wechsler intelligence scale for children* (4th ed.). San Antonio, TX: Pearson.

Wechsler, D. (2008). *Wechsler adult intelligence scale* (4th ed.). Bloomington, MN: Pearson.

Wechsler, D. (2012). *Wechsler preschool and primary scale of intelligence* (4th ed.). Bloomington, MN: Pearson.

Weiss, L. G., Chen, H., Harris, J. G., Holdnack, J. A., & Saklofske, D. H. (2010). WAIS-IV use in societal context. In L. G. Weiss, D. H. Saklofske, D. Coalson, & S. E. Raiford (Eds.), *WAIS-IV clinical use and interpretation: Scientist-practitioner perspectives* (pp. 97–139). Amsterdam, The Netherlands: Elsevier Academic Press.

Weiss, L. G., Harris, J. G., Prifitera, A., Courville, T., Rolfhus, E., Saklofske, D. H., & Holdnack, J. A. (2006). WISC-IV interpretation in societal context. In L. G. Weiss, D. H. Saklofske, A. Prifitera, & J. A. Holdnack, *WISC-IV advanced clinical interpretation* (pp. 1–57). Amsterdam, The Netherlands: Elsevier Academic Press.

Seven

WPPSI-IV CLINICAL APPLICATIONS

Susan Engi Raiford
Diane L. Coalson
Stephanie A. Tong

This chapter discusses the use of the WPPSI-IV with frequent referral questions in early childhood. Special group study results are used to highlight the clinical utility of the various composite scores. A broad overview of clinical and situational issues that influence early childhood intellectual assessment is presented at the conclusion of the chapter.

USE OF THE WPPSI-IV WITH COMMON EARLY CHILDHOOD REFERRAL QUESTIONS

The *Technical and Interpretive Manual* summarizes the data for small samples of children with the following clinical conditions: intellectually gifted, intellectual disability—mild severity, intellectual disability—moderate severity, developmental delay—cognitive, developmental risk factors, preliteracy concerns, attention-deficit/ hyperactivity disorder, disruptive behavior, expressive language disorder, mixed receptive-expressive language disorder, English language learners, autistic disorder, and Asperger's disorder. Where applicable, the studies utilize criteria specified in the *Diagnostic and Statistical Manual of Mental Disorders*, fourth edition, text revision (*DSM-IV-TR*; American Psychiatric Association, 2000) because the fifth edition (*DSM-5*; American Psychiatric Association, 2013) was not available at the time of data collection. No other clinical studies with the WPPSI-IV had been published at the time of this writing, so this chapter is limited to those special group studies from the *Technical and Interpretive Manual*.

As indicated in the *Technical and Interpretive Manual*, there are a number of limitations to these studies. They are based on samples of convenience rather than randomly selected samples, and may not be representative of the diagnostic category at large for that reason. Furthermore, the diagnoses originate from various clinical settings using different diagnostic procedures, rather than from a single location based on a consistent, specified protocol. Some samples do not include children at the younger extreme of the age range, and data are aggregated across the two age bands. As indicated in the *Technical and Interpretive Manual*, the sample sizes are small (mean sample size = 41; range N = 26 [disruptive behavior] to 72 [developmental delay—cognitive]). Some of the samples include children who are heterogeneous with respect to some participation criteria, including identification method (e.g., appropriate scores *or* receiving services to identify children who are intellectually gifted, children with intellectual disability, and children with developmental delay—cognitive), or medication status (e.g., ADHD).

Although these data are useful to begin developing an understanding of how the test functions with different clinical populations, they should not be used to make a differential diagnosis for a child. Data are aggregated at the group level, which may obscure individual differences based on other variables such as educational, medical, and psychosocial history. Furthermore, the groups are not separated by validated subtypes that typically occur. Hence, apply these results to understand an individual case with caution, considering the child's special circumstances carefully. A summary of the group data for the Full Scale IQ, primary index scores, mean of the primary index scores, and ancillary index scores is provided in Rapid References 7.1 and 7.2.

≡ Rapid Reference 7.1

Mean Full Scale IQ, Primary Index Scores, and Mean Primary Index Score for Special Group Samples

Special Group	N	FSIQ	VCI	VSI	FRI	WMI	PSI	MIS
Intellectually Gifted	56	127.2	128.1	120.2	121.5	118.4	**110.2**	119.7
Intellectual Disability—Mild	39	63.6	66.1	**65.1**	68.7	72.1	69.7	68.3
Intellectual Disability—Moderate	34	50.0	53.8	54.9	56.9	54.8	**53.3**	54.7
Developmental Delay—Cognitive	72	81.4	**81.7**	86.4	84.8	85.8	87.9	85.3

Developmental Risk Factors	42	85.9	87.1	88.4	89.7	85.8	**85.1**	87.2
Preliteracy Concerns	37	89.0	**89.9**	92.8	91.8	93.0	94.5	92.4
ADHD	53	93.4	94.4	99.6	95.0	94.9	**92.7**	95.3
Disruptive Behavior	26	91.8	96.3	97.2	95.0	**92.0**	92.6	94.6
Expressive Language Disorder	25	89.7	**86.1**	98.0	95.7	90.7	93.8	92.9
Mixed Receptive– Expressive Language Disorder	42	79.5	**78.3**	91.4	85.9	89.0	86.8	86.3
English Language Learners	33	95.2	**87.6**	102.8	98.6	98.7	104.0	98.3
Autistic Disorder	38	77.6	75.2	87.6	83.9	84.1	**73.7**	80.9
Asperger's Disorder	38	101.3	103.1	103.1	99.4	97.3	**93.0**	99.2

Note. The lowest mean primary index score for each special group appears in bold. FSIQ = Full Scale IQ; VCI = Verbal Comprehension Index; VSI = Visual Spatial Index; FRI = Fluid Reasoning Index; WMI = Working Memory Index; PSI = Processing Speed Index; MIS = Mean Primary Index Score. *Source:* Data are from the *Technical and Interpretive Manual* Tables 5.15–29.

≡ Rapid Reference 7.2

Mean Ancillary Index Scores for Special Group Samples

Special Group	N	VAI	NVI	GAI	CPI
Intellectually Gifted	56	124.1	123.2	129.3	**117.3**
Intellectual Disability—Mild	39	68.5	64.8	**62.6**	66.1
Intellectual Disability—Moderate	34	55.0	51.8	49.8	**47.6**
Developmental Delay—Cognitive	72	**81.3**	83.1	81.6	85.9
Developmental Risk Factors	42	90.2	86.3	86.1	**84.8**
Preliteracy Concerns	37	93.7	89.9	**89.4**	92.3
ADHD	53	97.3	93.6	94.6	**92.9**
Disruptive Behavior	26	92.2	91.7	95.4	**90.7**
Expressive Language Disorder	25	92.4	93.1	**90.5**	**90.5**
Mixed Receptive–Expressive Language Disorder	42	81.8	84.1	**78.8**	86.3
English Language Learners	33	**88.5**	100.6	92.5	102.4
Autistic Disorder	38	78.9	80.9	78.5	**75.9**
Asperger's Disorder	38	101.5	98.5	104.1	**94.2**

Note. The lowest ancillary index score for each sample appears in bold. VAI = Vocabulary Acquisition Index; NVI = Nonverbal Index; GAI = General Ability Index; CPI = Cognitive Proficiency Index. *Source:* Data are from the *Technical and Interpretive Manual* Tables 5.15 to 5.29.

Children With Intellectual Giftedness

Rapid Reference 7.3 indicates that the sample of 56 children who are intellectually gifted perform strongest on subtests involving crystallized knowledge and verbal reasoning, and weakest on processing speed tasks. These results are consistent with performance at the primary index level, where the Verbal Comprehension Index is highest and the Processing Speed Index is lowest. Prior studies with intellectually gifted individuals have consistently shown strengths in verbal comprehension and relatively weaker performance on processing speed (Raiford, Weiss, Rolfhus, & Coalson, 2005; Rimm, Gilman, & Silverman, 2008; Rowe, Kingsley, & Thompson, 2010; Wechsler, 2002, 2003, 2008). The WPPSI-IV intellectually gifted group results, however, differ from those of Rimm et al. (2008) and Rowe et al. (2010) because processing speed performance remains significantly higher than that of the general population.

Nevertheless, these results imply, as others (Lichtenberger & Kaufman, 2013; Shavinina, 2008) have suggested, that gifted individuals place a relative lack of emphasis on speed in favor of creative thought and accurate performance. Because of this trend, the estimate of intellectual ability of gifted individuals is lower if processing speed tasks contribute to a given composite score. For example, for the WPPSI-IV study, if the intellectually gifted group's mean Full Scale IQ excludes

≡ Rapid Reference 7.3

Highest and Lowest Mean Subtest Scaled Scores of Children With Intellectual Giftedness

Intellectually Gifted
N = 56; Female 51.8%
Ages 4.2–7:6, M = 6.2
FSIQ = 127.2

Highest Subtests	Mean Scaled Score
Vocabulary	15.3
Similarities	14.9
Information	14.8
Lowest Subtests	**Mean Scaled Score**
Bug Search	11.9
Cancellation	11.4
Animal Coding	11.4

Source: Data are from the *Technical and Interpretive Manual* Tables 5.15 to 5.29.

the contribution of processing speed through proration (omitting Bug Search), the result is a mean of 133 rather than 127.

Some gifted advocates assert that the General Ability Index, an estimate of global ability with reduced emphasis on working memory and processing speed, is an acceptable score for use in gifted program evaluations (National Association for Gifted Children, 2010; Rimm et al., 2008). There are indications that this is reasonable when using the WPPSI-IV as well. Although the Full Scale IQ was found a superior predictor of achievement (Rowe et al., 2010) relative to the General Ability Index for a group of children referred for inclusion in gifted programs, it was working memory (and not processing speed) that accounted for the improved prediction. However, these results are based upon the WISC-IV Working Memory Index. The WPPSI-IV Working Memory Index shows a weaker association with composite achievement scores (.29 to .47) on the Wechsler Individual Achievement Test–Third Edition (WIAT-III; Pearson, 2009) relative to the Working Memory Index scores from the WISC-IV (.57 to .71 with the WIAT-II; Pearson, 2001) or the WAIS-IV (.51 to .78 with the WIAT-II). Furthermore, recent research suggests that children who are intellectually gifted and participate in gifted education programs develop increased processing speed, compared to intellectually gifted peers who are in regular education programs (Duan, Shi, & Zhou, 2010). In that vein, it is notable that the children in the Rowe et al. (2010) investigation were referred to be tested for inclusion in gifted education at the time of intellectual ability testing, but were not participating in or had only very recently begun their gifted education coursework. Gifted education participation also was not a requirement for participation in the WPPSI-IV intellectually gifted special group study: Intellectual ability scores alone qualified a child for the study. Taken together, these results suggest that processing speed can improve with the proper instructional program among children who are intellectually gifted.

For this reason, the General Ability Index may better represent intellectual ability in the application process for gifted education programs if the Processing Speed Index is lower than the MIS at a significant and unusual level, or if Bug Search (or the subtest being substituted for Bug Search) is lower than the MSS-I at a significant and unusual level. The Full Scale IQ is also informative in this situation if the evaluation serves other purposes, such as appropriateness of placement in accelerated educational programs (e.g., honors, enriched, or advanced placement). The mean General Ability Index score for the intellectually gifted group is slightly higher than the mean Full Scale IQ (see Rapid Reference 7.2). Furthermore, the General Ability Index shows similar classification accuracy to the Full Scale IQ in groups of children who are intellectually gifted versus their matched controls. The *Technical and Interpretive Manual* provides the classification accuracy figures that are summarized in Rapid Reference 7.4.

≡ Rapid Reference 7.4

Classification Accuracy of the Full Scale IQ and the General Ability Index in Intellectually Gifted and Matched Control Groups

	Percentage of Children With Scores of 120 or Higher, by Group	
Score	Intellectually Gifted	Matched Control
FSIQ	85%	20%
GAI	84%	11%

Note. FSIQ = Full Scale IQ; GAI = General Ability Index.
Source: Data are from the *Technical and Interpretive Manual.*

Potential improvement in speed of information processing with participation in a gifted education program has important implications for the cognitive development of a child who is intellectually gifted. We believe it is important to assess processing speed in any evaluation for giftedness to permit the potential impact of gifted education on cognitive development to be understood for a given child.

Children With Intellectual Disability

Rapid Reference 7.5 indicates that the samples of 39 children with intellectual disability—mild and 34 children with intellectual disability—moderate vary in their strongest subtest-level performance, and variability within a cognitive domain is present within each group. Children with intellectual disability—mild perform strongest on subtests involving working memory and processing speed. Children with intellectual disability—moderate also show relatively strong performance on subtests involving processing speed, but a visual spatial task and a fluid reasoning task are also relative strengths. Children with intellectual disability—mild and moderate both perform weakest on subtests involving visual-spatial processing and crystallized knowledge. For children with intellectual disability—mild, performance on a verbal reasoning task is also relatively weak, whereas for children with intellectual disability—moderate, performance on a task involving lexical knowledge and receptive language is a relative weakness.

Consistent with the subtest level, the lowest means at the primary index level for the intellectual disability—mild group are on the Visual Spatial Index and the

≡ Rapid Reference 7.5

Highest and Lowest Mean Subtest Scaled Scores of Children With Intellectual Disability

Intellectual Disability—Mild		Intellectual Disability—Moderate	
N = 39; Male 66.7%		N = 34; Male 61.8%	
Ages 2:6–7:6, M = 5.3		Ages 2:6–7:6, M = 5.3	
FSIQ = 63.6		FSIQ = 50.0	
Highest Subtests	**Mean Scaled Score**	**Highest Subtests**	**Mean Scaled Score**
Zoo Locations	5.4	Animal Coding	3.1
Picture Memory	4.8	Object Assembly	2.7
Cancellation	4.5	Matrix Reasoning	2.6
Lowest Subtests	**Mean Scaled Score**	**Lowest Subtests**	**Mean Scaled Score**
Object Assembly	3.7	Receptive Vocabulary	1.8
Information	3.7	Block Design	1.8
Similarities	3.0	Information	1.5

Source: Data are from the *Technical and Interpretive Manual* Tables 5.15 to 5.29.

Verbal Comprehension Index. While the Verbal Comprehension Index is also one of the lowest intellectual disability—moderate group means, the Processing Speed Index is slightly lower. For the intellectual disability—mild group, the highest mean is the Working Memory Index. For the moderate group, the highest means are the Fluid Reasoning Index, at 56.9, and the Visual Spatial Index, at 54.9. All means for the primary index scores fall within the expected range for the level of severity being considered.

These results are consistent with prior studies that show relatively poor performance of children with intellectual disability on Verbal Comprehension subtests (Wechsler, 2002, 2003), which reflects the close relation of verbal and intellectual ability. These results are also consistent with other investigations that indicate visual spatial ability is a relative weakness for these children (Caffrey & Fuchs, 2007; Fontana, 2004; Wechsler, 2003).

The Nonverbal Index offers an estimate of global ability for children who have expressive issues. As many preschool children with intellectual disability present with significant language delays, the Nonverbal Index is an alternative to the Full

Scale IQ in such cases. The mean Nonverbal Index scores for the intellectual disability—mild and moderate groups are comparable to the Full Scale IQs (see Rapid Reference 7.2). Furthermore, the Nonverbal Index shows similar classification accuracy to the Full Scale IQ in groups of children with intellectual disability versus their matched controls. The *Technical and Interpretive Manual* provides the classification accuracy figures that are summarized in Rapid Reference 7.6.

Because the classification accuracy for the Nonverbal Index is similar to that of the Full Scale IQ, it may prove especially useful in evaluations of children with intellectual disability and substantial expressive language issues. One such example would be if total raw scores of 0 are obtained on both of the Verbal Comprehension subtests that contribute to the Full Scale IQ.

The *DSM-5* diagnostic criteria for intellectual disability severity levels deviate from those of the *DSM-IV-TR*, because the *DSM-5* severity levels are determined by descriptions of adaptive functioning in the conceptual, social, and practical domains rather than ranges of scores on intellectual ability tests. Moreover, the adaptive functioning criteria are descriptive in nature rather than tied to particular adaptive functioning score ranges. Until the new criteria are in use, it is not possible to predict how these changes will impact the typically observed strengths and weaknesses across severity level.

≡ Rapid Reference 7.6

Classification Accuracy of the Full Scale IQ and the Nonverbal Index in Intellectual Disability Groups and Matched Control Groups

	Percentage of Children With Scores of 75 or Lower, by Group		Percentage of Children With Scores of 60 or Lower, by Group	
Score	Intellectual Disability—Mild	Matched Control	Intellectual Disability— Moderate	Matched Control
FSIQ	97%	3%	81%	0%
NVI	97%	5%	85%	0%

Note. FSIQ = Full Scale IQ; NVI = Nonverbal Index.
Source: Data are from the Technical and Interpretive Manual.

Children With Developmental Delay—Cognitive and Developmental Risk Factors

The developmental delay—cognitive and developmental risk factors groups, despite similar names, differ importantly in their WPPSI-IV strengths and weaknesses. Children in the developmental delay—cognitive study have been identified with significant delays in the cognitive area, typically based on scores from some cognitive development or intellectual ability measure. The children in this particular study were previously identified with developmental delay—cognitive or produced full scale scores 1 to 2 standard deviations below the mean on an individually administered cognitive ability measure. In contrast, children in the developmental risk factors study were identified with biological or environmental risk factors by parent report (e.g., nutritional deprivation, fetal alcohol syndrome, low birth weight) that are known to increase risk of developmental delay and lower scores on intellectual ability measures (e.g., Baron et al., 2012; Raz, DeBastos, Newman, & Batton, 2012; Rose, Feldman, Jankowski, & Van Rossem, 2011).

Rapid Reference 7.7 highlights the differences in cognitive abilities between children with developmental delay—cognitive and children with developmental risk

≡ Rapid Reference 7.7

Highest and Lowest Mean Subtest Scaled Scores of Children With Developmental Delay—Cognitive and Developmental Risk Factors

Developmental Delay—Cognitive		Developmental Risk Factors	
$N = 72$; Male 63.9%		$N = 42$; Male 64.3%	
Ages 2:6–7:6, $M = 4.4$		Ages 2:6–7:6, $M = 5.3$	
FSIQ = 81.4		FSIQ = 85.9	
Highest Subtests	**Mean Scaled Score**	**Highest Subtests**	**Mean Scaled Score**
Bug Search	8.3	Similarities	8.4
Zoo Locations	7.9	Vocabulary	8.4
Object Assembly	7.5	Picture Naming	8.4
Lowest Subtests	**Mean Scaled Score**	**Lowest Subtests**	**Mean Scaled Score**
Similarities	6.1	Zoo Locations	7.5
Vocabulary	6.1	Animal Coding	7.4
Comprehension	5.4	Cancellation	7.0

Source: Data are from the Technical and Interpretive Manual Tables 5.15 to 5.29.

factors. The samples of 72 children with developmental delay—cognitive and 42 children with developmental risk factors vary quite dramatically in their strongest subtest-level performance. In fact, the groups show nearly opposite subtest strengths and weaknesses. Children with developmental delay—cognitive perform more similarly to children with intellectual disability than to children with developmental risk factors, in that two of their relative strengths occur on working memory and processing speed subtests and the other occurs on a visual spatial subtest. Children with developmental delay—cognitive perform lowest on subtests involving crystallized knowledge and verbal reasoning—both strengths for children with developmental risk factors. For children with developmental risk factors, a working memory subtest and two processing speed subtests are weaknesses (note that these areas are relative strengths for children with developmental delay—cognitive).

The differences between the two groups in terms of strengths and weaknesses are also evident at the primary index level. The lowest mean for the developmental delay—cognitive group is on the Verbal Comprehension Index, and the lowest mean for the developmental risk factors group is the Processing Speed Index. For the developmental delay—cognitive group, the highest means are the Processing Speed Index and the Visual Spatial Index, and for the developmental risk factors group, the highest means are the Fluid Reasoning Index and the Visual Spatial Index.

The relative weakness of the developmental delay—cognitive group on the Verbal Comprehension Index and subtests reflects the interplay of language and cognitive development for very young children (Brassard & Boehm, 2007; Ford, Kozey, & Negreiros, 2012) and are consistent with prior results that found children with developmental delay—cognitive score lowest on subtests with verbal demands (Hughes & McIntosh, 2002). The mean Processing Speed Index score of 87.9 is higher than that observed for the WPPSI-III Processing Speed Quotient (83.1) in the developmental delay study. This may be related to the modifications to the Processing Speed subtests to reduce motor demands, as well as to the differences in group composition between the studies: The WPPSI-III developmental delay group included children with developmental delays in areas other than cognitive. Children with motor delays were included in the WPPSI-III study, which also could contribute to the differing results.

The relative weaknesses of the developmental risk factors group in the areas of working memory and processing speed are consistent with prior results that found children with developmental risk factors had weaker performance in these areas (Rose et al., 2011). The mean Processing Speed Index (85.1) is a third of a standard deviation lower than that of the Processing Speed Quotient WPPSI-III developmental risk factors study (90.1). This difference may reflect the greater developmental appropriateness of the WPPSI-IV Processing Speed subtests, and

≣ Rapid Reference 7.8

Classification Accuracy of the Full Scale IQ and the Nonverbal
Index in Developmental Delay—Cognitive Group
and Matched Control Group

	Percentage of Children With Scores of 90 or Lower, by Group	
Score	Developmental Delay—Cognitive	Matched Control
FSIQ	90%	30%
NVI	76%	30%

Note. FSIQ = Full Scale IQ; NVI = Nonverbal Index.
Source: Data are from the *Technical and Interpretive Manual.*

therefore increased sensitivity to clinical conditions, because more children in the nonclinical group can perform the tasks successfully.

As with preschool children with intellectual disabilities, children with developmental delay—cognitive may sometimes present with significant language delays. The Nonverbal Index can therefore be a helpful addition to the Full Scale IQ in these situations. The mean Nonverbal Index for the developmental delay—cognitive group is comparable to the Full Scale IQ (see Rapid Reference 7.2). The Nonverbal Index shows somewhat lowered classification accuracy relative to the Full Scale IQ in groups of children with developmental delay—cognitive versus their matched controls. The *Technical and Interpretive Manual* provides the classification accuracy figures that are summarized in Rapid Reference 7.8.

Children With Preliteracy Concerns

Skills identified as developmental precursors of literacy include lexical development, phonological awareness, letter identification, and oral language (e.g., receptive and expressive vocabulary). The emergence of these behaviors prior to reading instruction in the schools predicts later reading achievement and disabilities (Burns et al., 2002; Catts, Gillispie, Leonard, Kail, & Miller, 2002; Lonigan, Burgess, & Anthony, 2000; Mann, Cowin, & Schoenheimer, 1989). Children were selected for the preliteracy concerns group on the basis of scores of less than or equal to 85 on the WIAT–III Early Reading Skills subtest, which is designed to assess phonological and phonological-orthographic relation awareness in young children. Some participants were originally identified on the basis of parent report of concerns or difficulties with reading, but subsequently obtained the requisite score on the Early Reading Skills subtest.

Rapid Reference 7.9 indicates that the sample of 37 children with preliteracy concerns perform strongest on subtests involving processing speed, receptive language skills, and visual spatial processing, and weakest on two subtests that involve crystallized knowledge and verbal reasoning. At the primary index level, the group's highest mean is on the Processing Speed Index, and the lowest occurs on the Verbal Comprehension Index. These results are consistent with prior research that indicates preliteracy concerns are associated with language issues, especially expressive and receptive vocabulary (Lonigan et al., 2000; Mann et al., 1989).

The General Ability Index group mean (89.4) is noticeably lower than that of the Cognitive Proficiency Index (92.3). The opposite pattern occurred on the WISC-IV special group study of children with reading disorder (Raiford et al., 2005): For that study, the Cognitive Proficiency Index was significantly higher than the General Ability Index. The difference may be related to the differences across the two tests in the working memory and the processing speed measures. The WPPSI-IV measures visual and visual spatial working memory, whereas the WISC-IV taps verbal working memory, and these domain-specific components of working memory appear to be differentially sensitive to reading problems (Borella, Carretti, & Pelegrina, 2010). The differential sensitivity could stem from a number of factors. First, the use of the ink dauber on the WPPSI-IV Processing Speed subtests reduces the fine motor skill

---

≡ Rapid Reference 7.9

Highest and Lowest Mean Subtest Scaled Scores of Children With Preliteracy Concerns

Preliteracy Concerns
N = 37; Female 54.1%
Ages 4:9–7:6, M = 6.2
FSIQ = 89.0

Highest Subtests	Mean Scaled Score
Cancellation	9.4
Receptive Vocabulary	9.1
Object Assembly	9.0
Lowest Subtests	**Mean Scaled Score**
Comprehension	8.3
Similarities	8.0

Source: Data are from the Technical and Interpretive Manual Tables 5.15 to 5.29.

demands relative to those required for the pencils that are utilized on the WISC-IV Processing Speed subtests. In addition, the WISC-IV Coding subtest draws more heavily on associative memory and requires memorization of a greater number associative pairs than does its WPPSI-IV counterpart, Animal Coding. It is possible that the increased associative memory demands of WISC-IV Coding (relative to Animal Coding) simulate early reading behaviors and thereby increase the sensitivity to childhood reading problems.

Despite the results at the group level, if a local education agency requires use of an ability–achievement discrepancy, and if working memory and processing speed are lowered due to the presence of specific learning disorder/disability, it may be more informative to utilize the General Ability Index to examine differences between ability and achievement. It is important to augment these results with an evaluation of a given child's strengths and weaknesses when conducting an evaluation for reading problems. The *DSM-5* requires specification of skill impairment (i.e., word reading accuracy, reading rate or fluency, reading comprehension) within the reading domain, and treatment should be linked to the specific skill impairment(s).

Children With Attention-Deficit/Hyperactivity Disorder and Disruptive Behavior

The *DSM-5* classifies attention-deficit/hyperactivity disorder as a neurodevelopmental disorder, in contrast to the *DSM-IV-TR*, which classified ADHD together with disruptive behavior disorders. Disruptive behavior disorders are now classified within a separate diagnostic category: Disruptive, impulse-control, and conduct disorders. Nevertheless, behaviors associated with oppositional-defiant disorder and conduct disorder sometimes overlap with those of ADHD, and disruptive behavior must be differentiated from ADHD.

Children were selected for the ADHD group based on parent ratings in the clinically significant range on the Brown Attention-Deficit Disorder Scales for Children and Adolescents (Brown, 2001) as well as a current diagnosis of ADHD. A psychostimulant medication washout of at least 24 hours was required prior to testing. Selection for the disruptive behavior group required a clinically significant score (≥ 65) on the parent-rated Emotional Self-Control scale of the Behavior Assessment System for Children–Second Edition (Reynolds & Kamphaus, 2004). A concurrent *DSM-IV-TR* diagnosis of either oppositional-defiant disorder or conduct disorder, or classification as emotionally disturbed using school district criteria due to disruptive behavior, was also required.

Rapid Reference 7.10 indicates that the samples of 53 children with attention-deficit/hyperactivity disorder and 26 children with disruptive behavior show different subtest-level strengths and weaknesses, but some similarities across

⁼ Rapid Reference 7.10

Highest and Lowest Mean Subtest Scaled Scores of Children with Attention-Deficit/Hyperactivity Disorder and Disruptive Behavior

Attention-Deficit/Hyperactivity Disorder		Disruptive Behavior	
$N = 53$; Male 75.5%		$N = 26$; Male 92.3%	
Ages 3:1–7:7, $M = 5.9$		Ages 4:7–7:2, $M = 6.2$	
FSIQ = 93.4		FSIQ = 91.8	

Highest Subtests	Mean Scaled Score	Highest Subtests	Mean Scaled Score
Object Assembly	10.2	Information	10
Picture Naming	9.6	Cancellation	9.8
Lowest Subtests	**Mean Scaled Score**	**Lowest Subtests**	**Mean Scaled Score**
Bug Search	8.7	Comprehension	8.3
Cancellation	8.7	Vocabulary	8.1
Animal Coding	8.5	Picture Naming	8
Comprehension	8.4	Bug Search	7.5

Source: Data are from the *Technical and Interpretive Manual* Tables 5.15 to 5.29.

the groups' performances are present as well. Both groups have processing speed measures among their lowest mean subtest scores.

The processing speed weaknesses are more pronounced and consistent in the ADHD group, with all three of the Processing Speed subtests appearing among the lowest four subtest scores. These findings are consistent with prior investigations in which processing speed emerged as a clear weakness for children with ADHD (Mayes, Calhoun, Chase, Mink, & Stagg, 2009; Mayes, Calhoun, Mayes, & Molitoris, 2012; Wechsler, 2003). However, the Working Memory subtests and Working Memory Index did not emerge as weaknesses, contrary to these other investigations. It is possible that the difference can be attributed to the differences between visual working memory, as measured on the WPPSI-IV, and verbal working memory, as measured on the WISC-IV and in these studies (Mayes et al., 2009, 2012; Wechsler, 2003). These differing results suggest that when evaluating children for ADHD, it is informative to obtain measures of both verbal and visual working memory to gain a complete picture of his or her cognitive strengths and weaknesses.

Comprehension is among the lowest mean subtest scores for each group. The disruptive behavior group shows weaknesses on two additional verbal subtests, consistent with prior investigations where verbal abilities were lowered for children with disruptive behavior disorders (Isen, 2010; Séguin, Parent, Tremblay, & Zelazo, 2009). The strongest performance for the ADHD group is on Object Assembly, followed by Picture Naming. For the disruptive behavior group, the highest mean scores are on Information and Cancellation.

The primary index level results for ADHD are consistent with those observed at the subtest level. The Processing Speed Index is the lowest mean score for the ADHD group, and the Visual Spatial Index is the highest. Somewhat unexpected is the relatively weak performance of the ADHD group on the Verbal Comprehension Index, which was significantly lower than the matched controls (Wechsler, 2012). For the disruptive behavior group, primary index level performance differs somewhat from that of the subtest level: The lowest mean score was the Working Memory Index and the highest was the Visual Spatial Index. Some prior studies, however, have found relatively weak working memory performance for children with disruptive behavior (Barker et al., 2011; Dougherty et al., 2007; Séguin et al., 2009).

As on the WISC-IV, the ADHD group has a higher mean General Ability Index score relative to those of the Full Scale IQ (Raiford et al., 2005) and Cognitive Proficiency Index (Weiss, Saklofske, Prifitera, & Holdnack, 2006). A similar result is observed for the group of children with disruptive behavior; however, the differences are more pronounced for this group. Deriving the General Ability Index for children with ADHD and disruptive behavior who are undergoing evaluation for learning problems may therefore be informative if a local or state education agency requires that an ability–achievement discrepancy be performed to determine eligibility for special education. As with any learning disability evaluation, it is important to augment these results with an evaluation of a given child's strengths and weaknesses. The *DSM-5* requires specification of skill impairment for any diagnosis of specific learning disorder/disability, and treatment should be linked to the specific skill impairment(s).

Children With Expressive Language Disorder and Mixed Receptive–Expressive Language Disorder

Rapid Reference 7.11 indicates that the samples of 25 children with expressive language disorder and 42 children with mixed receptive–expressive language disorder consistently show subtest-level weaknesses in tasks that require oral expression and lexical knowledge. Notably, Vocabulary and Comprehension place the greatest demands on expressive skills, and are among the lowest mean scores

≡ Rapid Reference 7.11

Highest and Lowest Mean Subtest Scaled Scores of Children With Expressive Language Disorder and Mixed Receptive–Expressive Language Disorder

Expressive Language Disorder	Mixed Receptive-Expressive Language Disorder
N = 25; Male 52.0%	N = 42; Male 64.3%
Ages 4:0–7:6, M = 5.6	Ages 4:0–7:6, M = 5.5
FSIQ = 89.7	FSIQ = 79.5

Highest Subtests	Mean Scaled Score	Highest Subtests	Mean Scaled Score
Matrix Reasoning	9.9	Object Assembly	8.9
Object Assembly	9.8	Animal Coding	8.2
Block Design	9.5	Picture Memory	8
		Zoo Locations	8

Lowest Subtests	Mean Scaled Score	Lowest Subtests	Mean Scaled Score
Vocabulary	7.6	Vocabulary	6
Comprehension	7.3	Comprehension	5.8
Similarities	7.2	Information	5.3

Source: Data are from the *Technical and Interpretive Manual* Tables 5.15 to 5.29.

for both groups. For both of the language disorder groups, the subtest-level strengths include tasks that do not require verbal responses and provide nonverbal task demonstration with minimal verbal instructions.

For children with expressive language disorder, the highest group means occur on Matrix Reasoning, Object Assembly, and Block Design. For children with mixed receptive-expressive language disorder, the highest group means are observed on Object Assembly, Animal Coding, Picture Memory, and Zoo Locations. For both groups, most of the subtest strengths involve manipulatives and do not require high amounts of lexical knowledge or verbal expression. The primary index level results are consistent with those observed at the subtest level. Both groups show the lowest mean score on the Verbal Comprehension Index and have as their highest mean score the Visual Spatial Index.

The *DSM-5* language disorder diagnostic criteria are substantially modified from those of the *DSM-IV-TR* by the collapse of the separate *DSM-IV-TR* expressive language disorder and mixed receptive–expressive language disorder diagnoses into a single *DSM-5* diagnosis of language disorder. To speculate about the impact of these changes on future special group studies, due to the generally consistent findings across the two groups one would expect a similar pattern of strengths and weaknesses in a collapsed language disorder group, with composite scores falling somewhat between those of the two groups and mostly in the low average range.

The Nonverbal Index has important applications for children with language disorders. For both groups, the Nonverbal Index is noticeably higher than the Full Scale IQ. While the Nonverbal Index is less language loaded than the Full Scale IQ, it still requires comprehension of spoken instructions for the contributing subtests. Still, the Nonverbal Index provides some estimate for these children of the impact of expressive requirements on the measurement of intellectual ability. When establishing a diagnosis of language disorder, standardized language testing is required to establish deficits in language comprehension or production, and the *DSM-5* recommends assessment of both receptive and expressive skills. Furthermore, intellectual ability testing may be required for children with suspected language disorder, because language disorder cannot be diagnosed until it is established that the language deficits are in excess of the intellectual limitations. If conducting such an evaluation, the Nonverbal Index may be the most informative composite score to establish the extent of intellectual limitations relative to language deficits. The Nonverbal Index removes expressive requirements from the estimate of intellectual ability. While using the Nonverbal Index does not completely eliminate all language skill requirements because receptive skills are necessary to comprehend the subtest instructions, the elimination of expressive requirements is useful to estimate the child's intellectual ability relative to his or her language skills.

Children Who Are English Language Learners

Intellectual ability assessment with children who are English language learners is a multifaceted process that involves discovery of the child's English and native language proficiency, as well as facility with models designed to individualize testing to be appropriate for the child's situation (Ortiz, Ochoa, & Dynda, 2012). Because children who are bilingual or are English language learners score lower than their matched controls on tasks requiring expressive responses, composite scores that are based in part on such tasks are not appropriate for these children. In fact, even subtests that require English comprehension are not language free but merely language reduced. However, language-reduced composite scores can be appropriately used, as long as they are interpreted with this in mind (Ortiz et al., 2012). Children were selected for the English language learners group if they were receiving school services for children with limited English proficiency, or if the parent/

guardian reported the child was an English language learner or gave an indication that the child had a preference to speak another language rather than English.

Rapid Reference 7.12 indicates that the sample of 33 children who are English language learners consistently show subtest-level weaknesses in tasks that require expressive responses. The English language learner group's strongest performance occurs on tasks that do not require verbal responses, provide nonverbal demonstration of the tasks with minimal verbal comprehension of instructions required, and involve manipulatives. The highest group means occur on Bug Search, Object Assembly, and Block Design. These subtests also involve manipulatives and do not require high amounts of lexical knowledge or verbal expression. The primary index level results are consistent with those observed at the subtest level. The lowest mean score occurs on the Verbal Comprehension Index, and the highest mean scores are on the Processing Speed Index and the Visual Spatial Index.

The Nonverbal Index group mean is noticeably higher than that of the Full Scale IQ and very close to the population mean of 100. These results suggest that the Nonverbal Index is a more appropriate estimate of global intellectual ability than is the Full Scale IQ for children who are English language learners, particularly if they can comprehend spoken instructions in English. We recommend its use over that of the Full Scale IQ for evaluations involving these children.

≡ Rapid Reference 7.12

Highest and Lowest Mean Subtest Scaled Scores of Children Who Are English Language Learners

English Language Learners
N = 33; Female 51.5%
Ages 2:7–7:6, M = 5.0
FSIQ = 95.2

Highest Subtests	Mean Scaled Score
Bug Search	11.3
Object Assembly	10.7
Block Design	10.2
Lowest Subtests	**Mean Scaled Score**
Picture Naming	7.6
Information	7.5
Comprehension	6.8

Source: Data are from the *Technical and Interpretive Manual* Tables 5.15 to 5.29.

Children With Autism Spectrum Disorders

Rapid Reference 7.13 indicates that the samples of 38 children with autistic disorder and 38 children with Asperger's disorder show important subtest-level differences in strengths and weaknesses, but some similarities are present as well. Consistent with the social impairment present in autism spectrum disorders, both groups have Comprehension as their greatest weakness. Both groups produced lower scores on tasks involving crystallized knowledge and processing speed. Consistently, the mean score values are noticeably higher in the Asperger's disorder group than in the autistic disorder group, likely indicative of the relatively preserved verbal functioning in children with Asperger's disorder. The two groups share visual spatial tasks as subtest-level strengths, but the Asperger's disorder group notably has two tasks that involve crystallized and lexical knowledge as strengths (Picture Naming and Information). The primary index level results are similar to those observed at the subtest level. Both groups have the Processing Speed Index as their lowest mean score, and the Visual Spatial Index as the highest. Taken together, these results are consistent with those of past studies, which have found relative strengths on visual–spatial tasks and weakness in processing speed (Mayes & Calhoun, 2008; Mayes

≡ Rapid Reference 7.13

Highest and Lowest Mean Subtest Scaled Scores of Children With Autism Spectrum Disorders

Autistic Disorder	Asperger's Disorder
N = 38; Male 78.9%	N = 38; Male 78.9%
Ages 2:10–7:6, M = 5.5	Ages 3:10–7:6, M = 6.2
FSIQ = 77.6	FSIQ = 101.3

Highest Subtests	Mean Scaled Score	Highest Subtests	Mean Scaled Score
Block Design	8.0	Picture Naming	11.0
Matrix Reasoning	7.7	Block Design	10.9
Object Assembly	7.6	Information	10.8
Lowest Subtests	**Mean Scaled Score**	**Lowest Subtests**	**Mean Scaled Score**
Comprehension	4.5	Comprehension	7.4
Cancellation	4.8	Vocabulary	8.3
Information	4.9	Bug Search	8.6

Source: Data are from the *Technical and Interpretive Manual* Tables 5.15 to 5.29.

et al., 2012; Wechsler, 2002, 2003) and lower performance on verbal subtests among children with autistic disorder (Klinger, O'Kelley, Mussey, Goldstein, & DeVries, 2012; Wechsler, 2002, 2003, 2008). The results differ from those of the WPPSI-III autistic disorder group in that the mean WPPSI-IV Processing Speed Index (73.7) is substantially lower than the mean WPPSI-III Processing Speed Quotient (82.5) in the analogous study. This difference is *not* related to inequitable intellectual ability levels across the two samples, because the mean Full Scale IQ scores for the autistic disorder groups are very similar across the two studies (WPPSI-III = 76.6; WPPSI-IV = 77.6). As previously stated, the difference may instead reflect the greater developmental appropriateness of the WPPSI-IV Processing Speed subtests, and therefore increased sensitivity to clinical conditions.

The mean Full Scale IQ for the Asperger's disorder group is substantially higher than that of the autistic disorder group; this difference is reflective of the substantial differences in verbal abilities across the two groups. The Nonverbal Index group mean difference (see Rapid Reference 7.2) is far less pronounced relative to the Full Scale IQ difference, although still greater than a standard deviation in standard score units (almost 18 points). As on the WISC-IV, both autistic disorder and Asperger's disorder groups have noticeably higher mean General Ability Index scores relative to the Full Scale IQ (Raiford et al., 2005) and Cognitive Proficiency Index (Weiss et al., 2006) mean scores.

As with the *DSM-5* language disorder diagnostic criteria, the autism spectrum disorder criteria represent a significant departure from those of the *DSM-IV-TR*, most notably through the collapse of the separate *DSM-IV-TR* autistic disorder and Asperger's disorder diagnoses into a single *DSM-5* diagnosis of autism spectrum disorder. The *DSM-5* indicates that individuals with well-established *DSM-IV-TR* diagnoses of autistic disorder, Asperger's disorder, or pervasive developmental disorder not otherwise specified should all receive diagnoses of autism spectrum disorder. Severity specifiers are used to describe the support (i.e., support, substantial support, or very substantial support) required for the social communication impairments and restrictive patterns of behavior. The presence and extent of intellectual and language impairment and catatonia—and involvement of medical, environmental, and genetic factors—are recorded within the diagnosis. Intellectual ability testing may be required for differential diagnosis with intellectual disability or to substantiate a secondary diagnosis of autism spectrum disorder definitively, because autism spectrum disorder cannot be diagnosed until it is established that the social communication deficits are in excess of the intellectual limitations. Future special group studies may produce similar results if separate groups are designated based on the severity specifiers and presence of intellectual and language impairment. A single, collapsed special group study for autism spectrum disorder would likely obscure important within-group differences.

When selecting the most appropriate score to represent the intellectual ability of a child with autism spectrum disorder, consider the purpose of the evaluation and the referral question, as well as the particular child's strengths and needs. If the evaluation involves simple determination of global level of intellectual functioning, the Full Scale IQ is most likely to be appropriate. If the evaluation is intended to facilitate differential diagnosis or establish comorbidity of autism spectrum disorder and intellectual disability, the *DSM-5* indicates that social communication and interaction must be impaired relative to the child's nonverbal skills. Therefore, the Nonverbal Index may be more informative in this situation.

Because specific learning disorder commonly co-occurs with autism spectrum disorder, one should consider the method of determination *and* the presence or absence of accompanying language impairment. If the child *does not* have significant accompanying language impairments, the General Ability Index, Visual Spatial Index, or Fluid Reasoning Index could be selected to represent intellectual ability if an ability–achievement discrepancy is required. The Verbal Comprehension Index, Visual Spatial Index, or Fluid Reasoning Index may also be selected as the processing strength for a pattern of strengths and weaknesses analysis in this situation. If the child *does* have significant accompanying language impairment, the Nonverbal Index, Visual Spatial Index, or Fluid Reasoning Index could be the best choice to represent intellectual ability for an ability–achievement discrepancy. In a pattern of strengths and weaknesses analysis for these children, the Visual Spatial Index or the Fluid Reasoning Index may be appropriate to select as the processing strength.

COMPARISONS OF THE GENERAL ABILITY INDEX TO THE FULL SCALE IQ AND THE COGNITIVE PROFICIENCY INDEX FOR THE SPECIAL GROUP SAMPLES

The General Ability Index provides an estimate of general intellectual ability that minimizes working memory and processing speed demands. Children with some neurodevelopmental issues can obtain relatively lower Full Scale IQ scores, because subtests from the working memory and/or processing speed scales contribute to the Full Scale IQ and are sensitive to these problems. For example, working memory displays sensitivity to specific learning disorders, ADHD, language disorders, and autism spectrum disorder (Archibald & Gathercole, 2006a, 2006b; Belleville, Ménard, Mottron, & Ménard, 2006; Passolunghi, 2006; Pickering, 2006; Roodenrys, 2006; Swanson, 2006), and processing speed is sensitive to specific learning disorders, ADHD, and autism spectrum disorder (Compton, Fuchs, Fuchs, Lambert, & Hamlett, 2012; Mayes & Calhoun, 2007, 2008).

The discrepancies between the General Ability Index and the Full Scale IQ and between the General Ability Index and the Cognitive Proficiency Index (for ages 4:0

to 7:7 only) are designed to provide information about the impact of reducing the influence of working memory and processing speed on the estimate of intellectual ability. If the difference between the General Ability Index and the Full Scale IQ is statistically significant and unusual, the influence of working memory and processing speed on intellectual ability may have resulted in a difference in the child's global performance. If the difference between the General Ability Index and the Cognitive Proficiency Index difference is statistically significant and unusual, general ability and cognitive proficiency may not be commensurate (Wechsler, 2012).

Rapid Reference 7.14 summarizes comparisons of the General Ability Index to the Full Scale IQ and to the Cognitive Proficiency Index for the special groups. Results are

≡ Rapid Reference 7.14

Comparisons of the General Ability Index to the Full Scale IQ and the Cognitive Proficiency Index for the Special Groups

Special Group	N	GAI	FSIQ	CPI	GAI–FSIQ Discrepancy	GAI–CPI Discrepancy
English Language Learners	33	92.5	95.2	102.4	−2.7	−9.9
Mixed Receptive–Expressive Language Disorder	42	78.8	79.5	86.3	−0.7	−7.5
Developmental Delay—Cognitive	72	81.6	81.4	85.9	0.2	−4.3
Intellectual Disability—Mild	39	62.6	63.6	66.1	−1.0	−3.5
Preliteracy Concerns	37	89.4	89.0	92.3	0.4	−2.9
Expressive Language Disorder	25	90.5	89.7	90.5	0.8	0
Developmental Risk Factors	42	86.1	85.9	84.8	0.2	1.3
ADHD	53	94.6	93.4	92.9	1.2	1.7
Intellectual Disability—Moderate	34	49.8	50.0	47.6	−0.2	2.2
Autistic Disorder	38	78.5	77.6	75.9	0.9	2.6
Disruptive Behavior	26	95.4	91.8	90.7	3.6	4.7
Asperger's Disorder	38	104.1	101.3	94.2	2.8	9.9
Intellectually Gifted	56	129.3	127.2	117.3	2.1	12.0

Note. GAI = General Ability Index; FSIQ = Full Scale IQ; CPI = Cognitive Proficiency Index.
Source: Data are from the Technical and Interpretive Manual Tables 5.15 to 5.29.

presented in order of the General Ability Index–Cognitive Proficiency Index discrepancy values. The differences between the General Ability Index and the Full Scale IQ are small, with none achieving statistical significance at the .05 level (4.01). Only the disruptive behavior group's General Ability Index–Full Scale IQ difference (3.6) achieved significance at the .10 level (3.35). The same is not true of the differences between the General Ability Index and the Cognitive Proficiency Index. Of the 13 special groups, 6 had a discrepancy of 4 or more points. The largest difference of 12 points is for children who are intellectually gifted (General Ability Index > Cognitive Proficiency Index). The special groups are approximately equally distributed across patterns of discrepancy, with 7 groups showing General Ability Index > Cognitive Proficiency Index patterns, and 5 showing General Ability Index < Cognitive Proficiency Index patterns. However, among these, only the intellectually gifted group discrepancy achieved statistical significance at the .05 level (10.46). The English language learners and Asperger's disorder score differences achieved statistical significance at the .10 level (8.75). Hence, the differences between general ability and cognitive proficiency in children from special groups are smaller than those observed for the WISC-IV and the WAIS-IV. This differential sensitivity may be related to the young age of the WPPSI-IV participants, for whom these differences may become more pronounced over time, the nature of the working memory task differences (i.e., visual on the WPPSI-IV and auditory on the WISC-IV and the WAIS-IV), or the reduced fine motor demands of the processing speed subtests relative to those of the WISC-IV or the WAIS-IV.

COMPARISON OF THE WORKING MEMORY INDEX TO THE PROCESSING SPEED INDEX FOR THE SPECIAL GROUP SAMPLES

Rapid Reference 7.15 lists the discrepancies between the Working Memory Index (WMI) and the Processing Speed Index (PSI) for the special groups, in order of WMI–PSI discrepancy values. Examining the WMI–PSI differences in the special groups indicates a mixed pattern of results. A WMI > PSI pattern is evident for 8 of the 13 special groups, and a WMI < PSI pattern is present for 5 groups. The largest discrepancies occur in the autistic disorder (10.4) and intellectually gifted groups (8.2), with WMI > PSI. None of these differences, however, achieve statistical significance at the .05 level (14.35). The largest discrepancies where WMI < PSI occur in the English language learners (5.3) and expressive language disorder (3.1) groups. The smallest differences between the WMI and the PSI occur in the disruptive behavior (.6) and developmental risk factors (.7) groups.

≡ Rapid Reference 7.15

Comparison of the Working Memory Index to the Processing Speed Index for the Special Groups

Special Group	N	WMI	PSI	WMI–PSI Discrepancy
English Language Learners	33	98.7	104.0	−5.3
Expressive Language Disorder	25	90.7	93.8	−3.1
Developmental Delay—Cognitive	72	85.8	87.9	−2.1
Preliteracy Concerns	37	93.0	94.5	−1.5
Disruptive Behavior	26	92.0	92.6	−0.6
Developmental Risk Factors	42	85.8	85.1	0.7
Intellectual Disability—Moderate	34	54.8	53.3	1.5
ADHD	53	94.9	92.7	2.2
Mixed Receptive–Expressive Language Disorder	42	89.0	86.8	2.2
Intellectual Disability—Mild	39	72.1	69.7	2.4
Asperger's Disorder	38	97.3	93.0	4.3
Intellectually Gifted	56	118.4	110.2	8.2
Autistic Disorder	38	84.1	73.7	10.4

Note. WMI = Working Memory Index; PSI = Processing Speed Index.
Source: Data are from the Technical and Interpretive Manual Tables 5.15 to 5.29.

The lack of a consistent WMI > PSI pattern across special groups is in contrast to results reported for the WAIS-IV (Lichtenberger & Kaufman, 2013). These differences could be related to the working memory domains measured by the WPPSI-IV Working Memory Index (visual) compared with the WAIS-IV Working Memory Index (verbal). The differing patterns could also be a result of the decreased motor demands of the WPPSI-IV Processing Speed subtests relative to those of the WAIS-IV; it is possible that the fine motor demands, particularly of WAIS-IV Coding, increase clinical sensitivity due to the co-occurrence of fine motor problems among individuals with clinical conditions. Another explanation could be related to the age differences across the two measures (i.e., very young children compared with adolescents and adults): Perhaps the WAIS-IV results reflect the impact of interventions over time that result in improved working memory, but not processing speed, in clinical populations.

CLINICAL SAMPLES WITH RELATIVELY HIGH OR LOW SCORES ON THE PROCESSING SPEED INDEX

The Processing Speed Index played a key role in the WISC-IV and the WAIS-IV special group studies, for which the majority of special groups had the Processing Speed Index as their highest or lowest index score (Flanagan & Kaufman, 2009; Lichtenberger & Kaufman, 2013). The same is true for the WPPSI-IV. Rapid Reference 7.16 lists the discrepancies between the Processing Speed Index and the mean of the other four primary index scores for the special groups with the Processing Speed Index as the highest or lowest primary index score, in order of discrepancy values.

The Processing Speed Index is the highest primary index score for 3 of the 13 special group studies: English language learners, developmental delay—cognitive, and preliteracy concerns. Among these groups, the largest discrepancy

≡ Rapid Reference 7.16

Comparisons of the Processing Speed Index to the Mean of the Remaining Four Primary Index Scores for the Special Groups That Scored Highest or Lowest on the PSI

Special Group	Mean of the Other Four Primary Index Scores	PSI	Difference
PSI as the Highest Primary Index Score			
English Language Learners	96.9	104.0	−7.1
Developmental Delay—Cognitive	84.7	87.9	−3.2
Preliteracy Concerns	91.9	94.5	−2.6
PSI as the Lowest Primary Index Score			
Intellectual Disability—Moderate	55.1	53.3	1.8
Developmental Risk Factors	87.8	85.1	2.7
ADHD	96.0	92.7	3.3
Asperger's Disorder	100.7	93.0	7.7
Autistic Disorder	82.7	73.7	9.0
Intellectually Gifted	122.1	110.2	11.9

Note. PSI = Processing Speed Index. The mean of the other four primary index scores is the same as the MIS–4E discussed in Chapter 4 of this book.
Source. Data are from the *Technical and Interpretive Manual* Tables 5.15 to 5.29.

(7.1) occurs in the English language learners group. The Processing Speed Index is the lowest primary index score for 6 of the 13 special group studies.

Among these groups, the intellectually gifted group shows the largest discrepancy (11.9). As mentioned previously, relatively low processing speed scores are typical of individuals who are intellectually gifted. The autism spectrum disorder groups (autistic disorder and Asperger's disorder) have the next largest discrepancies, between the Processing Speed Index and the mean of the other four index scores. Processing speed tasks are consistently found to be sensitive to autism spectrum disorders.

ISSUES IN EARLY CHILDHOOD INTELLECTUAL ASSESSMENT

Intellectual assessment of young children is a complex and challenging endeavor. There are many important aspects of the test, the practitioner, and the child that can influence the validity and applicability of results. These aspects are outlined in Rapid Reference 7.17 as samples of important factors to consider as you plan your WPPSI-IV

≡ Rapid Reference 7.17

Sample Test, Practitioner, and Child Factors That Affect Administration and Interpretation

Test Characteristics (Brassard & Boehm, 2007; Ford et al., 2012; Vig & Sanders, 2007)

- Are the materials developmentally appropriate given the child's motor skills?
- Which subtests are appropriate given the child's language skills?
- Are the floors and ceilings adequate given the child's expected performance?
- Is the planned testing time too long given the subtests I plan to administer? Do I need to plan for breaks?
- Is there evidence of clinical validity for this child's suspected issues or needs?
- Are there links between the WPPSI-IV and other measures I may need to administer (e.g., academic achievement measures for evaluations of early learning issues)?

Practitioner Training, Experience, and Complementary Assessment Techniques (Brassard & Boehm, 2007; Ford et al., 2012)

- Do I have adequate specialized training in assessing young children, or am I seeking supervision and training in this area?
- Am I familiar with relevant literature on early childhood, including cognitive, motor, language, and emotional development models, or receiving appropriate supervision and training in these areas?
- Am I experienced at pacing administration according to the child's needs and at reading signals that the child needs a break?
- Am I trained in observational and behavioral assessment and caregiver interviews to complement WPPSI-IV results?

(continued)

- Am I familiar with comprehensive interview techniques to obtain a thorough developmental history?
- Am I familiar with methods of discovering the child's current circumstances at home and other important environments, and integrating those with WPPSI-IV results to produce a useful report?

Child-Related Factors (Brassard & Boehm, 2007; Ford et al., 2012; Kaufman & Kaufman, 1977; Vig & Sanders, 2007)

- Does the child have a clinical condition that could impact his or her attention or concentration?
- Are responses available in another context or at another time, if not in the assessment session?
- Are the child's cognitive, language, and physical development and skills sufficient to understand directions, express answers, and perform tasks with manipulative components?
- Is the child familiar with materials similar to the test materials in his or her past experience?
- Has the child been exposed to test-like situations, or is the testing session likely an oddly unfamiliar situation?
- Is the child fatigued?
- Is the child emotionally distressed?
- Is the child uncomfortable with separation from a caregiver?

assessment and interpret results. More comprehensive information about intellectual assessment with young children is available in Brassard and Boehm (2007), Ford et al. (2012), Kaufman and Kaufman (1977), and Vig and Sanders (2007). It is critical to obtain adequate supervision, training, and/or consultation in early childhood assessment before assessing and interpreting the results of your first independent case.

🐟 TEST YOURSELF 🐟

I. **Which of the following statements is *not true* regarding the limitations of the WPPSI-IV clinical group studies?**

(a) They are based on randomly selected samples.

(b) They may not be representative of the diagnostic category.

(c) The diagnoses originate from various clinical settings using different diagnostic procedures.

(d) Some samples do not include children at the younger extreme of the age range.

(continued)

2. **Special group study data are useful to begin developing an understanding of how the WPPSI-IV functions with different populations**

   (a) And they should be used to make differential diagnoses because data are not aggregated at the group level.

   (b) And they should be used to make differential diagnoses because groups are separated by validated subtypes.

   (c) But they should not be used to make differential diagnoses because data are aggregated at the group level, which may obscure individual differences.

   (d) But they should not be used to make differential diagnoses because groups are separated by validated subtypes.

3. **Which of the following statements is *not true* regarding WPPSI-IV performance for children who are intellectually gifted?**

   (a) Strongest performance is on subtests involving crystallized knowledge and verbal reasoning.

   (b) Mean Full Scale IQ is slightly higher than mean General Ability Index.

   (c) Weakest subtest performance is on subtests involving processing speed tasks.

   (d) At the primary index level, performance on the Verbal Comprehension Index is highest.

4. **WPPSI-IV performance for children with intellectual disability indicates that**

   (a) Subtests involving crystallized knowledge are strengths for *both* the mild and moderate groups.

   (b) Subtests involving verbal reasoning are strengths for *both* the mild and moderate groups.

   (c) Subtests involving working memory and processing speed are strengths for the moderate group *only*.

   (d) Subtests involving working memory and processing speed are strengths for the mild group, and subtests involving processing speed are strengths for the moderate group.

5. **The WPPSI-IV Nonverbal Index**

   (a) Offers an estimate of global ability for children with expressive issues.

   (b) Is an alternative to the Full Scale IQ for children who present with significant language delays.

   (c) Shows similar classification accuracy to the Full Scale IQ in groups of children with intellectual disability.

   (d) All of the above are true statements regarding the WPPSI-IV Nonverbal Index.

6. **When comparing children with developmental delay—cognitive and children with developmental risk factors, the data indicate that**

   (a) Children with developmental risk factors perform more similarly to children with intellectual disability than to children with developmental delay—cognitive.

   (b) Children with developmental delay—cognitive perform more similarly to children with intellectual disability than to children with developmental risk factors.

(c) Children with developmental risk factors perform strongest on working memory tasks.

(d) Children with developmental delay—cognitive perform strongest on subtests involving crystallized knowledge.

7. **Which of the following is true about the results of the special group study with children with preliteracy concerns?**

(a) At the primary index level, the group's highest mean is on the Processing Speed Index and the lowest mean is on the Verbal Comprehension Index.

(b) Performance is strongest on subtests involving crystallized knowledge and weakest on subtests involving receptive language skills.

(c) Performance is strongest on subtests involving processing speed and weakest on subtests involving visual–spatial processing.

(d) The Cognitive Proficiency Index mean is notably lower than the General Ability Index mean.

8. **On the WPPSI-IV, children with attention-deficit/hyperactivity disorder**

(a) Show weaknesses on the Processing Speed and Working Memory subtests.

(b) Show weaknesses on the Processing Speed subtests and strengths on subtests involving verbal reasoning.

(c) Show weaknesses on the Processing Speed subtests, but not on the Working Memory subtests.

(d) Show weaknesses on the Working Memory subtests, but not on the Processing Speed subtests.

9. **For children with expressive language disorder and mixed receptive–expressive language disorder**

(a) Vocabulary and Comprehension are among the lowest subtest scores, which may reflect demands on expressive skills.

(b) Vocabulary and Information are among the lowest subtest scores, which may reflect acquired knowledge.

(c) Similarities and Comprehension are among the lowest subtest scores, which may reflect reasoning ability.

(d) Matrix Reasoning and Object Assembly are among the lowest subtest scores, which may reflect lower demands on verbal expression.

10. **The largest discrepancies occur between the Working Memory Index (WMI) and the Processing Speed Index (PSI) for the**

(a) ADHD and Asperger's special groups, with WMI < PSI.

(b) English language learners and expressive language disorder groups, with WMI > PSI.

(c) Disruptive behavior and developmental risk factors groups, with WMI < PSI.

(d) Autistic disorder and intellectually gifted groups, with WMI > PSI.

11. **The special group populations included in the WPPSI-IV *Technical and Interpretive Manual* utilize criteria specified in the *DSM-5*.**
True or False?

(continued)

12. The WPPSI-IV Processing Speed Index is the highest primary index score for 3 of the 13 special groups: English language learners, developmental delay—cognitive, and preliteracy concerns.
True or False?

Answers: 1. a; 2. c; 3. b; 4. d; 5. d; 6. b; 7. a; 8. e; 9. a; 10. d; 11. False; 12. True

REFERENCES

American Psychiatric Association. (2000). *Diagnostic and statistical manual of mental disorders* (4th ed., text rev.). Washington DC: Author.

American Psychiatric Association. (2013). *Diagnostic and statistical manual of mental disorders* (5th ed.). Arlington, VA: American Psychiatric Publishing.

Archibald, L. M. D., & Gathercole, S. E. (2006a). Short-term memory and working memory in specific language impairment. In T. P. Alloway & S. E. Gathercole (Eds.), *Working memory and neurodevelopmental disorders* (pp. 139–160). New York, NY: Psychology Press.

Archibald, L. M. D., & Gathercole, S. E. (2006b). Visuospatial immediate memory in specific language impairment. *Journal of Speech, Language, and Hearing Research, 49*, 265–277. doi: 10.1044/1092-4388(2006/022)

Barker, E. D., Tremblay, R. E., van Lier, P. A. C., Vitaro, F., Nagin, D. S., Assaad, J.-M., & Séguin, J. R. (2011). The neurocognition of conduct disorder behaviors: Specificity to physical aggression and theft after controlling for ADHD symptoms. *Aggressive Behavior, 37*, 63–72. doi: 10.1002/ab.20373

Baron, I. S., Brandt, J., Ahronovich, M. D., Baker, R., Erickson, K., & Litman, F. R. (2012). Selective deficit in spatial location memory in extremely low birth weight children at age six: The PETIT study. *Child Neuropsychology, 18*, 299–311. doi: 10.1080/09297049.2011.613815

Belleville, S., Ménard, É., Mottron, L., & Ménard, M.-C. (2006). Working memory in autism. In T. P. Alloway & S. E. Gathercole (Eds.), *Working memory and neurodevelopmental disorders* (pp. 213–238). New York, NY: Psychology Press.

Borella, E., Carretti, B., & Pelegrina, S. (2010). The specific role of inhibition in reading comprehension in good and poor comprehenders. *Journal of Learning Disabilities, 43*, 541–552. doi: 10.1177/0022219410371676

Brassard, M. R., & Boehm, A. E. (Eds.). (2007). *Preschool assessment: Principles and practices.* New York, NY: Guilford Press.

Brown, T. E. (2001). *Brown attention-deficit disorder scales for children and adolescents.* San Antonio, TX: Psychological Corporation.

Burns, M. K., Tucker, J. A., Hauser, A., Thelen, R. L., Holmes, K. J., & White, K. (2002). Minimum reading fluency rate necessary for comprehension: A potential criterion for curriculum-based assessments. *Assessment for Effective Intervention, 28*, 1–7.

Caffrey, E., & Fuchs, D. (2007). Differences in performance between students with learning disabilities and mild mental retardation: Implications for categorical instruction. *Learning Disabilities Research & Practice, 22*, 119–128.

Catts, H. W., Gillispie, M., Leonard, L. B., Kail, R. V., & Miller, C. A. (2002). The role of speed of processing, rapid naming, and phonological awareness in reading achievement. *Journal of Learning Disabilities, 35*, 510–525.

Compton, D. L., Fuchs, L. S., Fuchs, D., Lambert, W., & Hamlett, C. (2012). The cognitive and academic profiles of reading and mathematics learning disabilities. *Journal of Learning Disabilities, 45*, 79–95. doi: 10.1177/0022219410393012

Dougherty, D. M., Dew, R. E., Mathias, C. W., Marsh, D. M., Addicott, M. A., & Barratt, E. S. (2007). Impulsive and premeditated subtypes of aggression in conduct disorder: Difference in time estimation. *Aggressive Behavior, 33*, 574–582. doi: 10.1002/ab.20219

Duan, X., Shi, J., & Zhou, D. (2010). Developmental changes in processing speed: Influence of accelerated education for gifted children. *Gifted Child Quarterly, 54*, 85–91.

Flanagan, D. P., & Kaufman, A. S. (2009). *Essentials of WISC–IV assessment* (2nd ed.). Hoboken, NJ: Wiley.

Fontana, S. (2004). The instructional approach: Improving the performance of a person with moderate mental retardation in a reasoning task. *Journal of Cognitive Education and Psychology, 4*, 148–150.

Ford, L., Kozey, M. L., & Negreiros, J. (2012). Cognitive assessment in early childhood: Theoretical and practice perspectives. In D. P. Flanagan & P. L. Harrison (Eds.), *Contemporary intellectual assessment: Theories, tests, and issues* (3rd ed., pp. 585–622). New York, NY: Guilford Press.

Hughes, T. L., & McIntosh, D. E. (2002). Differential Ability Scales: Profiles of preschoolers with cognitive delay. *Psychology in the Schools, 39*, 19–29.

Isen, J. (2010). A meta-analytic assessment of Wechsler's P > V sign in antisocial populations. *Clinical Psychology Review, 30*, 423–435. doi: 10.1016/j.cpr.2010.02.003

Kaufman, A. S., & Kaufman, N. L. (1977). *Clinical evaluation of young children with the McCarthy Scales.* New York, NY: Grune & Stratton.

Klinger, L. G., O'Kelley, S. E., Mussey, J. L., Goldstein, S., & DeVries, M. (2012). Assessment of intellectual functioning in autism spectrum disorder. In D. P. Flanagan & P. L. Harrison (Eds.), *Contemporary intellectual assessment: Theories, tests, and issues* (3rd ed., pp. 670–686). New York, NY: Guilford Press.

Lichtenberger, E. O., & Kaufman, A. S. (2013). *Essentials of WAIS®–IV assessment* (2nd ed.). Hoboken, NJ: Wiley.

Lonigan, C. J., Burgess, S. R., & Anthony, J. L. (2000). Development of emergent literacy and early reading skills in preschool children: Evidence from a latent variable longitudinal study. *Developmental Psychology, 36*, 596–613.

Mann, V. A., Cowin, E., & Schoenheimer, J. (1989). Phonological processing, language comprehension, and reading ability. *Journal of Learning Disabilities, 22*, 76–89.

Mayes, S. D., & Calhoun, S. L. (2007). Learning, attention, writing, and processing speed in typical children and children with ADHD, autism, anxiety, depression, and oppositional-defiant disorder. *Child Neuropsychology, 13*, 469–193. doi: 10.1080/09297040601112773

Mayes, S. D., & Calhoun, S. L. (2008). WISC-IV and WIAT-II profiles in children with high-functioning autism. *Journal of Autism and Developmental Disorders, 38*, 429–439. doi: 10.1007/s10803-007-0410-4

Mayes, S. D., Calhoun, S. L., Chase, G. A., Mink, D. M., & Stagg, R. E. (2009). ADHD subtypes and co-occurring anxiety, depression, and oppositional defiant disorder: Differences in Gordon diagnostic system and Wechsler working memory and processing speed index scores. *Journal of Attention Disorders, 12*, 540–550. doi: 10.1177/1087054708320402

Mayes, S. D., Calhoun, S. L., Mayes, R. D., & Molitoris, S. (2012). Autism and ADHD: Overlapping and discriminating symptoms. *Research in Autism Spectrum Disorders, 6*, 277–285. doi: 10.1016/j.rasd.2011.05.009

National Association for Gifted Children. (2010, March). *Use of the WISC–IV for gifted identification* [NAGC Position Statement]. Retrieved from http://www.nagc.org/uploaded-Files/WISC%20IV%20Position%20Paper.pdf

Ortiz, S. O., Ochoa, S. H., & Dynda, A. M. (2012). Testing with culturally and linguistically diverse populations: Moving beyond the verbal–performance dichotomy into evidence-based practice. In D. P. Flanagan & P. L. Harrison (Eds.), *Contemporary intellectual assessment: Theories, tests, and issues* (3rd ed., pp. 526–552). New York, NY: Guilford Press.

Passolunghi, M. C. (2006). Working memory and arithmetic learning disability. In T. P. Alloway & S. E. Gathercole (Eds.), *Working memory and neurodevelopmental disorders* (pp. 113–138). New York, NY: Psychology Press.

Pearson. (2001). *Wechsler individual achievement test* (2nd ed.). San Antonio, TX: Author.

Pearson. (2009). *Wechsler individual achievement test* (3rd ed.). San Antonio, TX: Author.

Pickering, S. J. (2006). Working memory in dyslexia. In T. P. Alloway & S. E. Gathercole (Eds.), *Working memory and neurodevelopmental disorders* (pp. 7–40). New York, NY: Psychology Press.

Raiford, S. E., Weiss, L. G., Rolfhus, E., & Coalson, D. (2005). *General ability index* [WISC–IV Technical Report No. 4]. Retrieved from http://www.pearsonassessments.com/NR/rdonlyres/1439CDFE-6980-435F-93DA-05888C7CC082/0/80720_WISCIV_Hr_r4.pdf

Raz, S., DeBastos, A. K., Newman, J. B., & Batton, D. (2012). Intrauterine growth and neuropsychological performance in very low birth weight preschoolers. *Journal of the International Neuropsychological Society, 18*, 200–211. doi: 10.1017/S1355617711001767

Reynolds, C. R., & Kamphaus, R. W. (2004). *Behavior assessment system for children* (2nd ed.). Bloomington, MN: Pearson.

Rimm, S., Gilman, B., & Silverman, L. (2008). Alternative assessments with gifted and talented students. In J. L. VanTassel-Baska (Ed.), *Nontraditional applications of traditional testing* (pp. 175–202). Waco, TX: Prufrock Press.

Roodenrys, S. (2006). Working memory function in attention deficit hyperactivity disorder. In T. P. Alloway & S. E. Gathercole (Eds.), *Working memory and neurodevelopmental disorders* (pp. 187–211). New York, NY: Psychology Press.

Rose, S. A., Feldman, J. F., Jankowski, J. J., & Van Rossem, R. (2011). Basic information processing abilities at 11 years account for deficits in IQ associated with preterm birth. *Intelligence, 39*, 198–209. doi: 10.1016/j.intell.2011.03.003

Rowe, E. W., Kingsley, J. M., & Thompson, D. F. (2010). Predictive ability of the general ability index (GAI) versus the full scale IQ among gifted referrals. *School Psychology Quarterly, 25*, 119–128. doi: 10.1037/a0020148

Séguin, J. R., Parent, S., Tremblay, R. E., & Zelazo, P. D. (2009). Different neurocognitive functions regulating physical aggression and hyperactivity in early childhood. *Journal of Child Psychology and Psychiatry, 50*, 679–687. doi: 10.1111/j.1469-7610.2008.02030

Shavinina, L. V. (2008). How can we better identify the hidden intellectually-creative abilities of the gifted? *Psychology Science Quarterly, 50*, 112–133.

Swanson, H. L. (2006). Working memory and reading disabilities: Both phonological and executive processing deficits are important. In T. P. Alloway & S. E. Gathercole (Eds.), *Working memory and neurodevelopmental disorders* (pp. 59–88). New York, NY: Psychology Press.

Vig, S., & Sanders, M. (2007). Cognitive assessment. In M. R. Brassard & A. E. Boehm (Eds.), *Preschool assessment: Principles and practices* (pp. 383–419). New York, NY: Guilford Press.

Wechsler, D. (2002). *Wechsler preschool and primary scale of intelligence* (3rd ed.). San Antonio, TX: Pearson.

Wechsler, D. (2003). *Wechsler intelligence scale for children* (4th ed.). San Antonio, TX: Pearson.

Wechsler, D. (2008). *Wechsler adult intelligence scale* (4th ed.). Bloomington, MN: Pearson.

Wechsler, D. (2012). *Wechsler preschool and primary scale of intelligence* (4th ed.). Bloomington, MN: Pearson.

Weiss, L. G., Saklofske, D. H., Prifitera, A., & Holdnack, J. A. (2006). *WISC–IV advanced clinical interpretation*. Amsterdam, The Netherlands: Elsevier Academic Press.

Eight

ILLUSTRATIVE CASE REPORTS

hapters 1 through 7 have reviewed the key features of the WPPSI-IV and how to administer, score, and interpret the test. This chapter illustrates use of the WPPSI-IV in a comprehensive battery through case reports for two young children referred for psychological evaluations. The first case report presents the results of George R., a 7-year-old male referred for evaluation of intellectual giftedness. The second case report presents results for Jane B., a 7-year-old female referred for testing due to preliteracy concerns. These case reports demonstrate the integration of various aspects of the children's history and interview data, behavioral observations, and other tests. The reports also illustrate important information to include in each section and translation of results into recommendations. For both cases, identifying information has been altered to protect confidentiality. The Don't Forget box outlines the sections of a psychological evaluation report. Rapid References 8.1 to 8.8 inserted within the first report serve as reminders of information to provide in each section.

DON'T FORGET

Sections of a Psychological Evaluation Report

- Examiner/Agency Contact Information, Header, or Letterhead
- Identifying and Demographic Information
- Referral Question(s)
- Evaluation Methods and Procedures
- Background and History

(continued)

- Mental Status and Behavioral Observations
- Test Results and Interpretation
- Summary and Diagnostic Impressions
- Recommendations
- Practitioner's Signature, Name, and Credentials

CASE REPORT: GEORGE R.—INTELLECTUAL GIFTEDNESS AND HIGH ACHIEVEMENT

Case report authors: Susan E. Raiford, PhD; Clifton J. Wigtil, MA, MS Ed; and Diane L. Coalson, PhD

Identifying and Demographic Information

Name: George R.
Date of Birth: 6/3/2006
Age: 7 years 0 months 28 days
Race/Ethnicity: Hispanic
Parents: Mr. R. and Mrs. R.

School: B Elementary School
Grade: 2 (begins 9/2013)
Date of Testing: 7/1/2013
Date of Report: 7/8/2013
Examiner Name: Examiner C

≡ Rapid Reference 8.1

Identifying and Demographic Information Section

- Child's name
- Child's birth date
- Child's age
- Child's sex
- Child's race/ethnicity
- Parent/guardian name and relation
- Child's school (if applicable)
- Child's grade (if applicable)
- Child's admission date (if in program or hospitalized)
- Testing dates
- Examiner's name

Referral Questions

Mrs. R. requested an evaluation of George's intellectual ability to gain an objective appraisal of George's intellectual ability, cognitive strengths and weaknesses, and academic functioning, and to determine if gifted education and/or academic enrichment should be pursued in the fall. She became interested in obtaining assessment this summer when George was enrolled in a summer accelerated math and science program with two of his friends. In the course of helping them with home activities, Mrs. R. noticed that George appeared to learn the information much more quickly than his friends. Specific questions to be answered are:

- What is George's level of intellectual functioning?
- What are George's cognitive strengths and weaknesses?
- What is George's level of academic functioning?
- What are George's academic strengths and weaknesses?

≡ Rapid Reference 8.2

Referral Question Section

- Brief statement answering the question Why is an assessment requested?
- Referral source
- Relation of referral source to child
- Referral source's questions or symptoms
- Child's concerns (if applicable)
- List of specific questions to be answered

Evaluation Methods and Procedures

≡ Rapid Reference 8.3

Evaluation Methods and Procedures Section

List all evaluation procedures used, not just tests. Potential procedures might include:

- History and background review
- Prior testing results review (if any)
- Records review (if any)
- Interviews and consultation: referral source, parent/guardian or teacher, other professionals involved with child (all with appropriate consent)
- Clinical interview of child
- Mental status exam
- Behavioral observations
- Play assessment
- Formal testing

Evaluation methods and procedures used with George included:

- History and background review
- Parent interview
- Teacher interview
- Child interview
- Behavioral observations
- Wechsler Preschool and Primary Scale of Intelligence–Fourth Edition (WPPSI-IV). Note: Although the WPPSI-IV is not the test typically selected for 7-year-old gifted children, it was preferred because with five primary index scores it offers more information about specific cognitive domains relative to the WISC-IV, and one of the referral questions specified learning more about George's cognitive strengths and weaknesses.
- Wechsler Individual Achievement Test–Third Edition

Background and History

George is the firstborn to Mr. and Mrs. R., and is at present an only child. Mr. R. and Mrs. R. both work full time as information technology professionals. Mr. R. has a bachelor's degree, and Mrs. R. completed her master's degree last year. Both Mr. R. and Mrs. R. were born in the United States. George's paternal grandmother is a first-generation immigrant from Mexico; all other grandparents were born in the United States. Mr. R. speaks Spanish fluently, but Spanish is not spoken in the home and George speaks only English.

He was born 34.5 weeks into an uneventful pregnancy via natural childbirth delivery after Mrs. R.'s water broke prematurely. George was of normal length, head circumference, and weight for a full-term child despite his early arrival. His APGAR scores were within normal limits, and he had no complications other than slight jaundice.

Mrs. R. reported George reached developmental milestones either early or at a normal rate. He began to walk at 9 months, spoke his first words at 7 months, said sentences at 17 months, and was toilet trained at age 2. He was fed breast milk until age 1. George's medical history is unremarkable. His health is good other than mild colds, sinus infections, and allergies. His hearing and vision are within normal limits, and his last complete physical indicated he is at the 98th percentile for height and the 90th percentile for weight relative to other boys his age.

George's education began at 10 weeks when he entered full-time day care. He was enrolled in a private school at age 3, and he continues to second grade in the

≡ Rapid Reference 8.4

Background and History Section

Section is presented in narrative, paragraph form, with information gleaned from referral source, child interview, parent/guardian, teacher or daytime caregiver (if applicable), and prior records.

- Family background: Relevant current situation and history. Include any recent changes, significant milestone events such as separations, divorces, custody status, birth and age of siblings, place in birth order. Note evidence of relational issues with family members or peers. Note reporting source of all information. Note parent/guardian education level.
- Developmental history: Developmental milestones, dates, and reporting source.
- Medical history and records, and any recent notable changes. Medication, if relevant, that could impact results.
- Caregiving situation: Current daytime and nighttime caregiving situation, especially any recent changes. Specify after-school programs, day care, and who provides care when parent/guardian is working outside the home or otherwise unavailable (e.g., child care facility and type, parent/guardian, relative, neighbor, babysitter). Note richness of the caregiving situation that could be relevant to learning (e.g., reading at home; availability of books, educational games, and technology; parent/guardian expectations of the child's future achievement and educational attainment).
- Academic/educational background: Current situation and history, any recent changes, general level of performance, teacher awareness of evaluation, involvement with special education, school quality comments, caregiver support of educational needs. Note caregiver and parent/guardian general observations about learning if child is not yet enrolled in a school or preschool setting.
- Psychological symptoms not already reported and relevant to diagnostic evaluation.
- Prior testing results, diagnostic impressions, recommendations, and treatment (if applicable).
- Emotional functioning and peer relation perceptions.

same school in the fall. A typical day involves school drop-off at 7:00 a.m. and pickup at 4:30 p.m.

His day care providers indicated to his mother at that time that he engaged in early reading behaviors (e.g., recognizing letters and sight words, looking at books) at a very young age and showed more interest in reading than did his same-age peers. They also noted more interest in early math activities, such as learning numbers and counting, relative to his same-age peers. He was reading simple beginner books with some help at age 3. He continued to show strong interest in reading, math, and learning throughout preschool, kindergarten, and first grade.

His school reported he is achieving above grade level in every subject. His teacher indicates he is an active learner and typically learns information much more quickly than his classmates. His mother stated that currently he is learning addition and subtraction, and enjoys playing reading, math, and memory games on electronic devices, as well as playing with his iPad piano app and participating in age-group recreational soccer.

Before and after school and during the summers he is enrolled in extended learning at the private school. His parents enroll him in educational programs and camps during the summer when school is not in session and they are not on vacation. His extended learning program teacher stated that he is a very bright child and enjoys reading. Mr. and Mrs. R. report that they expect George to "go very far in life" and to achieve a graduate-level education.

According to his parents, George is an extraverted, conscientious, emotionally stable child who enjoys new experiences. Mrs. R. reported that he relates well with peers and is a leader. George stated he loves school, his teachers, and riding his bike, and has "lots of friends."

Mental Status and Behavioral Observations

George arrived on time and was oriented to person, place, time, and purpose of the meeting. He was accompanied by both parents. He was dressed and groomed neatly, and was of larger than average size for his age. Activity level, mannerisms, and eye contact were within normal limits. Speech revealed advanced vocabulary; for example, he used the word *assessment* appropriately. His reported mood was "good" and his affect was calm and mood congruent.

During testing, he was cooperative and appeared to give his best effort to the tasks. He showed little reaction to perceived success, but commented "Wait, oops" to himself when he perceived he had missed an item and returned to some items with spontaneous self-corrections. However, he did not appear anxious or distressed. For a speeded task involving visual matching where he was instructed to work as fast as possible without making mistakes, he rechecked several items in a deliberate manner before responding. During a task involving building block constructions and an activity that required him to complete puzzles, he talked aloud to himself during difficult items and verbally coached himself through the items to successful completion. He required almost no corrective feedback or prompting and learned tasks very quickly. He was actively engaged in the tasks and requested more information about some more complex verbal items that were presented. Given the effort, level of engagement, and persistence he displayed in the session, the results of the assessment are likely to reflect accurate estimates of intellectual and academic functioning.

≡ *Rapid Reference 8.5*

Mental Status and Behavioral Observations Section

Section is presented in narrative, paragraph form. Elaborate on only notable or relevant areas. Continue to observe throughout time with the child:

- Timeliness of arrival
- Orientation × 4 (i.e., person, place, time, purpose of meeting)
- Dress
- Height
- Weight
- Grooming
- Age-appropriateness of appearance, dress, and stature
- Activity level
- Speech
- Mannerisms
- Eye contact
- Impulsivity
- Mood reported
- Affect and whether mood is congruent
- Anxiety or mood symptoms
- Memory
- Cooperativeness, effort, and persistence
- Reactions to perceived success
- Reactions to perceived failure or frustration
- Problem-solving approach (e.g., trial and error, checking and rechecking answers, careful, reflective)
- Response styles (e.g., eager, impulsive, premature, hesitant, elaborated, succinct, reticent, incomplete)
- Adaptation to instruction and corrective feedback (e.g., requires single or multiple prompts, learns tasks quickly or requires repeated instructions, attends and focuses in response to prompting or requires multiple behavioral corrections)
- Interactive style (e.g., passive or active, requests more information or awaits feedback from examiner)
- Given the effort observed, are test results likely to be an accurate estimate, overestimate, or underestimate of functioning?

Test Results and Interpretation

Cognitive Functioning

Intellectual ability George was administered the Wechsler Preschool and Primary Scale of Intelligence–Fourth Edition (WPPSI-IV), an individually administered assessment of intellectual ability, to obtain comprehensive, objective information about his intellectual ability and his cognitive strengths and weaknesses (see Table 8.1 for a score summary, although scores can also be appended to the end of the report). The WPPSI-IV provides composite scores that represent global intellectual ability, as well as specific cognitive abilities in the areas of verbal comprehension, visual spatial processing, fluid reasoning, working memory, and processing speed.

The scores that best represent general intellectual ability for the purposes of this evaluation include the General Ability Index and the Full Scale IQ. The General Ability Index is recommended for gifted education admissions evaluations, and the Full Scale IQ is recommended for accelerated learning program admission.

≡ *Rapid Reference 8.6*

Test Results and Interpretation Section

- Section is presented in tables and in paragraph form. Use subheads to organize the domains assessed.
- In the tables, provide subtest/subscale and composite scores for instruments administered. Provide confidence intervals, percentile ranks, and descriptive classifications. Sample tables are provided on the CD that accompanies this book.
- In the paragraphs, avoid overreliance on numbers; focus on describing aspects of the domain measured, the child's range of functioning relative to normative groups, and intrapersonal strengths and weaknesses within the domain.
- Provide examples of how the child's real-world functioning may be impacted given the results.
- Describe the tasks; do not merely name the subtests.
- Comment on test validity measures or your impressions of test result validity.
- Describe results from other domains examined.
- Organize results into cognitive, academic, and socioemotional functioning sections, if applicable.
  - Cognitive Functioning (e.g., intellectual ability, attention and concentration, memory, executive functioning, thought processes)
  - Academic Functioning
  - Socioemotional Functioning (e.g., emotional functioning, interpersonal/social functioning, self concept, personality)

Table 8.1 George's WPPSI-IV Score Summary

Subtest	Scaled Score	Percentile Rank
Information	17	99
Similarities	18	99.6
(Vocabulary)	18	99.6
(Comprehension)	14	91
Block Design	10	50
Object Assembly	13	84
Matrix Reasoning	16	98
Picture Concepts	13	84
Picture Memory	9	37
Zoo Locations	13	84
Bug Search	7	16
Cancellation	9	37
(Animal Coding)	12	75

Subtests in parentheses do not contribute to composite scores.

Composite	Standard Score	Percentile Rank	95% Confidence Interval	Qualitative Description
Verbal Comprehension Index	143	99.8	134–147	Extremely High
Visual Spatial Index	109	73	99–117	Average
Fluid Reasoning Index	127	96	118–132	Very High
Working Memory Index	107	68	98–114	Average
Processing Speed Index	89	23	81–100	Low
Full Scale IQ	121	92	115–126	Very High
General Ability Index	133	99	125–138	Extremely High
Cognitive Proficiency Index	96	39	89–104	Average

George earned a General Ability Index of 133 (125 to 138 with 95% confidence) based on his performance on the four core subtests. His General Ability Index ranks him at the 99th percentile compared with other children his age and is considered in the Very High to Extremely High range of intellectual functioning. The General Ability Index measures global intellectual ability while reducing the influence of working memory and processing speed on its estimate. This is important when considering George's ability, because intellectually gifted children often perform less well in working memory and processing speed than in other areas; however, processing speed can improve after gifted education begins.

George's Full Scale IQ of 121 (115 to 126; 92nd percentile) is considered in the High to Very High range of intellectual functioning. The Full Scale IQ is the measure of global intellectual ability that is the best predictor of academic achievement scores in children with high intellectual ability. It is therefore helpful to consider this score in addition to the General Ability Index because George is being considered for accelerated learning programs. His General Ability Index and his Full Scale IQ scores show a significant and rare discrepancy (12 standard-score points) seen in less than 1% of the population, which suggests that the influence of working memory and processing speed on intellectual ability resulted in a difference in his overall performance, as reflected in the Full Scale IQ.

The Cognitive Proficiency Index summarizes performance in the areas of working memory and processing speed. Although George processes both verbal and visual information and reasons very well, he performs less well on tasks that involve holding and manipulating information in memory, and on tasks that involve rapid processing of information. His Cognitive Proficiency Index of 96 (89 to 104; 39th percentile) is in the Low to Average range compared to children the same age. His General Ability Index and his Cognitive Proficiency Index are significantly different, with only around 1% of children with similar overall ability level showing the same difference (37 standard-score points) between the two index scores. This suggests that his working memory and processing speed abilities are not equivalent to those in the areas of verbal comprehension, visual spatial processing, and fluid reasoning.

To more thoroughly understand his cognitive proficiency performance, it is important to also understand the cognitive abilities that contribute to that perform-ance: working memory and processing speed. The Working Memory Index represents visual and visual–spatial working memory, and ability to withstand proactive interference. His Working Memory Index of 107 (98 to 114; 68th percentile) is in the Average to High range. While still performing better than many children, he performed relatively lower in this area relative to his own overall performance on one Working Memory task, Picture Memory, that involves viewing stimulus pictures then selecting them from a number of response options on a page. This subtest score was significantly lower than his overall average core subtest score, and differences that large are rare, occurring in only 5% to 10% of children. His Picture Memory score was also significantly lower than his score on the other Working Memory subtest, Zoo Locations, which involves viewing animal cards in specified locations on a zoo layout for a brief time period, then replacing each card in its recalled location. A difference that large between these two subtests is observed in only about 14% of children.

The Processing Speed Index represents speed of information processing, especially quick scanning and discrimination of simple visual information. His Processing Speed Index of 89 (81 to 100, 23rd percentile) is in the Low to Average range compared to same-age peers. His processing speed appears to be an intrapersonal cognitive weakness, as his Processing Speed Index is significantly lower than the overall average of all specific cognitive areas measured by the test. The difference between his Processing Speed Index and the overall average of all specific cognitive areas occurs in only 5% of children at his ability level.

Two visual–motor tasks constitute the Processing Speed Index. For the first, Bug Search, he viewed a line drawing of bugs and marked the matching target bugs in the same row. While George performed higher than many children, his Bug Search performance was significantly lower than his own overall performance, occurring in only 1% to 2% of children. For the second task, Cancellation, he viewed two pages of clothing targets and other nontarget items, and marked as many clothing targets as possible within a time limit. Throughout both of these tasks, he appeared to be more concerned with accuracy than speed, evidenced in his checking and rechecking of responses before moving on. However, his performance was somewhat better on Cancellation than Bug Search. Interestingly, George performed better than 75% of his same-age peers on a third processing speed task that involved learning and indicating associations between animals and shapes, Animal Coding. He therefore displayed a pattern of improvement across the three subtests, suggesting that he may have adapted his response style to the demands of the situation by recognizing that speed was as important as accuracy to successful performance.

To understand more fully his global intellectual ability, and to discover his cognitive strengths, it is important to examine specific scores that represent different cognitive areas. The Verbal Comprehension Index measures acquired knowledge, verbal reasoning, and verbal concept formation. George's Verbal Comprehension Index of 143 (134 to 147; 99th percentile) is considered to be in the Extremely High range. Not surprisingly, the Verbal Comprehension Index is a significant intrapersonal strength relative to the overall average of all specific cognitive areas measured by the WPPSI-IV. Notably, the difference between his Verbal Comprehension Index and the average of his overall performance occurs in less than 1% of children at his ability level, which makes it a particularly impressive cognitive asset. On the Verbal Comprehension scale, he performed extremely well on the Information subtest, which involves responding verbally to questions about general-knowledge topics, and quite well on the Comprehension subtest, which involves responding to questions about general principles and social situations. He also demonstrated strong ability to describe how two words representing common objects or concepts are similar, on the Similarities subtest, and to define words, on the Vocabulary subtest. Both the Information and the Similarities subtest scores represented intrapersonal strengths relative to his overall average performance across 10 core subtests. These subtest scores were significantly higher than his average core subtest score, with differences that large or greater occurring in only 1% (Information versus the average) or less (Similarities versus the average) of children.

The Fluid Reasoning Index represents the ability to reason, conceptualize, and classify information, and is based on subtests that use visual stimuli. His Fluid Reasoning Index of 127 (118 to 132; 96th percentile), and is considered to be in the High to Extremely High range. The Fluid Reasoning Index is another significant intrapersonal strength relative to the overall average of all specific cognitive areas measured by the WPPSI-IV. The difference between his Fluid Reasoning Index and the average of his overall performance occurs in less than 10% of children at his ability level. He performed particularly well relative to his own overall performance on one Fluid Reasoning task, Matrix Reasoning, which involves selecting among visually presented response options the one that best completes a matrix. This subtest score was significantly higher than his overall average core subtest score, with differences that large or greater occurring in only 5% of children. In fact, his Matrix Reasoning score was also significantly and rarely higher than his score on the other Fluid Reasoning subtest, Picture Concepts, which involves forming a group with a shared element by selecting one picture from each of either two or three rows. A difference that large or greater between these two subtests is observed in only 20% of children.

The Visual Spatial Index measures visual spatial processing, part–whole relationships integration and synthesis, and visual–motor integration. George's Visual Spatial Index of 109 (99 to 117; 73rd percentile) is in the Average to High range. He reasoned aloud verbally while completing the block designs and the puzzles involved with this specific cognitive area, consistent with his strength in verbal reasoning and problem solving.

Academic Functioning
The Wechsler Individual Achievement Test–Third Edition (WIAT-III) was administered to provide an in-depth assessment of George's academic achievement in reading and mathematics skills (see Table 8.2 for a score summary). Results are interpreted using age-based norms.

Table 8.2 George's WIAT-III Score Summary

Subtest	Scaled Score	Percentile Rank	95% Confidence Interval
Early Reading Skills	118	88	105–131
Word Reading	115	84	111–119
Pseudoword Decoding	111	77	106–116
Reading Comprehension	125	95	116–134
Oral Reading Fluency	96	39	88–104
Oral Reading Accuracy	119	90	107–131
Oral Reading Rate	93	32	83–103
Math Problem Solving	112	79	102–122
Math Fluency—Addition	107	68	94–120
Math Fluency—Subtraction	110	75	100–120
Numerical Operations	114	82	105–123

Composite	Standard Score	Percentile Rank	95% Confidence Interval	Qualitative Description
Total Reading	118	88	114–122	Above Average
Basic Reading	114	82	111–117	Average
Mathematics	114	82	107–121	Average
Math Fluency	110	75	101–119	Average

Assessment in the area of reading included measures of early reading skills, single word reading, single word decoding, reading comprehension, and oral reading fluency. His Total Reading composite score, which is calculated from scores on reading comprehension, word reading, pseudoword decoding, and oral reading fluency tasks, was in the Average to Above Average range at 118 (114 to 122; 88th percentile). His Basic Reading composite score, solely based on word reading and pseudoword decoding activities, was also in the Average to Above Average range, 114 (111 to 117; 82nd percentile). Among all reading tasks, he scored most highly on reading comprehension, which involved reading a passage aloud or silently under untimed conditions and responding to open-ended questions about each passage. His score on this task was 125 (116 to 134; 95th percentile) and represented his highest score among all of the academic functioning subtests.

His performance on a task that required him to demonstrate early reading skills (for example, to name letters of the alphabet, produce rhyming words or words that begin or end with the same sounds, match letters with sounds, and match written words with pictures) was 118 (105 to 131 with 95% confidence), which is at the 88th percentile relative to others his age and is in the Average to Above Average range. His performance on an activity involving reading single words aloud was also in the Average to Above Average range, at 115 (111 to 119; 84th percentile). On a task that required him to read nonsense words, his score was a 111 and in the Average to Above Average range (106 to 116; 77th percentile). When reading passages out loud and responding verbally to questions about his understanding of the passages, he scored in the Average range with a 96 (88 to 104; 39th percentile). His Oral Reading Accuracy was in the Average to Above Average range (119, or 107 to 131; 90th percentile), however, and his Oral Reading Rate was in the Average range (83 to 103; 32nd percentile). He read the passages quite deliberately with apparent concern he would miss information or mispronounce a word.

Assessment in math skills included measures in the areas of math problem solving, math fluency, and numerical operations. His Mathematics composite score, derived from tasks requiring him to solve untimed math problems and written math problems related to basic skills and basic integer operations, was in the Average to Above Average range at 114 (107 to 121; 82nd percentile). His Math Fluency composite score, drawn from timed activities requiring him to solve written addition and subtraction problems within a time limit, was 110 (101 to 119; 75th percentile). His performance on a task that required him to solve untimed math problems related to basic skills such as counting and identifying shapes was in the Average to Above Average range at 112 (102 to 122; 79th percentile). When solving written addition and subtraction problems within a time limit to demonstrate math fluency, he performed in the Average to Above Average range, obtaining scores of 107 (94 to 120; 68th percentile) and 110 (100 to 120; 75th percentile). On an activity that required him to solve untimed written math problems related to basic skills and basic operations with integers, he scored 114 (105 to 123; 82nd percentile), which is in the Average to Above Average range.

Summary and Impressions

George is a 7-year-old boy who was assessed to gain an objective appraisal of his overall level of intellectual functioning, cognitive strengths and weaknesses, level of academic functioning, and academic strengths and weaknesses, and to determine if gifted or enriched education should be pursued in the fall after George demonstrated the ability to learn information from a summer math and science

≡ Rapid Reference 8.7

Summary and Diagnostic Impressions Section

- Presented in structured, organized paragraph and may include bulleted list to respond to referral questions.
- Integrate information already presented to provide a coherent description of the child that is relevant to his or her presenting issue.
- Provide brief and succinct response(s) to the referral question(s), in an organized fashion. Bulleted lists are easily located and skimmed.
- Do not ramble.
- Provide diagnostic impressions, if any. Use appropriate specifiers.

program very rapidly relative to his peers. The answers to each specific referral question are presented here.

Q: What is George's level of intellectual functioning?

A: George's General Ability Index of 133 (125 to 138; 99th percentile) is in the Very High to Extremely High range of intellectual functioning. It is often considered the best estimate of his overall intellectual functioning for the purposes of gifted admission evaluation. His Full Scale IQ of 121 (115 to 126; 92nd percentile) is in the High to Very High range of intellectual functioning. The Full Scale IQ is the measure of global intellectual ability that is the best predictor of academic achievement scores in children with high intellectual ability, so it is also important to include alongside the General Ability Index because George is being considered for accelerated learning programs.

Q: What are George's cognitive strengths and weaknesses?

A: George's greatest cognitive strengths lie in the areas of verbal comprehension and fluid reasoning. His Verbal Comprehension Index of 143 (134 to 147; 99th percentile) is in the Extremely High range. His Fluid Reasoning Index of 127 (118 to 132; 96th percentile) is also considered to be in the High to Extremely High range. Both the Verbal Comprehension Index and the Fluid Reasoning Index are significant intrapersonal strengths relative to the overall average of all specific cognitive areas.

George has a cognitive weakness in the area of processing speed. His Processing Speed Index of 89 (81 to 100; 23rd percentile) is in the Low to Average range. However, it is believed that this performance is in part due to George's greater concern with accuracy and thoroughness than with speed of completion. He demonstrated the ability to improve his processing speed performance with experience across multiple tasks.

Q: What is George's level of academic functioning?

A: George is performing in the Average to Above Average range in the areas of reading and math.

Q: What are George's academic strengths and weaknesses?

A: George has particular intrapersonal strengths in the area of Reading Comprehension, with a standard score of 125 (116 to 134; 95th percentile), which represented his highest score among all of the academic functioning subtests. He has strengths in the areas of Early Reading Skills, with a score of 118 (105 to 131; 88th percentile), and Oral Reading Accuracy, with a score of 119 (107 to 131; 90th percentile). His strongest performance in the math domain was for Numerical Operations, for which he scored 114 (105 to 123; 82nd percentile), which is in the Average to Above Average range. In terms of weaknesses, his lowest scoring areas were in Oral Reading Rate, which was in the Average range (83 to 103; 32nd percentile).

In summary, George's results suggest intellectual giftedness and powerful intrapersonal cognitive strengths in the areas of verbal comprehension and fluid reasoning. Results also indicate an intrapersonal cognitive area of weakness in the area of processing speed. He has consistently higher academic skill levels relative to other children his age in the areas of reading comprehension, early reading skills, word reading, oral reading accuracy, and numerical operations, and generally above average performance in almost all aspects of reading and math. His strongest academic skill, relative to his own overall performance, was in the area of reading comprehension. His weakest area relative to his own performance was in oral reading rate; however, this was still in the average range relative to other children his age. Furthermore, the weaker score was owed to a cautious style, and may have boosted his performance with respect to accuracy of oral reading.

Recommendations

1. Pursue gifted education through the gifted connections program at his private school using the results from this evaluation. Contact me if you need further assistance advocating for his educational needs or consulting with the school. Gifted education will ensure George has the opportunity to continue to maximize his intellectual potential, and it has been demonstrated that gifted education can improve processing speed over time. Request specifically an evaluation of creative thinking, as this is an important aspect of giftedness.

≡ *Rapid Reference 8.8*

Recommendations Section

- Presented in bulleted or numbered list format
- Organize recommendations according to referral questions, if more than one
- Group recommendations by relevant setting (e.g., home, classroom, programs, therapy)

2. Consider joining the National Association of Gifted Children (NAGC) or similar organization and the [state association withheld] and attending conferences on becoming a parent advocate for George's continued intellectual development.

3. Because encouraging creativity is critical as an aspect of gifted education, consider joining the Creativity Network within the NAGC. Advocate for creativity education for George, and teach him to solve problems creatively. When in a novel situation or facing a new problem, teach him to do the following (Treffinger, 2007):

   a. Define the problem.
   b. Generate options with which to approach or solve the new problem using various techniques, such as brainstorming, mixing and matching ideas, listing the key parts of the task, and trying to think of new ways to approach portions of it. Don't judge, but instead encourage generation of all of the options and as many as possible.
   c. Narrow down to the most promising ideas or solutions by rank ordering them, pairing them and forcing a choice, and evaluating them based on their short- and long-term pros and cons.
   d. Try the solutions that are chosen.
   e. Evaluate the outcome.
   f. Modify the solution or choose a different option if it wasn't working.

4. Find new ways to challenge George intellectually outside of school. Intellectually gifted children benefit greatly from these opportunities as they alleviate boredom and frustration if school is moving too slowly. Use his love of reading to introduce him to a wide range of both nonfiction (e.g., science) and fiction literature as he grows. Consider enrolling him in special reading programs. Continue to involve him in extracurricular experiences that will permit him to learn more about the world around

him, identify personal interests, and consider the possibilities that are open to him. Expose him to the arts and music. Consider enrollment in the school music programs in some capacity.

5. Because George has strong verbal abilities, he tends to talk himself through other types of tasks using those abilities. Encourage this practice. In particular, encourage him to use verbal skills to reason and problem solve, even talking aloud, in novel situations.

6. George's cautious style of responding and placing an emphasis on accuracy rather than speed should be taken into account in activities at school as well as at home. Whereas his processing speed is average relative to other children, he has strengths in other areas that will permit him to perform well above average given enough time. It is important to strengthen his higher order comprehension when reading. Ask questions about what he has read and work with him to ask questions that he may be able to answer if provided clues (and to provide them, but only if he struggles). If topics are too hard for him to answer with clues, then it may be helpful to give him an introduction to the topic by providing a way of thinking about it.

7. Pursue enrichment in regular classroom activities through involvement in the [product name omitted] program through the private school. Encourage involvement in the school science fair as well as in other additional activities to ensure he is properly challenged.

8. Consider accelerated learning in the area of reading by advocating for him to receive advanced coursework or more challenging assignments within his regular classroom, or perhaps, if permitted, to attend reading classes at the third-grade level in the fall. Because there is a tendency among adults to treat gifted children as little adults, some parents expect more maturity and social graces from their children, and this is sometimes used as a reason to deny access to gifted interventions, especially grade acceleration. However, a meta-analysis by Steenbergen-Hu and Moon (2011) found that grade advancement *does not affect* the child's social and emotional functioning; that is, they develop at the same rate as children who were not grade accelerated. It is normal for gifted children to have the emotional and social development of children their own age. Gifted children who receive educational interventions have been found to develop socially and emotionally at the same or better rate as gifted children who do not receive these interventions.

CASE REPORT: JANE B.—PRELITERACY CONCERNS

Case report authors: Kristina C. Breaux, PhD; Susan E. Raiford, PhD; and Diane L. Coalson, PhD

Identifying and Demographic Information

Name: Jane B.
Date of Birth: 1/3/2006
Age: 7 years 4 months
Race/Ethnicity: Caucasian
Parents: Mr. B. and Mrs. B.

School: C Elementary School
Grade: 2 (begins 9/2013)
Date of Testing: 7/1/2013
Date of Report: 7/8/2013
Examiner Name: Examiner C

Referral Questions

Mr. and Mrs. B. requested an evaluation to determine if Jane has intellectual or cognitive processing weaknesses that could be affecting her reading skill development, after her teacher indicated to them that she was behind grade level for reading skills at the end of first grade. They also hoped to learn more about her reading performance to determine the specific areas of focus for intervention and the best instructional approaches. Questions to be answered are

- What is Jane's level of intellectual functioning?
- What are Jane's cognitive strengths and weaknesses?
- What is Jane's general level of reading achievement?
- What is Jane's reading achievement in specific areas?
- Does Jane show a pattern of processing strengths and weaknesses across her cognitive and achievement profiles that is consistent with a specific learning disability?
- What approach to intervention is recommended?

Evaluation Methods and Procedures

Evaluation methods and procedures used with Jane included

- History and background review
- Parent interview
- Teacher interview
- Child interview
- Behavioral observations
- Wechsler Preschool and Primary Scale of Intelligence–Fourth Edition
- Wechsler Individual Achievement Test–Third Edition

- Kaufman Test of Educational Achievement–Second Edition (Naming Facility [RAN])

Background and History

Jane is the second child born to Mr. and Mrs. B. She has a sister two years her senior. Mr. and Mrs. B. are both employed full time; Mr. B. is a customer support specialist and Mrs. B. is a nurse. Mrs. B. works at a second job on Saturday mornings at a local lab. Mr. B. had a year and a half of college, and Mrs. B. has a CNA.

Jane was born after an uneventful pregnancy via C-section delivery. She was of normal length, head circumference, and weight. Her APGAR scores were within normal limits, and she had no complications.

Mrs. B. reported Jane reached developmental milestones within normal limits. She began to walk at 14 months, spoke her first words at around 12 months, said sentences at 26 months, and was fully toilet trained at age 3. She was fed breast milk until age 10 weeks. Her medical history is unremarkable. Her health is good other than mild colds and allergies. She had frequent ear infections as an infant and toddler, but did not require tubes. Her ear infections subsided shortly after she reached age 4. Her hearing and vision were within normal limits per an exam 1 year ago, and her last complete physical indicated she is within normal limits for height and weight relative to other girls her age.

Jane's education began at 3 years when she entered preschool. Prior to that, she was cared for in a neighbor's home when her parents were working. She was enrolled in kindergarten at age 5, then first grade at age 6, and she continues to second grade in the fall. Jane's typical day involves before-school day care drop-off at 7:00 a.m., transport to school by 8:15 a.m. by the day care staff, transport from school at 2:45 p.m. by the day care staff, pickup from the day care at 5:30 p.m., and dinner with both parents followed by bath and bedtime.

Mrs. B. recalls Jane had difficulty learning letters in preschool. Even now, prior to beginning the second grade, she sometimes confuses visually similar letters (e.g., b, d, p) when sounding out words. Mrs. B. has worked with her extensively at home, but she continued to have difficulty. Jane reportedly had little interest in reading but enjoyed looking at picture books. During this school year, Jane's teacher stated to Mrs. B. that Jane was not achieving at grade level in early reading skills, including some aspects of phonological awareness, or the ability to identify and manipulate the sounds with words, and phonics, or the ability to identify correspondence between letters and their sounds.

Mrs. B. and Teacher B both report that Jane is slow to recognize words on the page, and laboriously sounds out unfamiliar words. When reading a passage aloud, she tends to substitute visually similar words (e.g., crashed for crushed) without noticing that the sentence did not make sense. When she sounds out words, she often sounds them out even if she has read them previously on the same page. Her reading rate is reportedly "very slow" according to her mother and teacher. According to Teacher B, Jane understands less than other children after she has read a passage, and she displays a dislike of reading activities despite enjoying other aspects of and activities at school. Teacher B indicated that Jane is achieving at grade level in other areas. Teacher B describes Jane as a pleasant, curious child with many friends. According to her mother, Jane enjoys playing with dolls and dollhouses, playing outdoors, and playing Wii sports (e.g., bowling, soccer) in her free time. Mrs. B. said she expects Jane to graduate high school and to "have a good job, doing something she likes to do."

Jane's parents report that she is a somewhat introverted, conscientious, emotionally stable child who enjoys new experiences. Mrs. B. reported that she relates well with her female peers and has four or five close friends. Jane described school as "okay," and said she liked her teacher this past year. She listed her favorite subjects as "gym and dance." She named three close friends from school with whom she enjoys playing.

Mental Status and Behavioral Observations

Jane arrived on time and was oriented to person, place, time, and purpose of the meeting, stating she was here to "start getting better at reading." She was accompanied by her mother. She was dressed and groomed neatly and was of average size for her age. Activity level, mannerisms, and eye contact were within normal limits. Her use of vocabulary in conversation was within normal limits for age. Her reported mood prior to testing was "okay" and her affect was calm and mood congruent.

During testing, she was cooperative and appeared to give her best effort to the tasks. Given the effort, level of engagement, and persistence she displayed in the session, the results of the assessment are likely to reflect accurate estimates of intellectual and academic functioning. It is possible that past unpleasant experiences with reading tasks may have resulted in some level of disengagement and a slight underestimate of her reading skills; however, similar disengagement is likely to occur in the classroom as well. In reaction to perceived success, she became more engaged and smiled. She appeared unaware when she missed items on the intellectual test.

When she encountered reading-related tasks during the achievement portion of the evaluation, she appeared aware of lapses in her performance. She became distressed and anxious, lost focus, and asked for breaks frequently. On a speeded task involving visual search of an array of objects where she was instructed to locate all of the clothing, she appeared overwhelmed, surveying the entire array without stamping targets for several seconds at a time. She required prompting on a number of speeded tasks to work as fast as possible and to continue to the next item.

Test Results and Interpretation

Cognitive Functioning

Intellectual ability   To obtain comprehensive, objective information about her intellectual ability and her cognitive strengths and weaknesses (see Table 8.3 for a score summary), Jane was administered the Wechsler Preschool and Primary Scale of Intelligence–Fourth Edition (WPPSI-IV), an individually administered assessment of intellectual ability. The WPPSI-IV provides composite scores that represent global intellectual ability, as well as specific cognitive abilities in the areas of verbal comprehension, visual spatial processing, fluid reasoning, working memory, and processing speed.

The score that is most informative to represent intellectual ability for the purposes of this evaluation is the General Ability Index, which provides a measure of global intellectual ability while reducing the influence of working memory and processing speed on its estimate. The General Ability Index is recommended in situations where neurodevelopmental or other issues may interfere with working memory and processing speed abilities, and therefore obscure true differences between ability and achievement areas. Jane's reading difficulties suggest that the General Ability Index is the most appropriate score to utilize for the purpose of comparing cognitive ability and reading achievement. If, after consultation with the school district, it is determined that an ability–achievement discrepancy is required to qualify for special education services, the General Ability Index should be used in lieu of the Full Scale IQ because it reduces the influence of working memory and processing speed weaknesses commonly seen in children with reading problems.

Jane earned a General Ability Index of 99 (93 to 105 with 95% confidence) based on her performance on the four core subtests. Her General Ability Index ranks her at the 47th percentile, and is considered in the Average range of intellectual functioning.

Jane's Full Scale IQ of 94 (89 to 100; 34th percentile) is considered in the Average range of intellectual functioning. Her General Ability Index and her Full Scale IQ scores show a significant and rare discrepancy (5 standard-score points) seen in only 15% of the population, which suggests that the influence of working memory and processing speed on intellectual ability resulted in a difference in the overall performance estimate represented by the Full Scale IQ.

The Cognitive Proficiency Index summarizes performance in the areas of working memory and processing speed. Her Cognitive Proficiency Index of 82 (76 to 91; 39th percentile) is in the Low range. Her General Ability Index and Cognitive Proficiency Index are significantly different, with only around 7% of

Table 8.3 Jane's WPPSI-IV Score Summary

Subtest	Scaled Score	Percentile Rank
Information	8	25
Similarities	11	63
(Vocabulary)	9	37
(Comprehension)	10	50
(Receptive Vocabulary)	8	25
(Picture Naming)	11	63
Block Design	10	50
Object Assembly	9	37
Matrix Reasoning	10	50
Picture Concepts	16	98
Picture Memory	7	16
Zoo Locations	8	25
Bug Search	9	37
Cancellation	6	9
(Animal Coding)	11	63

Subtests in parentheses do not contribute to primary index scores or the Full Scale IQ.

Composite	Standard Score	Percentile Rank	95% Confidence Interval	Qualitative Description
Verbal Comprehension Index	96	39	89–103	Average
Visual Spatial Index	97	42	89–106	Average
Fluid Reasoning Index	117	87	109–123	High
Working Memory Index	84	14	77–93	Low
Processing Speed Index	86	18	78–97	Low
Full Scale IQ	94	34	89–100	Average
General Ability Index	99	47	93–105	Average
Cognitive Proficiency Index	82	12	76–91	Low
Vocabulary Acquisition Index	94	34	87–102	Average

children showing the same difference (17 standard-score points) or larger between the two index scores. This suggests that her working memory and processing speed abilities are not equivalent to those in the areas of verbal comprehension, visual spatial processing, and fluid reasoning. Although Jane processes both verbal and visual information in the Average range, and has relatively strong fluid reasoning skills, she shows lower performance on tasks that involve holding information in memory and performing simple operations to produce a response, and on tasks that involve rapid processing of information.

To more thoroughly understand her cognitive proficiency performance, it is important to also understand the cognitive abilities that contribute to that performance: working memory and processing speed. The Working Memory Index represents visual and visual–spatial working memory, and ability to withstand proactive interference. Her Working Memory Index of 84 (77 to 93; 14th percentile) is in the Very Low to Low range. Her working memory appears to be an intrapersonal cognitive weakness, as the corresponding index score is significantly lower than the overall average of her performance across all specific cognitive areas measured by the test. The difference between her Working Memory Index and her overall average of all specific cognitive ability scores occurs in less than 10% to 25% of children at her ability level. One of the tasks on which she scored lowest, Picture Memory, contributes to the Working Memory Index. It involves viewing stimulus pictures, and then selecting the stimulus picture from a number of response options on a page. The difference between this score and the average of her scores on other subtests was a significant and rare one, occurring in only 10% to 25% of children. This pattern of performance suggests a significant weakness on tasks requiring short-term memory for visual nonverbal stimuli and vigilance to manage interfering stimuli.

The Processing Speed Index represents speed of information processing, especially quick scanning and discrimination of simple visual information. Her Processing Speed Index of 86 (79 to 97; 18th percentile) is in the Low to Average range. Two visual–motor subtests constitute this index: Bug Search and Cancellation. Her performance on Bug Search was close to the average for children her age. For the Cancellation subtest, she was shown two 17 × 11 pages of clothing and other items, and was asked to mark as many clothing items as possible within a time limit. Relative to her average performance on 10 core subtests, this score was a weakness: Only 5% to 10% of children obtained a score that low or lower relative to their overall average. Among all parts of the test, this was her lowest score. A supplemental subtest, Animal Coding, was administered to provide additional information about her processing speed abilities. For this subtest, she was taught to associate pictured animals with shapes, and then mark the shape that corresponds to each pictured animal as quickly as possible. Her performance on Animal Coding was stronger relative to the other Processing Speed subtests. Hence, among these speeded visual nonverbal tasks, Jane demonstrated better performance on a task requiring associative learning than tasks requiring simple visual scanning and selective attention and vigilance.

To understand more fully Jane's global intellectual ability, and to discover her cognitive strengths, it is important to examine specific scores that represent different cognitive areas. The Fluid Reasoning Index represents the ability to reason, conceptualize, and classify information, and is based on subtests that use visual stimuli. Her Fluid Reasoning Index of 117 (109 to 123; 87th percentile) is in the High range and represents a significant strength relative to her overall performance. In fact, the difference between her average index-level performance and her Fluid Reasoning Index (21 standard-score points) occurs in less than 1% of the population. Among all parts of the test, she performed best on a task that contributes to the Fluid Reasoning Index, Picture Concepts, which involves selecting one picture from each of either two or three rows to form a group with a shared element. She demonstrated average performance on the other subtest that contributes to this index, Matrix Reasoning, which involves selecting among visually presented options the one that best completes a matrix. The difference between the two subtests was a significant and rare one, occurring in only 12.7% of children. This pattern of performance suggests a superior ability to identify pictured concepts that are most similar, suggesting strong categorical reasoning ability.

The Verbal Comprehension Index measures acquired knowledge, verbal reasoning, and verbal concept formation. Her Verbal Comprehension Index score of 96 (89 to 103; 39th percentile) is in the Average range and is consistent with her overall performance across other areas. Her performance on the two subtests that contribute to this index was disparate. She performed better on Similarities, a subtest for which she described how two words representing common objects or concepts are similar, than on Information, for which she responded to questions about general-knowledge topics. The difference between these two subtests was statistically significant, and a difference this large occurs in only 10% to 25% of children. This pattern of performance suggests a stronger ability to explain how two words/concepts are alike than to retrieve acquired knowledge from long-term memory. This result is consistent with her performance on Picture Concepts, which also requires categorical reasoning ability, but utilizes visual, rather than verbal, stimuli.

The Visual Spatial Index measures visual spatial processing, part–whole relationships integration and synthesis, and visual–motor integration. Her Visual Spatial Index of 97 (89 to 106; 42nd percentile) is in the Average range and is consistent with her overall performance across other areas. She performed consistently across the two subtests that constitute this index: Block Design, for which she viewed a model and used two-color blocks to reconstruct the design on the model, and Object Assembly, for which she assembled puzzle pieces within a time limit into a meaningful whole object that was named.

Overall, Jane's intellectual functioning is estimated to be in the Average range. With both verbal and nonverbal information, she displays strengths in categorical reasoning and associative learning; in other words, she has a strong ability to associate and find similarities between concepts or abstract stimuli, as demonstrated by her performance on Similarities, Picture Concepts, and Animal Coding. She tends to have difficulty on tasks requiring visual nonverbal working memory, or processing speed with selective attention and vigilance.

Academic Functioning

The Wechsler Individual Achievement Test–Third Edition (WIAT-III; Pearson, 2009) was administered to provide an in-depth assessment of Jane's academic achievement in reading. Assessment in the area of reading included measures of early reading skills, single word reading, single word decoding, reading comprehension, and oral reading fluency. Measures of oral language were also administered to evaluate whether global language comprehension may be impaired, and to assess oral expression skills that may impact reading achievement. One subtest from Form A of the Kaufman Test of Educational Achievement–Second Edition (KTEA-II; Kaufman & Kaufman, 2004), Naming Facility (RAN), was administered to assess rapid automatized naming, a cognitive process important to reading achievement. Results are interpreted using age-based norms (see Table 8.4 for a score summary).

Her Total Reading composite score of 83 (79 to 87; 13th percentile) is in the Below Average range. This composite is calculated from scores on Word Reading, Pseudoword Decoding, Reading Comprehension, and Oral Reading Fluency.

Her Basic Reading composite score of 89 (86 to 92; 23rd percentile) is in the Average range. This composite is composed of scores on Word Reading and Pseudoword Decoding. She scored in the lower end of the Average range when asked to read single words aloud on the Word Reading subtest, and when asked to read nonsense words on the Pseudoword Decoding subtest. Skills analysis results revealed a tendency to make errors on consonant blends/clusters and vowel teams. Some exception words with irregular patterns were also difficult for her.

Her Reading Comprehension and Fluency composite score of 79 (72 to 86; 8th percentile) is in the Below Average range. This score is composed of two subtest scores: Reading Comprehension and Oral Reading Fluency. She scored in the

Table 8.4 Jane's WIAT-III and KTEA-II (Form A) Score Summary

Subtest (Component Score)	Standard Score	Percentile Rank	95% Confidence Interval
WIAT-III Listening	81	10	69–93
Comprehension	86	18	
(Receptive Vocabulary)	81	10	
(Oral Discourse Comprehension)			
WIAT-III Oral Expression	96	39	85–107
(Expressive Vocabulary)	106	66	
(Oral Word Fluency)	99	47	
(Sentence Repetition)	87	19	
WIAT-III Early Reading Skills	88	21	75–101
WIAT-III Reading Comprehension	88	21	79–97
WIAT-III Word Reading	90	25	86–94
WIAT-III Pseudoword Decoding	89	23	84–94
WIAT-III Oral Reading Fluency	78	7	70–86
WIAT-III (Oral Reading Accuracy)	85	16	73–97
WIAT-III (Oral Reading Rate)	68	2	58–78
KTEA-II Naming Facility (RAN)	87	19	78–96

WIAT-III Composite Score	Standard Score	Percentile Rank	95% Confidence Interval	Qualitative Description
Oral Language	87	19	78–96	Average
Total Reading	83	13	78–86	Below Average
Basic Reading	89	23	86–92	Average
Reading Comprehension and Fluency	79	8	70–84	Below Average

lower end of the Average range on the Reading Comprehension subtest, which required her to read passages (either aloud or silently) under untimed conditions and answer open-ended comprehension questions. She chose to read aloud most of the time, and her reading was slow and labored. She appeared aware that she didn't fully comprehend a few of the passages, commenting that they "didn't make sense." She performed slightly better on literal than inferential questions. Jane scored in the Below Average range on the Oral Reading Fluency subtest, which involves reading passages aloud. Her reading rate on this subtest was in the Low range (2nd percentile), much lower than her reading accuracy, which was in the lower end of the Average range (16th percentile).

Her performance on the Early Reading Skills subtest was in the lower end of the Average range (21st percentile). On this subtest, she was asked to demonstrate early reading skills such as naming letters of the alphabet, matching letters with sounds, rhyming, recognizing words that begin or end with the same sound, blending sounds together to form words, and matching written words with pictures. Jane had some difficulty matching beginning/ending sounds on items involving three words/pictures.

Overall, Jane's reading performance is in the lower end of the Average range in most areas, including early reading skills, word recognition and decoding, and reading comprehension. Her lowest performance is in oral reading fluency (Below Average range), and oral reading rate (Low range) in particular.

To evaluate whether Jane has global language comprehension weaknesses, she was administered the Listening Comprehension subtest. She scored in the Below Average range. This subtest is composed of two components: Receptive Vocabulary and Oral Discourse Comprehension. On Receptive Vocabulary, she was asked to listen to a word and then point to the picture that best represents that concept. She scored in the lower end of the Average range. On Oral Discourse Comprehension, she was asked to listen to sentences and passages of increasing length and complexity, and orally respond to comprehension questions about each one. She scored in the Below Average range. She did well on the short sentence items, but had difficulty when the passages increased in length and complexity. She performed slightly better on literal than inferential questions.

Jane's performance on the Reading Comprehension and Listening Comprehension subtests suggests a weakness in language comprehension. Her performance on Reading Comprehension was somewhat stronger than on Listening Comprehension, perhaps in large part because she was able to re-read the text as needed to aid comprehension and review the passage when answering questions.

Across all parts of the test, Jane scored highest on the Oral Expression subtest and appeared to enjoy the tasks. Her overall performance was in the Average range. The subtest is composed of three components: Expressive Vocabulary, Oral Word Fluency, and Sentence Repetition. She performed strongest (solidly in the Average range) on Expressive Vocabulary and Oral Word Fluency. Expressive Vocabulary was administered to assess Jane's speaking vocabulary and word retrieval ability by asking her to say the word that best corresponds to a given picture and definition. Oral Word Fluency was administered to assess Jane's efficiency of word retrieval and flexibility of thought processes by asking her to name as many things as possible belonging to a given category (animals, for example) within 60 seconds. She performed in the lower end of the Average range on Sentence Repetition, which measures oral syntactic knowledge and short-term memory. Jane was asked to listen to sentences that increase in length and complexity and repeat each sentence verbatim. She only made one syntax error, but on several items she appeared to forget the last half of the sentence or the entire sentence. Jane's pattern of performance across the three components of the Oral Expression subtest indicates average word retrieval ability and speaking vocabulary with a relative weakness on a task requiring auditory verbal short-term memory. It is notable that her score on Receptive Vocabulary is 20 points lower than on Expressive Vocabulary (a component of the Oral Expression subtest), perhaps because Receptive Vocabulary places greater demands on visual nonverbal working memory by requiring interpretation of four pictures on each page, resisting distractors, and attention to visual detail.

Jane's performance on the KTEA-II Naming Facility (RAN) subtest, which required her to name objects, colors, and letters as quickly as possible, was in the low end of the Average range. Rapid automatic naming tasks require the same kinds of rapid identification and phonological retrieval skills that are necessary for fluent word identification. Jane's performance suggests that her rapid automatic naming ability is consistent with her performance on basic reading tasks and with her Low to Average performance on the WPPSI-IV Processing Speed Index and subtests. Hence, a rapid automatic naming weakness may be contributing to Jane's reading difficulties, but to a lesser degree than her weaknesses in working memory.

Pattern of Strengths and Weaknesses Analysis

Cognitive and achievement testing can be jointly used to examine a child's profile for signs of a specific learning disability. Children with specific learning disabilities typically show a pattern of cognitive processing strengths and weaknesses in addition to the achievement weakness. First, they often show a cognitive strength that is significantly different from their achievement weakness. Because fluid reasoning has not been shown to be strongly related to reading comprehension and fluency, Jane's strength in the area of fluid reasoning is not inconsistent with a specific learning disability in reading, with impairment in reading comprehension and fluency skills. A significant difference was found between her cognitive processing strength, the Fluid Reasoning Index, and her achievement weakness, Reading Comprehension and Fluency, which supports identification with a specific learning disability in reading comprehension and reading fluency.

The pattern of strengths and weaknesses also extends to the cognitive domain when specific learning disabilities are present. Typically, a child with a specific learning disability also shows a cognitive processing weakness that is significantly different from the cognitive processing strength. In Jane's case, her Working Memory Index represents a processing weakness, and it is significantly lower than her Fluid Reasoning Index. Research has established that a cognitive weakness in the area of working memory is common in children with specific learning disabilities in reading with skill deficits in reading comprehension and reading fluency. Hence, these results provide further support for a specific learning disability in the areas of reading fluency and reading comprehension.

Jane also demonstrates achievement weaknesses in other areas. With a cognitive processing strength of 117 in fluid reasoning, Reading Comprehension, Word Reading, Pseudoword Decoding, and Oral Reading Fluency could each represent the achievement weakness and would each be consistent with a specific learning disability in reading in those areas, with significant differences between those areas and the processing strength.

Summary and Impressions

Jane is a 7-year-old girl who was assessed to determine if she has intellectual or cognitive processing weaknesses that could be affecting her reading skill development or that might be consistent with a specific learning disability. Specific questions to be answered are

- What is Jane's level of intellectual functioning?
- What are Jane's cognitive strengths and weaknesses?
- What is Jane's general level of reading achievement?
- What is Jane's reading achievement in specific areas?
- Does she show a pattern of processing strengths and weaknesses across her cognitive and achievement profiles that is consistent with a specific learning disability?
- What approach to intervention is recommended?

The answers to each specific referral question are presented here.

Q: What is Jane's level of intellectual functioning?

A: Jane earned a General Ability Index of 99 (93 to 105; 47th percentile), which is in the Average range of intellectual functioning. After consultation with the school district, if it is determined that an ability–achievement discrepancy is required to qualify for special education services, the General Ability Index should be used in lieu of the Full Scale IQ because it reduces the influence of working memory and processing speed, cognitive processing weaknesses commonly seen with reading problems.

Q: What are Jane's cognitive strengths and weaknesses?

A: Jane's greatest cognitive strength lies in the area of fluid reasoning. Her Fluid Reasoning Index of 117 (109 to 123; 87th percentile) is in the High range and represents a significant strength relative to her own performance. In fact, the difference between her average index-level performance and her Fluid Reasoning Index (21 standard-score points) occurs in less than 1% of the population. The Fluid Reasoning Index is a significant intrapersonal strength relative to her overall average performance in all specific cognitive areas.

Jane has a cognitive weakness in the area of working memory. Her Working Memory Index of 84 (77 to 93; 14th percentile) is in the Very Low to Low range. Her working memory appears to be an intrapersonal cognitive weakness; the corresponding index score is significantly lower than the overall average of all specific cognitive areas measured by the test. The difference between her Working Memory Index and her overall average of all specific cognitive areas occurs in less than only 10% to 25% of children at her ability level.

Q: What is Jane's general level of reading achievement?

A: Overall, Jane's profile of reading performance indicates that she is functioning in the lower end of the Average range in most areas, but with performance in the Low to Below Average range on measures of fluency and rate.

Q: What is Jane's level of reading achievement in specific areas?

A: Jane shows her most concerning achievement weakness in the area of reading comprehension and fluency. Her lowest performance is in oral reading fluency, and specifically in oral reading rate. Her difficulties with language comprehension are more pronounced on measures of listening than reading.

Q: Does Jane show a pattern of processing strengths and weaknesses across her cognitive and achievement profiles that is consistent with a specific learning disability?

A: Yes. Because fluid reasoning has not been shown to be strongly related to reading comprehension and fluency, Jane's strength in the area of fluid reasoning is not inconsistent with a specific learning disability in reading comprehension and fluency. A significant difference was found between her cognitive processing strength, the Fluid Reasoning Index, and her primary achievement weakness, Reading Comprehension and Fluency, which supports identification of a specific learning disability. Her Working Memory Index represents a processing weakness, and it is significantly lower than her Fluid Reasoning Index. Research has established that a cognitive weakness in the area of working memory is observed in children with specific learning disabilities in reading with skill deficits in reading fluency and language comprehension. Jane also demonstrates achievement weaknesses in other areas. Her performance in

Basic Reading (including Word Reading and Pseudoword Decoding) is significantly different from her cognitive processing strength in Fluid Reasoning, and could also be consistent with a specific learning disability in reading (in settings that permit use of a standard score above 85 to represent an achievement weakness).

Q: What approach to intervention is recommended?

A: As a general approach, Jane's intervention plan should focus on improving all areas of reading (phonemic awareness, phonics, fluency, vocabulary, and comprehension) as well as listening comprehension. Given the reciprocal relationship between reading and spelling, it's recommended that all reading instruction incorporate spelling activities as well. Utilize activities that exploit her areas of strengths, especially fluid (categorical) reasoning, and teach strategies to help her compensate for working memory limitations (see Recommendations section for specific suggestions). Given Jane's working memory weaknesses, it's also recommended that her teachers and parents monitor her performance in math carefully because she may experience difficulty with word problems and procedural math as these curricular demands increase.

In summary, Jane's results suggest a specific learning disability in reading fluency and reading comprehension. Her greatest intrapersonal cognitive strength is in the area of fluid reasoning, with an intrapersonal cognitive area of weakness in the area of working memory. Her below average performance in the areas of reading fluency and language comprehension are unexpected given her average cognitive ability, but are consistent with a cognitive processing weakness in working memory. Her academic skill levels in the areas of early reading skills and basic reading are also lower than expected.

DSM-5 **Diagnostic Impression:** 315.00 specific learning disorder, with impairment in reading, with skill deficits in word reading accuracy, reading rate, reading fluency, and reading comprehension.

Recommendations

1. Pursue special education services for reading through her school, to begin in the fall, using the results from this evaluation. Special education services will help ensure that her need to develop reading skills is properly addressed. After consultation with the school district, if it is determined that an ability–achievement discrepancy is required to qualify for special education services, the General Ability Index should be used to summarize global intellectual ability in lieu of the Full Scale IQ because it reduces the influence of working memory and processing speed cognitive processing weaknesses commonly

seen with reading problems. Contact me if you need further assistance advocating for her educational needs or consulting with the school.

2. Capitalize on Jane's strength in fluid reasoning to stimulate her interest in reading and build comprehension.

   a. Encourage her to look for patterns and notice how words and concepts are similar (and different) in all areas of study.

   b. Ask her to discuss relations between the subjects of the paragraph, actions being performed in the book, or other examples of the category being described. For example, if a paragraph discusses where a dog sleeps, encourage her to discuss where a cat sleeps.

3. Teach strategies to help her monitor and strengthen her level of comprehension during and after listening and reading activities. In response to a listening or reading activity, consider utilizing methods such as the following:

   a. Teach Jane to form a habit of asking herself questions about what she learned, what did not make sense, and what she would still like to know, and asking questions of others to clarify her own understanding and find out more. Encourage Jane to express her intellectual curiosity in all areas of life—both at home and at school—through questioning.

   b. Request that Jane's parents and teachers repeat critical information and multistep instructions, and encourage Jane to ask for repetition as needed.

   c. Practice "reciprocal teaching" (Palincsar & Brown, 1984) whereby students take turns assuming different roles to employ four specific reading strategies to support comprehension: Questioning, Clarifying, Summarizing, and Predicting.

4. Improve phonemic awareness, reading fluency (accuracy, rate, automaticity of lexical access), decoding, and vocabulary at the level of the *word* using activities such as the following:

   a. Increase her familiarity with sight words using flash cards, lists, and/or sight word reading apps on your smartphone and tablet device. Practice sight words both at school and home, and consider charting her progress for both speed and accuracy to provide motivation and a visual indicator of success.

   b. Practice reading lists of words that have common features, such as initial consonant blends, and track both speed and accuracy. Encourage her to discover what the common feature is on each list, and always discuss what unfamiliar words mean and how to use the words in a sentence. After she learns to read the words, practice spelling them as well.

   c. Utilize letter cards to create a word and then change, delete, or add a letter/letter pattern to form a different word. To strengthen phonemic awareness, these cards may also be used for the "say it and move it" (Ball & Blachman, 1991) technique by having Jane say the sound that each letter/letter pattern makes as she moves each card.

d. Strengthen word analysis skills by recognizing morphemes like prefixes and suffixes as well as vowel combinations within words, and by learning to recognize syllable types. Read (and spell) groups of derived words (e.g., help, helpful, unhelpful, helping, helped, etc.). She may also practice cutting word cards to separate prefixes and suffixes. After reading these words in isolation, read them in short sentences to build fluency, vocabulary, and morpho-syntactic awareness.

e. To improve her visual inspection of words, provide tasks that require her to find the target word among orthographically similar words (e.g., *pedestrian*: pedstrian, pedestrian, pedestrien, pedestrin). This may be done under timed conditions to track speed of visual processing.

5. Improve oral reading fluency at the level of the *phrase* by having Jane practice reading phrase cards that can be made by printing phrases on notecards. Each card has a phrase such as *jumps over the fence* or *sitting in her chair*. The goal is to improve how quickly she can read them all accurately. If she makes a reading error, give a simple cue to encourage her to try again until the card is read correctly, and then proceed to the next card. Reading and re-reading these phrases will improve Jane's attention to morphology, syntax, prepositions, articles, and pronouns, and improve her ability to chunk meaningful units of text together fluently when reading in context.

6. Improve oral reading fluency at the level of the *sentence and paragraph*, and encourage Jane to pay greater attention to punctuation and period breaks to prevent sentences from running into each other and establish a natural reading prosody. Consider utilizing the following approaches to help Jane learn to read fluently with appropriate prosody and attention to punctuation:

a. Repeated reading is a simple but effective means of building reading fluency (Samuels, 1979).

b. Echo reading is a method whereby the teacher reads one to three sentences aloud as Jane follows along, and then Jane reads them.

c. The "neurological impress method" (Heckelman, 1969) involves having Jane and the teacher read aloud simultaneously. With repeated reading, the teacher may gradually allow Jane to take the lead as they read together.

d. Paired reading (Rasinski, 1995) is a similar, highly effective technique that Jane can practice at home whereby a parent reads a brief passage to

Jane, then the parent and child read it together several times, and finally, Jane reads the text to the parent and receives praise for a job well done.

7. Read paragraphs from simple beginner books aloud with her, allowing her to follow along. Seek to increase Jane's reading comprehension by discussing and asking questions about the text. Encourage Jane to also ask questions about what was read and to predict what will happen next in a story. Read highly predictable sentences or stories to encourage her to rely on comprehension to predict what word or type of word might come next. Incorporate both listening and reading comprehension activities and a wide range of texts including recipes, how-to, poetry, fiction, and nonfiction. Assess literal and inferential comprehension in different ways including oral (answer questions), written (mark yes/no, write about it), and other behaviors (pantomime/do what this says, follow instructions, etc.).

8. Provide a quiet area and time for practicing reading together on a daily basis. Allow her to choose among a small selection of books that interest to her and are at her reading level.

9. Use a variety of media to keep activities engaging and interesting, such as children's audio books on CD to strengthen listening comprehension, videos with text designed to teach sight words, audio books on your tablet or smartphone device that Jane can use to read along, or reading apps for young children. Begin at the pre-K and kindergarten levels and progress to first grade after success has been experienced.

10. When using reading to teach other academic skills, monitor her comprehension carefully to ensure she understands the content. For example, she may not easily understand mathematics word problems, and she may not comprehend written directions for writing or science activities without assistance.

11. Consider enrolling her in a research-supported working memory training program. Research suggests that high-quality working memory training methods may be beneficial as one component to a comprehensive approach to reading intervention. In addition to improving working memory in general (Holmes & Gathercole, 2013; Klingberg, 2010), working memory training may improve reading comprehension performance (Dahlin, 2011). Working memory is related to a wide variety of academic outcomes (Holmes & Gathercole, 2013; Klingberg, 2010).

12. Consider joining the Learning Disabilities Association of America (LDA) as well as the state chapter of that organization, and attending conferences

on becoming a parent advocate for Jane's continued development in the area of reading.

13. Monitor closely her academic performance over the next year. Children with learning disabilities in reading may also experience difficulty with math computations, spelling, and written language. Return for additional evaluation if necessary, or request evaluation of these areas through the school psychologist.

✒ TEST YOURSELF ✒

1. **What sources of information should be included in the Background and History section of a case report?**

2. **The information in the Mental Status and Behavioral Observations section of the case report should**
   a. List the most prominent to least prominent behaviors
   b. Elaborate on notable or relevant areas only
   c. Describe all behaviors in sequence of occurrence
   d. Focus on the child's cooperativeness and impulsivity

3. **The Summary and Impressions section of a case report should *not***
   a. Have brief responses to the referral questions
   b. Use bulleted lists
   c. Provide a coherent description of the child
   d. Detail the child's response style to subtest tasks

4. **What are the components that make up the Recommendations section of a case report?**

5. **Tables located in the Test Results and Interpretation section of a case report should include all of the following *except***
   a. Subtest raw scores
   b. Descriptive classifications
   c. Subtest composite scores
   d. Confidence intervals
   e. Percentile ranks

6. **The Mental Status and Behavioral Observations section of a case report should be fully complete before testing.**
   True or False?

Answers: 1. See Rapid Reference 8.4; 2. b; 3. d; 4. See Rapid Reference 8.8; 5. a; 6. False

REFERENCES

Ball, E. W., & Blachman, B. A. (1991). Does phoneme awareness training in kindergarten make a difference in early word recognition and developmental spelling? *Reading Research Quarterly, 26*, 49–66.

Dahlin, K. I. E. (2011). Effects of working memory training on reading in children with special needs. *Reading and Writing, 24*, 479–491.

Heckelman, R. G. (1969). A neurological-impress method of remedial-reading instruction. *Academic Therapy, 4*, 277–282.

Holmes, J., & Gathercole, S. E. (2013). Taking working memory training from the laboratory into schools. *Educational Psychology: An International Journal of Experimental Educational Psychology*, doi: 10.1080/01443410.2013.797338

Kaufman, A. S., & Kaufman, N. L. (2004). *Kaufman test of educational achievement* (2nd ed.). Bloomington, MN: Pearson.

Klingberg, T. (2010). Training and plasticity of working memory. *Trends in Cognitive Sciences, 14*, 317–324.

Palincsar, A. S., & Brown, A. L. (1984). Reciprocal teaching of comprehension-fostering and comprehension-monitoring activities. *Cognition and Instruction, 1*, 117–175.

Pearson. (2009). *Wechsler individual achievement test* (3rd ed.). Bloomington, MN: Author.

Rasinski, T.V. (1995). Fast start: A parent involvement reading program for primary grade students. In W. Linek & E. Sturtevant (Eds.), *Generations of literacy: The 17th yearbook of the College Reading Association* (pp. 301–312). Harrisonburg, VA: College Reading Association.

Samuels, S. J. (1979). The method of repeated readings. *Reading Teacher, 32*, 403–408.

Steenbergen-Hu, S., & Moon, S. (2011). The effects of acceleration on high-ability learners: A meta-analysis. *Gifted Child Quarterly, 55*, 39–53.

Treffinger, D. J. (2007). Creative problem solving (CPS): Powerful tools for managing change and developing talent. *Gifted and Talented International, 22*, 8–18.

About the CD-ROM

INTRODUCTION

This appendix provides you with information on the contents of the CD that accompanies this book. For the latest information, please refer to the AbouttheCD.txt located at the root of the CD.

System Requirements

Make sure that your computer meets the minimum system requirements listed in this section. If your computer doesn't match up to most of these requirements, you may have a problem using the contents of the CD.

- A computer with a web browser
- A CD-ROM drive
- Microsoft Word or Word Viewer or another program capable of reading Microsoft Word files.

Note: Many popular word processing programs are capable of reading Microsoft Word files. However, users should be aware that a slight amount of formatting might be lost when using a program other than Microsoft Word.

Using the CD with Windows

To access the content from the CD, follow these steps:

1. Insert the CD into your computer's CD-ROM drive.
2. Select Home.html from the list of files.
3. Read through the license agreement by clicking the License link near the top-right of the interface.
4. The interface appears. Simply select the material you want to view.

WHAT'S ON THE CD

The following sections provide a summary of the material you'll find on the CD.

Content

The CD includes:

- Appendix A: Subtest Specific Prompts
- Appendix B: Sample Tables for Reports
- Appendix C: Additional Index Score Norms
- WPPSI™-IV Interpretive Assistant 1.0, created by Susan Engi Raiford, PhD, and Ou Zhang, PhD

Applications

Adobe Reader

Included on this CD is a link to download Adobe Acrobat Reader for viewing PDF files. For more information and system requirements, please go to www.adobe.com.

Microsoft Word Viewer

Included on this CD is a link to download Microsoft Word Viewer on the "Chapter Files" link. Microsoft Word Viewer is a freeware viewer that allows you to view, but not edit, most Microsoft Word files. Certain features of Microsoft Word documents may not display as expected from within Word Viewer.

OpenOffice.org

Included on this CD is a link to download OpenOffice.org for viewing spreadsheet files. For more information and system requirements, please go to www.openoffice.org.

OpenOffice.org is a free multiplatform office productivity suite. It is similar to Microsoft Office or Lotus SmartSuite, but OpenOffice.org is absolutely free. It includes word processing, spreadsheet, presentation, and drawing applications that enable you to create professional documents, newsletters, reports, and presentations. It supports most file formats of other office software. You should be able to edit and view any files created with other office solutions.

Shareware programs are fully functional, trial versions of copyrighted programs. If you like particular programs, register with their authors for a nominal fee and receive licenses, enhanced versions, and technical support.

Freeware programs are copyrighted games, applications, and utilities that are free for personal use. Unlike shareware, these programs do not require a fee or provide technical support.

GNU software is governed by its own license, which is included inside the folder of the GNU product. See the GNU license for more details.

Trial, demo, or evaluation versions are usually limited either by time or functionality (such as being unable to save projects). Some trial versions are very sensitive to system date changes. If you alter your computer's date, the programs will time out and no longer be functional.

TROUBLESHOOTING

If you have difficulty installing or using any of the materials on the companion CD, try the following solutions:

- Turn off any antivirus software that you may have running. Installers sometimes mimic virus activity and can make your computer incorrectly believe that it is being infected by a virus. (Be sure to turn the antivirus software back on later.)
- Close all running programs. The more programs you are running, the less memory is available to other programs. Installers also typically update files and programs; if you keep other programs running, installation may not work properly.
- Reboot if necessary. If all else fails, rebooting your machine can often clear any conflicts in the system.

CUSTOMER CARE

If you have trouble with the CD-ROM, please call the Wiley Product Technical Support phone number at (800) 762-2974. Outside the United States, call 1 (317) 572-3994. You can also contact Wiley Product Technical Support at http://support.wiley.com. John Wiley & Sons will provide technical support only for installation and other general quality control items. For technical support on the applications themselves, consult the program's vendor or author. To place additional orders or to request information about other Wiley products, please call (877) 762-2974.

CUSTOMER NOTE: IF THIS BOOK IS ACCOMPANIED BY SOFTWARE, PLEASE READ THE FOLLOWING BEFORE OPENING THE PACKAGE

This software contains files to help you utilize the models described in the accompanying book. By opening the package, you are agreeing to be bound by the following agreement.

Author Index

Subject Index